FACTS ABOUT THE PRESIDENTS

gives a wealth of in ... everyone. Young and old, student and scholar alike, can benefit from this well-researched study of the men who held the highest office in the land.

Here, in one volume, are accurate records of the ancestry, religion, education and former occupations of all the Presidents; such personal data as their heights and weights, detailed marital statistics and the last words uttered by each before his death; and the texts of many of their greatest speeches and documents.

FACTS ABOUT THE PRESIDENTS

enables you to see these famous figures as men, and to learn what each did during his term as President. This unusual book, designed as a ready reference guide, will fascinate as well as instruct you and your entire family.

FACTS ABOUT THE PRESIDENTS was originally published by The H. W. Wilson Company.

OTHER BOOKS BY JOSEPH NATHAN KANE

American Counties
Famous First Facts
The Perma Quiz Book
The Second Perma Quiz Book

*Published in PERMABOOK editions.

FACTS ABOUT THE PRESIDENTS

A Compilation of
Biographical and Historical Data

JOSEPH NATHAN KANE

ABRIDGED BY THE AUTHOR

Illustrations by Jerry Allison

PERMABOOKS • NEW YORK

This Permabook edition, abridged for Pocket Books, Inc., by the author, is printed from brand-new plates made from completely reset, clear, easy-to-read type.

FACTS ABOUT THE PRESIDENTS

H. W. Wilson edition published September, 1959

PERMABOOK edition published June, 1960

1st printing.........................April, 1960

L

PERMABOOK editions are distributed in the U.S. by Affiliated Publishers, Inc., 630 Fifth Avenue, New York 20, N.Y.

 PERMABOOK editions are published in the United States by Pocket Books, Inc., and in Canada by Pocket Books of Canada, Ltd.—the world's largest publishers of low-priced adult books.

PREFACE

The Presidents of the United States, from George Washington to Dwight David Eisenhower, are subjects of continuing popular interest and scholarly research. About these thirty-three men countless books have been published—individual biographies, collective biographies, academic studies, political analyses, pictorial histories. *Facts About the Presidents* is a compilation which presents, in one volume, data concerning their lives, their backgrounds, their tenure of office—and much about the office itself. It would not be possible, obviously, to cover in one book every known fact about every President, but most of the facts likely to be sought by the general reader and by the specialist are included.

In Part I a chapter is devoted to each President in the chronological order in which he took office. The data in these chapters are arranged uniformly. A genealogical compilation presents vital material about the President's parents, brothers and sisters, wife, and children. Family history is followed by data on elections and the Vice President, as well as highlights of the President's life and administration.

In Part II material is presented in comparative form, with collective data and statistics on the Presidents as individuals and on the office of the presidency.

The determination of correct dates—thousands in a work of this nature—has been a great problem, and it has been a major task to supply those dates which are buried in musty records. The inclusion of complete dates, rather than just the year or month, has made the task still more difficult. Where first-hand sources are not available and where discrepancies appear in secondary sources, the dates have been omitted. It is hoped that future research or the discovery of new documents may unearth these unknown or obscure dates.

It should also be noted that many dates disagree with those previously printed. Such discrepancies do not indicate that the dates herein presented are incorrect but rather that the others may be in error. Should further research bring primary sources to light to contradict any of the dates in *Facts About the Presidents,* we will appreciate hearing of these documents so that they may be examined to determine whether the new data should be included in future editions.

Joseph Nathan Kane

May 1959

CONTENTS

Part II

COMPARATIVE DATA

The Presidents

The Presidency

Part I

BIOGRAPHICAL DATA
Washington—Eisenhower

G. Washington

GEORGE WASHINGTON

Born—Feb. 22, 1732

Birthplace—Pope's Creek, Westmoreland County, Va.

College attended—None

Religious denomination—Episcopalian

Ancestry—English

Occupation—Surveyor, planter

Date and place of marriage—Jan. 6, 1759, Kent County, Va.

Age at marriage—26 years, 318 days

Years married—40 years, 342 days

Political party—Federalist

State represented—Virginia

Term of office—Apr. 30, 1789-Mar. 3, 1797

Term served—7 years, 308 days

Administration—1st, 2nd

Congresses—1st, 2nd, 3rd, 4th

Age at inauguration—57 years, 67 days

Lived after term—2 years, 285 days

Occupation after term—Planter and General of the Army

Date of death—Dec. 14, 1799

Age at death—67 years, 295 days

Place of death—Mount Vernon, Va.

Burial place—Family vault, Mount Vernon, Va.

PARENTS

Father—Augustine Washington

Born—1694, Westmoreland, Va.

Married (1)—Jane Butler, Apr. 20, 1715

Married (2)—Mary Ball, Mar. 6, 1730

Occupation—Farmer, planter

For additional data see the end of this section and also specific subject headings in the Index.

3

Died—Apr. 12, 1743, King George County, Va.

Age at death—About 49 years

First wife of father—Jane Butler Washington

Born—*c.* 1700

Married—Apr. 20, 1715

Died—Nov. 24, 1728, Stafford County, Va.

Mother—Mary Ball Washington

Born—1708, Lancaster County, Va.

Married—Mar. 6, 1730

Died—Aug. 25, 1789, near Fredericksburg, Va.

Age at death—About 81 years

BROTHERS AND SISTERS

Augustine Washington was the father of ten children, four by his first wife and six by his second wife. George Washington was his fifth child and the first-born of Mary Ball Washington.

CHILDREN

None

MRS. GEORGE WASHINGTON

Name—Martha Dandridge Custis Washington

Born—June 21, 1731

Birthplace—New Kent County, Va.

Age at marriage to Washington—27 years, 199 days

Children by Washington—None

Mother—Frances Jones Dandridge

Father—Colonel John Dandridge

His occupation—Planter

Date of death—May 22, 1802

Age at death—70 years, 335 days

Place of death—Mount Vernon, Va.

Burial place—Mount Vernon, Va.

Years older than the President—246 days

Years she survived the President—2 years, 159 days

At the time of her marriage to Washington she was the widow of Daniel Parke Custis, by whom she had four children, two of whom died in infancy.

THE ELECTION OF 1789

When the first electors cast their ballots, there were no political organizations or political parties in existence. Each elector had to ballot for two persons. The one with the majority of votes was elected President and the next highest Vice President. No distinction was made between votes for President and Vice President until 1804.

The method of balloting and selecting the candidate is governed by Article 2, Section 1, Paragraph 3 of the Constitution:

The Electors shall meet in their respective States, and vote by Ballot for two persons, of whom one at least shall not be an Inhabitant of the same State with themselves. And they shall make a List of all the Persons voted for, and of the Number of Votes for each; which List they shall sign and certify, and transmit sealed to the Seat of the Government of the United States, directed to the President of the Senate. The President of the Senate shall, in the Presence of the Senate and the House of Representatives, open all the Certificates, and the Votes shall then be counted. The Person having the greatest Number of Votes shall be the President, if such a number be a Majority of the whole Number of Electors appointed; and if there be more than one who have such Majority, and have an equal number of Votes, then the House of Representatives shall immediately chuse by Ballot one of them for President; and if no Person has a Majority, then from the five highest on the List, the said House shall in like Manner chuse the President. But in chusing the President, the Votes shall be taken by States, the Representation from each State having one Vote; A quorum for this purpose shall consist of a Member or Members from two-thirds of the States, and a Majority of all the States shall be necessary to a Choice. In every Case, after the Choice of the President, the Person having the greatest Number of Votes of the Electors shall be the Vice President.

But if there should remain two or more who have equal Votes, the Senate shall chuse from them by Ballot the Vice President.

It was the intention of the Continental Congress that the newly formed government should convene on "the first Wednesday in March next" (March 4, 1789) at Federal Hall, New York City. Only eight of the twenty-six senators and thirteen of the sixty-five representatives presented themselves on that date and it was not until April 6, 1789, that a quorum was present. John Langdon, president of the Senate, received, opened, and counted the votes of the electors.

George Washington received one vote from each of the sixty-nine electors from the ten states and was the unanimous choice for President. The votes were cast by the states as follows: Massachusetts 10, Pennsylvania 10, Virginia 10, Connecticut 7, South Carolina 7, Maryland 6, New Jersey 6, Georgia 5, New Hampshire 5, and Delaware 3.

A committee from both houses was appointed to meet him: John Langdon of New Hampshire, Charles Carroll of Maryland, and William Samuel Johnson of Connecticut, representing the Senate; and Elias Boudinot of New Jersey, Richard Bland Lee of Virginia, Thomas Tudor Tucker of South Carolina, Egbert Benson of New York, and John Laurance of New York, representing the House.

Charles Thomson was appointed to notify George Washington that he had been elected President and Sylvanus Bourn was appointed to notify John Adams that he had been elected Vice President.

On April 14, 1789, Charles Thomson, secretary of the

Continental Congress, notified George Washington of his election, and on April 16, 1789, Washington left his home at Mount Vernon, Va., for the capital.

FULL ELECTORAL VOTE NOT CAST IN 1789

On February 4, 1789, the first presidential electors met in New York City. Ten states sent 69 electors. The electors of five states—Connecticut, Delaware, Georgia, New Jersey, and South Carolina—had been chosen by the state legislatures. Three states—Maryland, Pennsylvania, and Virginia—held popular elections. Massachusetts had a system combining popular election and appointment by the legislature. New Hampshire held a popular election, but none of the electors received a majority, and the electors finally chosen were those named by the state Senate.

Had all of the electors qualified, a total of 91 votes, instead of 69, would have been cast. New York had not yet chosen its 8 electors even though the seat of the new government was in New York. Consequently, New York's vote was not cast. The weather delayed the votes of 4 electors, 2 from Maryland and 2 from Virginia. As North

Carolina and Rhode Island had not as yet ratified the Constitution, they did not cast their 7 and 3 votes respectively. Thus, 22 of the 91 possible votes were not cast.

ADAMS ELECTED VICE PRESIDENT

Each elector cast 1 of his 2 votes for Washington, who thus received 69 of the 138 votes. The other 69 went to 11 others; John Adams of Massachusetts, the candidate with the greatest number, became Vice President. The other candidates included John Jay of New York, Robert Hanson Harrison of Maryland, John Rutledge of South Carolina, John Hancock of Massachusetts, George Clinton of New York, Samuel Huntington of Connecticut, John Milton of Georgia, James Armstrong of Georgia, Edward Telfair of Georgia, and Benjamin Lincoln of Georgia.

Adams received 34 votes as follows: Conn. 5 (of the 7 votes); Mass. 10; N.H. 5; N.J. 1 (of the 6 votes); Pa. 8 (of the 10 votes); Va. 5 (of the 10 votes).

The other candidates received the following votes:

Jay—Del. 3; N.J. 5 (of the 6 votes); Va. 1 (of the 10 votes)

Harrison—Md. 6

Rutledge—S.C. 6 (of the 7 votes)

Hancock—Pa. 2 (of the 10 votes); S.C. 1 (of the 7 votes); Va. 1 (of the 10 votes)

Clinton—Va. 3 (of the 10 votes)

Huntington—Conn. 2 (of the 7 votes)

Milton—Ga. 2 (of the 5 votes)

Armstrong—Ga. 1 (of the 5 votes)

Telfair—Ga. 1 (of the 5 votes)

Lincoln—Ga. 1 (of the 5 votes)

THE ELECTION OF 1792

Before the conclusion of George Washington's four-year term, it was necessary to elect a President for the second administration. George Washington and John Adams, who were known as Federalists, were advocates of a strong central government. Those in accord with their principles wanted them re-elected for a second term of four years.

Naturally, not all of the ideas and plans advocated by them were acceptable to everyone. Those who differed were known as Democratic Republicans or Republicans. As the Democratic Republicans were a minority group, they realized the futility of organizing to oppose Washington's reelection, and did not oppose him.

On November 6, 1792, George Washington received 132 of the 264 electoral votes cast, a unanimous election. The second highest vote, 77 votes, was for John Adams of Massachusetts, who was reelected Vice President. The balance of the 132 electoral votes was cast for George Clinton of New York (50 votes), Thomas Jefferson of Virginia (4 votes) and Aaron Burr of New York (1 vote).

APPOINTMENTS TO THE SUPREME COURT

Chief Justices

John Jay, N.Y., Sept. 26, 1789

John Rutledge, S.C., July 1, 1795

Oliver Ellsworth, Conn., Mar. 4, 1796

John Rutledge, commissioned July 1, 1795 (in recess), presided at the August term 1795. His nomination was rejected by the Senate on December 15, 1795.

Associate Justices

John Rutledge, S.C., Sept. 26, 1789

William Cushing, Mass., Sept. 27, 1789

Robert H. Harrison, Md., Sept. 28, 1789

James Wilson, Pa., Sept. 29, 1789

John Blair, Va., Sept. 30, 1789

James Iredell, N.C., Feb. 10, 1790

Thomas Johnson, Md., Aug. 5, 1791

William Paterson, N.J., March 4, 1793

Samuel Chase, Md., Jan. 27, 1796

William Cushing was commissioned as Chief Justice on Jan. 27, 1796, but declined to serve, continuing as Associate Justice.

ADMINISTRATION— IMPORTANT DATES

Apr. 1, 1789, first quorum, House of Representatives

Apr. 6, 1789, first quorum, U.S. Senate

June 1, 1789, first congressional act approved "to regulate the time and manner of administering certain oaths"

July 4, 1789, first tariff act, placing duties on imports to protect domestic industries

July 20, 1789, first federal navigation act, imposing duty on the tonnage of vessels

July 27, 1789, State Department created as Department of Foreign Affairs

Aug. 4, 1789, first federal bond issue authorized to refund domestic and state debt

Aug. 7, 1789, Department of War created

Sept. 2, 1789, Treasury Department established

Sept. 13, 1789, first loan to the U.S. Government negotiated by Alexander Hamilton with New York banks

Sept. 24, 1789, office of Attorney General established

Sept. 25, 1789, first ten amendments to the Constitution enacted by Congress

Sept. 29, 1789, first Congress adjourned after 210-day session

Nov. 21, 1789, twelfth state ratified the Constitution

Feb. 1, 1790, first session of U.S. Supreme Court

Mar. 1, 1790, first U.S. census authorized

May 29, 1790, Rhode Island adopted Constitution (last of the original thirteen to sign)

May 31, 1790, first copyright law signed

Aug. 9, 1790, *Columbia,* under Captain Robert Gray, returned to Boston, completing first trip around the world under U.S. flag

Jan. 10, 1791, Vermont ratified Constitution

Feb. 18, 1791, Vermont admitted as the 14th state

Feb. 25, 1791, Bank of the United States chartered

Mar. 3, 1791, District of Columbia established

Mar. 3, 1791, first internal revenue act

Mar. 4, 1791, Arthur St. Clair appointed commander-in-chief of federal troops

Apr. 7, 1791-June 12, 1791, George Washington made tour of the South

Nov. 4, 1791, General St. Clair surprised and defeated by Indians at Wabash River

Dec. 15, 1791, Bill of Rights, first ten amendments to the Constitution, ratified

Mar. 1, 1792, presidential succession act enacted

Mar. 1, 1792, Secretary of State Jefferson announced the adoption of the first ten amendments

Apr. 2, 1792, U.S. Mint established; coinage of various denominations authorized

Apr. 5, 1792, Washington vetoed apportionment bill

June 1, 1792, Kentucky admitted as the 15th state

Sept. 27, 1792, peace treaty signed with Wabash and Illinois Indians

Oct. 13, 1792, cornerstone of White House laid

Mar. 4, 1793, second inauguration, held at Philadelphia, Pa.

Apr. 22, 1793, neutrality proclamation issued by Washington

Sept. 18, 1793, cornerstone of Capitol laid

Mar. 14, 1794, Eli Whitney patented cotton gin

July-Nov. 1794, Whiskey Rebellion in western Pennsylvania

Aug. 20, 1794, General Wayne defeated Miami Indians at Fallen Timbers

Nov. 19, 1794, Jay's Treaty with Great Britain signed to settle terms of peace, amity, commerce, navigation, boundary claims and extradition

Feb. 7, 1795, Eleventh Amendment to Constitution ratified

Sept. 5, 1795, treaty of peace and amity with Algiers signed

May 19, 1796, first national game law approved

May 31, 1796, treaty with Six Nations concluded

June 1, 1796, Tennessee admitted as the 16th state

Nov. 4, 1796, treaty of peace, friendship, and navigation with Tripoli signed

Sept. 17, 1797, Washington issued his Farewell Address

IMPORTANT DATES IN HIS LIFE

1749, licensed as surveyor by College of William and Mary

July 20, 1749, official surveyor, Culpeper County, Va.

Nov. 6, 1752, appointed adjutant general of Virginia with rank of major

Mar. 15, 1754, lieutenant-colonel of Virginia regiment

June 5, 1754, colonel of Virginia regiment

May 10, 1755, appointed aide-de-camp (a volunteer position without rank) by General Braddock in French and Indian War

July 9, 1755, two horses were shot under him and four bullets pierced his coat in battle near Fort Duquesne, Pa.; withdrew remnants of Braddock's defeated army at the Monongahela to Fort Cumberland

Aug. 14, 1755, appointed by the legislature Colonel of the Virginia regiment and Commander-in-Chief of the Virginia forces protecting the frontier against the French and Indians

1755-1758, engaged in recruiting and organizing troops for colonial defense

1758, commanded successful expedition to Fort Duquesne

July 24, 1758, elected to House of Burgesses from Frederick County

Dec. 1758, resigned commission as colonel of the Virginia regiment and commander-in-chief of the Virginia forces

1758, resided at Mount Vernon, Va.

Oct. 1770, justice of the peace for Fairfax County

Aug. 1773, delegate to the Williamsburg Convention

Aug. 1774, member, First Virginia Provincial Convention

Aug. 5, 1774, elected delegate to First Continental Congress

Sept. 5, 1774, attended first session of Continental Congress at Philadelphia, Pa.

Mar. 25, 1775, Second Virginia Provincial Congress selected Washington to attend Second Continental Congress

June 15, 1775, Congress elected Washington as General and Commander-in-Chief of the Army of the United Colonies

July 3, 1775, assumed command at Cambridge, Mass.

Mar. 17, 1776, Boston evacuated by the British

Aug. 27, 1776, Battle of Long Island

Oct. 28, 1776, Battle of White Plains

Dec. 25, 1776, recrossed Delaware River

Dec. 26, 1776, Battle of Trenton

Jan. 3, 1777, Battle of Princeton

Sept. 11, 1777, Battle of Brandywine

Oct. 4, 1777, Battle of Germantown

Dec. 19, 1777, winter headquarters established at Valley Forge

Oct. 19, 1781, Cornwallis surrendered at Yorktown, Va.

May 8, 1783, dinner with Lord Carleton after conference. Washington received seventeen-gun salute

June 19, 1783, elected President General of the Society of the Cincinnati

Sept. 3, 1783, Treaty of Peace signed

Nov. 2, 1783, issued Farewell Orders to the armies

Nov. 25, 1783, reoccupied New York City after British occupation

Dec. 4, 1783, bade farewell to his officers at Fraunces Tavern

Dec. 23, 1783, surrendered his commission as commander-in-chief to Congress; returned to private life

May 25, 1787, delegate from Virginia to the Federal Convention. Elected president unanimously

Feb. 4, 1789, unanimously elected President of the United States for 1789-1793 term

Apr. 30, 1789, inaugurated President at Federal Hall, New York City

June 1, 1789, signed first act of Congress

Aug. 25, 1789, his mother, Mary Ball Washington, died at Fredericksburg, Va.

Dec. 5, 1792, unanimously reelected President

Mar. 4, 1793, inaugurated at Philadelphia, Pa., as President of the United States for a second term

Sept. 18, 1793, laid cornerstone

of the Capitol at Washington, D.C.

Mar. 3, 1797, expiration of his second term as President

July 3, 1798, President John Adams appointed him Lieutenant-General and Commander-in-Chief of the Army of the United States

July 13, 1798, accepted appointment

Dec. 14, 1799, died at Mount Vernon, Va.

Dec. 18, 1799, interred at Mount Vernon in vault he designed

GEORGE WASHINGTON

——was the only President who was inaugurated in two cities (New York City, April 30, 1789, and Philadelphia, Pa., March 4, 1793).

——was the only President who did not live in Washington, D.C.

——was the first and only President unanimously elected, having received 69 of the 69 electoral votes cast.

——was the first President to refuse a third term.

——was the first President born in Virginia.

——was the first President whose mother was alive when he was inaugurated.

——was the first President to marry a widow.

——was the first President whose mother was a second wife.

——was the first President to have stepbrothers.

WASHINGTON'S VICE PRESIDENT

Vice President—John Adams (1st V.P.)

For biographical information see John Adams, 2nd President.

ADDITIONAL DATA ON WASHINGTON

WASHINGTON WAS BORN ON FEBRUARY 11

George Washington was born on February 11, 1731, and celebrated his first nineteen birthdays on February 11.

An act of the British Parliament in 1750 discarded the Julian calendar and adopted the Gregorian calendar in its stead for Great Britain and the colonies. In the Julian calendar, the first day of the year had been March 25, but in the year 1751 the year ended on December 31 and the days between January 1 and March 24 were omitted from the calendar. This legal year contained only 282 days. The period from January 1 to March 24 was dated 1752.

Thus George Washington was 19 years old on February 11, 1750, but his twentieth birthday was on February 11, 1752, not 1751.

Since the vernal equinox had been displaced by 11 days in the Julian calendar, it was ordered that the difference be removed by the omission of 11 days from September 1752. There were no days dated September 3 to 13 inclusive; the day after September 2 was September 14. This required the addition of 11 days to compensate, and in 1753 George Washington celebrated his birthday on February 22 instead of on February 11.

BAPTISM

George Washington was baptized April 5, 1732 (1731 Old Style). His godfathers were Beverley Whiting and Captain Christopher Brooks and his godmother was Mrs. Mildred Gregory.

WASHINGTON OPERATED A FERRY

George Washington loaned $3,750 to Captain John Posey, who was unable to repay the amount and turned over his land, including a ferry and fishery, to Washington. Washington then ran the fishery, shipping fish in his own boats and selling them along the Atlantic seaboard.

The ferry, which he operated from 1769 to 1790, crossed the Potomac at a spot about a mile wide, landing at what is now Marshall Hall, Md. The schedule of rates as set up by the Virginia General Assembly was one shilling for an adult and a horse.

The rates were: for every coach, wagon, chariot, and driver, the same price as for six horses; for every four-wheeled chaise, phaeton and driver, the same price as for four horses; for every two-wheeled riding carriage, the same price as for two horses; for every hogshead of tobacco, the same price as for one horse; for every head of neat cattle, the same price as for one horse, and for every sheep, hog, goat or lamb, the same price as for one horse.

The ferry was abandoned in October 1790, a year and a half after Washington had become President. He submitted his reasons for discontinuing the service to the General Assembly which acceded to his request to be permitted to abandon the ferry service.

WASHINGTON ESCAPED KIDNAPPERS

Prior to George Washington's inauguration, while he was still commander-in-chief of the army, an attempt was made to kidnap or kill him. Involved in the conspiracy were the Tory governor of New York, William Tryon, the Tory mayor of New York City, David Matthews, and many others, including Thomas Hickey, one of Washington's bodyguard. Hickey was tried before a court-martial, which found him guilty. On June 28, 1776 Hickey was hanged on a field near the Bowery Lane in the presence of 20,000 persons.

The episode is recorded in General George Washington's orderly book on June 28, 1776 as follows: "The unhappy Fate of Thomas Hickey, executed this day for Mutiny, Sedition and Treachery; the General hopes will be a warning to every soldier, in the Army, to avoid those crimes and all others, so disgraceful to the character of a soldier and pernicious to his country, whose pay he receives and bread he eats."

WASHINGTON DISAPPROVED OF SWEARING

A General Order issued August 3, 1776, by General George Washington from his headquarters at New York stated:

The General is sorry to be informed that the foolish and wicked practice of profane cursing and swearing, a vice heretofore little known in an American army, is growing into fashion. He hopes the officers will, by example as well as influence, endeavor to check it, and that both they and the men will reflect, that we can have little hope of the blessing of Heaven on our arms, if we insult it by our impiety and folly. Added to this, it is a vice so mean and low, without any temptation, that every man of sense and character detests and despises it.

HONORARY DEGREES FOR WASHINGTON

The formal education of George Washington ceased before he was seventeen years of age; however, he did much studying on his own account. Although he lacked a college degree, five of the country's foremost colleges saw fit to confer honorary degrees upon him.

The first degree was the honorary degree of Doctor of Laws awarded by Harvard in 1776. Yale followed suit in 1781. The University of Pennsylvania made a similar award in 1783. Washington College of Chestertown, Md., and Brown University also conferred the honorary LL.D. degree in 1789 and 1790 respectively.

WASHINGTON REJECTED MONARCHY

The suggestion made by Colonel Lewis Nicola in a letter to General George Washington to the effect that Washington become king brought a stinging rebuke from the general. His answer from Newburgh, N.Y., dated May 22, 1782, follows:

With a mixture of great surprise and astonishment I have read with attention the Sentiments you have submitted to my perusal. Be assured Sir, no occurrence in the course of the War, has given me more painful sensations than your information of there being such ideas existing in the Army as you have expressed, and I must view with abhorrence, and reprehend with severity. For the present, the communication of them will rest in my bosom, unless some further agitation of the matter, shall make a disclosure necessary.

I am much at a loss to conceive what part of my conduct could have given encouragement to an address which to me seems big with the greatest mischiefs that can befall my Country.

If I am not deceived in the knowledge of myself, you could not have found a person to whom your schemes are more disagreeable: at the same time in justice to my own feelings I must add, that no Man possesses a more sincere wish to see ample justice done to the Army than I do, and as far as my powers and influence, in a constitutional way extend, they shall be employed to the utmost of my abilities to effect it, should there be any occasion. Let me conjure you then, if you have any regard for your Country, concern for yourself or posterity, or respect for me, to banish these thoughts from your Mind, and never communicate, as from yourself, or any one else, a sentiment of the like Nature.

WASHINGTON RAISED MULES

Although the exportation of full-blooded jacks from Spain was prohibited, Charles III of Spain sent George Washington two jacks and two jennets with a Spanish caretaker. They arrived at Boston on October 26,

1785. Only one of the jacks survived the trip; it was named Royal Gift by Washington and was used to breed heavy mules for draft purposes.

A Maltese jack sent by Lafayette to George Washington was named the Knight of Malta. It was used to breed lighter and nimbler mules for saddle and carriage use.

WASHINGTON BORROWED MONEY TO GO TO HIS FIRST INAUGURATION

Although George Washington was one of the richest men of his time he was "land-poor" and was obliged to borrow money to finance his trip to New York. He received a loan of 600 pounds from Richard Conway of Alexandria, Va., to whom he had written the following letter on March 4, 1789 from his home at Mount Vernon:

DEAR SIR,

Never till within these two years have I experienced the want of money. Short crops, and other causes not entirely within my control, make me feel it now very sensibly. To collect money without the intervention of Suits (and these are tedious) seems impracticable—and Land, which I have offered for sale, will not command Cash at an undervalue, if at all. Under this statement, I am inclined to do what I never expected to be driven to, that is, to borrow money on Interest. Five hundred pounds would enable me to discharge what I owe in Alexandria, etc., and to leave the State (if it shall not be in my power to remain home in retirement) without doing this, would be exceedingly disagreeable to me. Having thus fully and candidly explained myself, permit me to ask if it is in your power to supply me with the above or smaller Sum. Any security you may best like I can give, and you may be assured, that it is no more my inclination than it can be yours, to let it remain long unpaid. . . .

WASHINGTON ARRIVED IN NEW YORK BY BOAT

Thirteen pilots, all dressed in white sailor costume, rowed the barge which conveyed George Washington from Elizabeth Town, N.J., to New York City for his inauguration. The barge had a forty-seven-foot keel and carried two flags astern. It came out of the Kill van Kull into New York Bay, passed the Battery, and proceeded up the Hudson River to Murray's wharf at the foot of Wall Street.

A brief parade was held through Queen Street to the Franklin House. The order of march was as follows: 1, a troop of horse; 2, artillery and those remaining of the Legion under arms; 3, off-duty military officers in uniform; 4, The President's Guard, composed of the Grenadiers of the First Regiment; 5, the President, the governor and their suites; 6, the principal officers of the state; 7, the mayor of New York and the Corporation of New York; 8, the clergy; 9, the citizens.

FIRST INAUGURATION

George Washington took the oath of office as President of the United States on Thursday, April 30, 1789, out-of-doors on the balcony of the Senate Chamber at Federal Hall, Wall and Nassau Streets, New York City. The oath was administered by Robert R. Livingston, Chancellor of New York State. The Bible on which Washington took his oath was borrowed from St. John's Lodge, Free and Accepted Masons. His hand rested on Psalm 127:1 when he took the oath. He then proceeded to the Senate Chamber to deliver his inaugural address. After the ceremony, he was escorted to the President's House by a troop of cavalry, assistants, a committee of Representatives, a committee of the Senate and the gentlemen to be admitted to the Senate.

The evening celebration was opened and closed by thirteen skyrockets and thirteen cannon.

A weekly, the *U.S. Chronicle* of May 21, 1789, recorded:

The President of the United States, on the day of his inauguration, appeared dressed in a complete suit of Homespun Cloaths; the cloth was of a fine fabric, and as handsomely finished, as any European superfine cloth. A circumstance, which must be considered as not only highly flattering to our manufacturers in particular, but interesting to our countrymen in general.

His Excellency the Vice President appeared also in a suit of American manufacture and several members of both Houses are distinguished by the same token of attention to the manufacturing interests of their country.

After Chancellor Robert R. Livingston administered the oath of office to George Washington on April 30, 1789, he proclaimed, "Long live George Washington, the President of the United States."

FIRST INAUGURAL BALL

The first inaugural ball was held Thursday, May 7, 1789, in the Assembly Rooms on the east side of Broadway, a little above Wall Street, New York City. It was attended by President Washington, Vice President John Adams, the French and Spanish ministers, Chancellor Livingston, Baron Steuben, General Knox, John Jay, Alexander Hamilton and the majority of the House of Representatives and the Senate. Fans decorated with a medallion portrait of President Washington in profile were presented as souvenirs to the ladies. Martha Washington did not attend as she did not arrive in the city until the end of May.

WASHINGTON'S FIRST TERM 57 DAYS SHORT

As George Washington did not take the oath of office until April 30, 1789, his first term was 57 days shorter than it would have been had the inauguration taken place on March 4 as originally intended.

THE FIRST PRESIDENTIAL MANSION

George Washington lived at No. 1 Cherry Street, New York City, from April 23, 1789, to February 23, 1790. This residence has been referred to as the first presidential mansion. Residences were not supplied for our earliest Presidents.

CONGRESS IN SESSION AT NEW YORK AND PHILADELPHIA

The only Congress to meet at New York City was the First Congress. It held two sessions, the first from March 4, 1789, to September 29, 1789 (210 days), the second from January 4, 1790, to August 12, 1790 (221 days). A quorum was not present however until April 6, 1789.

The first session of Congress to meet at Philadelphia, Pa., was the third session of the First Congress, which was held from December 6, 1790, to March 3, 1791 (88 days). The first session of the Sixth Congress from December 2, 1799, to May 14, 1800 (164 days) was the last Congress to meet at Philadelphia.

HIS HIGHNESS, GEORGE WASHINGTON?

The committee appointed by the United States Senate on Thursday, April 23, 1789, to decide on the proper form of address for the President of the United States, reported on Thursday, May 14, 1789 "that in the opinion of the committee it will be proper thus to address the President: 'His Highness, the President of the United States of America, and Protector of their Liberties.'"

THE FIRST PRESIDENTIAL TOURS

President George Washington made the first presidential tour through the New England states from October 15 to November 13, 1789. He traveled in a hired coach accompanied by Major William Jackson, his aide-de-camp, Tobias Leer, his private secretary, six servants, nine horses, and a luggage wagon. He went as far north as Kittery, Maine (then part of Massachusetts). As Rhode Island and Vermont had not joined the new government at that time, he did not visit those states. Washington's first tour of the southern states was made from April 7 to June 12, 1791, during which time he left Mount Vernon, Virginia, on his 1,887-mile trip which took him north through Philadelphia, south through Virginia and the Carolinas into Georgia, and back to Mount Vernon.

SECOND INAUGURATION

The government having moved from New York City to Philadelphia, George Washington took the oath of office for his second term on Monday, March 4, 1793, in the Senate Chamber, Federal Hall, Philadelphia, Pa. Washington was the first President to be inaugurated at Philadelphia and the first inaugurated on March 4th. The oath was administered by William Cushing of Massachusetts, associate justice of the Supreme Court.

THE FIRST PRESIDENTIAL VETO

During his two terms of office, George Washington vetoed only two bills. His action on the first veto, dated April 5, 1792, was explained in the following letter to the members of the House of Representatives:

I have maturely considered the act passed by the two Houses entitled "An act for an apportionment of Representatives among the several States according to the first enumeration," and I return it to your House, wherein it originated, with the following objections:

First. The Constitution has prescribed that Representatives shall be apportioned among the several States according to their respective numbers, and there is no one proportion or divisor which, applied to the respective numbers of the States, will yield the number and allotment of representatives proposed by the bill.

Second. The Constitution has also provided that the number of representatives shall not exceed 1 for every 30,000, which restriction is by the context and by fair and obvious construction to be applied to the separate and respective numbers of the States; and the bill has allotted to eight of the States more than 1 for every 30,000.

His only other veto, dated February 28, 1797, rejected a bill to reduce the cavalry force of the army.

THE FIRST PRESIDENTIAL COMMISSION

The first presidential commission was appointed by Washington to deal with the rebellious elements in Washington and Alleghany counties, Pennsylvania. In his proclamation to Congress on August 7, 1794, he said: "I do hereby command all persons, being insurgents as aforesaid, on or before the first day of September next to disperse and retire peacefully to their respective abodes." In his sixth annual report, on November 19, 1794, he declared: "The report of the commissioners marks their firmness and abilities, and must unite all virtuous men, by shewing that the means of conciliation have been exhausted."

WASHINGTON DECLINED A THIRD TERM

Washington's second term of office expired on March 3, 1797. On September 17, 1796, he made his "Farewell Address," which was not delivered orally but released to the press. It was addressed to "Friends and Fellow Citizens" and began

The period for a new election of a citizen to administer the Executive Government of the United States being not far distant, and the time actually arrived when your thoughts must be employed in designating the person who is to be clothed with that important trust, it appears to me proper, especially as it may conduce to a more distinct expression of the public voice, that I should now apprise you of the resolution I have formed to decline being considered among the number of those out of whom a choice is to be made. . . .

WASHINGTON APPOINTED LIEUTENANT-GENERAL

On July 11, 1798, Secretary of War James McHenry delivered a letter from President John Adams to George Washington appointing Washington, with the advice and consent of the Senate, "Lieutenant-General and Commander-in-Chief of all the armies raised or to be raised for the service of the United States."

Washington's reply, dated July 13, 1798, from Mount Vernon, Va., was read in the Senate on July 18. He accepted

with the reserve only that I shall not be called into the field until the Army is in a situation to require my presence, or it becomes indispensable by the urgency of circumstances. I take the liberty also to mention, that I must decline having my acceptance considered as drawing after it any immediate charge upon the public, or that I can receive any emoluments annexed to the appointment, before entering into a situation to incur expense.

WASHINGTON LEFT HUGE ESTATE

George Washington was one of our richest Presidents. His estate was valued at more than a half million dollars.

In his last will and testament, dated July 9, 1799, he listed his assets. His land holdings exceeding 33,000 acres, consisted of 23,341 acres in Virginia, 5,000 acres in Kentucky, 3,051 acres in the Northwest Territory, 1,119 acres in Maryland, 1,000 acres in New York, 234 acres in Pennsylvania, and other property in Virginia and Washington, D.C., valued at $489,135. He also listed his stocks as worth $25,212. He valued his livestock, which consisted of 640 sheep, 329 cows, 42 mules, 20 working horses, pigs, etc., at $15,653. The value of these three items—acreage, stocks, and livestock—was estimated at $530,-000.

WASHINGTON OWNED LAND IN WASHINGTON, D.C.

On October 3, 1798, George Washington acquired two lots in the federal city (now Washington, D.C.). He described his purchase in his last will and testament as follows:

The two lots near the Capitol in Square 634, cost me $963 only, but in this price I was favoured on condition that I should build two brick houses, three storys high each:- without this reduction, the selling price of those lots would have cost me about $1,350. These lots with the buildings thereon when completed will stand me in $15,000 at least.

WASHINGTON'S SWORDS

In his will George Washington bequeathed five swords, one to each of his five nephews, with the admonition that none of these weapons should be unsheathed by the future owners for the purpose of shedding blood, "except it be for self-defence or in defence of their country and its rights and in the latter case to keep them unsheathed and prefer falling with them in their hands to the relinquishment thereof."

FIRST IN WAR, FIRST IN PEACE, FIRST IN THE HEARTS OF HIS COUNTRYMEN

This famous phrase was part of the "Funeral Oration Upon George Washington" delivered December 26, 1799, before the houses of Congress by General Henry Lee.

General Lee was familiarly known as "Light Horse Harry" and during the Revolutionary War commanded Lee's brigade, three troops of horses, which harassed and annoyed the British lines. He was the father of General Robert E. Lee, the Confederate general.

FIRST TOWN NAMED FOR WASHINGTON

The first town named for George Washington was Forks of Tar River, N.C., which changed its name to Washington in 1775. The town was originally formed November 20, 1771, by James Bonner, who owned all the land on which it was situated.

Washington, Ga., incorporated Jan. 23, 1780, was the first town incorporated with the name of Washington.

FIRST STAMP DEPICTING A PRESIDENT

The first President depicted on a United States postage stamp was George Washington, whose likeness appeared on the ten-cent black stamp. The issue was authorized March 3, 1847, to take effect July 1, 1847. The stamps were produced by Rawdon, Wright, Hatch & Edson. The issue was declared invalid as of July 1, 1851. (Some of the local postmasters' provisional stamps, however, bore a likeness of Washington.)

MOUNT VERNON NEUTRAL TERRITORY

In the Civil War, George Washington's home at Mount Vernon (named for Admiral Vernon, under whom George's brother, Lawrence, served in the capture of Porto Bello) was treated as neutral territory by arrangement between both sides. No armed soldiers ever invaded the home.

THE FIRST LADY

The first lady of the land was Martha Washington, known as Lady Washington. She never occupied the Executive Mansion at Washington, D.C., as it had not been completed during George Washington's administration. The seat of the government at the time of his first inauguration was at New York City; later it was moved to Philadelphia, Pa. The government did not furnish the President's House and the expense of furnishing was borne by George Washington. Mrs. Washington's social affairs were very formal and reserved.

John Adams

JOHN ADAMS

Born—Oct. 30, 1735

Birthplace—Braintree (now Quincy), Mass.

College attended—Harvard College, Cambridge, Mass.

Date of graduation—July 16, 1775, four-year course, Bachelor of Arts

Religion—Unitarian

Ancestry—English

Occupation—Lawyer

Date and place of marriage—Oct. 25, 1764, Weymouth, Mass.

Age at marriage—28 years, 360 days

Years married—54 years, 3 days

Political party—Federalist

State represented—Massachusetts

Term of office—Mar. 4, 1797- Mar. 3, 1801

Term served—4 years

Administration—3rd

Congresses—5th, 6th

Age at inauguration—61 years, 125 days

Lived after term—25 years, 122 days

Occupation after term—Writer

Date of death—July 4, 1826

Age at death—90 years, 247 days

Place of death—Quincy, Mass.

Burial place—First Unitarian Church, Quincy, Mass.

PARENTS

Father—John Adams

Born—Feb. 8, 1691

For additional data see the end of this section and also specific subject headings in the Index.

Married—Oct. 31, 1734

Occupation—Farmer, cord-wainer

Died—May 25, 1761

Age at death—70 years, 106 days

Mother—Susanna Boylston Adams

Born—Mar. 5, 1699

Died—Apr. 17, 1797

Age at death—98 years, 43 days

BROTHERS

John Adams was the oldest in a family of three boys.

CHILDREN

Abigail Amelia Adams, b. July 14, 1765, Braintree, Mass.; m. June 12, 1786, William Stephens Smith; d. Aug. 15, 1813

John Quincy Adams, b. July 11, 1767, Braintree, Mass.; m. July 26, 1797, Louisa Catherine Johnson; d. Feb. 23, 1848, Washington, D.C.

Susanna Adams, b. Dec. 28, 1768, Boston, Mass.; d. Feb. 4, 1770

Charles Adams, b. May 29, 1770, Boston, Mass.; m. Aug. 29, 1795, Sarah Smith; d. Nov. 30, 1800

Thomas Boylston Adams, b. Sept. 15, 1772, Quincy, Mass.;

m. May 16, 1805, Ann Harod; d. Mar. 12, 1832

MRS. JOHN ADAMS

Name—Abigail Smith Adams

Date of birth—Nov. 11, 1744

Birthplace—Weymouth, Mass.

Age at marriage—19 years, 348 days

Children—3 sons, 2 daughters

Mother—Elizabeth Quincy Smith

Father—William Smith

His occupation—Congregational minister

Date of death—Oct. 28, 1818

Age at death—73 years, 351 days

Place of death—Quincy, Mass.

Burial place—Quincy, Mass.

Years younger than the President—9 years, 12 days

Years the President survived her—7 years, 249 days

THE ELECTION OF 1796

After he had served his second four-year term, George Washington declined a third term for the presidency. This left the field wide open for numerous candidates.

When the electoral vote of 1796 was counted, 16 states cast 276 votes, 138 for President and

138 for Vice President. As there was no distinction between the votes, a situation developed that had not been anticipated by the framers of the Constitution. John Adams received 71 votes, a majority, and was elected President of the United States. The candidate receiving the next highest number of votes was Thomas Jefferson of Virginia, who had 68 votes and was elected Vice President. Adams was a Federalist and Jefferson was a Democratic-Republican. The President represented one political party and his Vice President stood for a rival party.

APPOINTMENTS TO THE SUPREME COURT

Chief Justice

John Marshall, Va., Jan. 31, 1801

Associate Justices

Bushrod Washington, Va., Sept. 29, 1798

Alfred Moore, N.C., Dec. 10, 1799

ADMINISTRATION— IMPORTANT DATES

May 10, 1797, first naval vessel, *United States,* launched, Philadelphia, Pa.

June 14, 1797, exportation of arms prohibited

Jan. 8, 1798, Adams informed Congress that 11th amendment had been adopted

Apr. 7, 1798, Mississippi Territory created

Apr. 25, 1798, "Hail Columbia" first sung in theatre

Apr. 30, 1798, Navy Department created

June 25, 1798, Alien Act passed

July 1798, yellow fever epidemic in Philadelphia; many officials moved to Trenton, N.J.

July 9, 1798-Sept. 30, 1800, conflict with France

July 11, 1798, U.S. Marine Corps created

July 13, 1798, Lieutenant General George Washington accepted office as commander-in-chief

July 14, 1798, Sedition Act passed

July 16, 1798, U.S. Public Health Service established

Oct. 2, 1798, treaty with Cherokee Indians

Nov. 16, 1798, governor of Kentucky signed law declaring the Alien and Sedition Acts unconstitutional

Dec. 21, 1798, Virginia resolution similarly declared the Alien and Sedition Acts unconstitutional

Jan. 14, 1799, Senate impeachment trial of Senator William Blount of Tennessee concluded; charges dismissed for want of jurisdiction (first impeachment proceedings against a U.S. senator)

Feb. 25, 1799, first federal forestry legislation to acquire timber lands for the U.S. Navy

Dec. 14, 1799, death of George Washington

Feb. 1800, capital removed from Philadelphia, Pa., to Washington, D.C.

Apr. 4, 1800, federal bankruptcy act passed

Apr. 24, 1800, Library of Congress established

Sept. 3, 1800, treaty with Napoleon Bonaparte

Oct. 1, 1800, Spain ceded Louisiana back to France by secret treaty of San Ildefonso

Nov. 17, 1800, first session of Congress at Washington, D.C.

Jan. 31, 1801, John Marshall began thirty-four-year period as chief justice of the United States

Nov. 29, 1802, Ohio admitted as the 17th state

IMPORTANT DATES IN HIS LIFE

1755, taught school at Worcester, Mass.

1758, admitted to the bar, practiced at Boston, Mass.

1768, Massachusetts legislature

Sept. 5, 1774, delegate to First Continental Congress

Nov. 28, 1774, revolutionary Provincial Congress of Massachusetts

May 10, 1775, delegate to Second Continental Congress

1776, one of committee of five to draft the Declaration of Independence

Aug. 2, 1776, signed Declaration of Independence; head of War Department; proposed George Washington as leader of the American Army

Apr. 8, 1778, reached Paris as commissioner to France, superseding Deane

Sept. 1, 1779, member of Massachusetts Constitutional Convention

Dec. 29, 1780, minister to the Netherlands; negotiated loan and Treaty of Amity and Commerce

May 14, 1785, minister to England (served until 1788)

Apr. 21, 1789, inaugurated Vice President at New York City

Mar. 4, 1793, inaugurated Vice President for a second term

Mar. 4, 1797-Mar. 3, 1801, President

Mar. 4, 1801, retired to Quincy, Mass.

Nov. 15, 1820, member of Second Constitutional Convention of Massachusetts

JOHN ADAMS

——was the first President born in Massachusetts.

——was the only President whose son was inaugurated President.

——was the second President whose mother was alive when he was inaugurated.

——was the first President to reside at Washington, D.C. When he moved into the President's House on November 1, 1800, it was not completed and not a single apartment was finished.

——was the first President to have children. He had three sons and two daughters.

——was the first President to have a justice of the Supreme Court administer the oath to him. He was sworn in on March 4, 1797, by Chief Justice Oliver Ellsworth.

——was the only President who was inaugurated at Philadelphia both as President and Vice President. On March 4, 1793, he was inaugurated as Vice President with George Washington as President, and on March 4, 1797, he was inaugurated President with Thomas Jefferson as his Vice President.

ADAMS' VICE PRESIDENT

Vice President—Thomas Jefferson (2nd V.P.)

For biographical information see Thomas Jefferson, 3rd President.

ADDITIONAL DATA ON ADAMS

ADAMS MARRIED BY FATHER-IN-LAW

The marriage of John Adams to Abigail Smith on October 25, 1764, at Weymouth, Mass., was performed by the father of the bride, the Reverend William Smith, a Congregational minister.

ADAMS SWORN IN AS WASHINGTON'S VICE PRESIDENT

John Adams entered upon his duties as Vice President of the United States on Tuesday, April 21, 1789, nine days before George Washington was inaugurated.

John Langdon of New Hampshire, who was president pro tempore of the Senate, introduced him to the senators as follows, "Sir; I have it in charge from the Senate to introduce you to the chair of this House; and, also to congratulate you on your appointment to the office of Vice President of the United States of America." He then conducted the Vice President to the chair, and John Adams addressed the Senate.

On Wednesday, June 3, 1789, the oath of office was administered to John Adams, who, in turn, administered the oath to the Senate members. The oath, "I . . . [name] do solemnly swear or affirm (as the case may be) that I will support the Constitution of the United States," was required by "an act to regulate the time and manner of administering certain oaths," June 1, 1789 (1 Stat.L.23), Chapter One, Statute One.

The oath as administered at present is, "I do solemnly swear (or affirm) that I will support and defend the Constitution of the United States against all enemies, foreign and domestic; that I will bear true faith and allegiance to the same; that I take this obligation freely, without any mental reservation or purpose of evasion, and that I will well and faithfully discharge the duties of the office on which I am about to enter. So help me God."

Adams made an inaugural address. He spoke about the successful formation of the federal union, the adoption of the federal Constitution, and the auspicious circumstances under which the new government came into operation "under the presidency of him who had led the American armies to victory and conducted by those who had contributed to achieve Independence."

THE ELECTION OF 1796 —BROTHERS ASPIRED TO THE VICE PRESIDENCY

Washington announced that he would not be a candidate for a third term. The electors cast 276 ballots for 13 candidates for the presidency and the vice presidency. One of them was George Washington, who received two votes even though he was not a candidate. Two of the other twelve were brothers, Thomas Pinckney of South Carolina, who received 59 votes, Charles Cotesworth Pinckney, of South Carolina, who received 1 vote. Since 138 of the votes cast were for the President and were apportioned 71 to John Adams and 68 to Thomas Jefferson, the two Pinckney brothers were really vice presidential candidates.

INAUGURATION

John Adams, the first Vice President to be elevated to the presidency, was the only President besides George Washington to be inaugurated at Philadelphia. He was the first President to whom the oath of office was administered by a Chief Justice. On Saturday, March 4, 1797, in the Chamber of the House of Representatives in Federal Hall, the oath was administered to John Adams by Oliver Ellsworth, chief justice of the United States. Adams was driven to the inauguration in a gilded coach drawn by six white horses.

SECRETARY OF THE NAVY APPOINTED BY ADAMS

The secretary of war was in charge of both the army and the navy, until May 21, 1798, when President John Adams appointed Benjamin Stoddert as the first secretary of the navy.

APPOINTMENT OF A GENERAL AUTHORIZED

The act of May 28, 1798 (1 Stat.L.558), "an act authorizing the President of the United States to raise a provisional army," empowered the President to appoint, by and with the advice and consent of the Senate, a commander of the army which may be raised by virtue of this act, and who being commissioned as lieutenant-general may be authorized to command the armies of the United States, and shall be entitled to the following pay and emoluments, viz.: two-hundred-and-fifty dollars monthly pay, fifty dollars monthly allowance for forage, when the same shall not be provided by the United States, and forty rations per day, or money in lieu thereof at the current price, who shall have authority to appoint, from time to time, such number of aids not exceeding four, and secretaries not exceeding two, as he may judge proper, each to have the rank, pay and emoluments of a lieutenant-colonel.

CONGRESS IN SESSION AT WASHINGTON

The first Congress to meet at Washington, D.C., was the Sixth Congress; the second session opened on November 17, 1800, and lasted until March 3, 1801 (107 days). The House of Representatives did not have a quorum until November 18, and the Senate did not have a quorum until November 21. On November 22, 1800, President John Adams read his fourth annual address to Congress.

ADAMS APPOINTED "MIDNIGHT JUDGES"

On February 13, 1801, Congress passed "an act to provide for the more convenient organization of the Courts of the United States" (2 Stat.L.89). It provided for the appointment of eighteen new judges. President John Adams sat at his desk until midnight, March 3, 1801, signing the appointment of Federalists to public offices.

The law was repealed during Jefferson's term and the judges lost their offices. The act of April 29, 1802, "an act to amend the Judicial System of the United States," voided the appointments.

ADAMS DEFEATED FOR REELECTION

John Adams was the first President of the United States who was defeated for reelection. After completing his term, 1797-1801, John Adams hoped to be reelected but the electors decided otherwise.

Thomas Jefferson received 73 electoral votes and was elected President and Aaron Burr, who had the same number of votes, was elected Vice President. The decision was referred to the House of Representatives. John Adams received 65 electoral votes, Charles Cotesworth Pinckney 64 votes and John Jay 1 vote.

ADAMS RECALLED SON

On January 31, 1801, John Adams recalled his son, John Quincy Adams, from his post as minister to Prussia to prevent President-elect Thomas Jefferson from dismissing him. On April 26, 1801, the recall reached John Quincy Adams, who returned to Philadelphia, Pa., on September 4, 1801.

Adams' letter to Secretary of State John Marshall stated:

I request you would cause to be prepared letters for me to sign, to the King of Prussia recalling Mr. John Quincy Adams as minister plenipotentiary from his court. . . . I wish you to make out one letter to go by the way of Hamburg, another by Holland, a third by France, a fourth through Mr. King in England, a fifth, if you please, by the way of Bremen or Stettin, or any channel most likely to convey it soon. It is my opinion this minister ought to be recalled from Prussia. . . . Besides, it is my opinion that it is my duty to call him home.

ABSENCE AT INAUGURATION OF SUCCESSOR

John Adams started the precedent of not attending the inauguration of his successor. When Thomas Jefferson was inaugurated on March 4, 1801, Adams absented himself rather than witness the success of his political rival. His son, John Quincy Adams, likewise refused to attend the inauguration services for Andrew Jackson and other Presidents also followed this example.

FATHER AND SON PRESIDENTS

John Adams and John Quincy Adams were the only father and son to be inaugurated Presidents of the United States. They each served one term. John Adams lived to see his son sworn in as President.

ADAMS' LAST WORDS

The last words attributed to John Adams were made by him without a full knowledge of the facts. Adams' last words were reported to have been "Thomas Jefferson still survives." He had not learned, nor had he any means of knowing, that Thomas Jefferson had died the same morning at 9:50 on July 4, 1826, at Monticello, Va.

ADAMS SUPPLIED VITAL INFORMATION

In a letter dated March 11, 1809, from Quincy, Mass., in response to a request for biographical material, John Adams wrote to Skelton Jones:

I was born in Quincy on the 19th of October 1735. . . .

The Fourth of March 1801. The causes of my retirement are to be found in the writings of Freneau, Markoe, Ned Church, Andrew Brown, Paine, Callender, Hamilton, Cobbet and John Ward Fennon and many others, but more especially in the circular letters of Members of Congress from the southern and middle States. Without a complete collection of all these libels, no faithful history of the last twenty years can ever be written, nor any adequate account given of the causes of my retirement from public life.

I have one head, four limbs and five senses, like any other

man, and nothing peculiar in any of them.

I have been married forty-four years to Miss Abigail Smith on the 25th of October 1764 in her father's house at Weymouth, the next town to his, and by her father who was a clergyman.

I have no miniature, and have been too much abused by painters ever to sit to any one again.

THE FIRST LADY AT THE EXECUTIVE MANSION

Mrs. John Adams, the first President's wife to live in the Executive Mansion, did not move to Washington, D.C., until November 1800, when the President's House was ready for occupancy. A New Year's reception was held there in 1801, the first reception at the White House. As Adams' term of office expired on March 3, 1801, Mrs. Adams resided at the Executive Mansion less than four months. She maintained the same strict etiquette as Martha Washington. She preferred the climate at Quincy, Mass., however, and she maintained her interests there, anticipating the time when her husband's term would be completed.

EXTRACT FROM FIRST LETTER FROM THE WHITE HOUSE BY A PRESIDENT (JOHN ADAMS TO HIS WIFE, ABIGAIL ADAMS)

President's House,
Washington City
2 November, 1800

MY DEAREST FRIEND,

We arrived here last night, or rather yesterday, at one o'clock, and here we dined and slept. . . . Besides, it is fit and proper that you and I should retire together, and not one before the other. Before I end my letter, I pray heaven to bestow the best of blessings on this house, and on all that shall hereafter inhabit it. May none but honest and wise men ever rule under this roof! I shall not attempt a description of it. You will form the best idea of it from inspection. . . .

I am, with unabated confidence and affection, yours,

JOHN ADAMS

MRS. ADAMS' IMPRESSION OF THE WHITE HOUSE (A LETTER TO HER DAUGHTER)

Washington,
21 November, 1800

MY DEAR CHILD:

I arrived here on Sunday

last, and without meeting with any accident worth noticing, except losing ourselves when we left Baltimore, and going eight or nine miles on the Frederick road, by which means we were obliged to go the other eight through woods, where we wandered two hours without finding a guide, or the path. . . . The house is made habitable, but there is not a single apartment finished, and all withinside, except the plastering has been done since Briesler came. We have not the least fence, yard, or other convenience, without, and the great unfinished audience room I make a drying-room of, to hang up the clothes in. The principal stairs are not up, and will not be this winter. . . .

Affectionately your mother,

A. ADAMS

Th.Jefferson.

THOMAS JEFFERSON

Born—Apr. 13, 1743

Birthplace—Shadwell, Goochland County, now Albemarle County, Va.

College attended—College of William and Mary, Williamsburg, Va.

Date of graduation—Apr. 25, 1762

Religion—No specific denomination

Ancestry—Welsh

Occupation—Lawyer, writer

Date and place of marriage—Jan. 1, 1772, Williamsburg, Va., at the Forest, the Wayles estate

Age at marriage—28 years, 263 days

Years married—10 years, 248 days

Political party—Democratic-Republican

State represented—Virginia

Term of office—Mar. 4, 1801-Mar. 3, 1809

Term served—8 years

Administration—4th, 5th

Congresses—7th, 8th, 9th, 10th

Age at inauguration—57 years, 325 days

Lived after term—17 years, 122 days

Occupation after term—Retired

Date of death—July 4, 1826

Age at death—83 years, 82 days

Place of death—Charlottesville, Va.

Burial place—Charlottesville, Va.

For additional data see the end of this section and also specific subject headings in the Index.

PARENTS

Father—Peter Jefferson

Born—Feb. 29, 1708

Married—Oct. 2, 1739

Occupation—Professor, land owner, planter, surveyor

Died—Aug. 17, 1757

Age at death—49 years, 170 days

Mother—Jane Randolph Jefferson

Born—Feb. 9, 1720, London, England

Died—Mar. 31, 1776

Age at death—56 years, 50 days

BROTHERS AND SISTERS

Thomas Jefferson was the third child in a family of ten.

CHILDREN

Martha Washington Jefferson, b. Sept. 27, 1772, Monticello, Va.; m. Feb. 23, 1790, Thomas Mann Randolph; d. Oct. 10, 1836

Jane Randolph Jefferson, b. Apr. 3, 1774; d. Sept. 1775

——Jefferson (son), b. May 28, 1777; d. June 14, 1777

Mary ("Marie," "Polly") Jefferson, b. Aug. 1, 1778; m. Oct. 13, 1797, John Wayles Eppes; d. Apr. 17, 1804

Lucy Elizabeth Jefferson, b. Nov. 3, 1780, Richmond, Va.; d. Apr. 15, 1781

Lucy Elizabeth Jefferson, b. May 8, 1782; d. Nov. 17, 1785, Eppington, Va.

MRS. THOMAS JEFFERSON

Name—Martha Wayles Skelton Jefferson

Date of birth—Oct. 19, 1748

Birthplace—Charles City County, Va.

Age at marriage—23 years, 74 days

Children by Jefferson—1 son, 5 daughters

Mother—Martha Eppes Wayles

Father—John Wayles

His occupation—Lawyer, planter

Date of death—Sept. 6, 1782

Age at death—33 years, 322 days

Place of death—Monticello, Va.

Burial place—Monticello, Va.

Years younger than the President—5 years, 189 days

Years the President survived her—43 years, 301 days

At the time of her marriage to Jefferson she was the widow of Bathurst Skelton, by whom she had one child—a son who was born Nov. 7, 1767, and who died June 10, 1771.

THE ELECTION OF 1800

The fourth national election was held on November 4, 1800. It showed that the loosely knitted political groups had begun to organize. The Federalists, still advocating a strong central government with only such political power for the various states as was absolutely necessary, began to encounter apparent dissatisfaction with their policies. The Federalist congressmen, in a congressional caucus which met in a Senate chamber, decided to support Adams for a second term with Charles Cotesworth Pinckney of South Carolina as a running mate.

Since both the President and the Vice President were elected by the same ballot, one faction of the Federalists hoped that Pinckney would receive the presidency and that Adams with the second greatest number of votes might become Vice President.

The Democratic-Republicans, believing that the states should yield to the federal government only that which was necessary, denounced the federal caucus but continued to work under it. At a congressional caucus held in Philadelphia, Pa., the Democratic-Republicans placed their hopes on Thomas Jefferson of Virginia and Aaron Burr of New York. At this caucus they adopted the first national platform ever formulated by a political party.

When the electoral votes of 1800 were counted, another unusual situation developed. The electors cast 276 votes. Of these, 73 were cast for Thomas Jefferson and 73 for Aaron Burr, both Democratic-Republicans. The Federalists cast 65 votes for John Adams, 64 votes for Charles Cotesworth Pinckney, and 1 vote for John Jay of New York.

Inasmuch as both Jefferson and Burr had each received 73 votes and tied for first place, the election was referred to the House of Representatives to decide which candidate would be the President and which would be the Vice President. The outcome was not as critical as the election of 1796, since both candidates were members of the same political faction. The issue was not whether the Federalists or the Democratic-Republicans should be in power, but which Democratic-Republican should be elected, Jefferson or Burr. It was not a contest of political factions but of personalities.

The balloting to decide the tie commenced on February 11, 1801. The representatives did not vote individually but by state groups, each state being entitled to one vote. On the first ballot, Jefferson had eight states and Burr six states, with Maryland and Vermont equally divided. As a majority was required, further ballots were taken. On February 17, the thirty-sixth ballot was taken to arrive at a choice. Ten states voted for Jefferson, four for Burr, and two voted blank. Jefferson was declared elected President and Burr his Vice President.

THE ELECTION OF 1804

In 1804, after Jefferson had served four years the Democratic-Republicans found Vice President Aaron Burr no longer acceptable. His catering to the Federalists for their support had lowered his standing with his own party, and his killing of Alexander Hamilton in a duel had made him *persona non grata* with the public. When the congressional caucus was held on February 25, 1804, the Democratic-Republicans decided to support Jefferson for a second term as President. They with-

drew their support of Burr and favored George Clinton, governor of New York for eighteen years, to supplant him as Vice President.

The Federalists, whose party strength was waning, held no congressional caucus and threw their support to Charles Cotesworth Pinckney of South Carolina for President and Rufus King of New York for Vice President.

Jefferson won a clear-cut victory and was elected President for a second term, carrying George Clinton with him as Vice President. He received 162 of the 176 electoral votes.

The election of November 6, 1804 was the first in which the President and the Vice President were voted for separately. This change in election procedure, authorized by the Twelfth Amendment to the Constitution, went into effect September 25, 1804, and superseded Article II, Section 1, paragraph three of the Constitution. The bill was passed by the Senate on December 3, 1803, by a vote of 22 yeas to 10 nays, and by the House of Representatives on December 9, 1803, by a vote of 83 yeas to 42 nays, with the Speaker, Nathaniel Macon of North Carolina, casting the deciding vote to make the necessary two-thirds majority. The amendment was submitted to the states, was ratified by three-fourths of them, and was declared in force on September 25, 1804. Connecticut, Delaware, Massachusetts, and New Hampshire rejected the amendment.

ELECTORAL VOTES
(176—17 states)

Jefferson received 92.05 per cent (162 votes—15 states) as follows: Ga. 6; Ky. 8; Md. 9 (of the 11 votes); Mass. 19; N.H. 7; N.J. 8; N.Y. 19; N.C. 14; Ohio 3; Pa. 20; R.I. 4; S.C. 10; Tenn. 5; Vt. 6; Va. 24.

Pinckney received 7.95 per cent (14 votes—2 states) as follows: Conn. 9; Del. 3; Md. 2 (of the 11 votes).

ADMINISTRATION— IMPORTANT DATES

June 10, 1801, Tripoli declared war against the United States

Feb. 6, 1802, war declared against Tripoli

Mar. 16, 1802, Army engineer corps created

Mar. 16, 1802, United States Military Academy authorized; opened July 4, 1802

Nov. 29, 1802, Ohio admitted as seventeenth state

Feb. 1803, Marbury *vs.* Madison —Supreme Court decision declaring portion of Judiciary Act of 1789 unconstitutional

Apr. 30, 1803, Louisiana Purchase made from France for $15 million

May 2, 1803, Louisiana Purchase treaty signed

Oct. 31, 1803, Captain Bainbridge of the *Philadelphia* ran on a reef pursuing Tripoli cruiser and was captured

Dec. 30, 1803, France formally ceded Louisiana to United States

Feb. 3, 1804, Lieutenant Decatur, aboard the *Philadelphia,* defeated Tripolitans

Mar. 12, 1804, Judge John Pickering impeached and removed from office in trial begun Mar. 3, 1803 (first impeachment of a federal judge)

May 14, 1804, Lewis and Clark expedition left St. Louis

July 12, 1804, Alexander Hamilton killed by Aaron Burr in a duel

Sept. 25, 1804, Twelfth Amendment to the Constitution ratified

Jan. 11, 1805, Michigan Territory created

Mar. 1, 1805, Supreme Court Justice Samuel Chase acquitted in impeachment trial begun Nov. 30, 1804 (first impeachment proceedings against a Supreme Court justice)

June 4, 1805, treaty of peace and amity signed with Tripoli

Nov. 15, 1805, Lewis and Clark reached Pacific Ocean

Mar. 29, 1806, Cumberland road construction to Ohio authorized

Nov. 13, 1806, Lieutenant Zebulon Pike discovered Colorado peak later named for him

Mar. 26, 1807, Territory of Orleans established

May 22, 1807-Oct. 20, 1807, trial of Aaron Burr at Richmond, Va., for conspiracy

June 1807, American ship *Chesapeake* fired upon by British *Leopard; Chesapeake* searched and British deserters seized

Aug. 7, 1807, Robert Fulton's steamboat *Clermont* made trip on Hudson River

Dec. 22, 1807, Embargo Act against international commerce

Jan. 1, 1808, law prohibiting importation of African slaves became effective

Nov. 10, 1808, Osage Treaty signed

Feb. 3, 1809, Illinois Territory established

Mar. 1, 1809, trade with Great Britain and France prohibited by nonintercourse act

APPOINTMENTS TO THE SUPREME COURT

Associate Justices

William Johnson, S.C., Mar. 26, 1804

Brockholst Livingston, N.Y., Nov. 10, 1806

Thomas Todd, Ky., Mar. 3, 1807

Levi Lincoln, Mass., Jan. 7, 1811 (declined to serve)

John Quincy Adams, Mass., Feb. 22, 1811 (declined to serve)

IMPORTANT DATES IN HIS LIFE

1757, inherited land and slaves on death of his father and took over responsibilities as head of the family

1767, admitted to the bar

May 11, 1769, member of Virginia House of Burgesses (served until 1774)

Apr. 1773, attended meeting of Committee of Correspondence

Mar. 1775, deputy delegate to Continental Congress

July 2, 1776, chairman of committee to prepare Declaration of Independence

June 1, 1779, elected governor of Virginia

June 2, 1780, reelected governor

June 1781, resigned governorship; offered post as peace commissioner by Continental

Congress but declined appointment

J:ne 1783, drafted constitution for Virginia

May 7, 1784, appointed minister plenipotentiary to France

Mar. 10, 1785, elected by Congress to succeed Franklin as minister to France

1785, minister to France; presented credentials to King of France on May 14

1786-1787, diplomatic missions in Paris and London

1789, prepared Charter of Rights for France

Sept. 26, 1789, confirmed as secretary of state

Oct. 22-Nov. 23, 1789, returned from France on the *Clermont,* disembarking at Norfolk, Va.

Feb. 14, 1790-Dec. 3, 1793, served as secretary of state

Jan. 1797, elected president of Philosophical Society

1800, prepared *Parliamentary Manual*

Mar. 4, 1801-Mar. 3, 1805, President (1st term)

May 2, 1803, Louisiana Purchase treaty signed

Mar. 4, 1805-Mar. 3, 1809, President (2nd term)

Sept. 1814, sold his library to Library of Congress

Mar. 29, 1819, rector of University of Virginia

Nov. 12, 1822, injured in fall (left forearm broken and wrist bones dislocated)

THOMAS JEFFERSON

——was the second President born in Virginia.

——was the second President to marry a widow.

——was the first widower inaugurated President.

——was the first President who had been a governor of a state.

——was the first President to have served in a cabinet.

——was the first President whose parents had twins.

——was the first President elected by the House of Representatives.

——was the first President inaugurated at Washington, D.C.

——was the first President who had served as secretary of state.

JEFFERSON'S VICE PRESIDENTS

FIRST TERM

Vice President—Aaron Burr (3rd V.P.)

Date of birth—Feb. 6, 1756

Birthplace—Newark, N.J.

Political party—Democratic-Republican

State represented—New York

Term of office—Mar. 4, 1801-
Mar. 3, 1805

Age at inauguration—45 years,
26 days

Occupation after term—Lawyer

Date of death—Sept. 14, 1836

Place of death—Staten Island,
N.Y.

Age at death—80 years, 220
days

Burial place—Princeton Cemetery, Princeton, N.J.

SECOND TERM

Vice President—George Clinton (4th V.P.)

Date of birth—July 26, 1739

Birthplace—Little Britain, N.Y.

Political party—Democratic-
Republican

State represented—New York

Term of office—Mar. 4, 1805-
Mar. 3, 1809

Age at inauguration—65 years,
221 days

Occupation after term—Died
in office during his term as
Madison's Vice President

Date of death—Apr. 20, 1812

Place of death—Washington,
D.C.

Age at death—72 years, 268
days

Burial place—Kingston, N.Y.

See also James Madison, 4th
President—Madison's Vice
Presidents.

VICE PRESIDENT CLINTON UNSUCCESSFUL IN THREE PREVIOUS ELECTIONS

George Clinton of New York,
who was elected Vice President
under Thomas Jefferson (second term, 1805-1809) and under
James Madison (first term,
1809-1813) had been unsuccessful in three previous elections.
In 1789 he received three votes
for the vice presidency; in 1793
he received fifty electoral votes;
and in 1797 he received seven
electoral votes.

ADDITIONAL DATA ON JEFFERSON

JEFFERSON ADVOCATED RELIGIOUS FREEDOM

One of Jefferson's greatest
achievements was the bill establishing religious freedom which
was drawn up by him and enacted by the Legislature of Virginia in 1779.

Section 2 stated:

We the General Assembly
of Virginia do enact that no
man shall be compelled to fre-

quent or support any religious worship, place, or ministry whatsoever, nor shall be enforced, restrained, molested, or burthened in his body or goods, or shall otherwise suffer, on account of his religious opinions or belief; but that all men shall be free to profess, and by argument to maintain, their opinions in matters of religion, and that the same shall in no wise diminish, enlarge, or affect their civil capacities.

JEFFERSON ADVOCATED DECIMAL SYSTEM OF CURRENCY

In April 1784 Thomas Jefferson wrote an important document entitled "Notes on the Establishment of a Money Unit and of a Coinage for the United States." The paper concluded:

My proposition then, is, that our notation of money shall be decimal, descending *ad libitum* of the person noting; that the Unit of this notation shall be a Dollar; that coins shall be accommodated to it from ten dollars to the hundredth of dollar; and that, to set this on foot, the resolutions be adopted which were proposed in the notes, only substituting *an enquiry into the fineness of the coins* in lieu of *an assay of them.*

GOVERNOR ELECTED PRESIDENT

Thomas Jefferson was the first governor of a state to be elected President. He was governor of Virginia from 1779 to 1781.

VICE PRESIDENT DEFEATED PRESIDENT

Thomas Jefferson was the only Vice President to defeat a President. In the election of 1800, Thomas Jefferson of Virginia and Aaron Burr of New York received 73 electoral votes, the election being decided in Jefferson's favor by the House of Representatives. Accordingly, Aaron Burr was made the Vice President. President John Adams received only 65 electoral votes and was defeated in his quest for reelection.

FIRST INAUGURATION

Thomas Jefferson was the first President to take the oath of office at Washington, D.C. It was a fair day and he walked to the Capitol from Mrs. Conrad's boarding house, one block away, accompanied by a group of riflemen, artillerymen, and civilians. The oath was administered on Wednesday, March 4, 1801, by Chief Justice John Marshall in the Senate Chamber in the Capitol. Only the north wing of the Capitol building had been completed and the center was unfinished. President John Adams drove out of the city at dawn, refusing to attend the inauguration of his successor to witness what he considered the dissolution of the republic.

JEFFERSON AT THE EXECUTIVE MANSION

The White House, which at the time of Jefferson's inauguration was called the President's House, was not fully completed. Jefferson described it as "a great stone house, big enough for two emperors, one pope and the grand lama in the bargain." Jefferson did not move into the official residence until March 19, 1801.

TROOPS REVIEWED FROM THE WHITE HOUSE

Thomas Jefferson held the first presidential review of military forces from his residence at the White House. On July 4, 1801, he reviewed the Marines, who were led by the Marine Band.

HAND-SHAKING INTRODUCED

On July 4, 1801, President Jefferson held a reception in the Blue Room at the White House which was attended by about one hundred guests. Jefferson introduced the custom of having the guests shake hands instead of bowing stiffly, a custom observed by Presidents Washington and Adams.

JEFFERSON SUBMITTED ANNUAL ADDRESS IN WRITING

When Thomas Jefferson prepared his first annual message to Congress, he sent it to that body on December 8, 1801, instead of addressing both houses in person as Washington and Adams had done. On the same date, he wrote the presiding officer of each house. The following letter was included with the message for the Senate:

Sir: The circumstances under which we find ourselves at this place rendering inconvenient the mode heretofore practiced of making by personal address the first communications between the legislative and executive branches, I have adopted that by message, as used on all subsequent occasions through the session. In doing this I have had principal regard to the convenience of the Legislature, to the economy of their time, to their relief from the embarrassment of immediate answers on subjects not yet fully before them, and to the benefits thence resulting to the public affairs. Trusting that a procedure founded in these motives will meet their approbation, I beg leave through you, sir, to communicate the inclosed message, with the documents accompanying it, to the honorable the Senate, and pray you to accept for yourself and them the homage of my high respect and consideration.

TH. JEFFERSON

UNITED STATES DOUBLED ITS AREA

The Louisiana Purchase contract, dated April 30, 1803, and signed on May 2, 1803, increased United States territory by approximately 846,000 square miles, practically doubling the area of the United States. Jefferson bought from Napoleon an area which was to become the entire states or substantial parts of Arkansas, Colorado, Iowa, Kansas, Louisiana, Minnesota, Missouri, Montana, Nebraska, North Dakota, Oklahoma, South Dakota, and Wyoming. The purchase price was $11,250,000, and the United States also assumed claims of Americans against France estimated at about $3,750,000.

SECOND INAUGURATION

Thomas Jefferson took the oath of office for his second term on Monday, March 4, 1805, in the Senate Chamber. Chief Justice John Marshall administered the oath. In the evening, a ceremony in the East Room of the Executive Mansion was attended by a large crowd which caused much disorder.

JEFFERSON ASSERTED PRESIDENT'S IMMUNITY TO COURTS

The lawyers defending Aaron Burr, who had been indicted for high treason, attempted to issue a *duces tecum* subpoena on June 10, 1807, on President Jefferson. In a letter to United States Attorney George Hay, dated June 20, 1807, President Jefferson wrote:

Let us apply the Judge's own doctrine to the case of himself and his brethren. The Sheriff of Henrico summons him from the bench to quell a riot somewhere in his country. The Federal judge is by the general law a part of the *posse* of the state sheriff. Would the judge abandon major duties to perform lesser ones? Again, the court of Orleans or Maine commands by subpoenas the attendance of all judges of the Supreme Court. Would they abandon their posts as judges and the interest of millions committed to them to serve the purposes of a single individual? The leading principle of our constitution is the independence of the legislature, executive and judiciary of each other; and none are more jealous of this than the judiciary. But would the executive be independent of the judiciary if he were subject to the commands of the latter and to imprisonment for disobedience; if the several courts could bandy him from pillar to post, keep him constantly trudging from north to south, and east to west, and withdraw him entirely from his constitutional duties?

JEFFERSON SIGNED
FIRST EMBARGO ACT

President Jefferson signed the first embargo act. It was passed December 22, 1807, (2 Stat.L.

451) by a vote of 82 to 44. Intended to prevent the United States from being drawn into the war between Britain and France, the act placed "an embargo on all ships and vessels in the ports and harbors of the United States" and required all American ships to refrain from international commerce. The act, signed by President Jefferson, stopped all foreign trade and was repealed on March 1, 1809. A later act was substituted, which stopped trade with England and France.

JEFFERSON WROTE
HIS OWN EPITAPH

Thomas Jefferson wrote the epitaph to be placed over his grave. He made no mention of his presidency. The inscription reads: "Here was buried Thomas Jefferson, author of the Declaration of American Independence, of the statute of Virginia for religious freedom, and father of the University of Virginia."

FIRST WIDOWER
TO BECOME
PRESIDENT

Thomas Jefferson was the first widower to become President of the United States. His wife, Martha Wayles Skelton, died 18 years, 179 days before he was inaugurated. Jefferson never remarried and was a widower 35 years, 302 days. Four of his six children died before he became President.

HOSTESSES AT THE WHITE HOUSE

Thomas Jefferson had been a widower for about eighteen years when he entered the White House. The duties of mistress of the White House were assumed by his daughters; one was Martha Washington Jefferson, the wife of Thomas Mann Randolph, and the other was Marie Jefferson, the wife of John Wayles Eppes. The unhealthy condition of the city of Washington, which was low and marshy, engendered disease, and his daughters preferred not to bring their children to the capital city. Mrs. James Madison, wife of the Secretary of State, generally presided at functions in the absence of Jefferson's daughters. Jefferson opposed the levees, or official receptions, which he thought were not democratic.

FIRST CHILD BORN IN THE WHITE HOUSE

James Madison Randolph, the grandson of President Thomas Jefferson, was the first child born in the White House. He was born January 17, 1806, and died January 23, 1834. His parents were Thomas Mann Randolph and Martha Jefferson Randolph, the daughter of President Jefferson.

James Madison

JAMES MADISON

Born—Mar. 16, 1751

Birthplace—Port Conway, Va.

College attended—College of New Jersey, now Princeton University, Princeton, N.J.

Date of graduation—Sept. 25, 1771, Bachelor of Arts (completed four-year course in three years)

Religion—Episcopalian

Ancestry—English

Occupation—Lawyer

Date and place of marriage—Sept. 15, 1794, Harewood, Jefferson County, Va.

Age at marriage—43 years, 183 days

Years married—41 years, 286 days

Political party—Democratic-Republican

State represented—Virginia

Term of office—Mar. 4, 1809-Mar. 3, 1817

Term served—8 years

Administration—6th, 7th

Congresses—11th, 12th, 13th, 14th

Age at inauguration—57 years, 353 days

Lived after term—19 years, 116 days

Occupation after term—Retired

Date of death—June 28, 1836

Age at death—85 years, 104 days

Place of death—Montpelier, Va.

Burial place—Family plot, Montpelier, Va.

For additional data see the end of this section and also specific subject headings in the Index.

PARENTS

Father—James Madison

Born—Mar. 27, 1723

Married—Sept. 15, 1749

Occupation—Justice of the peace, vestryman, land owner, farmer

Died—Feb. 27, 1801

Age at death—77 years, 337 days

Mother—Eleanor ("Nellie") Rose Conway Madison

Born—Jan. 9, 1731

Died—Feb. 11, 1829

Age at death—98 years, 33 days

BROTHERS AND SISTERS

James Madison was the oldest of twelve children.

CHILDREN

None

MRS. JAMES MADISON

Name—Dorothea ("Dolley," incorrectly "Dolly") Dandridge Payne Todd Madison

Date of birth—May 20, 1768

Birthplace—now Guilford County, N.C.

Age at marriage—26 years, 118 days

Children by Madison—None

Mother—Mary Coles Payne

Father—John Payne

His occupation—Farmer, planter

Date of death—July 12, 1849

Age at death—81 years, 53 days

Place of death—Washington, D.C.

Burial place—Montpelier, Va.

Years younger than the President—17 years, 65 days

Years she survived the President—13 years, 14 days

At the time of her marriage to Madison she was the widow of John Todd, by whom she had two sons, one of whom died in infancy.

THE ELECTION OF 1808

After he had served two terms (1801-1809) as President, Jefferson carried out the policy established by George Washington and refused to be a candidate for a third term. Jefferson favored James Monroe of Virginia as his successor, but the Democratic-Republican caucus decided in favor of James Madison, also of Virginia.

The Federalists, again without a congressional caucus, put up the same candidate, Charles Cotesworth Pinckney of South

Carolina, whom they had unsuccessfully run in 1804.

For the vice-presidency the Democratic-Republican votes were split among four candidates: George Clinton of New York (who had served under Jefferson), John Langdon of New Hampshire, James Madison, and James Monroe.

The Federalist candidate for the vice presidency was Rufus King of New York, who had been Pinckney's running mate in 1804.

ELECTORAL VOTES (175
votes—17 states)

Madison received 69.71 per cent (122 votes—12 states) as follows: Ga. 6; Ky. 7; Md. 9 (of the 11 votes); N.J. 8; N.Y. 13 (of the 19 votes); N.C. 11 (of the 14 votes); Ohio 3; Pa. 20; S.C. 10; Tenn. 5; Vt. 6; Va. 24.

Pinckney received 26.86 per cent (47 votes—5 states) as follows: Conn. 9; Del. 3; Md. 2 (of the 11 votes); Mass. 19; N.H. 7; N.C. 3 (of the 14 votes); R.I. 4.

Clinton received 3.43 per cent (6 votes—of the 19 N.Y. votes).

For the vice presidency Clinton received 113 votes as follows: Ga. 6; Ky. 7; Md. 9 (of the 11 votes); N.J. 8; N.Y. 13 (of the 19 votes); N.C. 11 (of the 14 votes); Pa. 20; S.C. 10; Tenn. 5, Va. 24.

King, the Federalist, received 47 votes as follows: Conn. 9; Del. 3; Md. 2 (of the 11 votes); Mass. 19; N.H. 7; N.C. 3 (of the 14 votes); R.I. 4.

The other Democratic-Republican candidates for the vice presidency received the following votes:

Langdon—Ohio 3; Vt. 6

Madison—N.Y. 3 (of the 19 votes)

Monroe—N.Y. 3 (of the 19 votes)

THE ELECTION OF 1812

After James Madison had served one term, the Democratic-Republicans in May 1812 chose to support him for a second term. George Clinton had died on April 12 while serving as Vice President and the party favored John Langdon of New Hampshire for that office. Langdon, however, declined to run because of his age (71), and Elbridge Gerry of Massachusetts was then selected for the vice presidency.

The Federalists in caucus at New York City decided to support the nomination of De Witt Clinton of New York and Jared Ingersoll of Pennsylvania.

ELECTORAL VOTES (217 votes—18 states)

Madison received 58.99 per cent (128 votes—11 states) as follows: Ga. 8; Ky. 12; La. 3; Md. 6 (of the 11 votes); N.C. 15; Ohio 7; Pa. 25; S.C. 11; Tenn. 8; Vt. 8; Va. 25.

Clinton received 41.01 per cent (89 votes—7 states) as follows: Conn. 9; Del. 4; Md. 5 (of the 11 votes); Mass. 22; N.H. 8; N.J. 8; N.Y. 29; R.I. 4.

Gerry received 131 votes for the vice presidency as follows: Ga. 8; Ky. 12; La. 3; Md. 6 (of the 11 votes); Mass. 2 (of the 22 votes); N.H. 1 (of the 8 votes); N.C. 15; Ohio 7; Pa. 25; S.C. 11; Tenn. 8; Vt. 8; Va. 25.

Ingersoll received 86 votes for the vice presidency as follows: Conn. 9; Del. 4; Md. 5 (of the 11 votes); Mass. 20 (of the 22 votes); N.H. 7 (of the 8 votes); N.J. 8; N.Y. 29; R.I. 4.

APPOINTMENTS TO THE SUPREME COURT

Associate Justices

Joseph Story, Mass., Nov. 18, 1811

Gabriel Duvall, Md., Nov. 18, 1811

ADMINISTRATION— IMPORTANT DATES

Sept. 30, 1809, General W. H. Harrison negotiated treaty with Indians for three million acres

1810-1811, British and French naval blockades during Napoleonic wars continued to harass American shipping

Oct. 1, 1811, arrival in New Orleans, La., of first steamboat to travel from Pittsburgh, Pa., to New Orleans

Nov. 7, 1811, General W. H. Harrison defeated Indian attackers at battle of Tippecanoe

Mar. 4, 1812, first war bond issue authorized

Apr. 20, 1812, death of George Clinton, first Vice President to die in office

Apr. 30, 1812, Louisiana admitted as the 18th state

June 4, 1812, Missouri Territory organized

June 18, 1812, war declared against Great Britain

June 30, 1812, first interest-bearing treasury notes authorized

Aug. 16, 1812, without firing a shot, General William Hull surrendered Detroit and Michigan Territory to the British under General Brock

Aug. 19, 1812, *Constitution,* under Captain Isaac Hull, defeated and burned the British *Guerrière* off Nova Scotia

Sept. 4, 1812, Captain Zachary Taylor defended Fort Harrison against Indian attack

Oct. 25, 1812, *United States*, under Captain Decatur, defeated the *Macedonian*

Mar. 25, 1813, *Essex*, on cruise around Cape Horn, engaged in first U.S. naval encounter in the Pacific Ocean

Sept. 10, 1813, Oliver Hazard Perry's naval victory on Lake Erie

Aug. 25, 1814, British captured Washington, D.C.

Sept. 11, 1814, defeat of British on Lake Champlain

Dec. 24, 1814, peace treaty signed with Great Britain

1815, treaties with Algiers, Tripoli, and Tunis

Jan. 8, 1815, battle of New Orleans

Jan. 30, 1815, Thomas Jefferson's library purchased for Library of Congress

July 4, 1815, cornerstone of first monument to George Washington laid at Baltimore, Md.

1816, public debt of the United States exceeded $1 million for the first time

Dec. 11, 1816, Indiana admitted as the 19th state

Feb. 5, 1817, first gas light company incorporated, Baltimore, Md.

IMPORTANT DATES IN HIS LIFE

1763-1767, attended Donald Robertson's school, King and Queen County, Va.

1767-1768, private instruction from the Reverend Thomas Martin

1769-1772, student at Princeton (graduated 1771); one-year post-graduate course

17——, admitted to the bar

1772-1774, in ill health, continued studies at home

Dec. 1774, member of Committee of Safety

May 6, 1776, delegate to Williamsburg convention which declared for independence and set up state government

17——, drafted Virginia guarantee of religious liberty

1776-1777, member of Virginia legislature

1777, elected to Virginia State Council

Jan. 14, 1778, member of executive council to direct Virginia's activities in the Revolution

Dec. 14, 1779, elected by Virginia Legislature to Continental Congress

Mar. 20, 1780-Feb. 25, 1783, member of Continental Congress

1784-1786, member of Virginia legislature

1786-1788, member of Continental Congress

Feb.-Apr. 1787, attended Congress at New York

May 2, 1787, left for Federal Convention at Philadelphia

June 2, 1788, member of Virginia Ratification Convention

Mar. 4, 1789-Mar. 3, 1797, U.S. House of Representatives (from Virginia)

1794, declined Washington's invitation to join mission to France and position as secretary of state

May 2, 1801-Mar. 3, 1809, secretary of state under Jefferson

Mar. 4, 1809-Mar. 3, 1813, President (1st term)

Mar. 4, 1813-Mar. 3, 1817, President (2nd term)

1817, retired to estate at Montpelier, Va.

1826, Rector, University of Virginia

1829, delegate to Virginia Constitutional Convention

JAMES MADISON

——was the third President born in Virginia.

——was the third President whose mother was alive when he was inaugurated.

——was the third President to marry a widow.

——was the first President who had been a congressman.

——was the first President regularly to wear trousers instead of knee breeches.

——was the last surviving signer of the Constitution.

MADISON'S VICE PRESIDENTS

FIRST TERM

Vice President—George Clinton (4th V.P.)

Term of office—Mar. 4, 1809-Apr. 20, 1812

Age at inauguration—69 years, 221 days

Occupation after term—Died in office

For additional data on Clinton see Thomas Jefferson, 3rd President—Jefferson's Vice Presidents.

SECOND TERM

Vice President—Elbridge Gerry (5th V.P.)

Date of birth—July 17, 1744

Birthplace—Marblehead, Mass.

Political party—Democratic-Republican

State represented—Massachusetts

Term of office—Mar. 4, 1813-Nov. 23, 1814

Age at inauguration—68 years, 230 days

Occupation after term—Died in office

Date of death—Nov. 23, 1814

Place of death—Washington, D.C.

Age at death—70 years, 129 days

Burial place—Washington, D.C.

ADDITIONAL DATA ON MADISON

FIRST INAUGURATION

James Madison took the oath of office on Saturday, March 4, 1809. It was administered by Chief Justice John Marshall in the Chamber of the House of Representatives. Madison was the first President whose complete costume was made in the United States. He wore a jacket of oxford cloth which came from Hartford, Conn., and merino wool breeches fashioned from cloth made at the farm of Chancellor Robert R. Livingston of New York. He wore silk stockings and black shoes, which were made in Massachusetts.

The inaugural ball, held at Long's Hotel on Capitol Hill, was the first one at Washington, D.C. Dancing commenced at 7 P.M.

CONSCIENCE FUND ESTABLISHED

In 1811, during Madison's administration, the "Conscience Fund" was started by an unknown person who sent an anonymous letter containing five dollars, since he had, he claimed, defrauded the government of that sum. Other deposits received that year increased the total to $250. No further deposits were received until 1827 when $6 was forwarded anonymously. For statistical and accounting purposes, the funds are listed by the government as "miscellaneous receipts."

WHITE HOUSE WEDDING

The first wedding in the White House took place March 29, 1812, when Mrs. Lucy Payne Washington, a sister of Mrs. James Madison and the widow of George Steptoe Washington, was married to Justice Thomas Todd of the United States Supreme Court.

SECOND INAUGURATION

James Madison took his second oath of office on Thursday, March 4, 1813. It was administered by Chief Justice John Marshall in the Chamber of the

House of Representatives. The inaugural ball was held at Long's Hotel.

JEWISH DIPLOMATIC REPRESENTATIVE APPOINTED

During James Madison's administration, Mordecai Manuel Noah, a Jew, was appointed United States consul with diplomatic powers to Tunis. He served from 1813 to 1816 and was the first Jewish diplomatic representative of the United States.

MADISON AT SCENE OF BATTLE

President James Madison was the only President to face enemy gunfire while in office and the first and only President to exercise actively his authority as commander-in-chief.

On August 19, 1814, General Robert Ross, in command of British regulars, and Admiral George Cockburn, commanding the Marines, landed at Benedict, Md., on the Patuxent River. They started a forty-mile march to Washington, D.C. Five days later, at Bladensburg, Md., they encountered and routed the militia and marines under General William Henry Winder, who fled to Georgetown after a losing battle. President James Madison on August 25 assumed command of Commodore Joshua Barney's battery, known as "Barney's Battery," stationed a half-mile north of Bladensburg, Md., to forestall the capture of Washington by the British.

MADISON FLED FROM THE CAPITAL

On August 24, 1814, the British entered Washington, D.C. and found the officials of the government had fled. On August 24 and 25 the British burned the Capitol, the President's House, and numerous other buildings. The damage might have been more extensive had the British known how completely the defenders had been routed. Unable to understand the lack of defense at the Capitol, the British officers feared that they were being drawn too far away from their ships and supplies and were walking into a trap. Afraid of being cut off from their base, they returned, thus ending the holocaust.

MADISON MOVED TO OCTAGON HOUSE

After the British had burned the White House in 1814, Colonel John Tayloe dispatched a courier offering President Madison the use of his home, the Octagon House. For more than a year, Madison made it his official residence. The building, known as the Octagon House, was not octagon-shaped. It had two rectangular wings connected by a circular tower.

MADISON'S VICE PRESIDENTS DIED IN OFFICE

James Madison was the only President whose administration suffered the death of two Vice Presidents.

George Clinton, who had served four years during the second term of Thomas Jefferson and three years and forty-seven days during the first term of James Madison, died in Washington, D.C., on April 20, 1812, at the age of 72.

On May 12, 1812, a Democratic-Republican caucus decided upon Senator John Langdon of New Hampshire as the party's vice presidential nominee. He received 64 of the 82 votes cast, but refused to accept the nomination because of his age (71). A second caucus nominated Elbridge Gerry of Massachusetts, who received 74 of the 77 votes cast. Gerry, who

was over 68 and thus only 3 years younger than Langdon, was elected Vice President to serve during Madison's second term, 1813-1817. But he did not live to complete the term. He died on November 23, 1814, at the age of 70, having served one year and 264 days. (Langdon, who died September 18, 1819, at the age of 78, survived Gerry by almost five years.)

ONLY ONE VICE PRESIDENT BURIED AT WASHINGTON, D.C.

The only Vice President buried at Washington, D.C., was Elbridge Gerry. He was buried in the Washington Parish Burial Ground, better known as the Congressional Cemetery, comprising about thirty acres of ground on the north bank of the Anacostia River. He died November 23, 1814 at Washington, D.C.

THE GERRYMANDER

The only Vice President whose name has been adopted as part of the English language was Elbridge Gerry. On February 11, 1812, when he was the governor of the Commonwealth of Massachusetts, he signed an act which rearranged the senatorial districts so that the Federalists were massed together in one or two districts, leaving the other districts controlled by a safe majority of Democratic-Republicans.

It is claimed that when Gilbert Stuart, the painter, saw a colored map of the redistricting hanging in the Boston office of Benjamin Russell, Federalist editor of the *Columbian Centinel,* he added a few strokes and said "This will do for a salamander." Russell said "Call it a gerrymander." Thus the word was born which became a Federalist war cry. Ironically, however, Governor Gerry had not sponsored the bill and had signed it reluctantly.

THE FIRST LADY

When James Madison assumed the presidency in 1809, the duties of first lady fell upon his wife, Dolley, whose experience as hostess at White House social functions during Jefferson's administration had prepared her well for the task.

MRS. MADISON VOTED SEAT IN HOUSE OF REPRESENTATIVES

Dolley Madison was observed seated in the visitors' gallery of the House of Representatives. Romulus Saunders, a representative from North Carolina, introduced a resolution to grant Mrs. Madison a seat within the House. The measure was immediately and unanimously passed.

The widow of President Madison wrote a letter dated January 9, 1844, which was read in the House the following day. She stated:

Permit me to thank you, gentlemen, as the Committee on the part of the House of Representatives, for the great gratification you have this day conferred on me, by the delivery of the favor from that honorable body allowing me a seat within its hall. I shall be ever proud to recollect it, as a token of their remembrance, collectively and individually, of one who had gone before us.

JAMES MONROE

James Monroe

JAMES MONROE

Born—Apr. 28, 1758

Birthplace — Westmoreland County, Va.

College attended—College of William and Mary, Williamsburg, Va.

Date of graduation—1776

Religion—Episcopalian

Ancestry—Scotch

Occupation—Lawyer

Date and place of marriage—Feb. 16, 1786, New York, N.Y.

Age at marriage—27 years, 294 days

Years married—44 years, 219 days

Political party—Democratic-Republican

State represented—Virginia

Term of office—Mar. 4, 1817-Mar. 3, 1825

Term served—8 years

Administration—8th, 9th

Congresses—15th, 16th, 17th, 18th

Age at inauguration—58 years, 310 days

Lived after term—6 years, 122 days

Occupation after term—Writer

Date of death—July 4, 1831

Age at death—73 years, 67 days

Place of death—New York, N.Y.

Burial place—Hollywood Cemetery, Richmond, Va.

For additional data see the end of this section and also specific subject headings in the Index.

PARENTS

Father—Spence Monroe

Married—1752

Occupation—Circuit judge, farmer

Died—1774

Mother—Elizabeth Jones Monroe

BROTHERS AND SISTERS

James Monroe was the eldest of five children.

CHILDREN

Eliza Kortright Monroe, b. Dec. 1786; m. Oct. 17, 1808, George Hay; d. 1835(?)

—— Monroe (son), b. May 1799; d. Sept. 28, 1801

Maria Hester Monroe, b. 1803; m. Mar. 9, 1820, Samuel Lawrence Gouverneur in White House, Washington, D.C.; d. 1850, Oak Hill, Va.

MRS. JAMES MONROE

Name—Elizabeth Kortright Monroe

Date of birth—June 30, 1768

Birthplace—New York, N.Y.

Age at marriage—17 years, 231 days

Children—2 daughters, 1 son

Mother—Hannah Aspinwall Kortright

Father—Captain Lawrence Kortright

His occupation—Former officer in British Army

Date of death—Sept. 23, 1830

Age at death—62 years, 85 days

Place of death—Oak Hill, Va.

Burial place—Richmond, Va.

Years younger than the President—10 years, 63 days

Years the President survived her—284 days

THE ELECTION OF 1816

After Madison had served two full terms, the Democratic-Republican party was divided between William Harris Crawford and James Monroe, the latter securing the party endorsement by the vote of 65 to 54. James Monroe's running mate was Daniel D. Tompkins of New York. Burr and other extremists denounced the caucus system. They declared that Virginia was trying to dominate the presidential succession.

The Federalists made no nominations but supported Rufus King of New York for the presidency. Their electoral vote for the vice presidency was split among four candidates—John Eager Howard of Maryland, James Ross of Pennsylvania,

John Marshall of Virginia, and Robert Goodloe Harper of Maryland.

ELECTORAL VOTES (217 —19 states)

Monroe received 84.33 per cent (183 votes—16 states) as follows: Ga. 8; Ind. 3; Ky. 12; La. 3; Md. 8; N.H. 8; N.J. 8; N.Y. 29; N.C. 15; Ohio 8; Pa. 25; R.I. 4; S.C. 11; Tenn. 8; Vt. 8; Va. 25.

King received 15.67 per cent (34 votes—3 states) as follows: Conn. 9; Del. 3; Mass. 22.

For the vice presidency Tompkins received 183.

The Federalist candidates for the vice presidency received the following votes:

Howard—Mass. 22

Ross—Conn. 5 (of the 9 votes)

Marshall—Conn. 4 (of the 9 votes)

Harper—Del. 3

THE ELECTION OF 1820

James Monroe was so popular during his first term, 1817-1821, that an "era of good feeling" swept the nation. All of the 232 electors, with only one exception, voted for Monroe for a second term. William Plumer, Sr., of New Hampshire, one of the electors, cast his vote for

John Quincy Adams in protest against a unanimous election. He was not opposed to Monroe but felt that no one other than George Washington should have the honor of a unanimous election. (Some sources, however, maintain that he opposed the Virginia dynasty of Presidents.)

The electoral vote for Vice President was split among five candidates: Daniel D. Tompkins of New York (seeking re-election), Richard Stockton of New Jersey, Daniel Rodney of Delaware, Robert Goodloe Harper of Maryland, and Richard Rush of Pennsylvania.

Three electors died and their respective states—Mississippi, Pennsylvania, and Tennessee—did not replace them and as a result failed to cast full electoral votes for President and Vice President.

ELECTORAL VOTES (235 —24 states)

Monroe received 99.57 per cent (231 votes—24 states) as follows: Ala. 3; Conn. 9; Del. 4; Ga. 8; Ill. 3; Ind. 3; Ky. 12; La. 3; Me. 9; Md. 11; Mass. 15; Miss. 2; Mo. 3; N.H. 7 (of the 8 votes); N.J. 8; N.Y. 29; N.C. 15; Ohio 8; Pa. 24; R.I. 4; S.C. 11; Tenn. 7; Vt. 8; Va. 25.

Adams received .43 per cent (1 vote—of the 9 N.H. votes).

For the vice presidency Tompkins received 218 votes as follows: Ala. 3; Conn. 9; Ga. 8; Ill. 3; Ind. 3; Ky. 12; La. 3; Me. 9; Md. 10 (of the 11 votes); Mass. 7 (of the 15 votes); Miss. 2; Mo. 3; N.H. 7 (of the 8 votes); N.J. 8; N.Y. 29; N.C. 15; Ohio 8; Pa. 24; R.I. 4; S.C. 11; Tenn. 7; Vt. 8; Va. 25.

The other candidates for the vice presidency received the following votes:

Stockton—Mass. 8 (of the 15 votes)

Rodney—Del. 4

Harper—Md. 1 (of the 11 votes)

Rush—N.H. 1 (of the 8 votes)

APPOINTMENT TO THE SUPREME COURT

Associate Justice

Smith Thompson, N.Y., Sept. 1, 1823

ADMINISTRATION— IMPORTANT DATES

July 4, 1817, Erie Canal construction began

Nov. 1817, first Seminole war began

Dec. 10, 1817, Mississippi admitted as the 20th state

Apr. 4, 1818, legislation established flag of the United States

May 28, 1818, Andrew Jackson captured Pensacola, Fla.

Oct. 19, 1818, treaty with Chickasaw Indians

Dec. 3, 1818, Illinois admitted as the 21st state

1819, financial panic

1819, McCulloch *vs.* Maryland and Dartmouth College cases —Supreme Court affirmed its power to set aside acts of state legislatures if unconstitutional

Feb. 22, 1819, Florida purchased from Spain

May 22, 1819, *Savannah,* first American steamship to cross the Atlantic ocean, left Savannah, Ga.

Dec. 14, 1819, Alabama admitted as the 22nd state

Mar. 3, 1820, Missouri Compromise—Maine admitted as a separate state; Missouri admitted as slave state; slavery prohibited in Louisiana Purchase north of 36° 30'.

Mar. 15, 1820, Maine admitted as the 23rd state

May 1820, first high school opened, Boston, Mass.

May 31, 1821, first Catholic cathedral dedicated, Baltimore, Md.

Aug. 10, 1821, Missouri admitted as the 24th state

Dec. 2, 1823, Monroe Doctrine proclaimed

1824, Clay's "American system" proposed—higher protective tariff and internal improvements in transportation

1824 Gibbons *vs.* Ogden case— Supreme Court declared a state law unconstitutional

Aug. 15, 1824, Lafayette landed in United States to begin tour

IMPORTANT DATES IN HIS LIFE

17——, pursued classical studies

17——, left College of William and Mary to join the army

Sept. 28, 1775, second lieutenant, Third Virginia Regiment, under General Hugh Mercer

June 24, 1776, first lieutenant

Sept. 16, 1776, wounded at Battle of Harlem Heights, N.Y.

Oct. 28, 1776, fought at White Plains, N.Y.

Dec. 26, 1776, wounded at Trenton, N.J.; promoted to rank of captain by General George Washington for "bravery under fire"

Sept. 11, 1777, fought at Brandywine, Pa.

Oct. 4, 1777, fought at Germantown, Pa.

Nov. 20, 1777, volunteer aide with rank of major on staff of General Lord Stirling

June 28, 1778, fought at Monmouth, N.J.

1780, military commissioner for Virginia, with rank of lieutenant colonel (appointed by Governor Thomas Jefferson)

Dec. 20, 1780, resigned as commissioner

1780, elected to Virginia Legislature

1781-1783, on Governor Jefferson's council

Oct. 21, 1782, member of Virginia House of Delegates

Dec. 13, 1783-1786, member of Continental Congress

17——, resumed study of law in office of Thomas Jefferson

Oct. 1786, admitted to the bar of the Courts of Appeal and Chancery; practiced at Fredericksburg, Va.

1786, member of Virginia Assembly

June 2, 1788, delegate to Virginia state convention to frame the Federal Constitution

Nov. 9, 1790-May 27, 1794, U.S. Senate (from Virginia)

May 28, 1794-Dec. 30, 1796, minister plenipotentiary to France (appointed by Washington)

1799-1803, governor of Virginia

Jan. 12-July 12, 1803, minister plenipotentiary to France (appointed by Jefferson)

Apr. 18, 1803, minister plenipotentiary to England

Feb. 14, 1804, headed diplomatic mission to Spain

May 21, 1805, left Spanish court for London

May 12, 1806, commissioner to negotiate treaty with England

1808, returned to the U.S.

1810, member of Virginia Assembly

1811, governor of Virginia

Apr. 6, 1811-Mar. 3, 1817, secretary of state under Madison

Aug. 30, 1814, secretary of war, ad interim

Sept. 27, 1814, secretary of war

Mar. 1, 1815, secretary of war, ad interim

Mar. 4, 1817-Mar. 3, 1821, President (1st term)

Mar. 4, 1821-Mar. 3, 1825, President (2nd term)

Mar. 1825, retired to his farm at Loudon County, Va.

1826, regent, University of Virginia, Charlottesville

Oct. 5, 1829, chairman of Virginia Constitutional Convention, Richmond

1831, moved to New York City

JAMES MONROE

——was the fourth President born in Virginia.

——was the first President who was inaugurated on March 5 (March 4 was a Sunday).

——was the first President who had been a senator.

——was the last of the Virginia regime of Presidents (Washington, Jefferson, Madison, Monroe).

——was the first President inaugurated outdoors.

MONROE'S VICE PRESIDENT

Vice President—Daniel D. Tompkins (6th V.P.)

Date of birth—June 21, 1774

Birthplace—Fox Meadows (now Scarsdale), N.Y.

Political party—Democratic-Republican

State represented—New York

Term of office—Mar. 4, 1817-Mar. 3, 1825

Age at inauguration—42 years, 256 days

Occupation after term—Lawyer

Date of death—June 11, 1825

Place of death—Tompkinsville, Staten Island, N.Y.

Age at death –50 years, 355 days

Burial place—New York City

ADDITIONAL DATA ON MONROE

FIRST INAUGURATION

James Monroe took his oath of office on Tuesday, March 4,

1817. It was administered by Chief Justice John Marshall on the platform erected on the east portico of the Capitol. As the result of a controversy between the Senate and the House of Representatives over the distribution of seats, it was decided that the inaugural be held outdoors. This was the first of the outdoor inaugurals.

Monroe rode to the Capitol accompanied by an escort of citizens. After the ceremonies, he went to the Octagon House, at Eighteenth Street and New York Avenue, where he resided as the White House had been burned by the British during Madison's administration. He was accompanied by an escort of Marines, Georgia riflemen, artillerymen and two companies of infantry from Alexandria, Va.

In the evening a reception was held at Davis' Hotel.

SECOND INAUGURATION

As March 4, 1821 fell on a Sunday, James Monroe did not take office until Monday, March 5. Because of snow and rain, Monroe took his oath of office in the Chamber of the Hall of Representatives. The oath was administered to him by Chief Justice John Marshall.

This was the first postponement of an inauguration.

The Marine Band played, introducing a new trend followed in all later inaugurations.

SENATOR ELECTED PRESIDENT

James Monroe was the first senator to become President of the United States. He served as senator from Virginia from November 9, 1790 to May 27, 1794, filling the vacancy caused by the death of William Grayson on March 12, 1790.

THE MONROE DOCTRINE

Extract from President Monroe's Annual Message, Washington, D.C., December 2, 1823:

The citizens of the United States cherish sentiments the most friendly in favor of the liberty and happiness of their fellow-men on that side of the Atlantic. In the wars of the European powers, in matters relating to themselves, we have never taken any part, nor does it comport with our policy to do so. It is only when our rights are invaded, or seriously menaced, that we resent injuries or make preparations for our defence. With the movements in this hemisphere, we are, of necessity, more immediately connected, and by causes which must be obvious to all enlightened and impartial observers. The political system of the allied powers is essentially different, in this respect, from that of America. This difference proceeds from that which exists in their respective Governments. And to the defence of our own, which has been achieved by the loss of so much blood and treasure, and matured by the wisdom of their most enlightened citizens, and under which we have enjoyed unexampled felicity, this whole nation is devoted. . . .

We owe it, therefore, to candor and to the amicable relations existing between the United States and those powers, to declare, that we should consider any attempt on their part to extend their system to any portion of this hemisphere, as dangerous to our peace and safety.

With the existing colonies or dependencies of any European power, we have not interfered, and shall not interfere. But, with the Governments who have declared their independence, and maintained it, and whose independence we have, on great consideration, and on just principles, acknowledged, we could not view any interposition for the purpose of oppressing them, or controlling, in any other manner, their destiny, by any European power, in any other light than as the manifestation of an unfriendly disposition towards the United States.

In the war between those new Governments and Spain, we declared our neutrality at the time of their recognition, and to this we have adhered, and shall continue to adhere, provided no change shall occur, which, in the judgement of the competent authorities of this Government, shall make a corresponding change on the part of the United States, indispensable to their security.

AFRICA HONORED MONROE

Upper Guinea, West Africa, was acquired by the American Colonization Society, founded in 1817 for the purpose of colonizing free Negroes from the United States. On August 15, 1824, the name of the country was changed to Liberia and its capital city was named Monrovia in honor of President James Monroe.

THE FIRST LADY

Mrs. Monroe had accompanied her husband to his posts in England and France and was familiar with political life. She became the first lady in 1817 and was an amiable hostess. Her health failed in later years, however, and she secluded herself from the throng. She discontinued the custom of returning calls.

J. Q. Adams

JOHN QUINCY ADAMS

Born—July 11, 1767

Birthplace—Braintree (now Quincy), Mass.

College attended—Harvard College, Cambridge, Mass.

Date of graduation—July 18, 1787, Bachelor of Arts

Religion—Unitarian

Ancestry—English

Occupation—Lawyer

Date and place of marriage—July 26, 1797, London, England

Age at marriage—30 years, 15 days

Years married—50 years, 212 days

Political party—Democratic-Republican

State represented—Massachusetts

Term of office—Mar. 4, 1825-Mar. 3, 1829

Term served—4 years

Administration—10th

Congresses—19th, 20th

Age at inauguration—57 years, 236 days

Lived after term—18 years, 356 days

Occupation after term—Congressman

Date of death—Feb. 23, 1848

Age at death—80 years, 227 days

Place of death—Washington, D.C.

Burial place—First Unitarian Church, Quincy, Mass.

For additional data see the end of this section and also specific subject headings in the Index.

PARENTS

Father—John Adams

Born—Oct. 30, 1735, Braintree, Mass.

Married—Oct. 25, 1764

Occupation—Lawyer, President of the United States

Died—July 4, 1826, Quincy, Mass.

Age at death—90 years, 247 days

Mother—Abigail Smith Adams

Born—Nov. 11, 1744

Died—Oct. 28, 1818, Quincy, Mass.

Age at death—73 years, 351 days

BROTHERS AND SISTERS

John Quincy Adams was the second child in a family of five.

CHILDREN

George Washington Adams, b. Apr. 13, 1801, Berlin, Germany; d. Apr. 30, 1829, on steamer in Long Island Sound, lost at sea

John Adams, b. July 4, 1803, Boston, Mass.; m. Feb. 25, 1828, Mary Catherine Hellen in the White House, Washington, D.C.; d. Oct. 23, 1834, Washington, D.C.

Charles Francis Adams, b. Aug. 18, 1807, Boston, Mass.; m. Sept. 3, 1829, Abigail Brown Brooks; d. Nov. 21, 1886, Boston, Mass.

Louisa Catherine Adams, b. 1811, St. Petersburg, Russia; d. 1812

MRS. JOHN QUINCY ADAMS

Name—Louisa Catherine Johnson Adams

Date of birth—Feb. 12, 1775

Birthplace—London, England

Age at marriage—22 years, 164 days

Children—3 sons, 1 daughter

Mother—Catherine Nuth Johnson

Father—Joshua Johnson

His occupation—U.S. Consul

Date of death—May 14, 1852

Age at death—77 years, 91 days

Place of death—Washington, D.C.

Burial place—Quincy, Mass.

Years younger than the President—7 years, 216 days

Years she survived the President—4 years, 80 days

THE ELECTION OF 1824

The last of the congressional caucuses met in 1824 in the

chamber of the House of Representatives. William Harris Crawford of Georgia was chosen as the presidential candidate.

The selection was not popular with the various state legislatures, which asserted themselves and decided that they were no longer bound to endorse the congressional choices. The legislature of Tennessee placed Andrew Jackson in nomination on July 22, 1822, and other state legislatures proposed their choices.

The election of 1824 was a contest of individuals rather than political parties. There were four candidates—each representing a different faction of the Democratic-Republican Party.

ELECTION RESULTS, NOV. 2, 1824— PRESIDENTIAL CANDIDATES

Andrew Jackson, Tenn., 153,544

John Quincy Adams, Mass., 108,740

Henry Clay, Ky., 47,136

William Harris Crawford, Ga., 46,618

ELECTORAL VOTES (261 —24 states)

Jackson received 37.93 per cent (99 votes—11 states) as follows: Ala. 5; Ill. 2 (of the 3 votes); Ind. 5; La. 3 (of the 5 votes); Md. 7 (of the 11 votes); Miss. 3; N.J. 8; N.Y. 1 (of the 36 votes); N.C. 15; Pa. 28; S.C. 11; Tenn. 11.

Adams received 32.18 per cent (84 votes—7 states) as follows: Conn. 8; Del. 1 (of the 3 votes); Ill. 1 (of the 3 votes); La. 2 (of the 5 votes); Me. 9; Md. 3 (of the 11 votes); Mass. 15; N.H. 8; N.Y. 26 (of the 36 votes); R.I. 4; Vt. 7.

Crawford received 15.71 per cent (41 votes—3 states) as follows: Ga. 9; Del. 2 (of the 3 votes); Md. 1 (of the 11 votes); N.Y. 5 (of the 36 votes); Va. 24.

Clay received 14.18 per cent (37 votes—3 states) as follows: Ky. 14; Mo. 3; Ohio 16; N.Y. 4 (of the 36 votes).

As no candidate for the presidency received a majority of the electoral votes, it again devolved upon the House of Representatives to choose a President from the three leading contenders. Twenty-four tellers, one from each state, were appointed to examine the ballots. Clay's supporters threw their strength to Adams, with the result that Adams was elected. Adams received 13 votes, Jackson 7 votes, and Crawford 4 votes.

VICE PRESIDENTIAL CANDIDATES

There were six vice presidential candidates: John Caldwell Calhoun of South Carolina, Nathan Sanford of New York, Nathaniel Macon of North Carolina, Andrew Jackson of Tennessee, Martin Van Buren of New York, and Henry Clay of Kentucky. Since one elector failed to cast his vote, the total number of votes was 260 instead of 261.

Calhoun received 182 votes as follows: Ala. 5; Del. 1 (of the 3 votes); Ill. 3; Ind. 5; Ky. 7 (of the 14 votes); La. 5; Md. 10 (of the 11 votes); Me. 9; Mass. 15; Miss. 3; N.H. 7; N.J. 8; N.Y. 29 (of the 36 votes); N.C. 15; Pa. 28; R.I. 3; S.C. 11; Tenn. 11; Vt. 7.

Sanford received 30 votes as follows: Ky. 7 (of the 14 votes); N.Y. 7 (of the 36 votes); Ohio 16.

Macon received the 24 Va. votes.

Jackson received 13 votes as follows: Conn. 8; Md. 1 (of the 11 votes); Mo. 3; N.H. 1.

Van Buren received the 9 Ga. votes.

Clay received 2 of the 3 Del. votes.

APPOINTMENT TO THE SUPREME COURT

Associate Justice

Robert Trimble, Ky., May 9, 1826

ADMINISTRATION— IMPORTANT DATES

June 17, 1825, Bunker Hill Monument cornerstone laid by General Lafayette

Oct. 26, 1825, Erie Canal opened for traffic

Mar. 24, 1826, General Congress of South American States convened at Panama

July 4, 1826, John Adams and Thomas Jefferson died

1828, South Carolina Exposition on nullification of federal tariffs

July 4, 1828, construction of Baltimore and Ohio Railroad begun

IMPORTANT DATES IN HIS LIFE

1778, attended school at Paris

Aug. 1779, returned to the United States

1780, made fourth trip across Atlantic

1780, attended school at Amsterdam, Holland; entered University of Leyden

July 1781, accompanied Francis

Dana, minister to Russia, as his private secretary

1782, made a six-month trip alone to Sweden, Denmark, northern Germany, and France

Sept. 3, 1783, present at signing of Treaty of Paris

17——, secretary to his father, John Adams, minister to Great Britain

1785, returned to the United States

1786, entered Harvard College

1788, graduated from Harvard College; studied law in office of Theophilus Parsons

1791, admitted to the bar, practiced in Boston, Mass.

1791-17——, wrote pamphlets and articles under the pseudonyms of Publicola, Marcellus, Columbus, etc.

May 30, 1794, appointed minister to the Netherlands by George Washington

1796, minister plenipotentiary to Portugal

June 1, 1797, minister plenipotentiary to Prussia

Mar. 14, 1798, commissioned to make a commercial treaty with Sweden (mission terminated when Jefferson became President)

1801, resumed law practice, Boston, Mass.

1802, member of Massachusetts Senate

Mar. 4, 1803-June 8, 1808, U.S. Senate (from Massachusetts)

1805, professor of rhetoric and belles-lettres, Harvard College

1808, resigned from Senate when Massachusetts legislature chose James Lloyd to succeed him

1809-1814, minister to Russia

1811, nominated to Supreme Court, but declined

1814, sent by President Madison to negotiate terms of peace with England (War of 1812); commissioners met at Ghent in Aug. 1814; signed Treaty of Ghent, Dec. 24, 1814, ending War of 1812

1815, Adams, Clay, and Gallatin negotiated a commercial treaty with England (completed July 13)

1815-1817, minister to England

Sept. 22, 1817-Mar. 3, 1825, secretary of state

Mar. 4, 1825-Mar. 3, 1829, President

1828, unsuccessful candidate for reelection to the presidency on the Whig ticket

1829, retired to farm

Mar. 4, 1831-Feb. 23, 1848, U.S. House of Representatives (from Massachusetts)

1834, unsuccessful candidate for governor of Massachusetts as nominee of the Anti-Masonic party

1846, paralysis; confined at home four months

1848, paralysis, second attack, in Speaker's Room, House of Representatives

JOHN QUINCY ADAMS

——was the second President born in Massachusetts.
——was the first President elected a member of Phi Beta Kappa.
——was the first President to wear long trousers at his inauguration.
——was the President least interested in clothes. It is said that he wore the same hat ten years.
——was the first President elected without receiving the plurality of the popular votes.
——was the first and only President to have a son whose given name was George Washington.
——was the first President who was married abroad.

ADAMS' VICE PRESIDENT

Vice President—John Caldwell Calhoun (7th V.P.)

Date of birth—Mar. 18, 1782

Birthplace—Abbeville District, S.C.

Political party—Democratic-Republican

State represented—South Carolina

Term of office—Mar. 4, 1825-Mar. 3, 1829

Age at inauguration—42 years, 351 days

Occupation after term—Vice President under Andrew Jackson

Date of death—Mar. 31, 1850

Place of death—Washington, D.C.

Age at death—68 years, 13 days

Burial place—Charleston, S.C.

ADDITIONAL DATA ON ADAMS

INAUGURATION

John Quincy Adams took the oath of office on Friday, March 4, 1825, at noon in the Hall of the House of Representatives (the same room in which he was to die on February 23, 1848). The oath was administered by Chief Justice John Marshall. Adams was accompanied to the Capitol by a military escort. After the ceremony, he returned to his residence at 1333 F Street, where a reception was held; later he went to the White House.

An inaugural ball was held that evening at Louis Carusi's Assembly Room, known also as the City Assembly Rooms.

ADAMS THE SON OF A PRESIDENT

John Quincy Adams was the only President whose father had also been a President. Like his father, he served only one term.

FORMER PRESIDENTS STILL LIVING

When John Quincy Adams took the oath of office as President of the United States on March 4, 1825, all of the former Presidents, with the exception of George Washington, were living: John Adams, Thomas Jefferson, James Madison, and James Monroe.

ADAMS SUFFERED WORST DEFEAT

The most badly defeated presidential candidate, excluding those nominated by the minor parties, was John Quincy Adams. In the election of 1820, he received only one electoral vote, which was cast by an elector from New Hampshire, whereas James Monroe received 231 of the 232 electoral votes.

PRESIDENT BECAME CONGRESSMAN

After serving as President, John Quincy Adams became a congressman. He represented the Plymouth, Mass., district, serving as a Whig congressman in the Twenty-second and the eight succeeding Congresses, from March 4, 1831, to February 23, 1848, when he died. He served ten days less than seventeen years.

FIRST VICE PRESIDENT BORN A CITIZEN OF THE UNITED STATES

John Caldwell Calhoun, Vice President under John Quincy Adams and Andrew Jackson, was the first Vice President not born a British subject. He was born March 18, 1782, near Calhoun Mills, Abbeville District, S.C.

VICE PRESIDENT RESIGNED TO BECOME SENATOR

John Caldwell Calhoun, Vice President from March 4, 1825, to December 28, 1832, resigned to become a senator from South Carolina. He had been elected to the United States Senate on December 12, 1832, to fill the vacancy caused by the resignation of Robert Young Hayne, who became governor of South Carolina. Calhoun was reelected in 1834 and 1840 and served from December 29, 1832, until his resignation, effective March

3, 1843. He later served as secretary of state and afterward was reelected to the Senate, where he served from November 26, 1845, until his death in Washington, D.C., on March 31, 1850.

THE FIRST LADY

The sixth in succession as lady of the Executive Mansion was Louisa Catherine Adams, who acted as hostess when her husband assumed the presidency in 1825. She ruled with little regard to politics and her hospitality was warm and sincere. The frugality and severity of the two previous administrations was replaced by an era of gracious living in which the choicest foods and the rarest wines were always served.

ANDREW JACKSON

Andrew Jackson

ANDREW JACKSON

Born—Mar. 15, 1767

Birthplace—Waxhaw, S.C.

College attended—None

Religion—Presbyterian

Ancestry—Scotch-Irish

Occupation—Soldier

Date and place of marriage—
Aug. 1791, Natchez, Miss.
(Jan. 17, 1794, Nashville,
Tenn.—second ceremony)

Age at marriage—24 years

Years married—37 years

Political party—Democratic
(Democratic-Republican)

State represented—Tennessee

Term of office—Mar. 4, 1829-
Mar. 3, 1837

Term served—8 years

Administration—11th, 12th

Congresses—21st, 22nd, 23rd,
24th

Age at inauguration—61 years,
354 days

Lived after term—8 years, 96
days

Date of death—June 8, 1845

Age at death—78 years, 85 days

Place of death—Nashville,
Tenn.

Burial place—The Hermitage
estate, Nashville, Tenn.

PARENTS

Father—Andrew Jackson

Born—Ireland

Occupation—Linen weaver (in
Ireland), farmer

Died—Mar. 1767

Mother—Elizabeth Hutchinson
Jackson

For additional data see the end of this section and also specific
subject headings in the Index.

Born—Ireland

Died—1780, Charleston, S.C.

BROTHERS AND SISTERS

Andrew Jackson was the third child in a family of three.

CHILDREN

None

MRS. ANDREW JACKSON

Name—Rachel Donelson Robards Jackson

Date of birth—June 15 (?), 1767

Birthplace—Halifax County, Va.

Age at marriage—24 years

Children—None

Mother—Rachel Stockley Donelson

Father—Colonel John Donelson

His occupation—Surveyor

Date of death—Dec. 22, 1828

Age at death—61 years, 190 days

Place of death—Nashville, Tenn.

Burial place—Nashville, Tenn.

Years younger than the President—92 days

Years the President survived her—16 years, 168 days

Rachel Donelson married Captain Lewis Robards March 1, 1785. In 1790 the legislature of Virginia granted Robards the right to sue for divorce—a grant which she mistakenly assumed was a divorce. She married Jackson in 1791, learned later that the proceeding had not been completed, and was remarried to Jackson in 1794 after Robards had received the divorce decree.

THE ELECTION OF 1828

Jackson's supporters claimed that the caucus system defeated the purposes of the Constitution, which envisaged electors voting as they pleased, and that the power of selection had passed from the electors to an extra-legal body. They argued that the popular vote showed that the congressional caucus was not representative of the wishes of the people.

In 1828 a new policy was instituted. It was the first election in which the nominations were all made by state legislatures instead of congressional caucuses. It was also the first in which the popular vote (November 4, 1828) was a real factor in the selection of electors.

The Democratic-Republicans, known also as Republicans or Democrats, were split into factions. Jackson's supporters (who tended more and more to call themselves Democrats) felt that he had been deprived of the election in 1825 and were determined to elect him in 1828. It was not only a personal matter, but a geographical struggle as well. The Adams-Clay adherents (who soon joined the remaining Federalists to form the National Republican Party) nominated two candidates from the North, Adams of Massachusetts and Rush of Pennsylvania. The Democrats nominated two from the South, Jackson of Tennessee and Calhoun of South Carolina.

The system of choosing candidates by congressional caucus was now a thing of the past, and the new system showed the will of the people. Jackson carried 15 of the 24 states.

ELECTION RESULTS, NOV. 4, 1828—PRESIDENTIAL AND VICE PRESIDENTIAL CANDIDATES

Jackson-Calhoun faction (Democratic Party) (647,286 votes)

Andrew Jackson, Tenn.
John Caldwell Calhoun, S.C.

Adams-Clay faction (Federalist or National Republican Party) (508,064 votes)

John Quincy Adams, Mass.
Richard Rush, Pa.

ELECTORAL VOTES (261 —24 states)

Jackson received 68.20 per cent (178 votes—15 states) as follows: Ala. 5; Ga. 9; Ill. 3; Ind. 5; Ky. 14; La. 5; Me. 1 (of the 9 votes); Md. 5 (of the 11 votes); Miss. 3; Mo. 3; N.Y. 20 (of the 36 votes); N.C. 15; Ohio 16; Pa. 28; S.C. 11; Tenn. 11; Va. 24.

For the vice presidency Calhoun received 171 votes and William Smith (also of South Carolina) received 7 votes.

Adams received 31.80 per cent (83 votes—9 states) as follows: Conn. 8; Del. 3; Me. 8 (of the 9 votes); Md. 6 (of the 11 votes); Mass. 15; N.H. 8; N.J. 8; N.Y. 16 (of the 36 votes); R.I. 4; Vt. 7.

For the vice presidency Rush received 83 votes.

THE ELECTION OF 1832

NOMINATIONS FOR TERM 1833-1837

Democratic (Democratic-Republican) Party Convention (1st)

May 21-23, 1832, The Athenaeum, Baltimore, Md.

Nominated for President—Andrew Jackson, Tenn.

Nominated for Vice President—Martin Van Buren, N.Y.

First Ballot: Andrew Jackson, Tenn.

National Republican Party Convention

December 12-15, 1831, The Athenaeum, Baltimore, Md.

Nominated for President—Henry Clay, Ky.

Nominated for Vice President—John Sergeant, Pa.

First ballot: Henry Clay, Ky.

ELECTION RESULTS, NOV. 6, 1832—PRESIDENTIAL AND VICE PRESIDENTIAL CANDIDATES

Democratic (Democratic-Republican) Party (687,502 votes)

Andrew Jackson, Tenn.
Martin Van Buren, N.Y.

National Republican Party (530,189 votes)

Henry Clay, Ky.
John Sergeant, Pa.

Independent Party

John Floyd, Va.
Henry Lee, Mass.

Anti-Masonic Party

William Wirt, Md.
Amos Ellmaker, Pa.

ELECTORAL VOTES (286 —24 states)

Jackson received 76.57 per cent (219 votes—16 states) as follows: Ala. 7; Ga. 11; Ill. 5; Ind. 9; La. 5; Me. 10; Md. 3 (of the 8 votes); Miss. 4; Mo. 4; N.H. 7; N.J. 8; N.Y. 42; N.C. 15; Ohio 21; Pa. 30; Tenn. 15; Va. 23.

Clay received 17.13 per cent (49 votes—6 states) as follows: Conn. 8; Del. 3; Ky. 15; Md. 5 (of the 8 votes); Mass. 14; R.I. 4.

Floyd received 3.85 per cent (1 state): S.C. 11.

Wirt received 2.45 per cent (1 state): Vt. 7.

For the vice presidency Martin Van Buren received 189 votes and William Wilkins of Pennsylvania received 30 votes, the Democratic vote for the vice presidency being divided.

APPOINTMENTS TO THE SUPREME COURT

Chief Justice

Roger Brooke Taney, Md., Mar. 15, 1836

Associate Justices

John McLean, Ohio, Mar. 7, 1829

Henry Baldwin, Pa., Jan. 6, 1830

James Moore Wayne, Ga., Jan. 9, 1835

Philip Pendleton Barbour, Va., Mar. 15, 1836

ADMINISTRATION— IMPORTANT DATES

Aug. 9, 1829, "Stourbridge Lion," first locomotive for railroad use, in service

Oct. 17, 1829, Delaware River and Chesapeake Bay canal formally opened

1830, Webster-Hayne debates on states' rights

June 8, 1830, *Vincennes*, first warship to circumnavigate the world, returned to New York City

1832, Jackson vetoed renewal of charter of the Bank of the United States

June 6, 1832, Black Hawk war began with attack on Apple River Fort, Ill.

June 28, 1832, cholera epidemic broke out at New York City

July 4, 1832, "America" first sung publicly, Boston, Mass.

Nov. 24, 1832, South Carolina declared federal tariff acts null and void; compromise reached to save Union sent to Charleston and action was suspended

Dec. 28, 1832, Vice President Calhoun resigned

1833, Jackson removed government deposits from Bank of the United States

Mar. 20, 1833, treaty with Siam signed—first treaty with a Far Eastern nation

Sept. 3, 1833, first daily newspaper, *Sun*, New York City

June 21, 1834, McCormick's reaper patented

June 24, 1834, appointment of Roger B. Taney as secretary of the treasury rejected by Senate—first rejection of cabinet appointee

Nov. 2, 1835, Second Seminole War begun by Osceola

Dec. 16, 1835, fire in New York City destroyed 600 buildings

Mar. 1, 1836, Texas adopted declaration of independence

Mar. 6, 1836, slaughter of defenders of the Alamo

Apr. 21, 1836, Texans defeated Mexicans at San Jacinto battlefield

May 14, 1836, Wilkes expedition to the South Seas authorized

June 15, 1836, Arkansas admitted as the 25th state

July 4, 1836, Wisconsin Territory organized

July 11, 1836, Jackson issued specie circular requiring payment for public lands in coin

Jan. 26, 1837, Michigan admitted as the 26th state

IMPORTANT DATES
IN HIS LIFE

1784, studied law, Salisbury, N.C.

Nov. 21, 1787, admitted to the bar (practiced in McLeanville, N.C., and Tennessee)

Oct. 1788, solicitor of western district of North Carolina (comprising what is now Tennessee)

Jan. 1796, delegate to Tennessee State Constitutional Convention, Knoxville

Dec. 5, 1796-Mar. 3, 1797, U.S. House of Representatives (from Tennessee)

Mar. 4, 1797-April 1798, U.S. Senate (from Tennessee)

1798-July 24, 1804, judge, Supreme Court of Tennessee

1801, major general of militia for western district of Tennessee

1804, moved to the Hermitage, near Nashville, Tenn.; engaged in planting and mercantile pursuits

June 5, 1806, killed Charles Dickinson in duel

1812, commander of Tennessee militia; served against Creek Indians

1812-1814, major general of volunteers

Aug. 30, 1813, expedition against Creek Indians who massacred garrison at Fort Meigs, Ala.

Mar. 27, 1814, defeated Creek Indians at Horseshoe Bend of the Tallapoosa

Apr. 19, 1814, commissioned brigadier general, U.S. Army

May 1, 1814, promoted to major general

Aug. 9, 1814, negotiated treaty with the Creek Indians

Nov. 7, 1814, captured Pensacola and Fort Michael; British retreated

Jan. 8, 1815, defeated British under General Pakenham at Battle of New Orleans, not aware that a peace treaty had been signed at Ghent

Feb. 27, 1815, received thanks of Congress; awarded a gold medal by resolution

Dec. 26, 1817, ordered by Secretary of War Calhoun to attack the Seminoles

Mar. 1818, captured St. Marks, Fla., and defeated the Seminoles

Mar. 10-July 18, 1821, governor of Florida

Mar. 4, 1823-Oct. 14, 1825, U.S. Senate (from Tennessee); resigned

1824, unsuccessful candidate for the presidency; won plurality of electoral votes, but House of Representatives chose John Quincy Adams

Mar. 4, 1829-Mar. 3, 1837, President

ANDREW JACKSON

——was the first President born in a log cabin.

——was the first President born in South Carolina.

——was the first President whose birthplace was in dispute. It was claimed that his birthplace was Union County, N.C.; Berkeley County, Va.; Augusta County, Va. (now W.Va.); York County, Pa.; England; Ireland; and on the high seas.

——was the first President born west of the Allegheny Mountains.

——was the first President to marry a woman who had been divorced.

——was the second widower inaugurated President.

——was the first presidential candidate named by a national nominating convention.

——was the first President elected from a state other than his native state.

——was the first President to ride on a railroad train. On June 6, 1833, he took the stagecoach from Washington, D.C., to Ellicott's Mill, Md., where he boarded a Baltimore and Ohio train for Baltimore, Md. It was a pleasure trip. (John Quincy Adams, however, had made a trip on the same line a few months earlier when he was no longer President.)

——was the oldest President when he left office. At the completion of his second four-year term, he was 69 years, 354 days old.

——was the first President to receive a plurality of popular votes but failed to win the election (1824).

——could, most likely, have been elected for a third term, but as none of his predecessors had served more than two terms he refused to be a candidate again and supported Van Buren for the presidency.

JACKSON'S VICE PRESIDENTS

FIRST TERM

Vice President—John Caldwell Calhoun (7th V.P.)

Political party—Democratic (Democratic-Republican)

Term of office—Mar. 4, 1829-Dec. 28, 1832

Age at inauguration—46 years, 351 days

Occupation after term—U.S. Senate

For additional data on Calhoun see John Quincy Adams, 6th President—Adams' Vice President.

SECOND TERM

Vice President—Martin Van Buren (8th V.P.)

For biographical information see Martin Van Buren, 8th President.

ADDITIONAL DATA ON JACKSON

ANDREW JACKSON, DUELIST

There are many estimates of the number of brawls and duels in which Andrew Jackson is believed to have participated. Some sources maintain that the figure approximates one hundred.

History records one duel in which Andrew Jackson killed his opponent. Charles Dickinson, one of the best pistol shots in the United States, made some derogatory remarks about Mrs. Jackson. Andrew Jackson challenged him to a duel. They met on May 30, 1806, at Harrison's Mills on Red River in Logan County, Ky. They stood twenty-four feet apart with pistols pointed downwards. At the signal, Dickinson fired first, breaking some of Jackson's ribs and

grazing his breastbone. Jackson, without flinching, maintained his position and fired. His shot proved mortal.

In 1812, Andrew Jackson was wounded in a gun battle at Knoxville, Tenn., by a bullet fired by Jesse Benton. It was feared that Jackson's arm would have to be amputated. In 1832, an operation was performed and the bullet which had been imbedded in Jackson's arm for twenty years was removed.

FIRST INAUGURATION

Like his father, John Adams, John Quincy Adams, the outgoing President, refused to participate in the inaugural ceremonies of his successor. Andrew Jackson took the oath of office on Wednesday, March 4, 1829, on the east portico of the White House. The oath was administered by Chief Justice John Marshall. The firing of cannon announced the conclusion of the ceremonies.

It was a warm and spring-like day. Andrew Jackson was an imposing figure as he rode down Pennsylvania Avenue leading a parade which included war veterans, many of whom had fought in the Revolution. As Jackson was in mourning for his wife, who had died on December 22, 1828, no ceremonies were planned. In the evening a reception was held for the public at the White House. A crowd of twenty thousand people jammed the building, ruining rugs, furniture and glassware, and causing thousands of dollars' worth of damage. It was a boisterous reception. Jackson was a man of the people, the first President not descended from an old aristocratic family.

NOMINATION OF VAN BUREN NOT CONFIRMED BY THE SENATE

President Andrew Jackson's nomination of Martin Van Buren to the post of minister to Great Britain in August 1831 was not confirmed by the Senate. Van Buren therefore relinquished his post and returned from England.

CANDIDATES NOMINATED BY CONVENTIONS

The election of 1832 was the first in which all the candidates were nominated by national conventions. The Democratic Party chose Jackson and Van Buren, the National Republican Party Clay and Sergeant, and the Anti-Masonic Party Wirt and Ellmaker.

CONVENTION ENACTED TWO-THIRDS RULE

The two-thirds rule requiring nominees to obtain two thirds of the votes was enacted by the Democratic-Republican National Convention at Baltimore, Md., on May 22, 1832:

Resolved: That each state be entitled, in the nomination to be made of a candidate for the vice presidency, to a number of votes equal to the number to which they will be entitled in the electoral college, under the new apportionment, in voting for President and Vice President; and that two thirds of the whole number of the votes in the convention shall be necessary to constitute a choice.

VICE PRESIDENT VAN BUREN NOMINATED AT A NATIONAL CONVENTION

As the nomination of President Andrew Jackson was assured at the Democratic-Republican Party Convention held May 21-23, 1832, at the Athenaeum, Baltimore, Md., the purpose of the convention was to select a vice presidential candidate to replace John Caldwell

Calhoun, who had resigned the vice presidency to serve his state in the Senate. Richard Mentor Johnson received 26 votes, Philip Pendleton Barbour received 49 votes, and Martin Van Buren 208 votes of the 283 votes cast. This made Van Buren the running mate of Andrew Jackson and the first Vice President selected at a national convention.

JACKSON DENOUNCED NULLIFICATION ATTEMPT

South Carolina in convention assembled passed an ordinance which declared:

The several acts and parts of the acts of the Congress of the United States, purporting to be laws for the imposing of duties and imposts on the importation of foreign commodities, and now having actual operation and effect within the United States, and more especially "two acts for the same purposes, passed on the 29th of May, 1828, and on the 14th of July 1832," are unauthorized by the Constitution of the United States, and violate the true meaning and intent thereof, and are null and void, and no law.

President Jackson issued a proclamation on December 10, 1832, in which he stated, in part:

I consider, then, the power to annul a law of the United States, assumed by one state, incompatible with the existence of the Union, contradicted expressly by the letter of the Constitution, unauthorized by its spirit, inconsistent with every principle on which it was founded, and destructive of the great object for which it was formed.

The dispute ended in a compromise which provided for gradual reduction of the tariff, and South Carolina withdrew the ordinance.

SECOND INAUGURATION

Andrew Jackson took the oath of office for his second term on Monday, March 4, 1833, in the House of Representatives. John Marshall, the chief justice, administered the oath (the ninth presidential oath administered by him).

HARVARD CONFERRED LL.D. ON JACKSON

The honorary degree of LL.D. was conferred on President Andrew Jackson by Harvard, Cambridge, Mass., on June 26, 1833. A distinguished alumnus, former President John Quincy Adams, expressed his disapproval of the award on June 18, to Josiah Quincy, President of Harvard College:

> As myself an affectionate child of our alma mater, I would not be present to witness her disgrace in conferring her highest literary honors upon a barbarian who could not write a sentence of grammar and hardly could spell his own name.

SENATE REJECTED JACKSON CABINET APPOINTEE

The first cabinet appointee rejected by the Senate was Roger Brooke Taney of Frederick, Md., who was proposed by President Andrew Jackson for secretary of the treasury. He was rejected by a vote of 28 to 18 on June 24, 1834.

JACKSON ESCAPED ASSASSINATION

The first attempt upon the life of a President was made January 30, 1835, upon President Andrew Jackson in the rotunda of the Capitol while he attended the funeral services for Representative Warren Ransom Davis

of South Carolina. As Jackson was about to go to the portico, Richard Lawrence, a mentally unbalanced house painter, fired two pistols at him from a distance of only six feet. Both weapons missed fire and Jackson was unhurt.

Lawrence was tried April 11, 1835, in the United States Circuit Court at Washington, D.C., and was committed to jail and mental hospitals for life. He suffered from chronic monomania and was found insane at the time of his act.

JACKSON APPOINTED CATHOLIC CHIEF JUSTICE

The first Catholic chief justice of the Supreme Court of the United States was Roger Brooke Taney of Frederick, Md., who was appointed on March 28, 1836, by President Andrew Jackson to succeed John Marshall as chief justice.

JACKSON REFUNDED TAXES

A surplus of $37 million accumulated during President Jackson's administration. On June 23, 1836, Congress voted to permit the government to disburse all but $5 million to the states in proportion to their representation in Congress. About $28 million was distributed in three installments. The panic of 1837 caused a sudden shift in government finances, and revenues decreased to such an extent that payments of the balance were discontinued.

JACKSON'S KITCHEN CABINET

Jackson had a coterie of advisers who met with him unofficially in the kitchen or rear of the White House to discuss public affairs. Referred to as "Jackson's kitchen cabinet," they held no government positions and had no official standing. Among those who were in this group were Andrew Jackson Donelson, his ward and private secretary; Amos Kendall of Kentucky, later postmaster general; General Duff Green, editor of the *United States Telegraph;* Francis P. Blair, editor of the Washington, D.C., *Globe;* Isaac Hill, senator from New Hampshire, and Major William B. Lewis of Nashville, Tenn.

JACKSON'S AGE AT RETIREMENT

Andrew Jackson was the oldest President to retire from the presidency. He took office when he was 61 years and 354 days

old, served eight years, and was 69 years and 354 days old when he left office. (President Eisenhower, at the conclusion of his second term, will be slightly older—70 years and 98 days.)

HOSTESSES AT THE WHITE HOUSE

As Rachel Donelson Robards Jackson had died of a heart attack before her husband was inaugurated and as they had no children, President Jackson assigned the duties of hostess at the White House to Emily Donelson, his wife's niece, who was the youngest child of Major Andrew Jackson Donelson. Her four children were all born in the White House. She developed tuberculosis and in 1836 returned to her home in Tennessee. Also serving at various times as hostess was Sarah York Jackson, wife of Andrew Jackson's foster son.

EXTRACT FROM ANDREW JACKSON'S WILL

June 7, 1843
The Hermitage

First, I bequeath my body to the dust whence it comes, and my soul to God who gave it, hoping for a happy immortality through the atoning merits of our Lord, Jesus Christ, the Saviour of the world. My desire is, that my body be buried by the side of my dear departed wife, in the garden at the Hermitage, in the vault prepared in the garden, and all expenses paid by my executor hereafter named. . . .

JACKSON WILLED HIS PISTOLS TO GENERAL ARMSTRONG

The famous pistols carried by Jackson are mentioned in his last will and testament:

As a memento of my high regard for Gen'l. Robert Armstrong as a gentleman, patriot and soldier, as well as for his meritorious military services under my command during the late British and Indian war, and remembering the gallant bearing of him and his gallant little band at Enotochopco Creek, when, falling desperately wounded, he called out —"My brave fellows, some may fall, but save the cannon" —as a memento of all these things, I give and bequeath to him my case of pistols and sword worn by me throughout my military career, well satisfied that in his hands they will never be disgraced—that they will never be used or drawn without occasion, nor sheathed but with honour.

JACKSON'S FINE RETURNED

On March 31, 1815, Judge Hall of the United States District Court at New Orleans fined Andrew Jackson $1,000 for contempt in declaring martial law during the defense of New Orleans. On January 8, 1844, the House of Representatives voted (158 to 28) to return the $1,000 with interest at 6 per cent.

MARTIN VAN BUREN

Born—Dec. 5, 1782

Birthplace—Kinderhook, N.Y.

College attended—None

Religious denomination—Dutch Reformed

Ancestry—Dutch

Occupation—Lawyer

Date and place of marriage—Feb. 21, 1807, Catskill, N.Y.

Age at marriage—24 years, 78 days

Years married—11 years, 349 days

Political party—Democratic (Democratic-Republican)

State represented—New York

Term of office—Mar. 4, 1837-Mar. 3, 1841

Term served—4 years

Administration—13th

Congresses—25th, 26th

Age at inauguration—54 years, 89 days

Lived after term—21 years, 142 days

Date of death—July 24, 1862

Age at death—79 years, 231 days

Place of death—Kinderhook, N.Y.

Burial place—Kinderhook Cemetery, Kinderhook, N.Y.

PARENTS

Father—Abraham Van Buren

Born—Feb. 17, 1737, Albany, N.Y.

Married—1776

Occupation—Farmer, innkeeper, captain in 7th Regiment Albany County Militia

For additional data see the end of this section and also specific subject headings in the Index.

Died—Apr. 8, 1817

Age at death—80 years, 40 days

Mother—Maria Goes Hoes Van Alen Van Buren

Born—1747(?) (baptized Jan. 16, 1747)

Died—Feb. 16, 1817 (or 1818)

BROTHERS AND SISTERS

Martin Van Buren was the third child in a family of five.

CHILDREN

Abraham Van Buren, b. Nov. 27, 1807, Kinderhook, N.Y.; m. Nov. 1838, Angelica Singleton; d. Mar. 15, 1873, New York, N.Y.

John Van Buren, b. Feb. 18, 1810, Hudson, N.Y.; m. June 22, 1841, Elizabeth Van der Poel; d. Oct. 13, 1866, at sea

Martin Van Buren, b. Dec. 20, 1812, unmarried, d. Mar. 19, 1855, Paris

Smith Thompson Van Buren, b. Jan. 16, 1817, m. June 18, 1842, Ellen King James; m. Feb. 1, 1855, Henrietta Irving; d. 1876

MRS. MARTIN VAN BUREN

Name—Hannah Hoes Van Buren

Date of birth—Mar. 8, 1783

Birthplace—Kinderhook, N.Y.

Age at marriage—23 years, 350 days

Children—4 sons

Date of death—Feb. 5, 1819

Age at death—35 years, 334 days

Place of death—Albany, N.Y.

Burial place—Kinderhook, N.Y.

Years younger than the President—93 days

Years the President survived her—43 years, 169 days

THE ELECTION OF 1836

NOMINATIONS FOR TERM 1837-1841

Democratic (Democratic-Republican) Party Convention (2nd)

May 20-22, 1835, First Presbyterian Church, Baltimore, Md.

Nominated for President—Martin Van Buren, N.Y.

Nominated for Vice President—Richard Mentor Johnson, Ky.

First ballot: 265, Martin Van Buren, N.Y.

Nomination made unanimous

Whig Party Convention (state convention)

December 14, 1835, Harrisburg, Pa.

Nominated for President—William Henry Harrison, Ohio
Nominated for Vice President—Francis Granger, N.Y.

The Anti-Masons and others opposed to Van Buren rallied to Harrison's support at this and other state conventions which confirmed Harrison's nomination. But the Whig Party (which had absorbed the short-lived National Republican Party) held no national convention and its electoral votes were divided among four presidential candidates.

ELECTION RESULTS, NOV. 1, 1836—PRESIDENTIAL AND VICE PRESIDENTIAL CANDIDATES

Democratic (Democratic-Republican) Party (762,678 votes)

Martin Van Buren, N.Y.
Richard Mentor Johnson, Ky.

Whig Party (735,561 votes)

Presidential candidates

William Henry Harrison, Ohio
Hugh Lawson White, Tenn.
Daniel Webster, Mass.
Willie Person Mangum, N.C.

Vice presidential candidates

Francis Granger, N.Y.
John Tyler, Va.
William Smith, Ala.

ELECTORAL VOTES

(294—26 states)

Van Buren received 57.82 per cent (170 votes—15 states) as follows: Ala. 7; Ark. 3; Conn. 8; Ill. 5; La. 5; Me. 10; Mich. 3; Miss. 4; Mo. 4; N.H. 7; N.Y. 42; N.C. 15; Pa. 30; R.I. 4; Va. 23.

Harrison received 24.83 per cent (73 votes—7 states) as follows: Del. 3; Ind. 9; Ky. 15; Md. 10; N.J. 8; Ohio 21; Vt. 7.

White received 8.85 per cent (26 votes—2 states) as follows: Ga. 11; Tenn. 15.

Webster received 4.76 per cent (1 state): Mass. 14.

Mangum received 3.74 per cent (1 state): S.C. 11.

For the vice presidency Johnson received 147 votes, Granger 77 votes, Tyler 47 votes, and Smith 23 votes. Since no candidate had a majority, the election devolved upon the Senate, and Johnson was elected by a vote of 33 to 16.

APPOINTMENTS TO THE SUPREME COURT

Associate Justices

William Smith, Ala., Mar. 8, 1837 (declined to serve)
John Catron, Tenn., Mar. 8, 1837
John McKinley, Ala., Apr. 22, 1837

Peter Vivian Daniel, Va., Mar. 3, 1841

ADMINISTRATION— IMPORTANT DATES

Mar. 6, 1837, General Jessup concluded agreement with Seminole Indian chiefs

Mar. 17, 1837, Republic of Texas adopted constitution

Spring 1837, financial panic of 1837

June 17, 1837, rubber patent obtained by Charles Goodyear

July 29, 1837, Chippewa treaty signed

Aug. 25, 1837, Texas petition for annexation refused

Oct. 12, 1837, $10 million in Treasury notes authorized to relieve distress

Oct. 21, 1837, Osceola, Seminole chief seized while under flag of truce

Dec. 25, 1837, Seminoles defeated by General Zachary Taylor at Okeechobee swamp

Jan. 5, 1838, Van Buren issued neutrality proclamation in Great Britain-Canada dispute

Jan. 8, 1838, Alfred Vail transmitted telegraph message using dots and dashes

Jan. 26, 1838, Osceola died in prison

Jan. 26, 1838, Tennessee forbade liquor sales

Apr. 25, 1838, boundary treaty with Texas signed

June 12, 1838, Iowa territorial government authorized

Aug. 18, 1838, Charles Wilkes left Hampton Roads, Va., on scientific expedition to the South Seas

Feb. 23, 1839, express service organized, Boston, Mass.

Mar. 3, 1839, President authorized to send troops to Maine to protect frontiersmen in Aroostook war

Feb. 1, 1840, Baltimore College of Dental Surgery, first dental school, incorporated

July 4, 1840, independent treasury system created; subtreasuries established in New York, Boston, Charleston, and St. Louis

IMPORTANT DATES IN HIS LIFE

1796-1802, worked in law office of Francis Sylvester

1802, studied law in New York City with William P. Van Ness

1803, admitted to the bar, practiced in Kinderhook, N.Y.

1807, counselor of Supreme Court, N.Y.

Feb. 20, 1808, appointed surrogate of Columbia County, N.Y. by Governor Tompkins (his first public office)

1809, moved to Hudson, N.Y.

1813-1820, New York State Senate

1815-1819, attorney general, New York State

Mar. 4, 1821-Dec. 20, 1828, U.S. Senate (from New York); resigned

Aug. 28, 1821, delegate to 3rd New York State constitutional convention

Jan. 1, 1829-Mar. 12, 1829, governor of New York; resigned

Mar. 28, 1829-May 23, 1831, secretary of state under Jackson; resigned

June 25, 1831, appointed minister to Great Britain

Jan. 25, 1832, Senate rejected his nomination; returned to U.S.

Mar. 4, 1833-Mar. 3, 1837, Vice President of the United States under Jackson

Mar. 4, 1837-Mar. 3, 1841, President

1840, unsuccessful Democratic nominee for reelection to the presidency; lost even his own state

1844, unsuccessful Democratic candidate for nomination; received highest number of votes but not two-thirds majority

1848, unsuccessful Free Soil nominee for the presidency, not receiving any electoral votes; withdrew from public life; returned to his home, Lindenwald, at Kinderhook, N.Y.

MARTIN VAN BUREN

——was the first President born in New York.

——was the third widower inaugurated President.

——was the first President whose son died in a foreign country.

——was the eighth President and eighth Vice President of the United States.

——lived to see eight Presidents from eight different states succeed him.

——was the last Vice President to succeed to the Presidency whose succession was not due to the death of a President. The only other Vice Presidents similarly elected were John Adams in 1796 and Thomas Jefferson in 1800.

——brought his four sons with him when he went to the White House in 1837. They were 20, 25, 27, and 30 years of age.

VAN BUREN'S VICE PRESIDENT

Vice President—Richard Mentor Johnson (9th V.P.)

Date of birth—Oct. 17, 1780

Birthplace—Floyd's Station, Ky.

Political party—Democratic
(Democratic-Republican)

State represented—Kentucky

Term of office—Mar. 4, 1837-
Mar. 3, 1841

Age at inauguration—56 years,
138 days

Occupation after term—Re-
tired; served in Kentucky legislature

Date of death—Nov. 19, 1850

Place of death—Frankfort, Ky.

Age at death—70 years, 33 days

Burial place—Frankfort, Ky.

ADDITIONAL DATA ON VAN BUREN

FIRST PRESIDENT BORN AN AMERICAN CITIZEN

The first President born a citizen of the United States and therefore never a British subject was Martin Van Buren. He was born December 5, 1782.

VAN BUREN CHANGED JOBS

In fourteen weeks Martin Van Buren held three important positions. On December 20, 1828, he gave up the office of United States senator. Eleven days later, he was governor of New York State. Sixty-four days later, he was made secretary of state under President Andrew Jackson, resigning the governorship on March 12 and assuming his new post on March 28.

INAUGURATION

Martin Van Buren took the oath of office on Saturday, March 4, 1837, on the east portico of the White House. Chief Justice Roger Brooke Taney administered the oath. As Van Buren and Jackson rode to the Capitol in a beautiful phaeton built from wood obtained from the frigate *Constitution,* they were accompanied by cavalrymen and infantrymen, as well as delegations from political organizations.

For several hours crowds visited the White House to greet the new President and pay their respects to Andrew Jackson.

This inauguration was of great political importance. The chief justice of the United States Supreme Court, whose earlier appointments as secretary of the treasury and associate justice had not been confirmed by the Senate, swore in as President of the United States a man whose appointment as United States minister to Great Britain had likewise not been approved by the Senate.

VAN BUREN'S VICE PRESIDENT—FIRST VICE PRESIDENT ELECTED BY THE SENATE

In the election of 1836, Richard Mentor Johnson of Kentucky received 147 of the 294 electoral votes for the vice presidency; Francis Granger of New York, 77 votes; John Tyler of Virginia, 47 votes; and William Smith of Alabama, 23 votes. There was no choice for Vice President by the people; the election devolved upon the Senate of the United States. Johnson received 33 votes, Granger received 16 votes, and Johnson was declared elected Vice President.

The twelfth amendment to the Constitution provided that:

> If no person have a majority, then from the two highest numbers on the list, the Senate shall choose the Vice President; a quorum for the purpose shall consist of two thirds of the whole number of Senators, and a majority of the whole number shall be necessary to a choice.

YOUNGEST SPEAKER OF THE HOUSE

The youngest Speaker of the House of Representatives was Robert Mercer Taliaferro Hunter of Virginia, who was 30 years and 7 months old when he became Speaker. He was elected Speaker of the First Session of the Twenty-Sixth Congress on December 16, 1839.

VAN BUREN SOUGHT REELECTION

Martin Van Buren, who served as President from 1837 to 1841, made three unsuccessful attempts to be reelected. He was renominated by the Democrats in 1840 but was defeated by the Whig candidate, William Henry Harrison. Van Buren won in only seven of the twenty-six states.

In the 1844 convention, he received 146 of the 266 votes on the first nominating ballot, but the two-thirds rule was in effect and 177 votes were required for choice. He could not muster sufficient strength and the nomination was captured on the ninth ballot by a "dark horse," James Knox Polk.

The Democrats did not consider him as their candidate in 1848, but the antislavery faction of the party formed the Free Soil Party and ran Van Buren for President. In this election, his fourth candidacy, he received not a single electoral vote and less than 11 per cent of the popular vote.

HOSTESS AT THE WHITE HOUSE

Hannah Van Buren died about nineteen years before Martin Van Buren became President. The mistress of the White House during his administration was Angelica Van Buren, the wife of Abraham Van Buren, President Van Buren's son and private secretary.

THREE PRESIDENTS SERVED IN SAME YEAR

Martin Van Buren completed his four-year term on March 3, 1841. On March 4, 1841, William Henry Harrison was inaugurated. Harrison died on April 4, 1841, and on April 6, 1841, John Tyler was inaugurated President, the third President in one year.

WILLIAM HENRY HARRISON

W. H. Harrison

WILLIAM HENRY HARRISON

Born—Feb. 9, 1773

Birthplace—Berkeley, Charles City County, Va.

College attended—Hampden-Sydney College, Hampden-Sydney, Va.

Date of graduation—None (attended college 1787-1790)

Religious denomination—Episcopalian

Ancestry—English

Occupation—Soldier

Date and place of marriage—Nov. 25, 1795, North Bend, Ohio

Age at marriage—22 years, 289 days

Years married—45 years, 130 days

Political party—Whig

State represented—Ohio

Term of office—Mar. 4, 1841-Apr. 4, 1841

Term served—32 days

Administration—14th

Congress—27th

Age at inauguration—68 years, 23 days

Lived after term—Died in office

Date of death—Apr. 4, 1841

Age at death—68 years, 54 days

Place of death—Washington, D.C.

Burial place—William Henry Harrison Memorial State Park, North Bend, Ohio

PARENTS

Father—Benjamin Harrison

Born—Apr. 5, 1726, Berkeley, Va.

For additional data see the end of this section and also specific subject headings in the Index.

Married—1748

Occupation—Politics, statesman

Died—Apr. 24, 1791, City Point, Va.

Age at death—65 years, 19 days

Mother—Elizabeth Bassett Harrison

Born—Dec. 13, 1730, Berkeley, Va.

Died—1792, Berkeley, Va.

Age at death—62 years

BROTHERS AND SISTERS

William Henry Harrison was the seventh child in a family of seven.

CHILDREN

Elizabeth Bassett Harrison, b. Sept. 29, 1796, Fort Washington, Ohio; m. June 29, 1814, John Cleves Short; d. Sept. 26, 1846

John Cleves Symmes Harrison, b. Oct. 28, 1798, Vincennes, Ind.; m. Sept. 29, 1819, Clarissa Pike; d. Oct. 30, 1830

Lucy Singleton Harrison, b. Sept. 1800, Richmond, Va.; m. Sept. 30, 1819, David K. Este; d. Apr. 7, 1826, Cincinnati, Ohio

William Henry Harrison, b. Sept. 3, 1802, Vincennes, Ind.; m. Feb. 18, 1824, Jane Findlay Irwin; d. Feb. 6, 1838, North Bend, Ohio

John Scott Harrison, b. Oct. 4, 1804, Vincennes, Ind.; m. 1824, Lucretia Knapp Johnson; m. Aug. 12, 1831, Elizabeth Ramsey Irwin; d. May 25, 1878, Point Farm, Ind.

Benjamin Harrison, b. 1806, Vincennes, Ind.; m. Louisa Bonner; m. Mary Raney; d. June 9, 1840

Mary Symmes Harrison, b. Jan. 22, 1809, Vincennes, Ind.; m. Mar. 5, 1829, John Henry Fitzhugh Thornton; d. Nov. 16, 1842

Carter Bassett Harrison, b. Oct. 26, 1811, Vincennes, Ind.; m. June 16, 1836, Mary Anne Sutherland, Hamilton, Ohio; d. Aug. 12, 1839

Anna Tuthill Harrison, b. Oct. 28, 1813, Cincinnati, Ohio; m. June 16, 1836, William Henry Harrison Taylor; d. July 5, 1845

James Findlay Harrison, b. 1814, North Bend, Ohio; d. 1817, North Bend, Ohio

MRS. WILLIAM HENRY HARRISON

Name—Anna Tuthill Symmes Harrison

Born—July 25, 1775

Birthplace—Morristown, N.J.

Age at marriage—20 years, 123 days

Children—6 sons, 4 daughters

Mother—Susan Livingston Symmes

Father—John Cleves Symmes

His occupation—Judge, landowner

Date of death—Feb. 25, 1864

Age at death—88 years, 215 days

Place of death—North Bend, Ohio

Burial place—North Bend, Ohio

Years younger than the President—2 years, 166 days

Years she survived the President—22 years, 327 days

THE ELECTION OF 1840

NOMINATIONS FOR TERM 1841-1845

Whig Party Convention

May 4-5, 1840, First Lutheran Church, Baltimore, Md.

Nominated for President—William Henry Harrison, Ohio

Nominated for Vice President—John Tyler, Va.

Harrison was nominated on the second ballot.

This was the first national convention to adopt the unit rule by which all the votes of a state delegation are cast for the candidate who receives a majority of the state's votes.

Democratic (Democratic-Republican) Party Convention (3rd)

May 5-7, 1840, Hall of the Musical Association, Baltimore, Md.

Nominated for President—Martin Van Buren, N.Y.

Nomination unanimous on the first ballot

The nomination for the vice presidency was not made at this convention. Each state proposed its own nominee. Candidates running on the Democratic ticket for the vice presidency included the following:

Richard Mentor Johnson, Ky.
Littleton Waller Tazewell, Va.
James Knox Polk, Tenn.

ELECTION RESULTS, NOV. 3, 1840—PRESIDENTIAL AND VICE PRESIDENTIAL CANDIDATES

Whig Party (1,275,016 votes)

William Henry Harrison, Ohio
John Tyler, Va.

Democratic (Democratic-Republican) Party (1,129,102 votes)

Martin Van Buren, N.Y.
Richard Mentor Johnson, Ky.

Liberty (Abolitionist) Party

James Gillespie Birney, N.Y.
Thomas Earle, Pa.

ELECTORAL VOTES (294 —26 states)

Harrison received 79.60 per cent (234 votes—19 states) as follows: Conn. 8; Del. 3; Ga. 11; Ind. 9; Ky. 15; La. 5; Me. 10; Md. 10; Mass. 14; Mich. 3; Miss. 4; N.J. 8; N.Y. 42; N.C. 15; Ohio 21; Pa. 30; R.I. 4; Tenn. 15; Vt. 7.

Van Buren received 20.40 per cent (60 votes—7 states) as follows: Ala. 7; Ark. 3; Ill. 5; Mo. 4; N.H. 7; S.C. 11; Va. 23.

For the vice presidency the 60 Democratic votes were divided as follows: Johnson received 48 votes, Tazewell received 11 votes, and Polk received 1 vote.

ADMINISTRATION— IMPORTANT DATES

Mar. 9, 1841, decision by Supreme Court freed Negroes taken from Spanish ship *Amistad* after they had seized

the ship (defense argued by John Quincy Adams)

Mar. 12, 1841, British minister made formal demand for release of Alexander McLeod, Canadian deputy sheriff involved in death of American citizen during Canadian rebellion (1837)

Mar. 17, 1841, Claims Convention signed with Peru

Mar. 27, 1841, steam fire-engine publicly tested, New York, N.Y.

IMPORTANT DATES IN HIS LIFE

1791, regularly enrolled in the Medical Department of the University of Pennsylvania

1791, left school to fight Indians

Aug. 16, 1791, commissioned ensign in the First Infantry by General George Washington

June 2, 1792, commissioned a second lieutenant

1793, aide-de-camp under General Anthony Wayne

1793, general orders issued thanking him and others for their part in expedition that erected Fort Recovery

June 30, 1794, served in Indian war

Aug. 20, 1794, fought in battle of Miami Rapids

May 15, 1797, promoted to captain; given command of Fort Washington

June 1, 1798, resigned with rank of captain

1798-1799, secretary of the Northwest Territory (appointed at $1,200 a year by President John Adams; resigned in Oct. 1799)

Mar. 4, 1799-May 14, 1800, U.S. House of Representatives (delegate from the Territory Northwest of the River Ohio)

1801-1813, territorial governor of Indiana and superintendent of Indian Affairs (appointed by President John Adams; reappointed by Presidents Jefferson and Madison)

Nov. 7, 1811, defeated Indians under the Prophet, brother of Chief Tecumseh, at Tippecanoe, on the Wabash River (American casualties: 108 killed and wounded)

1811, complimented by President Madison; votes of thanks extended to him by legislatures of Kentucky and Indiana

Aug. 22, 1812, commissioned major general of Kentucky militia in War of 1812

Sept. 2, 1812, commissioned brigadier general in U.S. Army

Mar. 2, 1813, commissioned major general in chief command of the Northwest

Oct. 5, 1813, defeated the British and Indians in the battle of the Thames in which Tecumseh was killed

May 31, 1814, resigned from the army

1814, appointed head commissioner to treat with the Indians

Oct. 8, 1816-Mar. 3, 1819, U.S. House of Representatives (from Ohio)

Mar. 24, 1818, received gold medal from Congress for his victory at the battle of the Thames

Dec. 6, 1819-1821, Ohio Senate

1822, unsuccessful candidate for U.S. House of Representatives

Mar. 4, 1825-May 20, 1828, U.S. Senate (from Ohio)

May 24, 1828-Sept. 26, 1829, envoy extraordinary and minister plenipotentiary to Colombia

1829, retired to his farm at North Bend, Ohio

1829-1836, county recorder, clerk of county court, president of county agricultural society

Nov. 8, 1836, unsuccessful Whig candidate for the presidency

Mar. 4-Apr. 4, 1841, President

WILLIAM HENRY HARRISON

——served the shortest term as President, from March 4, 1841, to April 4, 1841.

——was the first President to die in office. He died on April 4, 1841, in the White House.

——was the second President elected from a state other than his native state.

——was the fifth President born in Virginia.

——was the last President born before the American Revolution. He was born February 9, 1773.

——was the only President whose father was a signer of the Declaration of Independence.

——was the oldest President inaugurated. He was 68 years and 23 days old when he took the oath of office.

——was the first and only President who studied to become a doctor. He was regularly enrolled in the Medical Department of the University of Pennsylvania and completed sixteen weeks of a thirty-two week course.

——was the only President whose grandson (Benjamin Harrison) also became a President.

——was the first President to lie in state in the White House.

HARRISON'S VICE PRESIDENT

Vice President—John Tyler (10th V.P.)

For biographical information see John Tyler, 10th President.

ADDITIONAL DATA ON HARRISON

HARRISON ARRIVED BY TRAIN

William Henry Harrison was the first President-elect to arrive by railroad at Washington, D.C., for his inauguration. Harrison left Baltimore, Md., February 9, 1841, on his sixty-eighth birthday. He boarded a Baltimore and Ohio Railroad train and arrived at Washington, D.C., where he registered at Gadsby's Hotel.

HARRISON'S PROPHETIC FAREWELL

In a speech delivered January 26, 1841, at Cincinnati, Ohio, Harrison said: "Gentlemen and fellow citizens. . . . Perhaps this may be the last time I may have the pleasure of speaking to you on earth or seeing you. I will bid you farewell, if forever, fare thee well."

INAUGURATION

William Henry Harrison, the oldest President inaugurated, took the oath of office on Thursday, March 4, 1841, on the east portico of the Capitol. The oath was administered by Chief Justice Taney. Harrison rode a white horse to the Capitol, refusing to wear hat or coat despite the cold and stormy weather. He read his 8,578-word inaugural address, the longest on record, taking about one hour and forty-five minutes.

After the ceremony, he led the inaugural parade to the White House. Numerous floats depicting log cabins and cider barrels were highlights of the parade. Great crowds flocked to the White House.

In the evening, Harrison attended three inaugural balls, one known as the "Native American Inaugural Ball"; another on Louisiana Avenue in a converted theatre known as the new Washington Assembly Room; and the third the People's Tippecanoe Ball at Carusi's Saloon between 10th and 11th Streets on C Street, attended by a thousand people who paid ten dollars each.

Harrison caught cold at the ceremonies and was prostrated by a chill on March 27, 1841.

He died of pleurisy fever (pneumonia) at thirty minutes past one on Sunday morning, April 4, 1841.

THE FIRST LADY

Anna Symmes Harrison, the wife of William Henry Harrison, was taken ill one month before the inauguration and did not accompany her husband to Washington. Mrs. Harrison intended to follow later but was not able to go to Washington during her husband's brief term. Harrison's daughter-in-law, Mrs. Jane Irwin Harrison, the wife of Colonel William Henry Harrison, Jr., accompanied the President to Washington and acted temporarily as mistress of the White House. There was practically no social activity at the White House in the short time Harrison presided there.

HARRISON'S FAMILY IN OFFICE

Benjamin Harrison of Virginia, one of the signers of the Declaration of Independence and a member of the Continental Congress from 1774 to 1778, was the father of William Henry Harrison.

Carter Bassett Harrison of

Virginia, who served in the Third, Fourth, and Fifth Congresses from March 4, 1793 to March 3, 1799, was a brother of William Henry Harrison.

John Scott Harrison, a Whig representative from Ohio in the 34th and 35th Congresses from March 4, 1853 to March 3, 1857, was a son of William Henry Harrison.

Benjamin Harrison, a Republican senator from March 4, 1881 to March 3, 1887 and President of the United States from March 4, 1889 to March 3, 1893, was a grandson of William Henry Harrison.

JOHN TYLER

John Tyler

JOHN TYLER

Born—Mar. 29, 1790

Birthplace—Charles City County, Va.

College attended—College of William and Mary, Williamsburg, Va.

Date of graduation—July 4, 1807

Religion—Episcopalian

Ancestry—English

Occupation—Lawyer

Date and place of first marriage—Mar. 29, 1813, New Kent County, Va.

Age at marriage—23 years

Years married—29 years, 165 days

Date and place of second marriage—June 26, 1844, New York, N.Y.

Age at second marriage—54 years, 89 days

Years married—17 years, 206 days

Political party—Whig (originally Democratic)

State represented—Virginia

Term of office—Apr. 6, 1841-Mar. 3, 1845 (Tyler succeeded to the presidency on the death of William Henry Harrison.)

Term served—3 years, 332 days

Administration—14th

Congresses—27th, 28th

Age at inauguration—51 years, 8 days

Lived after term—16 years, 320 days

Occupation after term—Lawyer

Date of death—Jan. 18, 1862

Age at death—71 years, 295 days

Place of death—Richmond, Va.

For additional data see the end of this section and also specific subject headings in the Index.

Burial place—Hollywood Cemetery, Richmond, Va.

PARENTS

Father—John Tyler

Born—Feb. 28, 1747, Yarmouth, James City County, Va.

Married—1776, Weyanoke, Va.

Occupation—Lawyer, judge, governor

Died—Jan. 6, 1813, Charles City County, Va.

Age at death—65 years, 312 days

Mother—Mary Marot Armistead Tyler

Born—1761

Died—Apr. 1797

Age at death—36 years

BROTHERS AND SISTERS

John Tyler was the sixth child in a family of eight.

CHILDREN

By first wife, Letitia Christian Tyler

Mary Tyler, b. Apr. 15, 1815; m. Dec. 14, 1835, Henry Lightfoot Jones; d. June 17, 1848

Robert Tyler, b. Sept. 9, 1816; m. Sept. 12, 1839, Elizabeth Priscilla Cooper; d. Dec. 3, 1877

John Tyler, b. Apr. 27, 1819; m. Oct. 25, 1838, Martha Rochelle; d. Jan. 26, 1896

Letitia Tyler, b. May 11, 1821; m. James A. Semple; d. Dec. 28, 1907

Elizabeth Tyler, b. July 11, 1823; m. Jan. 31, 1842, William Nevison Waller at the White House, Washington, D.C.; d. June 1, 1850

Anne Contesse Tyler, b. Apr. 1825; d. July 1825

Alice Tyler, b. Mar. 23, 1827; m. 1850, Rev. Henry Mandeville Denison; d. June 8, 1854

Tazewell Tyler, b. Dec. 6, 1830; m. Dec. 1857, Nannie Bridges; d. Jan. 8, 1874

By second wife, Julia Gardiner

David Gardiner Tyler, b. July 12, 1846, Charles City County, Va.; m. June 6, 1894, Mary Morris Jones; d. Sept. 5, 1927, Richmond, Va.

John Alexander Tyler, b. Apr. 7, 1848; m. Sarah Gardiner; d. Sept. 1, 1883

Julia Tyler, b. Dec. 25, 1849 (or 1850); m. June 26, 1869, William H. Spencer; d. May 8, 1871

Lachlan Tyler, b. Dec. 2, 1851; m. Georgia Powell; d. Jan. 26, 1902, New York, N.Y.

Lyon Gardiner Tyler, b. Aug. 1853, Charles City County, Va.; m. Nov. 14, 1878, Annie Baker Tucker; m. Sept. 12, 1923, Susan Ruffin; Richmond, Va.; d. Feb. 12, 1935, Charles City County, Va.

Robert Fitzwalter Tyler, b. Mar. 12, 1856; m. Fannie Glinn; d. Dec. 30, 1927, Richmond, Va.

Pearl Tyler, b. June 20, 1860; m. Major William Mumford Ellis; d. June 30, 1947, Elliston, Va.

MRS. JOHN TYLER (first wife)

Name—Letitia Christian Tyler

Date of birth—Nov. 12, 1790

Birthplace—"Cedar Grove," New Kent County, Va.

Age at marriage—22 years, 137 days

Children—5 daughters, 3 sons

Mother—Mary Brown Christian

Father—Colonel Robert Christian

His occupation—Planter

Date of death—Sept. 10, 1842

Age at death—51 years, 302 days

Place of death—White House, Washington, D.C.

Burial place—Cedar Grove, Va.

Years younger than the President—228 days

Years the President survived her—19 years, 130 days

MRS. JOHN TYLER (second wife)

Name—Julia Gardiner Tyler

Date of birth—May 4, 1820

Birthplace—Gardiner's Island, N.Y.

Age at marriage—24 years, 53 days

Children—5 boys, 2 girls

Mother—Juliana McLachlen Gardiner

Father—David Gardiner

His occupation—Senator (New York)

Date of death—July 10, 1889

Age at death—69 years, 67 days

Place of death—Richmond, Va.

Burial place—Richmond, Va.

Years younger than the President—30 years, 36 days

Years she survived the President—27 years, 173 days

APPOINTMENT TO THE SUPREME COURT

Associate Justice

Samuel Nelson, N.Y., Feb. 13, 1845

ADMINISTRATION— IMPORTANT DATES

Aug. 13, 1841, independent treasury act repealed

Sept. 11, 1841, cabinet resigned, except secretary of state

1842, gold discovered, San Fernando Mission, Calif.

Feb. 1, 1842, Coast Guard commandant appointed

Feb. 15, 1842, adhesive postage stamps used, New York, N.Y.

Feb. 21, 1842, sewing machine patented, J. J. Greenough

Mar. 31, 1842, Henry Clay resigned after forty years in Congress

June 10, 1842, Wilkes expedition returned

Aug. 9, 1842, Webster-Ashburton treaty with Great Britain signed, settling Maine boundary

Aug. 14, 1842, end of Seminole War announced by Colonel Worth

Aug. 22, 1842, Northeastern boundary treaty ratified by the Senate

Aug. 26, 1842, start of fiscal year changed from Jan. 1 to July 1

Aug. 30, 1842, tariff placed upon opium imports

Aug. 31, 1842, Bureau of Medicine and Surgery of the Navy authorized

Oct. 18, 1842, underwater cable laid in New York Harbor

Nov. 22, 1842, Mount Saint Helens, Wash., erupted

Mar. 3, 1843, Congress appropriated $30,000 to test the telegraph

May 2, 1843, organization of Oregon government attempted

June 17, 1843, Bunker Hill monument dedicated

Nov. 13, 1843, Mount Rainier, Wash., erupted

Feb. 28, 1844, explosion on warship *Princeton*

May 25, 1844, first news dispatch sent by telegraph to Baltimore *Patriot*

June 15, 1844, Charles Goodyear obtained patent on vulcanized rubber

July 3, 1844, treaty of peace, amity and commerce signed with China

Jan. 3, 1845, uniform election day established

Mar. 1, 1845, annexation of Texas by joint resolution of Congress

Mar. 3, 1845, first legislation passed over a presidential veto

Mar. 3, 1845, Florida admitted as the 27th state

IMPORTANT DATES IN HIS LIFE

1807, graduated from College of William and Mary, which he had entered at age of twelve

1809, admitted to the bar; practiced in Charles City County, Va.

1811-1816, Virginia House of Delegates

1813, captain of a military company

1816, member of Virginia Council of State

Dec. 16, 1817-Mar. 3, 1821, U.S. House of Representatives (from Virginia)

1820, declined renomination because of ill health

18——, rector and chancellor of College of William and Mary

1823-1825, Virginia House of Delegates

Dec. 1, 1825-1827, governor of Virginia

Mar. 4, 1827-Feb. 29, 1836, U.S. Senate (from Virginia)

1829, 1830, delegate to Virginia constitutional conventions

Mar. 3, 1835-July 1, 1836, president pro tempore of the Senate

1835, unsuccessful candidate for Vice President on Whig ticket

1838, president of Virginia African Colonization Society

1839, Virginia House of Delegates

Mar. 4, 1841-Apr. 4, 1841, Vice President

Apr. 6, 1841-Mar. 3, 1845, President (took office on death of William Henry Harrison)

1844, proposed as presidential candidate by secessionist Democratic convention

1859, chancellor of College of William and Mary

Mar. 1, 1861, member of Virginia secession convention

July 20, 1861, delegate to Confederate Provisional Congress

JOHN TYLER

——was the sixth President born in Virginia.

——was the first President whose wife died while he was in office.

——was the first Vice President elevated to the presidency through the death of a Chief Executive. He was elected as a Whig to the vice presidency and took office March 4, 1841. Upon the death of President William Henry Harrison, Tyler took the oath of office as President of the United States on April 6, 1841.

——was the first President to marry while in office. He remarried on June 26, 1844.

——was the first President to marry on his birthday.

——was the first President whose father had been a governor of a state (Virginia).

ADDITIONAL DATA ON TYLER

SENATOR TYLER OPPOSED STATE MANDATE

Tyler refused to obey a resolution of the Virginia legislature demanding that he vote for the Benton resolution, and resigned his seat in the Senate on February 29, 1836.

President Jackson had removed Secretary of the Treasury Duane for refusing to check out the deposits in the United States Bank, and for this action he had been censured by the Senate. Senator Thomas Hart Benton of Missouri moved to have the Senate expunge the censure.

INAUGURATION

John Tyler was the first Vice President to succeed to the presidency through the death of a President. He was at Williamsburg, Va., when he received the news that President William Henry Harrison had died on April 4, 1841. Tyler returned to Washington, D.C., on April 6, 1841, at 4 A.M. At 12 noon on April 6 the oath was administered by William Cranch, Chief Justice of the United States Circuit Court of the District of Columbia, at the Indian Queen Hotel, Washington, D.C.

TYLER PROCLAIMED MEMORIAL FOR HARRISON

On April 13, 1841, one week after his succession to the presidency, John Tyler issued a proclamation recommending

to the people of the United States of every religious denomination that, according to their several modes and forms of worships, they observe a day of fasting and prayer by such religious services as may be suitable on the occasion; and I recommend Friday the 14th of May next, for that purpose. . . .

TYLER CABINET RESIGNED

On September 9, 1841, President Tyler vetoed a bill "to provide for the better collection, safekeeping, and disbursement of the public revenues by means of a corporation to be styled the Fiscal Corporation of the United States." This action was disapproved of by his cabinet, and the secretaries of the treasury, war and navy, as well as the attorney general and the postmaster general, resigned. The only cabinet member who retained his post was Secretary of State Daniel Webster.

TYLER ESCAPED DEATH ABOARD THE "PRINCETON"

About four hundred visitors, including President Tyler, the members of the Cabinet, the diplomatic corps, members of Congress, and their families visited the U.S.S. *Princeton,* the first propeller-driven warship, on February 28, 1844. She proceeded from Alexandria, Va., down the Potomac River. Below Fort Washington, the ship's "Peacemaker," a ten-ton gun, fifteen feet long with a twelve-inch bore, fired a 225-pound ball.

On the return trip, when the ship was about fifteen miles below Washington, D.C., the gun was fired again, with a 25-pound charge. Although the gun had been tested at 49 pounds and had been frequently fired successfully with a 30-pound charge, it exploded and burst at the breech. Thomas Walker Gilmer, secretary of the navy; Abel Parker Upshur, secretary of state; Commodore Kennon of the *Princeton*; David Gardiner, a former state senator of New York; Virgil Maxcy, a former United States chargé d'affaires in Belgium; and Tyler's Negro servant were killed. Seventeen seamen were wounded and many others were stunned, including Captain Robert Field Stockton

of the *Princeton.* President Tyler was below decks when the explosion took place.

The bodies were brought to the Executive Mansion and the coffins were placed in the East Room. As the explosion was an accident, the captain and the officers were exonerated from blame.

CONGRESS OVERRODE VETO

The first legislation passed over a President's veto was an act (S.66, 2 sess. 28 Cong.) "relating to revenue cutters and steamers." It provided that no revenue cutter could be built unless an appropriation was first made by law. President Tyler vetoed the bill, on the ground contracts for two revenue cutters had already been let, one to a firm in Richmond, Va., and the other to a Pittsburgh, Pa., contractor. He vetoed the bill on February 20, 1845. It was reconsidered by the Senate and House on March 3, 1845. The former passed it without debate over his veto, 41 to 1, and the House by a vote of 127 to 30.

HOSTESSES AT THE WHITE HOUSE

Letitia Christian Tyler was still suffering from the effects of a paralytic attack when her husband became President. As she was unable to act as mistress of the White House, Priscilla Cooper Tyler, the wife of their eldest son, acted in that capacity.

During the seventeen months that Letitia Tyler was the first lady, she appeared in public at the White House only once. On January 31, 1842, she attended the marriage of her daughter, Elizabeth, to William Nevison Waller. Less than eight months later, on September 10, 1842, Mrs. Tyler died.

PRESIDENT TYLER REMARRIED

John Tyler was the first President to marry while in office. After the death of his first wife, he remained a widower for a little over twenty-one months and then married Julia Gardiner on June 26, 1844, at the Church of the Ascension, New York, N.Y. She was the first lady of the land for a little over eight months until James Knox Polk became President.

TYLER PRESIDED AT PEACE CONFERENCE

Former President Tyler was president of the peace conference which met in secret session from February 4 to Febru-

ary 27, 1861 at Washington, D.C. The conference presented to the delegates on February 15 a report which was adopted February 26. The conference was attended by 133 commissioners from 22 states. The free states represented were Connecticut, Illinois, Indiana, Iowa, Kansas, Maine, Massachusetts, New Hampshire, New Jersey, New York, Ohio, Pennsylvania, Rhode Island, Vermont and Wisconsin; the slave states represented were Delaware, Kentucky, Maryland, Missouri, North Carolina, Tennessee and Virginia.

The report of the conference was submitted to Congress which considered it and finally rejected it.

TYLER IN CONFEDERATE CONGRESS

John Tyler served as a member of the Confederate States Congress. On August 1, 1861, he was a delegate to the Provisional Congress of the Confederate States. He was elected a member of the House of Representatives of the permanent Confederate Congress on November 7, 1861, but never took his seat, as he died January 18, 1862, at Richmond, Va., before the Congress assembled.

TYLER'S DEATH IGNORED

When former President John Tyler died at Richmond, Va., on January 18, 1862, the government made no announcement or proclamation of his death and no official notice of his demise was taken.

GOVERNMENT AUTHORIZED TYLER MONUMENT FIFTY YEARS AFTER HIS DEATH

On March 4, 1911, Congress authorized the erection of a monument to Tyler's memory and on August 24, 1912, appropriated $10,000 for it. It was completed June 9, 1915, and dedicated October 12, 1915, at Hollywood Cemetery, Cherry and Albemarle Streets, Richmond, Va. Five senators and five congressmen represented the United States at the ceremonies.

TYLER HONORED HIS HORSE

In Sherwood, Charles City County, Va., John Tyler had a grave dug for his horse, "The General," over which was the following inscription:

Here lies the body of my good horse, "The General." For twenty years he bore me around the circuit of my practice, and in all that time he never made a blunder. Would that his master could say the same! John Tyler.

JAMES KNOX POLK

Born—Nov. 2, 1795

Birthplace—Near Pineville, Mecklenburg County, N.C.

College attended—University of North Carolina, Chapel Hill, N.C.

Date of graduation—June 4, 1818, Bachelor of Arts

Religion—Presbyterian

Ancestry—Scotch-Irish

Occupation—Lawyer

Date and place of marriage—Jan. 1, 1824, Murfreesboro, Tenn.

Age at marriage—28 years, 60 days

Years married—25 years, 165 days

Political party—Democratic

State represented—Tennessee

Term of office—Mar. 4, 1845-Mar. 3, 1849

Term served—4 years

Administration—15th

Congresses—29th, 30th

Age at inauguration—49 years, 122 days

Lived after term—103 days

Occupation after term—Retired because of illness

Date of death—June 15, 1849

Age at death—53 years, 225 days

Place of death—Nashville, Tenn.

Burial place—State Capitol Grounds, Nashville, Tenn.

PARENTS

Father—Samuel Polk

Born—July 5, 1772, Tryon, N.C.

For additional data see the end of this section and also specific subject headings in the Index.

Married—Dec. 25, 1794, Mecklenburg County, N.C.

Occupation—Planter, farmer

Died—Nov. 5, 1827, Maury County, Tenn.

Age at death—55 years, 123 days

Mother—Jane Knox Polk

Born—Nov. 15, 1776

Died—Jan. 11, 1852, Maury County, Tenn.

Age at death—75 years, 57 days

BROTHERS AND SISTERS

James Knox Polk was the oldest child in a family of ten.

CHILDREN

None

MRS. JAMES KNOX POLK

Name—Sarah Childress Polk

Date of birth—Sept. 4, 1803

Birthplace—Murfreesboro, Tenn.

Age at marriage—20 years, 119 days

Children—None

Mother—Elizabeth Childress

Father—Captain Joel Childress

His occupation—Planter

Date of death—Aug. 14, 1891

Age at death—87 years, 344 days

Place of death—Nashville, Tenn.

Burial place—Nashville, Tenn.

Years younger than the President—7 years, 306 days

Years she survived the President—42 years, 60 days

THE ELECTION OF 1844

NOMINATIONS FOR TERM 1845-1849

Democratic Party Convention (4th)

May 27-30, 1844, Odd Fellows' Hall, Baltimore, Md.

Nominated for President—James Knox Polk, Tenn.

Nominated for Vice President—George Mifflin Dallas, Pa.

Total number of votes: 266

Number necessary for nomination: 177

Polk received his first vote on the eighth ballot and was nominated unanimously on the ninth ballot.

Silas Wright of New York was nominated for the vice presidency, receiving 258 votes, while Levi Woodbury of New Hampshire received 8 votes. Wright declined the nomination and George Mifflin Dallas became the vice presidential nominee.

Whig Party Convention

May 1, 1844, Universalist Church, Baltimore, Md.

Nominated for President— Henry Clay, Ky.

Nominated for Vice President— Theodore Frelinghuysen, N.J.

Clay was nominated on the first ballot by acclamation.

National Democratic Tyler Convention

May 27-28, 1844, Calvert Hall, Baltimore, Md.

Nominated for President—John Tyler, Va.

A group of Democrats opposed to the nominations of the major parties endeavored to establish a separate ticket and party. A committee was appointed to nominate a vice presidential candidate.

ELECTION RESULTS, NOV. 5, 1844—PRESIDENTIAL AND VICE PRESIDENTIAL CANDIDATES

Democratic Party (1,337,243 votes)

James Knox Polk, Tenn.
George Mifflin Dallas, Pa.

Whig Party (1,299,062 votes)

Henry Clay, Ky.
Theodore Frelinghuysen, N.J.

Liberty Party (62,300 votes)

James Gillespie Birney, N.Y.
Thomas Morris, Ohio

ELECTORAL VOTES (275 —26 states)

Polk received 61.82 per cent (170 votes—15 states) as follows: Ala. 9; Ark. 3; Ga. 10; Ill. 9; Ind. 12; La. 6; Me. 9; Mich. 5; Miss. 6; Mo. 7; N.H. 6; N.Y. 36; Pa. 26; S.C. 9; Va. 17.

Clay received 38.18 per cent (105 votes—11 states) as follows: Conn. 6; Del. 3; Ky. 12; Md. 8; Mass. 12; N.J. 7; N.C. 11; Ohio 23; R.I. 4; Tenn. 13; Vt. 6.

APPOINTMENTS TO THE SUPREME COURT

Associate Justices

Levi Woodbury, N.H., Sept. 20, 1845

Robert Cooper Grier, Pa., Aug. 4, 1846

ADMINISTRATION— IMPORTANT DATES

Oct. 10, 1845, United States Naval Academy opened

Dec. 29, 1845, Texas admitted as the 28th state

1846, Howe patented sewing machine

Jan. 23, 1846, uniform election day established

Mar. 4, 1846, Michigan legislature abolished death penalty (first state to do so)

Apr. 25, 1846, first skirmish in Mexican War

May 8, 1846, Battle of Palo Alto

May 9, 1846, Battle of Resaca de la Palma

May 13, 1846, United States formally declared war against Mexico

June 15, 1846, treaty concluded with Great Britain establishing Oregon boundary on the 49th parallel; in force Aug. 1846

Aug. 8, 1846, defeat in Senate of Wilmot Proviso calling for exclusion of slavery from any territory acquired from Mexico

Sept. 24, 1846, Battle of Monterey

Dec. 28, 1846, Iowa admitted as the 29th state

1847, conquest of California by American forces

Feb. 23, 1847, Battle of Buena Vista

Mar. 29, 1847, General Winfield Scott captured Vera Cruz

Apr. 18, 1847, Battle of Cerro Gordo

May 5, 1847, American Medical Association organized

Sept. 8, 1847, Battle of Molino del Rey

Sept. 13, 1847, Battle of Chapultepec

Sept. 14, 1847, fall of Mexico City to General Scott

Jan. 24, 1848, gold discovered in California by James W. Marshall; beginning of gold rush which reached its height in 1849

Feb. 2, 1848, treaty of Guadalupe Hidalgo signed with Mexico; Mexico recognized Rio Grande as boundary and ceded, for $15 million, territory that became California, New Mexico, Arizona, Nevada, Utah, and parts of Colorado and Wyoming

May 29, 1848, Wisconsin admitted as the 30th state

July 4, 1848, President Polk laid cornerstone of the Washington Monument

July 19-20, 1848, women's rights convention, Seneca Falls, N.Y.

Aug. 14, 1848, Oregon admitted as a territory

Mar. 3, 1849, Department of Interior created

IMPORTANT DATES IN HIS LIFE

1806, moved to Tennessee, settling in what is now Maury County

1818, graduated from University of North Carolina

1820, admitted to the bar; practiced at Columbia, Tenn.

1821-1823, chief clerk of Tennessee Senate

1823-1825, Tennessee House of Representatives

Mar. 4, 1825-Mar. 3, 1839, U.S. House of Representatives (from Tennessee)

Dec. 7, 1835-Mar. 3, 1839, Speaker of the House of Representatives

1839-1841, governor of Tennessee

Mar. 4, 1845-Mar. 3, 1849, President

1849, declined to be a candidate for reelection; retired to Nashville

JAMES KNOX POLK

——was the first President born in North Carolina.

——was the third President elected from a state other than his native state.

——was the fourth President whose mother was alive when he was inaugurated.

——was the first President who was survived by his mother.

POLK'S VICE PRESIDENT

Vice President—George Mifflin Dallas (11th V.P.)

Date of birth—July 10, 1792

Birthplace—Philadelphia, Pa.

Political party—Democratic

State represented—Pennsylvania

Term of office—Mar. 4, 1845-Mar. 3, 1849

Age at inauguration—52 years, 237 days

Occupation after term—Governmental positions

Date of death—Dec. 31, 1864

Place of death—Philadelphia, Pa.

Age at death—72 years, 174 days

Burial place—Philadelphia, Pa.

ADDITIONAL DATA ON POLK

NEWS OF POLK'S NOMINATION TELEGRAPHED

The first use of the telegraph in politics occurred on May 29, 1844, when news was flashed to Washington, D.C., from Baltimore, Md., that Polk had been nominated for the presidency on the Democratic ticket. The Washington *National Intelligencer* reported:

During the whole day, a crowd of persons, including a number of Members of Congress, were in attendance at the Capitol to receive the reports by telegraph of news from Baltimore, which were made at successive intervals with striking despatch and accuracy, and were received by the auditors, as the responses of the ancient Oracle may be supposed to have been, with emotions corresponding to the various and opposite sentiments of those comprising the assembly. Whatever variety of impression the news made upon the auditory, however, there was but one sentiment concerning the telegraph itself, which was that of mingled delight and wonder.

Twenty minutes after Polk had been nominated, a telegram was sent to the convention from Washington, D.C.

The Democratic members of Congress to their Democratic brethren in convention assembled. Three cheers for James K. Polk.

POLK THE FIRST "DARK HORSE" ELECTED

Polk was not even considered as a candidate for the presidency at the Democratic national convention held at Odd Fellows' Hall, Baltimore, Md. from May 27 to May 30, 1844. His name was not mentioned during the first seven ballots and not a single vote was cast for him. A stalemate existed between former President Martin Van Buren and Lewis Cass of Michigan. On the eighth ballot (May 29, 1844), Polk was suggested as a compromise candidate and received 44 votes, while Van Buren had 104 votes and Cass 114 votes. Two votes each were also cast for Buchanan and Calhoun. On the ninth ballot, amid indescribable confusion, the convention stampeded for Polk. State after state that had supported Van Buren or Cass cast its votes for Polk, and before the final tally his nomination was declared unanimous, as he had received 266 of the 266 votes cast.

INAUGURATION

James Knox Polk took the oath of office on Tuesday, March 4, 1845, on the east portico of the Capitol. Chief Justice Taney administered the oath. Although it rained, Polk delivered his inaugural address outdoors, and a large military parade took place. This was the first presidential inauguration reported by telegraph. Samuel F. B. Morse, using a telegraph key installed on the platform, sent the news by wire to Baltimore, Md. Two inaugural balls were held.

POLK THE FIRST PRESIDENT WHO HAD BEEN A SPEAKER OF THE HOUSE

James Knox Polk was the first Speaker of the House of Representatives who became a President of the United States. He served as Speaker of the 24th Congress (first session, December 7, 1835 to July 4, 1836, 211 days; second session, December 5, 1836 to March 3, 1837, 89 days). He also served as Speaker of the 25th Congress (first session, September 4, 1837 to October 16, 1837, 43 days; second session, December 4, 1837 to July 9, 1838, 218 days; and third session, December 3, 1838 to March 3, 1839, 91 days).

ELECTION DAY MADE UNIFORM

Originally, there was no uniform date for national elections. Each state could fix its own date, but all elections were required to be held at least thirty-four days before the first Wednesday in December, which was the date of the meeting of the presidential electors.

As a result, repeaters could go from state to state and vote. In 1844, the last year under this system, elections were held on the first Monday in November in Alabama, Arkansas, Connecticut, Georgia, Illinois, Indiana, Kentucky, Maine, Maryland, Michigan, Mississippi, Missouri, North Carolina, Rhode Island and Virginia. On the second Monday in November, elections were held in Massachusetts and New Hampshire. The first Tuesday in November was the date when elections were held in Delaware, Louisiana, Tennessee and Vermont. In New Jersey, election day was the first Tuesday in November and the next day. In New York, the day for election was the first Tuesday after the first Monday in November. Other dates were employed by Ohio, Pennsylvania, and South Carolina.

On January 23, 1845, an act was passed (5 Stat.L.721) appointing the first Tuesday after the first Monday in November of every even-numbered year. As a result, the date has varied between November 2 and November 8. The law applied to all states except Maine, where the voting was earlier.

The first Tuesday after the first Monday was decided upon in order to eliminate the possibility of an Election Day falling on the first day of November, a day often inconvenient to merchants balancing their books for the month. Monday also was found objectionable as, prior to the establishment of good roads, it often took more than a day for the voter to reach the polling place. As this might have necessitated voters' leaving their homes on Sunday, the day of rest, it was found preferable to have Election Day fall on Tuesdays instead of on Mondays.

POLK RELIEVED AT CONCLUSION OF PRESIDENTIAL TERM

President Polk made the following notation in his diary on February 13, 1849:

I am heartily rejoiced that my term is so near its close. I will soon cease to be a servant and become a sovereign. As a private citizen, I will have no one but myself to serve, and will exercise a part of the sovereign power of the country. I am sure I will be happier in this condition than in the exalted station I now hold.

Under the date of Sunday, March 4, 1849, Polk wrote in his diary:

I feel exceedingly relieved that I am now free from all public cares. I am sure I shall be a happier man in my retirement than I have been during the four years I have filled the highest office in the gift of my countrymen.

THE FIRST LADY

As Sarah Childress Polk had no children, her interests were not divided and her entire time was devoted to her husband. She made a great effort to act as a capable mistress of the White House, but was grave and formal and maintained great dignity. A devout Presbyterian, she banned dancing and the serving of alcoholic refreshments, believing that both were not in keeping with the standards necessary in the White House. She carefully guarded the purse strings and did away with extravagance. Although the social set of Washington did not approve, the nation as a whole did not condemn her. Her policy was greatly admired by the strict religious elements in the nation.

POLK BAPTIZED A WEEK BEFORE HIS DEATH

Fulfilling a promise that he had made, Polk was baptized June 9, 1849, by the Reverend Mr. McFerren, a Methodist minister.

Polk died June 15, 1849, in the presence of the Reverend Dr. Edgar, a Presbyterian minister, and the Reverend Dr. Mack.

ZACHARY TAYLOR

Zachary Taylor

ZACHARY TAYLOR

Born—Nov. 24, 1784

Birthplace—Montebello, Orange County, Va.

College attended—None

Religion—Episcopalian

Ancestry—English

Occupation—Soldier

Date and place of marriage—June 21, 1810, near Louisville, Ky.

Age at marriage—25 years, 209 days

Years married—40 years, 18 days

Political party—Whig

State represented—Louisiana

Term of office—Mar. 4, 1849-July 9, 1850

Term served—1 year, 127 days

Administration—16th

Congress—31st

Age at inauguration—64 years, 100 days

Lived after term—Died in office

Date of death—July 9, 1850

Age at death—65 years, 227 days

Place of death—Washington, D.C.

Burial place—Springfield, Ky.

PARENTS

Father—Lieutenant Colonel Richard Taylor

Born—Apr. 3, 1744, Orange County, Va.

Married—Aug. 20, 1779

Occupation—Farmer, soldier

Died—Jan. 19, 1829, near Lexington, Ky.

Age at death—84 years, 291 days

Mother—Sarah Dabney Strother Taylor

Born—Dec. 14, 1760

Died—Dec. 13, 1822

Age at death—61 years, 364 days

BROTHERS AND SISTERS

Zachary Taylor was the third child in a family of nine.

For additional data see the end of this section and also specific subject headings in the Index.

CHILDREN

Anne Margaret Mackall Taylor, b. Apr. 9, 1811, Jefferson County, Ky.; m. Sept. 20, 1829, Robert Crooke Wood, Prairie du Chien, Michigan Territory; d. Dec. 2, 1875, Freiburg, Germany

Sarah Knox Taylor, b. Mar. 6, 1814, Fort Knox, Missouri Territory; m. June 17, 1835, Jefferson Davis, near Lexington, Ky.; d. Sept. 15, 1835, near St. Francisville, La.

Octavia Pannel Taylor, b. Aug. 16, 1816, Jefferson County, Ky.; d. July 8, 1820, Bayou Sara, La.

Margaret Smith Taylor, b. July 27, 1819, Jefferson County, Ky.; d. Oct. 22, 1820, Bayou Sara, La.

Mary Elizabeth ("Betty") Taylor, b. Apr. 20, 1824, Jefferson County, Ky.; m. Dec. 5, 1848, William Wallace Smith Bliss, Baton Rouge, La.; m. Feb. 11, 1858, Philip Pendleton Dandridge; d. July 26, 1909, Winchester, Va.

Richard Taylor, b. Jan. 27, 1826, near Louisville, Ky.; m. Feb. 10, 1851, Louise Marie Myrthé Bringier, New Orleans, La.; d. Apr. 12, 1879, New York, N.Y.

MRS. ZACHARY TAYLOR

Name—Margaret Mackall Smith Taylor

Date of birth—Sept. 21, 1788

Birthplace—Calvert County, Md.

Age at marriage—21 years, 273 days

Children—5 daughters, 1 son

Mother—Ann Mackall Smith

Father—Walter Smith

His occupation—Planter

Date of death—Aug. 18, 1852

Age at death—63 years, 331 days

Place of death—Near Pascagoula, Miss.

Burial place—Springfield, Ky.

Years younger than the President—3 years, 301 days

Years she survived the President—2 years, 40 days

THE ELECTION OF 1848

NOMINATIONS FOR TERM 1849-1853

Whig Party Convention

June 7-9, 1848, Museum Building, Philadelphia, Pa.

Nominated for President—Zachary Taylor, La.

Nominated for Vice President—Millard Fillmore, N.Y.

Taylor was nominated on the fourth ballot.

Total number of votes: first ballot 279; fourth ballot, 280

Number necessary for nomination: 140

Democratic Party Convention (5th)

May 22-26, 1848, Universalist Church, Baltimore, Md.

Nominated for President—Lewis Cass, Mich.

Nominated for Vice President —William Orlando Butler, Ky.

Cass was nominated on the fourth ballot.

Total number of votes: first ballot, 251; fourth ballot, 254

Number necessary for nomination: 168

Free Soil (Democratic) Party Convention

Aug. 9-10, 1848, Buffalo, N.Y.

Nominated for President—Martin Van Buren, N.Y.

Nominated for Vice President— Charles Francis Adams, Mass.

ELECTION RESULTS, NOV. 7, 1848—PRESIDENTIAL AND VICE PRESIDENTIAL CANDIDATES

Whig Party (1,360,099 votes)

Zachary Taylor, La.
Millard Fillmore, N.Y.

Democratic Party (1,220,544 votes)

Lewis Cass, Mich.
William Orlando Butler, Ky.

Free Soil (Democratic Party) (291,263 votes)

Martin Van Buren, N.Y.
Charles Francis Adams, Mass.

ELECTORAL VOTES (290 —30 states)

Taylor received 56.21 per cent (163 votes—15 states) as follows: Conn. 6; Del. 3; Fla. 3; Ga. 10; Ky. 12; La. 6; Md. 8; Mass. 12; N.J. 7; N.Y. 36; N.C. 11; Pa. 26; R.I. 4; Tenn. 13; Vt. 6.

Cass received 43.79 per cent (127 votes—15 states) as follows: Ala. 9; Ark. 3; Ill. 9; Ind. 12; Iowa 4; Me. 9; Mich. 5; Miss. 6; Mo. 7; N.H. 6; Ohio 23; S.C. 9; Tex. 4; Va. 17; Wis. 4.

ADMINISTRATION— IMPORTANT DATES

Apr. 10, 1849, safety pin patented by Walter Hunt

May 22, 1849, Abraham Lincoln obtained a patent on inflated cylinders "for buoying vessels over shoals"

Dec. 20, 1849, treaty with Hawaiian Islands

1850, private mint authorized, Mt. Ophir, Calif.

Apr. 19, 1850, Clayton-Bulwer treaty with Great Britain ratified

July 2, 1850, gas mask patented by Benjamin J. Lane

Aug.-Sept. 1850, measures constituting Clay Compromise of 1850 passed, providing for admission of California as free state; formation of territories of New Mexico and Utah, with option on slavery at time of admission as states; abolition of slave trade in District of Columbia; drastic fugitive slave bill

IMPORTANT DATES IN HIS LIFE

May 3, 1808, appointed first lieutenant, 7th Infantry

Nov. 30, 1810, appointed captain

July 1, 1811, in charge of Fort Knox at Vincennes in Indian territory

Sept. 1812, defended Fort Harrison against Tecumseh

Sept. 5, 1812, brevet rank of major conferred for gallant conduct at the defense of Fort Harrison

May 15, 1814, major, 26th Infantry

June 15, 1815, after the War of 1812, retained as captain of the 7th Infantry; declined and received honorable discharge

May 17, 1816, reinstated as major, 3rd Infantry

Apr. 20, 1819, lieutenant colonel, 4th Infantry

1821, stationed at Cantonment Bay, St. Louis, Miss.

Nov. 9, 1822, established Fort Jesup, La.

Dec. 1822, in charge of Cantonment Robertson near Baton Rouge, La.

May 1828, commanded Fort Snelling, unorganized territory, Minnesota

July 18, 1829, commanded Fort Crawford, Michigan territory (now Wisconsin)

Apr. 4, 1832, colonel, First Regiment

Aug. 2, 1832, Indians defeated at Bad Axe, ending the Black Hawk War

Dec. 25, 1837, brevet brigadier general for distinguished service at the battle of Okeechobee against the Seminole Indians

June 17, 1844, assumed command of Fort Jesup

Apr. 24, 1846, Mexicans crossed Rio Grande, clashed with a scouting party

May 8, 1846, Mexicans routed, battle of Palo Alto

May 9, 1846, Mexicans routed, Resaca de la Palma

May 18, 1846, Mexican army fled Matamoras, which was occupied without bloodshed

May 28, 1846, brevet major general for his zealous and distinguished services in Mexico

June 29, 1846, major general of the line

July 18, 1846, received thanks of Congress "for the fortitude, skill, enterprise and courage which have distinguished the recent operations on the Rio Grande"

Sept. 25, 1846, Monterey surrendered; Mexicans left city

Feb. 23, 1847, defeated Santa Anna at battle of Buena Vista (La Angostura)

July 18, 1848, nominated for the presidency by the Whigs

Jan. 31, 1849, resigned from the army

Mar. 4, 1849-July 9, 1850, President

ZACHARY TAYLOR

——was the seventh President born in Virginia.

——was the second President to die in office.

——was the second President inaugurated on March 5 (March 4 was a Sunday).

——was the fourth President elected from a state other than his native state.

——was the second President to die in the White House.

TAYLOR'S VICE PRESIDENT

Vice President—Millard Fillmore (12th V.P.)

For biographical information see Millard Fillmore, 13th President.

TAYLOR THE THIRD PRESIDENT BORN AFTER REVOLUTION

Zachary Taylor was the third President born after the Revolutionary War. The two Presidents who preceded him in office were also born after the war and after Taylor.

The final draft of the treaty of peace was made on September 3, 1787. Taylor, the twelfth President, was born November 24, 1784, about six years before John Tyler (March 29, 1790), the tenth President, and about eleven years before James Knox Polk (November 2, 1795), the eleventh President.

TAYLOR THE FIRST PRESIDENT REPRESENTING A STATE WEST OF THE MISSISSIPPI

Zachary Taylor of Louisiana was the first President elected from a state west of the Mississippi River. He was, however, born in Virginia.

TAYLOR UNWITTINGLY REFUSED LETTER OF NOMINATION

The reason attributed to Zachary Taylor's not answering the letter sent by the Whigs notifying him at Baton Rouge, La., of his nomination for the presidency was that it arrived "postage due." Taylor refused to accept all unpaid mail. At that time, the Post Office carried "collect letters" which could be sent without the prepayment of postage.

BALLOTLESS PRESIDENT ELECTED

Zachary Taylor was too busy soldiering to vote. He served in the War of 1812, in the Indian wars against the Black Hawks and the Seminoles, and against the Mexicans. He never stayed in one place long enough to qualify as a voter, and being in the army, had not voted for forty years. His first vote was cast when he was sixty-two years of age.

CLAY TRIED FIFTH TIME FOR THE PRESIDENCY

Henry Clay's fifth attempt for the Whig Party nomination was made in 1848 at the Philadelphia convention. He failed to secure the necessary number of votes and the nomination was won by Zachary Taylor, who also won the election. At the Baltimore convention in 1840, Clay had tried in vain for the Whig Party nomination, the nominee that year being William Henry Harrison, who was elected President.

On three other occasions, Henry Clay was a presidential nominee, losing the election each time. He was defeated for the presidency in 1824 by John Quincy Adams, in 1832 by Andrew Jackson, and in 1844 by James Knox Polk.

Henry Clay made numerous speeches while he was a Senator from Kentucky stating that he was opposed to secession or separation from the union and advocating compromise measures. William Preston, a member of the Kentucky legislature, told Clay that his views would interfere with his chances of becoming President. Clay answered: "Sir, I would rather be right than be President."

INAUGURATION

Zachary Taylor took the oath of office on the east portico of the Capitol on Monday, March 5, 1849, as March 4 fell on a

Sunday, the second time in inaugural history. One hundred marshals escorted the presidential carriage from Willard's Hotel to the Capitol. Thirty thousand persons witnessed the inauguration. After a parade lasting one hour, a reception was held in the afternoon at the White House. Three different inaugural balls were held, each attended by President Taylor.

HORSE PASTURED ON WHITE HOUSE LAWN

When Zachary Taylor moved into the White House, he had his favorite mount, Whitey, accompany him. The horse that had served the general in the Mexican War at Buena Vista, Palo Alto, and other battles was given the freedom of the White House lawn. When President Taylor was buried, old Whitey followed his master's body in the funeral procession.

INTERIOR DEPARTMENT ESTABLISHED

On March 3, 1849, "an act to establish the Home Department" was passed. On March 8, 1849, President Taylor appointed Thomas Ewing of Ohio, who served until July 23, 1850. The name of the department was later changed to the Depart-

ment of Interior. It is concerned principally with the management, conservation, and development of the natural resources of the United States. These resources include the public lands and the Federal range, water and power resources, oil, gas and other mineral resources, certain foreign resources, fish and wildlife resources, and the national park system.

WAS ATCHISON PRESIDENT?

Many people have claimed that David Rice Atchison was President of the United States.

As March 4, 1849, fell on a Sunday, Zachary Taylor did not take his oath of office as President until Monday, March 5, 1849. Polk's four-year term constitutionally ended at noon on March 4, 1849. Vice President George Mifflin Dallas resigned as president of the Senate on Friday, March 2, 1849, and Senator David Rice Atchison of Missouri was elected president of the Senate pro tempore on March 2. He was nominated by Thomas Hart Benton.

Atchison presided over the Senate the following day and late into the night. On March 5, he was reelected president of the Senate pro tempore for the purpose of administering the oath of office to the senators-elect.

Article II of the Constitution contains the following provision:

In Case of the Removal of the President from Office, or of his Death, Resignation, or Inability to discharge the Powers and Duties of the said Office, the Same shall devolve on the Vice President, and the Congress may by Law provide for the Case of Removal, Death, Resignation or Inability, both of the President and the Vice President, declaring what Officer shall then act as President, and such Officer shall act accordingly, until the Disability be removed, or a President shall be elected.

Although Atchison was never a Vice President and never lived in the White House, and signed no acts of Congress, many insist that he was President of the United States for one day.

He died in 1886 and Missouri appropriated $15,000 for his monument, which bears this inscription, "David Rice Atchison, 1807-1886. President of U.S. one day. Lawyer, statesman and jurist."

THE FIRST LADY

Mrs. Margaret Smith Taylor refused to appear at public functions. She was about sixty-one years of age when her husband became President on March 4, 1849. She was in ill health and her third and youngest daughter, Elizabeth, who was married to William Wallace Bliss, acted for her. Taylor became ill on July 4, 1850, and died five days later, having served about sixteen months. Mrs. Taylor, who had traveled from one military post to another during her husband's early years in the army, preferred to live a quiet, simple life, avoiding all gaiety and excitement.

MILLARD FILLMORE

Millard Fillmore

MILLARD FILLMORE

Born—Jan. 7, 1800

Birthplace—Summerhill, Cayuga County, N.Y.

College attended—None

Religion—Unitarian

Ancestry—English

Occupation—Lawyer

Date and place of first marriage—Feb. 5, 1826, Moravia, N.Y.

Age at marriage—26 years, 29 days

Years married—27 years, 53 days

Date and place of second marriage—Feb. 10, 1858, Albany, N.Y.

Age at second marriage—58 years, 34 days

Years married—16 years, 36 days

Political party—Whig

State represented—New York

Term of office—July 10, 1850-Mar. 3, 1853 (Fillmore succeeded to the presidency on the death of Zachary Taylor.)

Term served—2 years, 236 days

Administration—16th

Congresses—31st, 32nd

Age at inauguration—50 years, 184 days

Lived after term—21 years, 4 days

Occupation after term—Chancellor of University of Buffalo

Date of death—Mar. 8, 1874

Age at death—74 years, 60 days

Place of death—Buffalo, N.Y

Burial place—Forest Lawn Cemetery, Buffalo, N.Y.

For additional data see the end of this section and also specific subject headings in the Index.

PARENTS

Father—Nathaniel Fillmore

Born—Apr. 19, 1771, Bennington, Vt.

Married (1)—Phoebe Millard

Married (2)—Eunice Love

Occupation—Farmer, magistrate

Died—Mar. 28, 1863

Age at death—91 years, 343 days

Mother—Phoebe Millard Fillmore

Born—1780, Pittsfield, Mass.

Died—May 2, 1831

Age at death—About 51 years

Second wife of father—Eunice Love Fillmore

Married—May 2, 1834

BROTHERS AND SISTERS

Millard Fillmore was the second child in a family of nine.

CHILDREN

By first wife, Abigail Powers Fillmore

Millard Powers Fillmore, b. Apr. 25, 1828, Aurora, N.Y.; d. Nov. 15, 1889, Buffalo, N.Y.

Mary Abigail Fillmore, b. Mar. 27, 1832, Buffalo, N.Y.; d. July 26, 1854, Aurora, N.Y.

By second wife, Caroline Carmichael McIntosh Fillmore

None

MRS. MILLARD FILLMORE (first wife)

Name—Abigail Powers Fillmore

Date of birth—Mar. 13, 1798

Birthplace—Stillwater, N.Y.

Age at marriage—27 years, 329 days

Children—1 son, 1 daughter

Mother—Abigail Newland Powers

Father—Reverend Lemuel Powers

His occupation—Baptist clergyman

Date of death—Mar. 30, 1853

Age at death—55 years, 17 days

Place of death—Washington, D.C.

Burial place—Buffalo, N.Y.

Years older than the President—1 year, 300 days

Years the President survived her—20 years, 343 days

MRS. MILLARD FILLMORE (second wife)

Name—Caroline Carmichael McIntosh Fillmore

Date of birth—Oct. 21, 1813

Birthplace—Morristown, N.J.

Age at marriage—44 years, 112 days

Children—None

Mother—Temperance Blachley Carmichael

Father—Charles Carmichael

Date of death—Aug. 11, 1881

Age at death—67 years, 294 days

Place of death—Buffalo, N.Y.

Burial place—Buffalo, N.Y.

Years younger than the President—13 years, 287 days

Years she survived the President—7 years, 156 days

The second Mrs. Fillmore was the widow of Ezekiel C. McIntosh of Albany, N.Y.

APPOINTMENT TO THE SUPREME COURT

Associate Justice

Benjamin Robbins Curtis, Mass., Sept. 22, 1851

ADMINISTRATION— IMPORTANT DATES

Sept. 9, 1850, California admitted as the 31st state

Sept. 11, 1850, first American performance of Jenny Lind, "the Swedish Nightingale," at New York City

Sept. 18, 1850, fugitive slave law enacted

July 4, 1851, cornerstone laid for the south house extension of the Capitol

Dec. 5, 1851, General Louis Kossuth, Hungarian patriot, arrived; celebration at New York City, Dec. 6

Dec. 24, 1851, Capitol at Washington, D.C., partly destroyed by fire

Nov. 1852, Commodore Matthew C. Perry sent on expedition to open the ports of Japan to commerce

Mar. 2, 1853, Washington Territory created out of northern part of Oregon

Mar. 3, 1853, federal assay office building authorized

IMPORTANT DATES IN HIS LIFE

18——, attended primitive rural schools and was self-instructed

1815, apprenticed to wool carder and clothdresser

1818, taught school at Scott, N.Y.

1823, admitted to the bar; practiced in East Aurora, N.Y.

1829-1831, New York State Assembly (Anti-Masonic party)

1830, moved to Buffalo, N.Y.

Mar. 4, 1833-Mar. 3, 1835, U.S. House of Representatives (from New York)

Mar. 4, 1837-Mar. 3, 1843, U.S. House of Representatives (from New York)

1842, declined to be a candidate for renomination

1844, unsuccessful Whig candidate for governor of New York

18——, commanded a corps of Home Guard during the Mexican War

1846, chancellor of the University of Buffalo

Jan. 1, 1848-Feb. 20, 1849, New York State Controller

Mar. 4, 1849-July 9, 1850, Vice President

July 10, 1850-Mar. 3, 1853, President (took office on death of Zachary Taylor)

June 1852, unsuccessful aspirant for Whig presidential nomination

Nov. 1856, unsuccessful candidate for the presidency on the American ("Know-Nothing") Party and the Whig Party tickets

MILLARD FILLMORE

——was the second President born in New York.

——was the second President whose father was alive when he was inaugurated.

——was the second President to remarry.

——was the fourth President to marry a widow.

——was the first President to have a stepmother.

ADDITIONAL DATA ON FILLMORE

INAUGURATION

Millard Fillmore, succeeding President Zachary Taylor, who died on July 9, 1850, was the second Vice President to succeed to the presidency on the death of a President. At noon on Wednesday, July 10, 1850, Judge William Cranch, chief justice of the United States Circuit Court of the District of Columbia, administered the oath to Fillmore in the Hall of the House of Representatives.

BOOKS FOR THE PRESIDENT

According to contemporary reports, when President Millard Fillmore took office, the White House had no books, not even a Bible. His wife, Abigail Powers Fillmore, a former schoolteacher and a voracious reader, converted a large room on the second floor into a library, and the appropriation act of March 3, 1851 (9 Stat.L.613) authorized "for purchase of books for library at the Executive Mansion two hundred and fifty dollars to be expended under the direction of the President of the United States."

FILLMORE SOUGHT RE-NOMINATION AND REELECTION

Millard Fillmore served until the completion of the term ending March 3, 1853. He was an aspirant for the presidential nomination at the Whig convention held in Baltimore in June 1852, but the Whigs nominated General Winfield Scott.

Four years later, Fillmore was nominated for the presidency by the American Party (the "Know-Nothing" Party), but was defeated in the election. He received approximately 875,000 votes against 1,341,000 for John Charles Fremont, the first presidential candidate of the newly formed Republican Party, and 1,838,000 for James Buchanan, the Democrat, who was elected.

The platform adopted by the American Party on February 21, 1856, at Philadelphia, Pa., contained the following sections:

Americans must rule America; and to this end *native-born* citizens should be selected for all state, federal, and municipal offices of government employment, in preference to all others.

A change in the laws of naturalization, making a continued residence of twenty-one years, of all not heretofore provided for, an indispensable requisite for citizenship hereafter, and excluding all paupers and persons convicted of crime from landing upon our shores; but no interference with the vested rights of foreigners.

THE FIRST LADY

Mrs. Abigail Powers Fillmore was an invalid when her husband succeeded to the presidency. Her daughter, Mary Abigail Fillmore, assumed the functions of first lady. Mrs. Fillmore died less than a month after her husband ended his term of office, having contracted a chill while attending the inauguration of President Franklin Pierce.

Frank Pierce

FRANKLIN PIERCE

Born—Nov. 23, 1804

Birthplace—Hillsborough, N.H. (now Hillsboro)

College attended—Bowdoin College, Brunswick, Me.

Date of graduation—Sept. 1, 1824, four-year course, Bachelor of Arts

Religion—Episcopalian

Ancestry—English

Occupation—Lawyer

Date and place of marriage—Nov. 10, 1834, Amherst, Mass.

Age at marriage—29 years, 352 days

Years married—29 years, 22 days

Political party—Democratic

State represented—New Hampshire

Term of office—Mar. 4, 1853-Mar. 3, 1857

Term served—4 years

Administration—17th

Congresses—33rd, 34th

Age at inauguration—48 years, 101 days

Lived after term—12 years, 218 days

Occupation after term—Retired; traveled

Date of death—Oct. 8, 1869

Age at death—64 years, 319 days

Place of death—Concord, N.H.

Burial place—Old North Cemetery, Concord, N.H.

PARENTS

Father—General Benjamin Pierce

Born—Dec. 25, 1757, Chelmsford, Mass.

For additional data see the end of this section and also specific subject headings in the Index.

Married (1)—Elizabeth Andrews

Married (2)—Anna Kendrick

Occupation—Soldier, farmer, tavern owner, governor

Died—Apr. 1, 1839

Age at death—81 years, 97 days

First wife of father—Elizabeth Andrews

Born—1768

Married—May 24, 1787

Died—Aug. 13, 1788

Age at death—20 years

Mother—Anna Kendrick Pierce

Born—1768

Married—Feb. 1, 1790

Died—Dec. 1838

Age at death—70 years

BROTHERS AND SISTERS

Franklin Pierce was the seventh child of his father, the sixth of eight children of a second marriage.

CHILDREN

Franklin Pierce, b. Feb. 2, 1836, Hillsborough, N.H.; d. Feb. 5, 1836, Hillsborough, N.H.

Frank Robert Pierce, b. Aug. 27, 1839, Concord, N.H.; d. Nov. 14, 1843, Concord, N.H.

Benjamin Pierce, b. Apr. 13, 1841, Concord, N.H.; d. Jan. 6, 1853, near Andover, Mass.

MRS. FRANKLIN PIERCE

Name—Jane Means Appleton Pierce

Date of birth—Mar. 12, 1806

Birthplace—Hampton, N.H.

Age at marriage—28 years, 243 days

Children—3 sons

Mother—Elizabeth Appleton

Father—Jesse Appleton

His occupation—Congregational minister

Date of death—Dec. 2, 1863

Age at death—57 years, 265 days

Place of death—Andover, Mass.

Burial place—Concord, N.H.

Years younger than the President—1 year, 109 days

Years the President survived her—5 years, 310 days

THE ELECTION OF 1852

NOMINATIONS FOR TERM 1853-1857

Democratic Party Convention (6th)

June 1-5, 1852, Maryland Institute Hall, Baltimore, Md.

Nominated for President—Franklin Pierce, N.H.

Nominated for Vice President—

William Rufus De Vane
King, Ala.

Pierce was nominated on the
forty-ninth ballot.

Total number of votes : first ballot, 287 ; forty-ninth ballot,
289

Whig Party Convention

June 17-20, 1852, Maryland In-
stitute Hall, Baltimore, Md.
Nominated for President—Win-
field Scott, N.J.
Nominated for Vice President—
William Alexander Graham,
N.C.

Scott was nominated on the
fifty-third ballot.

Total number of votes : first ballot, 293 ; fifty-third ballot, 292

ELECTION RESULTS, NOV. 2, 1852—PRESIDENTIAL AND VICE PRESIDENTIAL CANDIDATES

Democratic Party (1,601,274 votes)

Franklin Pierce, N.H.
William Rufus De Vane King,
Ala.

Whig Party (1,386,580 votes)

Winfield Scott, N.J.
William Alexander Graham,
N.C.

Free Soil Party (155,825 votes)

John Parker Hale, N.H.
George Washington Julian, Ind.

ELECTORAL VOTES (296 —31 states)

Pierce received 85.81 per cent
(254 votes—27 states) as fol-
lows : Ala. 9 ; Ark. 4 ; Calif. 4 ;
Conn. 6 ; Del. 3 ; Fla. 3 ; Ga. 10 ;
Ill. 11 ; Ind. 13 ; Iowa 4 ; La. 6 ;
Me. 8 ; Md. 8 ; Mich. 6 ; Miss. 7 ;
Mo. 9 ; N.H. 5 ; N.J. 7 ; N.Y.
35 ; N.C. 10 ; Ohio 23 ; Pa. 27 ;
R.I. 4 ; S.C. 8 ; Tex. 4 ; Va. 15 ;
Wis. 5.
Scott received 14.19 per cent
(42 votes—4 states) as follows :
Ky. 12 ; Mass. 13 ; Tenn. 12 ; Vt.
5.

APPOINTMENT TO THE SUPREME COURT

Associate Justice

John Archibald Campbell, Ala.,
Mar. 22, 1853

ADMINISTRATION— IMPORTANT DATES

May 31, 1853, Elisha Kent Kane
expedition to Arctic left New
York City
June 1853, first stamped enve-
lopes issued
July 14, 1853, President Pierce
opened Crystal Palace Exposition, New York, N.Y.

Sept. 19, 1853, patent on sleeping car issued to H. B. Myer

Mar. 8, 1854, Perry's treaty with Japan ratified

May 22, 1854, Congress enacted Kansas-Nebraska Act permitting state option on slavery, nullifying the Missouri Compromise

June 30, 1854, Gadsden Purchase treaty proclaimed; United States acquired border territory from Mexico

Oct. 1854, Ostend Manifesto, issued by U.S. ministers to England, France, and Spain, urged American acquisition of Cuba from Spain by purchase or force

1855, first postal directory published

Aug. 19, 1856, Gail Borden obtained condensed milk patent

Sept. 4, 1856, first American flag flown in Japan by Consul General Townsend Harris

1857, financial panic

Feb. 24, 1857, first perforated postage stamps used

IMPORTANT DATES IN HIS LIFE

18——, attended the academies of Hancock and Francestown, N.H.

18——, prepared for college at Exeter

Sept. 1, 1824, graduated from Bowdoin College, Brunswick, Me.

1827, admitted to the bar; practiced at Hillsborough, N.H.

June 3, 1829-1833, New Hampshire House of Representatives

1832, speaker, New Hampshire House of Representatives

Mar. 4, 1833-Mar. 3, 1837, U.S. House of Representatives (from New Hampshire)

Mar. 4, 1837-Feb. 28, 1842, U.S. Senate (from New Hampshire)

1842, resigned to practice law at Concord, N.H.

1846, declined appointment as U.S. attorney general under President Polk

1847, enlisted as private in Mexican War

Feb. 16, 1847, became colonel of 9th Regiment, Infantry

Mar. 3, 1847, commissioned brigadier general

Apr. 12, 1847, served at Cerro Gordo

May 27, 1847, sailed for Mexico City

June 27, 1847, landed in Mexico

Aug. 19, 1847, injured at Contreras when horse took fright

Sept.-Dec., 1847, in Mexico City

Sept. 13, 1847, served at Chapultepec

Mar. 20, 1848, resigned from army

18——, declined senatorial appointment made by the governor of New Hampshire

18——, declined to run as governor of New Hampshire

Nov. 6, 1850, member and president of New Hampshire Fifth State Constitutional Convention

1852, Democratic nominee for the presidency

Mar. 4, 1853-Mar. 3, 1857, President

1856, unsuccessful candidate for Democratic nomination for the presidency

Nov. 1857, made European tour, visiting Portugal, Spain, France, Switzerland, Italy, Austria, Germany, Belgium, and England

May 1860, received one complimentary vote at Democratic convention

FRANKLIN PIERCE

——was the first President born in New Hampshire.

——was the first President born in the nineteenth century (November 23, 1804).

——was the first President who did not read his inaugural address but instead delivered it as an oration.

PIERCE'S VICE PRESIDENT

Vice President—William Rufus De Vane King (13th V.P.)

Date of birth—Apr. 7, 1786

Birthplace—Sampson County, N.C.

Political party—Democratic

State represented—Alabama

Term of office—Mar. 4, 1853-Apr. 18, 1853

Age at inauguration—66 years, 331 days

Occupation after term—Died in office

Date of death—Apr. 18, 1853

Place of death—Cahawba, Ala.

Age at death—67 years, 11 days

Burial place—Selma, Ala.

ADDITIONAL DATA ON PIERCE

PIERCE A "DARK HORSE" CANDIDATE

Franklin Pierce, the Democratic nominee for President in 1852, was not considered as a candidate until the thirty-fifth ballot, when Virginia cast fifteen votes for him. On the forty-eighth ballot, he received 55 votes. On the forty-ninth ballot, there was a sudden surge in his favor and he received 283 of the 289 votes cast, thereby winning the nomination.

PIERCE DEFEATED GENERAL SCOTT

Franklin Pierce carried 27 of the 31 states and defeated General Winfield Scott, the Whig Party nominee. Pierce, a brigadier general in the Mexican War, served under General Scott and was with him during his march to and capture of Mexico City on September 14, 1847. Pierce enlisted in the war as a private and was enrolled in a company of volunteers organized at Concord, N.H. He was commissioned a colonel in the Ninth Regiment and on March 3, 1847, was commissioned a brigadier in the volunteer army.

INAUGURATION

Franklin Pierce was inaugurated on Friday, March 4, 1853, and took the oath of office on the east portico of the Capitol. A raw northeasterly wind blew over the fast melting snow.

The oath was administered by Chief Justice Taney. In taking the oath Pierce availed himself of an option provided in Article Two, section one of the Constitution. Instead of the usual "I do solemnly swear," he said, "I do solemnly affirm," the only President to "affirm" instead of "swear."

Pierce delivered his 3,319-word inaugural address without reference to notes and was the first President to deliver his speech as an oration instead of

reading it. Over eighty thousand spectators flocked to Washington, but as it commenced to snow during the ceremonies, only about fifteen thousand remained to hear the address.

The cost of putting up and taking down the grandstand in front of the Capitol was $322, including the pay of sixteen extra policemen.

A reception was held at the White House. The inaugural ball at Jackson Hall was canceled since Pierce was in mourning for his son, who had been killed in a railroad accident on January 6. Mrs. Pierce did not go to Washington for the inauguration.

FULL CABINET RETAINED

Franklin Pierce was the only President to retain the same cabinet for four years without any changes, replacements, resignations, or vacancies due to illness or death. His seven cabinet members remained in office until the completion of his term March 3, 1857.

VICE PRESIDENT KING NEVER SERVED

William Rufus De Vane King, who was elected Vice President of the United States in 1852 under Franklin Pierce, had the oath of office administered to him in Havana, Cuba, by William L. Sharkey, United States Consul at Havana. This was permitted by a special act of Congress. Of all the Presidents and Vice Presidents, King was the first and only one to take the oath in a foreign country.

King died April 18, 1853, and as the first session of the Thirty-third Congress was not held until December 5, 1853, he never performed any of the duties of his office and therefore never presided over the Senate.

VICE PRESIDENT KING SERVED IN BOTH HOUSES AND REPRESENTED TWO STATES

King was the only Vice President of the United States to serve in both houses of Congress. In each house he represented a different state. He was a representative from North Carolina from March 4, 1811, to November 4, 1816, and a senator from Alabama from December 14, 1819, to April 15, 1844, and again from July 1, 1848, to December 20, 1852.

133 BALLOTS NEEDED TO ELECT SPEAKER

The Thirty-fourth Congress assembled on Monday, December 3, 1855, to elect a Speaker of the House of Representatives. It was not until the 133rd ballot, on February 2, 1856, that Nathaniel Prentice Banks of Massachusetts was elected Speaker.

THE FIRST LADY

When Jane Appleton Pierce became mistress of the White House on March 4, 1853, she entered upon her duties with a troubled heart. Less than two months before the inauguration, her third and youngest son had been killed in a railroad accident. Her three children died before they had reached their teens. Her grief was so great that she lost interest in other matters. She always dressed in black while in the White House.

The second wife of Mrs. Pierce's uncle, Mrs. Abby Kent Means, acted as White House hostess.

James Buchanan

JAMES BUCHANAN

Born—Apr. 23, 1791

Birthplace—Cove Gap, Pa.

College attended—Dickinson College, Carlisle, Pa.

Date of graduation—Sept. 27, 1809, two-year course

Religion—Presbyterian

Ancestry—Scotch-Irish

Occupation—Lawyer

Marital status—Bachelor

Political party—Democratic

State represented—Pennsylvania

Term of office—Mar. 4, 1857-Mar. 3, 1861

Term served—4 years

Administration—18th

Congresses—35th, 36th

Age at inauguration—65 years, 315 days

Lived after term—7 years, 89 days

Occupation after term—Writing

Date of death—June 1, 1868

Age at death—77 years, 39 days

Place of death—Lancaster, Pa.

Burial place—Woodward Hill Cemetery, Lancaster, Pa.

PARENTS

Father—James Buchanan

Born—1761, County Donegal, Ireland

Married—Apr. 16, 1788

Occupation—Merchant, farmer

Died—June 11, 1821

Age at death—60 years

Mother—Elizabeth Speer Buchanan

For additional data see the end of this section and also specific subject headings in the Index.

Born—1767

Died—May 14, 1833, Greensburg, Pa.

Age at death—66 years

BROTHERS AND SISTERS

James Buchanan was the second child in a family of eleven.

THE ELECTION OF 1856

NOMINATIONS FOR TERM 1857-1861

Democratic Party Convention (7th)

June 2-6, 1856, Smith and Nixon's Hall, Cincinnati, Ohio
Nominated for President—James Buchanan, Pa.
Nominated for Vice President—John Cabell Breckinridge, Ky.

Buchanan was nominated on the seventeenth ballot, receiving all of the 296 votes cast.

Nomination made unanimous

Republican Party Convention (1st)

June 17-19, 1856, Music Fund Hall, Philadelphia, Pa.
Nominated for President—John Charles Fremont, Calif.
Nominated for Vice President—William Lewis Dayton, N.J.

Fremont was nominated on the first official ballot.

Total number of votes: first informal ballot, 553; first official ballot, 558

Nomination made unanimous

ELECTION RESULTS, NOV. 4, 1856—PRESIDENTIAL AND VICE PRESIDENTIAL CANDIDATES

Democratic Party (1,838,169 votes)

James Buchanan, Pa.
John Cabell Breckinridge, Ky.

Republican Party (1,341,264 votes)

John Charles Fremont, Calif.
William Lewis Dayton, N.J.

American Party (874,534 votes)

Millard Fillmore, N.Y.
Andrew Jackson Donelson, Tenn.

ELECTORAL VOTES (296 —31 states)

Buchanan received 58.79 per cent (174 votes—19 states) as follows: Ala. 9; Ark. 4; Calif. 4; Del. 3; Fla. 3; Ga. 10; Ill. 11; Ind. 13; Ky. 12; La. 6;

Miss. 7; Mo. 9; N.J. 7; N.C. 10; Pa. 27; S.C. 8; Tenn. 12; Tex. 4; Va. 15.

Fremont received 38.51 per cent (114 votes—11 states) as follows: Conn. 6; Iowa 4; Me. 8; Mass. 13; Mich. 6; N.H. 5; N.Y. 35; Ohio 23; R.I. 4; Vt. 5; Wis. 5.

Fillmore received 2.70 per cent (1 state): Md. 8.

APPOINTMENT TO THE SUPREME COURT

Associate Justice

Nathan Clifford, Me., Jan. 12, 1858

ADMINISTRATION— IMPORTANT DATES

Mar. 6, 1857, Chief Justice Taney announced Dred Scott decision rendering the Missouri Compromise unconstitutional

May 11, 1858, Minnesota admitted as the 32nd state

Aug. 1858, Lincoln-Douglas debates

Aug. 5, 1858, Atlantic cable completed

Aug. 16, 1858, James Buchanan and Queen Victoria exchanged greetings by means of the Atlantic cable

Feb. 14, 1859, Oregon admitted as the 33rd state

Aug. 27, 1859, oil discovered in Pennsylvania

Oct. 16, 1859, Harpers Ferry, Va., raided by John Brown

Apr. 3, 1860, Pony Express service began between St. Joseph, Mo., and Sacramento, Calif.

Sept. 20, 1860, Prince of Wales arrived at Detroit, Mich., from Canada, traveling as Baron Renfrew

Dec. 1860-Feb. 1861, futile compromise attempts to save the Union

Dec. 20, 1860, South Carolina seceded from the Union

Jan.-Feb. 1861, secession of Mississippi, Florida, Alabama, Georgia, Louisiana, Texas

Jan. 29, 1861, Kansas admitted as the 34th state

Feb. 4, 1861, Confederate States organized

IMPORTANT DATES IN HIS LIFE

Nov. 17, 1812, admitted to the bar; practiced at Lancaster, Pa.

18——, served under Major Charles Sterret Ridgely of Baltimore in War of 1812

Dec. 6, 1814-Oct. 1815, Pennsylvania House of Representatives

1816, unsuccessful candidate for

U.S. House of Representatives

18——, became a Jacksonian Democrat when Federalist Party went out of existence

Mar. 4, 1821-Mar. 3, 1831, U.S. House of Representatives (from Pennsylvania)

Jan. 4, 1832-Aug. 5, 1833, U.S. minister to Russia

Dec. 6, 1834-Mar. 5, 1845, U.S. Senate (from Pennsylvania)

May 29, 1844, unsuccessful aspirant to Democratic presidential nomination

Mar. 6, 1845-Mar. 6, 1849, secretary of state in cabinet of President Polk

May 25, 1848, unsuccessful aspirant to Democratic presidential nomination

1849, retired to Wheatland, his twenty-two-acre estate near Lancaster, Pa.

June 4, 1852, unsuccessful aspirant to Democratic presidential nomination

Apr. 11, 1853, envoy extraordinary and minister plenipotentiary to Great Britain

Mar. 4, 1857-Mar. 3, 1861, President

JAMES BUCHANAN

——was the first President born in Pennsylvania.

——was the only President to remain a bachelor.

BUCHANAN'S VICE PRESIDENT

Vice President—John Cabell Breckinridge (14th V.P.)

Date of birth—Jan. 21, 1821

Birthplace—near Lexington, Ky.

Political party—Democratic

State represented—Kentucky

Term of office—Mar. 4, 1857-Mar. 3, 1861

Age at inauguration—36 years, 42 days

Occupation after term—Military service in Confederate Army, lawyer

Date of death—May 17, 1875

Place of death—Lexington, Ky.

Age at death—54 years, 116 days

Burial place—Lexington, Ky.

ADDITIONAL DATA ON BUCHANAN

BUCHANAN WAS ENGAGED TO MARRY

In the summer of 1819, James Buchanan, twenty-eight, was engaged to twenty-three-year-old Ann Caroline Coleman, the daughter of Robert Coleman of Lancaster, Pa. While on a visit in Philadelphia, Pa., she took an overdose of laudanum and died there on December 9, 1819. She was buried December 12,

1819, in the St. James Episcopal churchyard at Lancaster, Pa.

BACHELOR ELECTED PRESIDENT

James Buchanan was the first bachelor elected President of the United States and the only one to remain unmarried.

Grover Cleveland, also a bachelor, was elected as the twenty-second President, but on June 2, 1886, he married his ward, Frances Folsom, in a ceremony performed in the White House.

INAUGURATION

James Buchanan was inaugurated on Wednesday, March 4, 1857, the oath of office being administered by Chief Justice Taney on the east portico of the Capitol.

A big parade containing impressive floats attracted great crowds. Models of battleships, the Goddess of Liberty, and historical scenes were depicted on the floats.

A special building to accommodate six thousand persons was erected at a cost of $15,000 on Judiciary Square for the inaugural ball. The building, which contained two rooms, one for dancing and one for the supper, was 235 feet long, 77 feet wide, and 20 feet high, and had a white ceiling studded with gold stars. The walls were red, white, and blue. The music was furnished by an orchestra of 40. Food was lavishly served. At the supper, 400 gallons of oysters were consumed, 60 saddles of mutton, 4 saddles of venison, 125 tongues, 75 hams, 500 quarts of chicken salad, 500 quarts of jellies, 1200 quarts of ice cream, and a cake four feet high. Over $3,000 was spent for wine.

BUCHANAN TIRED OF PRESIDENCY

Buchanan, in a letter to Mrs. James Knox Polk on September 19, 1859, wrote:

I am now in my sixty-ninth year and am heartily tired of my position as president. I shall leave it in the beginning of March 1861, should a kind Providence prolong my days until that period, with much greater satisfaction than when entering on the duties of the office.

YOUNGEST VICE PRESIDENT

John Cabell Breckinridge of Kentucky, who served as Vice President under President James Buchanan, was the youngest man to become Vice President. He was inaugurated on March 4, 1857, when he was 36 years, 1 month, and 11 days old.

HOSTESS AT THE WHITE HOUSE

Since James Buchanan was a bachelor, Harriet Lane, the daughter of his sister Jane Lane, served as mistress of the White House during his administration. Her mother had died when she was seven and her father when she was nine. During her uncle's presidential term, she married Henry Elliott Johnson of Baltimore, Md.

ABRAHAM LINCOLN

A. Lincoln

ABRAHAM LINCOLN

Born—Feb. 12, 1809

Birthplace—Hodgenville, Hardin County (now Larue County), Ky.

College attended—None

Religion—No specific denomination

Ancestry—English

Occupation—Lawyer

Date and place of marriage—Nov. 4, 1842, Springfield, Ill.

Age at marriage—33 years, 265 days

Years married—22 years, 162 days

Political party—Republican

State represented—Illinois

Term of office—Mar. 4, 1861-Apr. 15, 1865

Term served—4 years, 42 days

Administrations—19th, 20th

Congresses—37th, 38th, 39th

Age at inauguration—52 years, 20 days

Lived after term—Died in office

Date of death—Apr. 15, 1865

Age at death—56 years, 62 days

Place of death—Washington, D.C.

Burial place—Oak Ridge Cemetery, Springfield, Ill.

PARENTS

Father—Thomas Lincoln

Born—Jan. 6, 1778, Rockingham County, Va.

Married (1)—Nancy Hanks

Married (2)—Sarah Bush Johnston

Occupation—Farmer, carpenter, wheelwright

For additional data see the end of this section and also specific subject headings in the Index.

Died—Jan. 17, 1851, Coles County, Ill.

Age at death—73 years, 11 days

Mother—Nancy Hanks Lincoln

Born—Feb. 5, 1784, Campbell County, Va.

Married—June 12, 1806, Beechland, Ky.

Died—Oct. 5, 1818, Spencer County, Ind.

Age at death—34 years, 242 days

Second wife of father—Sarah Bush Johnston Lincoln

Born—Dec. 12, 1788, Hardin County, Ky.

Married—Dec. 2, 1819, Elizabethtown, Ky.

Died—Apr. 10, 1869, Charleston, Ill.

Age at death—80 years, 119 days

At the time of her marriage to Thomas Lincoln, Sarah Bush Johnston was the widow of Daniel Johnston, by whom she had four children. Her marriage to Johnston took place Mar. 13, 1806, and his death Oct. 1818.

BROTHERS AND SISTERS

Abraham Lincoln was the second child of his father's first wife.

CHILDREN

Robert Todd Lincoln, b. Aug. 1, 1843, Springfield, Ill.; m. Sept. 24, 1868, Mary Harlan, Washington, D.C.; d. July 25, 1926, Manchester, Vt.

Edward Baker Lincoln, b. Mar. 10, 1846, Springfield, Ill.; d. Feb. 1, 1850, Springfield, Ill.

William Wallace Lincoln, b. Dec. 21, 1850, Springfield, Ill.; d. Feb. 20, 1862, at the White House, Washington, D.C.

Thomas (Tad) Lincoln, b. Apr. 4, 1853, Springfield, Ill.; d. July 15, 1871, Chicago, Ill.

MRS. ABRAHAM LINCOLN

Name—Mary Todd Lincoln

Date of birth—Dec. 13, 1818

Birthplace—Lexington, Ky.

Age at marriage—23 years, 326 days

Children—4 sons

Mother—Eliza Ann Parker Todd

Father—Robert Smith Todd

His occupation—Banker, manufacturer, merchant, farmer

Date of death—July 16, 1882

Age at death—63 years, 215 days

Place of death—Springfield, Ill.

Burial place—Springfield, Ill.

Years younger than the President—9 years, 304 days

Years she survived the President—17 years, 92 days

THE ELECTION OF 1860

NOMINATIONS FOR TERM 1861-1865

Republican Party Convention (2nd)

May 16-18, 1860, the Wigwam, Chicago, Ill.

Nominated for President—Abraham Lincoln, Ill.

Nominated for Vice President—Hannibal Hamlin, Me.

Lincoln was nominated on the third ballot.

Total number of votes: 465

Number necessary for nomination: 233

Before the third ballot was completed, a shift in votes brought Lincoln's total to 364 votes.

Democratic Party Convention (8th)

April 23-28, 30, and May 1-3, 1860, the Hall of the South Carolina Institute, Charleston, S.C.

Nominated for President—No nomination made

Nominated for Vice President—No nomination made

Total number of votes: first ballot, 252½; fifty-seventh ballot, 252

Number necessary for nomination: 202

Unable to reach a decision on the fifty-seventh ballot, the convention adjourned to meet at Baltimore, Md., on June 18, 1860.

Democratic Party Convention (Northern or Douglas Democrats)

June 18-23, 1860, Front Street Theatre, Baltimore, Md.

Nominated for President—Stephen Arnold Douglas, Ill.

Nominated for Vice President—Herschel Vespasian Johnson, Ga.

Douglas was nominated on the second ballot.

Total number of votes: first ballot, 190½; second ballot, 194½

Nomination made unanimous

National Democratic Party Convention (Independent Democratic Party)

June 23, 1860, Maryland Institute Hall, Baltimore, Md.

Nominated for President—John Cabell Breckinridge, Ky.

Nominated for Vice President—Joseph Lane, Ore.

Breckinridge was nominated on the first ballot.

Total number of votes: 105
Nomination made unanimous

ELECTION RESULTS, NOV. 6, 1860—PRESIDENTIAL AND VICE PRESIDENTIAL CANDIDATES

Republican Party (1,866,452 votes)

Abraham Lincoln, Ill.
Hannibal Hamlin, Me.

Democratic Party (Northern Democrats) (1,375,157 votes)

Stephen Arnold Douglas, Ill.
Herschel Vespasian Johnson, Ga.

Democratic Party (Southern Democrats) (847,953 votes)

John Cabell Breckinridge, Ky.
Joseph Lane, Ore.

Constitutional Union Party (590,631 votes)

John Bell, Tenn.
Edward Everett, Mass.

ELECTORAL VOTES (303 —33 states)

Lincoln received 59.41 per cent (180 votes—18 states) as follows: Calif. 4; Conn. 6; Ill. 11; Ind. 13; Iowa 4; Me. 8; Mass. 13; Mich. 6; Minn. 4; N.H. 5; N.J. 4 (of the 7 votes); N.Y. 35; Ohio 23; Ore. 3; Pa. 27; R.I. 4; Vt. 5; Wis. 5.

Breckinridge received 23.76 per cent (72 votes—11 states) as follows: Ala. 9; Ark. 4; Del. 3; Fla. 3; Ga. 10; La. 6; Md. 8; Miss. 7; N.C. 10; S.C. 8; Tex. 4.

Bell received 12.87 per cent (39 votes—3 states) as follows: Ky. 12; Tenn. 12; Va. 15.

Douglas received 3.96 votes (12 votes—1 state) as follows: Mo. 9; N.J. 3 (of the 7 votes).

THE ELECTION OF 1864

NOMINATIONS FOR TERM 1865-1869

Republican Party Convention (National Union Convention) (3rd)

June 7-8, 1864, Front Street Theatre, Baltimore, Md.
Nominated for President—Abraham Lincoln, Ill.
Nominated for Vice President—Andrew Johnson, Tenn.

Abraham Lincoln was nominated on the first ballot.

Total number of votes: 506
Nomination made unanimous

Democratic Party Convention (9th)

August 29-31, 1864, the Amphitheatre, Chicago, Ill.

Nominated for President— George Brinton McClellan, N.Y.

Nominated for Vice President —George Hunt Pendleton, Ohio

George Brinton McClellan was nominated on the first ballot.

Total number of votes: 226
Number necessary for nomination: 151
Nomination made unanimous

ELECTION RESULTS, NOV. 8, 1864—PRESIDENTIAL AND VICE PRESIDENTIAL CANDIDATES

Republican Party (2,213,635 votes)

Abraham Lincoln, Ill.
Andrew Johnson, Tenn.

Democratic Party (1,805,237 votes)

George Brinton McClellan, N.Y.
George Hunt Pendleton, Ohio

ELECTORAL VOTES (233 —25 states)

Lincoln received 90.99 per cent (212 votes—22 states) as follows: Calif. 5; Conn. 6; Ill. 16; Ind. 13; Iowa 8; Kan. 3; Me. 7; Md. 7; Mass. 12; Mich. 8; Minn. 4; Mo. 11; Nev. 2;

N.H. 5; N.Y. 33; Ohio 21; Ore. 3; Pa. 26; R.I. 4; Vt. 5; W.Va. 5; Wis. 8.

McClellan received 9.01 per cent (21 votes—3 states) as follows: Del. 3; Ky. 11; N.J. 7.

Eleven Confederate states with 80 votes did not vote: Ala. 8; Ark. 5; Fla. 3; Ga. 9; La. 7; Miss. 7; N.C. 9; S.C. 6; Tenn. 10; Tex. 6; Va. 10.

APPOINTMENTS TO THE SUPREME COURT

Chief Justice

Salmon Portland Chase, Ohio, Dec. 6, 1864

Associate Justices

Noah Haynes Swayne, Ohio, Jan. 24, 1862
Samuel Freeman Miller, Iowa, July 16, 1862
David Davis, Ill., Oct. 17, 1862
Stephen Johnson Field, Calif., Mar. 10, 1863

ADMINISTRATION— IMPORTANT DATES

Feb. 1861, plot to assassinate President-elect Lincoln at Baltimore, Md.
Apr.-June 1861, secession of Virginia, Arkansas, North Carolina, Tennessee
Apr. 12, 1861, first attack in Civil War at Fort Sumter, S.C.

Apr. 15, 1861, President Lincoln issued call for 75,000 volunteers

Apr. 19, 1861, riot at Baltimore, Md.

May 3, 1861, call for 42,034 volunteers for three years

June 3, 1861, first bloodshed in Civil War, Philippi, W.Va.

July 21, 1861, First Battle of Bull Run

Aug. 16, 1861, proclamation prohibiting intercourse between loyal and seceding states

Nov. 8, 1861, *Trent* affair— Confederate agents Mason and Slidell taken from British steamer *Trent* by Union ship

Mar. 9, 1862, battle between *Monitor* and *Merrimac*

Mar. 11, 1862, President Lincoln assumed command of the Army and the Navy

Apr. 6-7, 1862, Battle of Shiloh

Apr. 16, 1862, slavery abolished in the District of Columbia

May 20, 1862, Homestead Act approved

July 2, 1862, Morrill land-grant college act approved

Aug. 30, 1862, Second Battle of Bull Run

Sept. 17, 1862, Battle of Antietam

Sept. 22, 1862, preliminary Emancipation Proclamation issued

Jan. 1, 1863, Emancipation Proclamation issued

Feb. 25, 1863, national banking system created

May 1-4, 1863, Battle of Chancellorsville

June 1863, occupation of Mexico by French troops led to American protests

June 19, 1863, West Virginia admitted as the 35th state

July 1-3, 1863, Battle of Gettysburg

July 4, 1863, surrender of Vicksburg

Sept. 19-20, 1863, Battle of Chickamauga

Nov. 19, 1863, Lincoln delivered Gettysburg Address

Nov. 24-25, 1863, Battle of Chattanooga

May 5-7, 1864, Battle of the Wilderness

June 19, 1864, U.S. warship *Kearsarge* sank the British-built Confederate ship *Alabama*, which had preyed upon American vessels

Sept. 2, 1864, General Sherman captured Atlanta

Oct. 31, 1864, Nevada admitted as the 36th state

Nov. 15, 1864, burning of Atlanta; beginning of Sherman's march to the sea

Apr. 3, 1865, evacuation of Richmond

Apr. 9, 1865, General Robert E. Lee surrendered to General Ulysses S. Grant at Appomattox Courthouse, Va.

IMPORTANT DATES IN HIS LIFE

1816, family moved from Kentucky to Indiana

July 1827, hired to operate a ferry across the Anderson River in Spencer County, Ind.

Apr. 1828, hired to pilot a flatboat from Rockport, Ind., to New Orleans, La.

Mar. 1, 1830, family moved from Indiana to Illinois

Mar. 1831, hired to build a flatboat at Sangamon Town, Ill., and take a load of produce to New Orleans

1832, volunteer, Sangamon Rifle Co., Richland, Ill.; reenlisted as private; mustered out June 16; returned to New Salem, Ill.; unsuccessful in general merchandise business with partner

Aug. 6, 1832, unsuccessful candidate for Illinois House of Representatives

Mar. 6, 1833, received saloon license to dispense liquor at Springfield, Ill. (Berry and Lincoln)

May 7, 1833, appointed postmaster, New Salem, Ill.

Dec. 7, 1835-Feb. 7, 1836, Illinois General Assembly

1837, moved to Springfield, Ill.

Mar. 1, 1837, admitted to the bar

Mar. 4, 1847-Mar. 3, 1849, U.S. House of Representatives (from Illinois) (only Whig elected from Illinois)

Feb. 8, 1855, unsuccessful candidate for senator from Illinois on Whig ticket

June 19, 1856, unsuccessful aspirant to the Republican vice presidential nomination at Philadelphia convention; received 110 votes

Aug.-Oct. 1858, Lincoln-Douglas debates in Illinois (senatorial campaign)

Nov. 2, 1858, unsuccessful candidate for senator from Illinois on Republican ticket

May 18, 1860, nominated for the presidency, Republican convention, Chicago, Ill.

Nov. 6, 1860, elected as first Republican President

Mar. 4, 1861-Mar. 3, 1865, President (first term)

Nov. 19, 1863, delivered Gettysburg Address

Nov. 8, 1864, reelected President

Mar. 4, 1865, inaugurated President for second term ending Mar. 3, 1869

Apr. 14, 1865, assassinated at Ford's Theatre, Washington, D.C.; died at 7:22 A.M., Apr. 15

ABRAHAM LINCOLN

——was the first President born in Kentucky.

——was the third President to die in office.

——was the first President assassinated.

——was the fifth President elected from a state other than his native state.

LINCOLN'S VICE PRESIDENTS

FIRST TERM

Vice President—Hannibal Hamlin (15th V.P.)

Date of birth—Aug. 27, 1809

Birthplace—Paris, Me.

Political party—Republican (after 1856)

State represented—Maine

Term of office—Mar. 4, 1861- Mar. 3, 1865

Age at inauguration—51 years, 189 days

Occupation after term—U.S. senator, minister to Spain

Date of death—July 4, 1891

Place of death—Bangor, Me.

Age at death—81 years, 311 days

Burial place—Bangor, Me.

SECOND TERM

Vice President—Andrew Johnson (16th V.P.)

For biographical information see Andrew Johnson, 17th President.

ADDITIONAL DATA ON LINCOLN

FIRST PRESIDENT BORN OUTSIDE ORIGINAL THIRTEEN STATES

Abraham Lincoln was the first President born beyond the boundaries of the original thirteen states. He was born near Hodgenville, in Hardin County, now Larue County, Ky.

LINCOLN ENLISTED AS A SOLDIER

On April 16, 1832, Governor John Reynolds called the Illinois militia to duty. When the notice reached New Salem on April 19, 1832, Lincoln gave up his job as a clerk and enlisted. On April 21, 1832, he was elected captain of his company.

The call for troops was issued as follows:

Your Country Requires Your Services

The Indians have assumed a hostile attitude and have invaded the State in violation of the treaty of last summer. The British band of Sacs and other hostile Indians, headed by Black Hawk, are in possession of the Rock River country, to the great terror of the frontier inhabitants. . . .

No citizen ought to remain inactive when his country is invaded and the helpless part of the community are in danger.

His company was enrolled at Beardstown, Ill., in state service on April 28 and into federal service on May 9. When mustered out on May 27, Lincoln reenlisted as a private in Captain Elijah Iles' company. This enlistment expired June 16, while Lincoln was at Fort Wilbourn, and he reenlisted in the company under the command of Captain Jacob M. Early. On July 10, he was mustered out of service at White Water, Wis.

LINCOLN A PATENTEE

On March 10, 1849, Abraham Lincoln of Springfield, Ill., applied for a patent on "a new and improved manner of combining adjustable buoyant air chambers with a steamboat or other vessel for the purpose of enabling their draught of water to be readily lessened to enable them to pass over bars, or through shallow water, without discharging their cargoes."

A waterproof fabric or India-rubber cloth in the form of a cylinder was placed at the sides of a vessel. When inflated with air, the buoyant cylinder chamber expanded and increased the size of the hull, decreasing the relative proportionate weight of the boat. When not inflated, the cylinder contracted and occupied little space.

The Patent Office awarded Lincoln U.S. Patent No. 6,469 on May 22, 1849, for "buoying vessels over shoals."

This was the first and only patent obtained by a President. It was never put into practical use.

"LINCOLN'S LOST SPEECH"

The Kansas-Nebraska Bill which became a law May 30, 1854, provided that the two new territories could determine whether they wanted to be free states or slave states. This act repealed the Missouri Compromise, an act of Congress passed in February 1820, which had admitted Missouri as a slave state and prohibited the extension of slavery to the remainder of the Louisiana territory north of the 36° 30' line.

Slavery agitators sacked the town of Lawrence, Kans., on May 21, 1856. Lives were lost, homes burned, printing presses destroyed. The slavery question aroused the nation and when the Illinois Republican Party held its first convention at Bloomington, Ill. on May 29, 1856, Lincoln was called upon to speak. His denunciation of slavery thrilled the newspaper reporters, and they listened instead of taking notes. As no verbatim account exists, this speech is known as "Lincoln's Lost Speech."

LINCOLN DEFEATED IN RACE FOR VICE PRESIDENTIAL NOMINATION

On June 19, 1856, at the first Republican Party convention, held at Philadelphia, Pa., Abraham Lincoln ran for the vice presidential nomination. He received 110 votes (Illinois 33, Indiana 26, California 12, Pennsylvania 11, New Hampshire 8, Massachusetts 7, Michigan 5, New York 3, Ohio 2, Rhode Island 2 and Maine 1). He was defeated on the first ballot, as William Lewis Dayton of New Jersey received 253 votes. Another candidate for the office of Vice President was Nathaniel Prentice Banks of Massachusetts, who received 46 votes.

LINCOLN'S MODESTY

Some authorities have claimed that Abraham Lincoln, by his own admission, was not fit to be President, an opinion based upon Lincoln's letter to Thomas J.

Pickett, of Rock Island, Ill., dated April 16, 1859. Lincoln wrote him: "I do not think myself fit for the Presidency. I certainly am flattered, and grateful that some partial friends think of me in that connection."

FIRST CONVENTION BUILDING ERECTED

The first building especially constructed to house a political convention was the "Wigwam" on Lake Street, Chicago, Ill., built for the second Republican Party convention, which met May 16, 17, and 18, 1860. The main floor was reserved for delegates. A balcony was provided for spectators. The building was equipped with telegraph equipment. The Wigwam, decorated with flags, flowers, evergreens, and statuary, accommodated ten thousand persons. William Boyington was the architect.

LINCOLN SUPPORTERS PACKED THE WIGWAM

The Republican Convention of 1860 was the first to which the general public was admitted. While the supporters of William Henry Seward of New York were parading through the city with a brass band prior to the time set for nominating, the followers of Abraham Lincoln of Illinois filled the spectators' seats in the convention hall, leaving only a few places for the thousands of Seward followers seeking admission.

LINCOLN NOT EX- PECTED TO WIN NOMINATION

Reporting the prospects of the various candidates at the Republican convention of 1860, the Washington, D.C., *Evening Star* of May 16, 1860, said: "Lincoln is urged by the delegates from Illinois, but his alleged want of administrative ability is the objection raised against him. After a complimentary vote for him, Illinois will likely go for [Edward] Bates."

KENTUCKY IGNORED FAVORITE SONS

Kentucky cast its twelve electoral votes in the election of 1860 for John Bell of Tennessee despite the fact that the two other presidential candidates, Abraham Lincoln and John Cabell Breckinridge, were born in Kentucky.

LINCOLN'S BEARD

Abraham Lincoln was the first President to wear a beard, which he began to grow shortly after his election in 1860. Many of his supporters had suggested that he would look more dignified with a beard, and while he was campaigning he received the following letter:

Westfield,
Chautauqua Co., N.Y.
October 15, 1860

Hon. A B Lincoln

Dear Sir

I am a little girl 11 years old, but want you should be President of the United States very much so I hope you wont think me very bold to write to such a great man as you are.

Have you any little girls about as large as I am if so give them my love and tell her to write me if you cannot answer this letter. I have got four brothers and part of them will vote for you any way and if you will let your whiskers grow I will try to get the rest of them to vote for you. You would look a great deal better for your face is so thin. All the ladies like whiskers and they would tease their husbands to vote for you and then you would be President.

GRACE BEDELL

Lincoln replied to her letter as follows:

Private
Springfield, Ill.
Oct. 19, 1860

Miss Grace Bedell
Westfield, N.Y.

My dear little Miss:

Your very agreeable letter to the 15th is received. I regret the necessity of saying I have no daughters. I have three sons, one seventeen, one nine, and one seven years of age. They, with their mother, constitute my whole family. As to the whiskers, having never worn any, do you not think people would call it a piece of silly affectation if I were to begin it now?

Your very sincere well-wisher,

A. Lincoln

When the train bearing Lincoln to the White House stopped at a station near Westfield, Lincoln told the assembled crowd about his correspondent. He asked if she was present. When she came forward, he picked her up, kissed her, and told the crowd, "She wrote me that she thought I'd look better if I wore whiskers."

LINCOLN'S ADIEU TO SPRINGFIELD, ILLINOIS

On February 11, 1861, from the rear of the railroad car transporting him to Washington, D.C., for his inauguration, President-elect Lincoln made a prophetic speech to his fellow Springfield townsfolk who had gathered in the morning rain to bid him farewell. His speech as reported follows:

My friends: No one, not in my situation, can appreciate my feeling of sadness at this parting. To this place, and the kindness of these people, I owe everything. . . . Here my children have been born, and one is buried. I now leave, not knowing when or whether I may return, with a task before me greater than that which rested on Washington.

ATTEMPT MADE TO ASSASSINATE LINCOLN IN 1861

An attempt to assassinate Lincoln was made in 1861. Lincoln's inaugural train left Springfield, Ill., on February 11, 1861, bound for Washington, D.C., and conspirators planned to kill him at the Calvert Street Depot, Baltimore, Md. A commotion was to be staged which would engage the attention of the police during which time the assassin would carry out his plan. The plot was discovered and the crime prevented by Allan Pinkerton, a detective assigned to guard Lincoln.

FIRST INAUGURATION

Abraham Lincoln was inaugurated on Monday, March 4, 1861, on the east portico of the Capitol. It was the seventh time that Chief Justice Taney administered the oath of office to a President.

Former President Buchanan greeted the incoming President by saying, "If you are as happy, my dear sir, on entering this house as I am on leaving it and returning home, you are the happiest man on earth."

Lincoln was the first President whose military escort was really a guard instead of an honorary escort.

The intense feeling between the North and the South marred the occasion, but a large military parade seemed to lend assurance to the nervous populace. After the ceremonies, Lincoln returned to the White House to watch the parade. One of the floats carried thirty-four young girls, each one representing a state in the union. As the float passed in front of Lincoln, the girls rushed over to him and he kissed all of them.

Lincoln did not attend the inaugural ball, which was held in a frame building called, for the occasion, "the White Muslin Palace of Aladdin."

FIVE FORMER PRESIDENTS ALIVE WHEN LINCOLN WAS INAUGURATED

When President Abraham Lincoln took the oath of office on March 4, 1861, as the sixteenth President of the United States, five former Presidents of the United States were alive: Martin Van Buren, John Tyler, Millard Fillmore, Franklin Pierce, and James Buchanan.

KENTUCKY PRESIDENTS OF 1861

Abraham Lincoln, inaugurated President of the United States on March 4, 1861, was born in Hodgenville, Hardin County, Ky., on February 12, 1809.

Jefferson Davis, chosen President of the Confederate States of America by the provisional Confederate congress on February 18, 1861, was born in Fairview, Todd County (formerly Christian County), Ky., on June 3, 1808.

CONFEDERATE STATES ADOPT CONSTITUTION

During President Lincoln's first term, the first formal attempts at a united secession government were made when the

Constitution of the Confederate States of America was adopted by the seceding southern states on March 11, 1861, at Montgomery, Ala. It contained the following preamble:

> We, the people of the Confederate States, each State acting in its sovereign and independent character, in order to form a permanent federal government, establish justice, insure domestic tranquillity, and secure the blessings of liberty to ourselves and our posterity—invoking the favor and guidance of Almighty God—do ordain and establish this Constitution for the Confederate States of America.

CHARLES FRANCIS ADAMS APPOINTED AMBASSADOR TO ENGLAND

President Lincoln appointed Charles Francis Adams as envoy extraordinary and minister plenipotentiary to England on March 20, 1861. Adams was the third member of his family to receive this coveted appointment. His father, President John Quincy Adams, and his grandfather, President John Adams, had also served as ambassadors to Great Britain.

FIRST PRESIDENTIAL EXECUTIVE ORDER

The first presidential executive order to be numbered was Order No. 1 signed by President Lincoln on October 20, 1862. This order established a provisional court in Louisiana. It was not the first executive order issued by a President, but the first one in the files of the Department of State.

LINCOLN PROCLAIMED ANNUAL THANKSGIVING DAY

Thanksgiving Day proclamations had been issued on numerous earlier occasions. Governor William Bradford in 1621 proclaimed a day for the Massachusetts colonists to offer thanks to God for their lives, their food, their clothing, etc. During the Revolutionary War, numerous days of thanksgiving were appointed for prayer and fasting by the Continental Congress. November 26, 1789 was set aside by President Washington to thank God for the newly formed government and the blessings which accompanied it. Other Thanksgiving days were set aside to commemorate special occasions such as the conclusion of a war.

The first of the national Thanksgiving Day proclamations was issued by Abraham Lincoln in 1863, on October 3, the month and day of George Washington's first Thanksgiving Day proclamation. President Andrew Johnson continued the custom, which was followed by the succeeding Presidents, until President Franklin Delano Roosevelt made a change.

LINCOLN'S GETTYSBURG ADDRESS

Delivered on November 19, 1863, this immortal address commemorated the battle fought at Gettysburg, July 1-3, 1863.

Fourscore and seven years ago our fathers brought forth on this continent a new nation, conceived in liberty, and dedicated to the proposition that all men are created equal.

Now we are engaged in a great civil war, testing whether that nation, or any nation so conceived and so dedicated, can long endure. We are met on a great battlefield of that war. We have come to dedicate a portion of that field as a final resting-place for those who here gave their lives that that nation might live. It is altogether fitting and proper that we should do this.

But, in a larger sense, we cannot dedicate—we cannot consecrate—we cannot hallow —this ground. The brave men, living and dead, who struggled here, have consecrated it far above our poor power to add or detract. The world will little note nor long remember what we say here, but it can never forget what they did here. It is for us, the living, rather, to be dedicated here to the unfinished work which they who fought here have thus far so nobly advanced. It is rather for us to be here dedicated to the great task remaining before us—that from these honored dead we take increased devotion to that cause for which they gave the last full measure of devotion; that we here highly resolve that these dead shall not have died in vain; that this nation, under God, shall have a new birth of freedom; and that government of the people, by the people, for the people, shall not perish from the earth.

FIRST AMNESTY PROCLAMATION

The first amnesty proclamation to citizens was issued by President Abraham Lincoln on December 8, 1863. He issued a similar proclamation on March 26, 1864.

President Andrew Johnson issued supplementary proclamations on May 29, 1865; September 27, 1867; July 4, 1868; and December 25, 1868.

REPUBLICAN FACTION DISAPPROVED OF SECOND TERM

Although Lincoln was chosen unanimously on the first ballot at the Republican convention of 1864, not all the Republicans had favored his candidacy for a second term. A group of Republican dissenters held a convention at Cleveland, Ohio, on May 31, 1864, and nominated John Charles Fremont for the presidency and John Cochrane of New York for the vice presidency. Both nominees withdrew on September 21, 1864, urging the reelection of Abraham Lincoln.

LINCOLN WON 1864 SOLDIER VOTE

In the 1864 election, Lincoln received 77.5 per cent of the soldier vote, compared with 22.5 per cent cast for Major General George Brinton McClellan, general-in-chief of the armies of the United States and commander of the Army of the Potomac. The vote was 116,887 for Lincoln and 33,748 for McClellan.

The states which provided for soldier votes were California, Iowa, Kentucky, Maine, Maryland, Michigan, New Hampshire, Ohio, Pennsylvania, Vermont, and Wisconsin. No provision was made allowing the soldiers to vote in Connecticut, Delaware, Illinois, Indiana, Massachusetts, Missouri, Nevada, New Jersey, New York, Oregon, Rhode Island, and West Virginia. The votes of Kansas and Minnesota soldiers were not counted as they arrived too late.

The 1864 election was the first in which the army vote was tabulated.

LINCOLN'S LETTER TO MRS. BIXBY

Perhaps the most famous letter in American literature was Lincoln's letter to Mrs. Lydia Bixby of Boston, written at the request of Governor Andrew of Massachusetts. The letter, dated November 21, 1864, was sent to Adjutant General Schouler, who delivered it on November 25 to Mrs. Bixby. It reads:

I have been shown in the files of the War Department a statement of the Adjutant General that you are the mother of five sons who have died gloriously on the field of battle. I feel how weak and fruitless must be any word of mine which should attempt to beguile you from the grief of a loss so overwhelming. But I cannot refrain from tendering you the consolation that may be found in the thanks of the republic they died to save. I pray that our Heavenly Father may assuage the anguish of your bereavement, and leave you only the cherished memory of the loved and lost, and the solemn pride that must be yours to have laid so costly a sacrifice upon the altar of freedom.

> Yours very sincerely and respectfully,
>
> A. LINCOLN.

The reports upon which Lincoln based his consoling letter were inaccurate. Charles N. Bixby was killed at the second battle of Fredericksburg, May 3, 1863. Henry Cromwell Bixby, first reported missing and later as killed, was captured and honorably discharged on December 19, 1864. Edward Bixby deserted from Company C, 1st Massachusetts Heavy Artillery, and went to sea to escape the penalty for desertion. Oliver Cromwell Bixby was killed in action in the Crater fight before Petersburg, Va., on July 30, 1864. George Way Bixby was captured on July 30, 1864, and deserted to the enemy at Salisbury, N.C.

SECOND INAUGURATION

Abraham Lincoln was inaugurated on Saturday, March 4, 1865, on the east portico of the Capitol. The oath was administered by Chief Justice Salmon Portland Chase. The morning was stormy, but the weather cleared by afternoon.

This was the first inauguration in which Negroes participated. Negro civic associations and a battalion of Negro soldiers formed part of the Lincoln escort. For security reasons, Lincoln did not ride in the military procession to the Capitol. Enthusiasm gripped the people as the war was drawing to a close.

At the inaugural ball, held on Monday, March 6, Mrs. Lincoln wore a white silk and lace dress with a headdress, an ensemble that cost over $2,000.

LINCOLN ASSASSINATED

The first assassination of a President was the murder of Lincoln on Good Friday, April 14, 1865, by John Wilkes Booth, an actor and southern sympathizer. President Lincoln drove to Ford's Theatre on Tenth Street, between E and F streets, Washington, D.C., with Mrs. Lincoln, Major Henry Reed Rathbone, and Clara Harris, Rathbone's fiancée. They were viewing a performance of *Our American Cousin,* a three-act comedy by Tom Taylor starring Laura Keene, when at about 10:30 P.M. Booth fired the fatal shot. Lincoln was carried across the street to William Peterson's boarding house at 453 Tenth Street, and put in the room of William Clark, a boarder. He died at 21 minutes 55 seconds past 7 A.M. on April 15, 1865.

Booth, who had fled after the crime, was shot April 26, 1865, in a barn by Sergeant Boston Corbett.

FUNERAL PROCESSION AND INTERMENT

Abraham Lincoln was the first President to rest in state at the United States Capitol rotunda. His body was taken first to the White House, where it remained from April 15 to April 18, after which it was removed to the Capitol rotunda, where it was displayed from April 19 to April 20. On April 21, it was taken to the railroad station, where it was conveyed to Springfield, Ill.

The funeral procession took twelve days, stops along the route being made at Baltimore, Harrisburg, Philadelphia, New York City, Albany, Utica, Syracuse, Cleveland, Columbus, Indianapolis, and Chicago, where people paid their respects before the train arrived at Springfield, Ill. Lincoln was buried on May 4, 1865, in Oakland Cemetery, Springfield.

Lincoln was moved seventeen times from the night of April 14, 1865, when he was carried from Ford's Theatre to the Peterson house across the street, until his body was finally laid to rest in a solid block of concrete in the Lincoln tomb at Springfield in 1901.

THE FIRST LADY

Mary Todd Lincoln served as hostess of the White House in a very simple and quiet manner. The war years placed a pall on social functions. Much of her time was devoted to war work.

LINCOLN'S WIFE AND THE SOUTH

Lincoln's wife, Mary Ann Todd Lincoln, born in Lexington, Ky., was the subject of much speculation. Her patriotism was questioned by many.

Her brother, George Rogers Clark Todd, was a surgeon in the Confederate army.

Her half-brother, Samuel Briggs Todd, a soldier in the Confederate army, was killed at the Battle of Shiloh, Tenn., April 6-7, 1862. Another half-brother, David H. Todd, an officer, died from wounds received at Vicksburg, Miss., and another, Alexander H. Todd, was killed at Baton Rouge, La., August 20, 1862.

The husband of Emilie, her half-sister, was Confederate Brigadier General Ben Hardin Helm, killed September 20, 1863, at Chickamauga, Ga.

Two other brothers-in-law were also in the Confederate service.

President Lincoln appeared before the Senate members of the Committee on the Conduct of the War, and made this statement:

I, Abraham Lincoln, President of the United States, appear of my own volition before this committee of the Senate, to say I, of my own knowledge, know that it is untrue that any of my family hold treasonable relations with the enemy.

MRS. LINCOLN COMMITTED

In 1875 a Court of Inquest ordered that Mrs. Lincoln "be committed to a state hospital for the insane." She was confined to the Bellevue Place Sanatorium, a private sanitorium at Batavia, Ill., from May 20, 1875, to September 10, 1875.

THIEVES TRIED TO STEAL LINCOLN'S BODY

On November 7, 1876, a gang of thieves and counterfeiters broke into Lincoln's tomb at Springfield, Ill., tore open the sarcophagus and partially pulled out the Lincoln casket. They intended to cart the casket by wagon, bury it in the sand dunes of Indiana, and demand $200,000 for its return. They intended also to demand the freedom of Benjamin Boyd, an engraver of counterfeit plates, who was confined in the penitentiary at Joliet, Ill. A Pinkerton detective to whom they had confided their plans agreed to help them. Instead he notified the Secret Service, worked with the conspirators and gave the signal which enabled the Secret Service to make the arrests. As there was no penalty at that time for such an offense, they were charged with breaking the lock and sentenced to serve a year in the penitentiary. The next legislature enacted a law which made body-stealing punishable by imprisonment for from one to ten years.

LINCOLN'S SON AT THE SCENE OF THREE AS-SASSINATIONS

Robert Todd Lincoln, Lincoln's oldest son, was at Ford's Theatre, Washington, D.C., on April 14, 1865, the night his father was shot by John Wilkes Booth.

On July 2, 1881, Lincoln, then secretary of war in President Garfield's cabinet, went to the railroad station at Washington to tell the President that pressure of business prevented him from accompanying the President to Elberon, N.J. When Lincoln arrived at the station, Garfield had just been shot by Charles J. Guiteau.

Twenty years later, Lincoln received an invitation from President William McKinley to meet him on September 6, 1901, at the Pan-American Exposition at Buffalo, N.Y. When Lincoln arrived there, he saw a group gathered about the President, who had just been mortally wounded by Leon Czolgosz.

ANDREW JOHNSON

Andrew Johnson

ANDREW JOHNSON

Born—Dec. 29, 1808

Birthplace—Raleigh, N.C.

College attended—None

Religion—No specific denomination

Ancestry—English

Occupation—Tailor, legislator

Date and place of marriage—May 5, 1827, Greeneville, Tenn.

Age at marriage—18 years, 127 days

Years married—48 years, 87 days

Political party—Democratic (elected Vice President on Republican ticket)

State represented—Tennessee

Term of office—Apr. 15, 1865-Mar. 3, 1869 (Johnson succeeded to the presidency on the death of Abraham Lincoln.)

Term served—3 years, 323 days

Administration—20th

Congresses—39th, 40th

Age at inauguration—56 years, 107 days

Lived after term—6 years, 149 days

Occupation after term—U.S. senator

Date of death—July 31, 1875

Age at death—66 years, 214 days

Place of death—Carter's Station, Tenn.

Burial place—Andrew Johnson National Cemetery, Greeneville, Tenn.

For additional data see the end of this section and also specific subject headings in the Index.

PARENTS

Father—Jacob Johnson

Born—Apr. 1778

Married—Sept. 9, 1801 (date of marriage bond)

Occupation—Sexton, porter, constable

Died—Jan. 4, 1812, Raleigh, N.C.

Age at death—33 years

Mother—Mary McDonough Johnson

Born—July 17, 1783

Died—Feb. 13, 1856

Age at death—72 years, 211 days

After the death of Jacob Johnson, Mary McDonough Johnson married Turner Dougherty of Raleigh, N.C.

BROTHERS AND SISTERS

Andrew Johnson was the third child in a family of three.

CHILDREN

Martha Johnson, b. Oct. 25, 1828, Greeneville, Tenn.; m. Dec. 13, 1855, David Trotter Patterson, Greeneville, Tenn.; d. July 10, 1901, Greeneville, Tenn.

Charles Johnson, b. Feb. 19, 1830, Greeneville, Tenn.; d. Apr. 4, 1863, near Nashville, Tenn.

Mary Johnson, b. May 8, 1832, Greeneville, Tenn. · m. Apr. 7, 1852, Daniel Stover; m. William R. Brown; d. Apr. 19, 1883, Bluff City, Tenn.

Robert Johnson, b. Feb. 22, 1834, Greeneville, Tenn.; d. Apr. 22, 1869, Greeneville, Tenn.

Andrew Johnson, b. Aug. 5, 1852, Greeneville, Tenn.; m. Bessie May Rumbough; d. Mar. 12, 1879, Elizabethtown, Tenn.

MRS. ANDREW JOHNSON

Name—Eliza McCardle Johnson

Date of birth—Oct. 4, 1810

Birthplace—Leesburg, Tenn.

Age at marriage—16 years, 213 days

Children—3 sons, 2 daughters

Father's occupation—Shoemaker

Date of death—Jan. 15, 1876

Age at death—65 years, 103 days

Place of death—Greene County, Tenn.

Burial place—Greeneville, Tenn.

Years younger than the President—1 year, 279 days

Years she survived the President—168 days

tion ratified, establishing rights of citizens

ADMINISTRATION— IMPORTANT DATES

Apr. 26, 1865, General Joseph E. Johnston surrendered at Durham Station, N.C. to General William T. Sherman

May 10, 1865, Confederate President Jefferson Davis captured by federal troops

May 26, 1865, General Edmund Kirby-Smith, commander of Trans-Mississippi Department, surrendered at New Orleans, La., to Major General E. S. Canby (last major Confederate commander to surrender)

Dec. 18, 1865, Thirteenth Amendment to the Constitution ratified, abolishing slavery

1867, Reconstruction Acts passed despite President Johnson's opposition

Mar. 1, 1867, Nebraska admitted as the 37th state

Mar. 30, 1867, Territory of Alaska ceded by treaty with Russia

May 16, 1868, President Johnson acquitted at impeachment trial before U.S. Senate

July 28, 1868, Fourteenth Amendment to the Constitu-

IMPORTANT DATES IN HIS LIFE

Feb. 18, 1822, bound out as an apprentice to a tailor, James J. Selby, Wake County, N.C.

1824, opened tailor shop, Laurens, S.C.

1828, became leader of a workingmen's party which he organized; elected alderman of Greeneville, Tenn.; reelected in 1829

1830-1833, mayor of Greeneville, Tenn. (three terms)

1833, trustee of Rhea Academy

Oct. 5, 1835, nominated himself for the Tennessee legislature; elected; served two years

1837, opposed bond issue and was defeated for reelection

1839, reelected to legislature

Oct. 4, 1841, elected to Tennessee Senate

Mar. 4, 1843-Mar. 3, 1853, U.S. House of Representatives (from Tennessee)

Oct. 3, 1853, elected governor of Tennessee

1855, reelected governor

Oct. 8, 1857-Mar. 4, 1862, U.S. Senate (from Tennessee)

Mar. 4, 1862-Mar. 3, 1865, military governor of Tennessee with rank of brigadier general of volunteers (appointed by President Lincoln)

1864, nominated as vice presidential candidate by National Union Party at Baltimore, Md.

Mar. 4, 1865-Apr. 15, 1865, Vice President

Apr. 15, 1865-Mar. 3, 1869, President (took office on death of Abraham Lincoln)

Mar. 13, 1868, impeachment trial in U.S. Senate

May 26, 1868, acquitted

1868, unsuccessful candidate for nomination to the presidency on the Democratic ticket

1869, unsuccessful candidate for U.S. Senate (from Tennessee)

1872, unsuccessful candidate for U.S. House of Representatives (from Tennessee)

1874, elected to U.S. Senate

Mar. 4-July 31, 1875, U.S. Senate

ANDREW JOHNSON

——was the second President born in North Carolina.

——was the sixth President elected from a state other than his native state.

——married at a younger age than any other President.

——was the first and only President against whom impeachment proceedings were brought.

——was the first President whose early background was not military or legal.

ADDITIONAL DATA ON JOHNSON

JOHNSON TAUGHT ABC'S BY HIS WIFE

Andrew Johnson never attended school and was scarcely able to read when he met Eliza McCardle, whom he married on May 5, 1827. He was about seventeen years of age when she taught him how to write.

JOHNSON DEFIED ENEMIES

Several threats were made against the life of Andrew Johnson while he was campaigning for a second term as governor of Tennessee. While addressing an enthusiastic crowd, Johnson, it is recorded, drew a pistol and laid it on the table so that everyone could see it. He addressed his audience as follows:

Fellow-citizens, I have been informed that part of the business to be transacted on the present occasion is the assassination of the individual who now has the honor of addressing you. I beg respectfully to propose that this be the first business in order. Therefore if any man has come here to-night for the purpose indicated, I do not say to him let him speak, but let him shoot.

JOHNSON DEFENDED THE UNION

Senator Andrew Johnson of Tennessee made a stirring speech in favor of the union on the floor of the Senate on December 18, 1860. He said:

I am in the Union, and intend to stay in it. I intend to hold on to the Union, and the guarantees under which the Union has grown; and I do not intend to be driven from it, nor out of it, by . . . unconstitutional enactments.

The following day, Johnson said:

Then, let us stand by the Constitution; and in preserving the Constitution we shall save the Union; and in saving the Union we save this, the greatest government on earth.

"WHAT WILL THE ARISTOCRATS DO?"

When Andrew Johnson was told that he, a former tailor, had been nominated on the same ticket with Abraham Lincoln, a former rail splitter, it is reported that he said, "What will the aristocrats do?"

JOHNSON INAUGU-RATED VICE PRESIDENT

One of the most unusual events in American history occurred on March 4, 1865, when Andrew Johnson was inaugurated Vice President of the United States. Not fully recovered from the effects of typhoid fever, he had doctored himself with intoxicating liquor. He walked arm-in-arm with Hannibal Hamlin, the former Vice President, into the stuffy Senate Chamber, the galleries of which were packed with guests.

His face was flushed and his balance unsteady. Before taking the vice presidential oath, he delivered a peculiar harangue in which he stressed his lowly origin. The liquor had gone to his head. Although this was the most humiliating event that had ever occurred at an inauguration, Johnson was not disgraced. Even his enemies forgave him since it was known Johnson was not a drinking man.

OATH OF OFFICE

The death of Lincoln profoundly shocked the nation. The

oath of office as Lincoln's successor was quietly administered to Andrew Johnson at 10 A.M., on Saturday, April 15, 1865, at the Kirkwood House, Washington, D.C. Chief Justice Chase went to Johnson's suite to administer the oath.

The following is an extract from Johnson's inaugural address:

> I have long labored to ameliorate and elevate the condition of the great mass of the American people. Toil and an honest advocacy of the great principles of free government have been my lot. Duties have been mine; consequences are God's. This has been the foundation of my political creed, and I feel that in the end the government will triumph and that these great principles will be permanently established.

DAY OF MOURNING FOR LINCOLN

On April 25, 1865, President Johnson issued the following proclamation:

> Thursday, the 25th of May next, [is] to be observed, wherever in the United States the flag of the country may be respected, as a day of humiliation and mourning, and I recommend my fellow-citizens then to assemble in their respective places of worship, there to unite in solemn service to Almighty God in memory of the good man who has been removed, so that all shall be occupied at the same time in contemplation of his virtues and in sorrow for his sudden and violent end.

On April 29, 1865, President Johnson issued a further proclamation changing the date to Thursday, June 1, 1865, as his attention had since been called to "the fact that the day aforesaid is sacred to large numbers of Christians as one of rejoicing for the ascension of the Savior."

GOVERNMENT OFFERED REWARDS FOR ARREST

On May 2, 1865, President Andrew Johnson issued a proclamation offering rewards for the arrest of the persons presumed to be connected with the assassination of President Lincoln and the attempted assassination of William H. Seward, secretary of state. The rewards were $100,000 for Jefferson Davis, $25,000 for Clement C. Clay, $25,000 for Jacob Thompson, $25,000 for George N. Sanders, $25,000 for Beverley

Tucker, and $10,000 for William C. Cleary.

VISIT OF A QUEEN

Andrew Johnson was the first President to receive the visit of a queen. Queen Emma, widow of King Kamehameha IV of the Sandwich Islands (Hawaii), sailed from England on the Cunard ship *Java* and arrived in New York City on August 8, 1866. She was received on August 14, 1866, by President Johnson and introduced to his official family.

IMPEACHMENT PROCEEDINGS

Johnson's attempt to carry out Lincoln's policies of reconstruction and reconciliation brought him into bitter conflict with the Radical Republicans in Congress.

The Tenure of Office Act of March 2, 1867, prohibited the President from removing a cabinet officer without Senate approval. On August 12, 1867, in defiance of this act, President Johnson dismissed a cabinet officer, Secretary of War Edwin McMasters Stanton, a Radical Republican. The President appointed General of the Army Ulysses Simpson Grant to act ad interim.

The Senate declared Stanton's removal from office illegal and in its session of January 13, 1868, ordered Stanton reinstated. Grant returned to his army duties and Stanton again returned to head the War Department.

On February 21, 1868, President Johnson replaced Stanton by Brevet Major General Lorenzo Thomas, to whom he wrote: "You are hereby authorized and empowered to act as Secretary of War ad interim, and will immediately enter upon the discharge of the duties pertaining to that office."

Impeachment proceedings were instituted against President Johnson by the House of Representatives on February 24, 1868, with the following resolution: "Resolved: that Andrew Johnson be impeached of high crimes and misdemeanors." The charges brought against him were usurpation of the law, corrupt use of the veto power, interference at elections, and misdemeanors.

The impeachment proceedings were held from March 13 to May 26, 1868, with Chief Justice Salmon Portland Chase of the United States presiding in the Senate chambers.

Associate Justice Samuel Nelson of the Supreme Court administered the following oath to the chief justice: "I do solemnly swear that in all things appertaining to the trial of the impeachment of Andrew Johnson, President of the United States, now pending, I will do impartial justice according to the Constitution and laws. So help me God." This oath was then administered by the chief justice to the fifty-four members of the Senate.

Thirty-five senators voted for conviction, nineteen for acquittal. As a two-thirds vote was necessary for conviction, Johnson was acquitted by one vote.

JOHNSON'S FEUD WITH GRANT

President Johnson wrote an angry letter to General Grant, who had given up his ad interim appointment as secretary of war and returned to his army duties, thereby allowing Stanton to return to the War Department. Johnson accused Grant of violating his word.

Grant replied that he considered Congress the final authority and that he had never given the President any intimation that he would disobey the law. He concluded his letter dated February 3, 1868, by stating:

And now, Mr. President, when my honor as a soldier and integrity as a man have been so violently assailed, pardon me for saying that I can but regard this whole matter from beginning to end as an attempt to involve me in a resistance of law for which you hesitated to assume the responsibility, and thus destroy my character before the country.

When Grant was inaugurated President of the United States on March 4, 1869, Johnson refused to ride with him to his inaugural and therefore did not witness Grant's induction into office.

PRESIDENT BECOMES SENATOR

The first President to become a senator after his term of office was Andrew Johnson. He was elected senator from Tennessee and served from March 4, 1875, until his death on July 31, 1875. He had made an unsuccessful attempt to become a senator in 1869, and another unsuccessful attempt in 1872 to win a seat as a representative in the 43rd Congress.

When Johnson took his seat in the 44th Congress he was one of seventy-four senators. Only fourteen of these senators had taken part in his trial of 1868. Twelve of them had voted "guilty" and two of them "not guilty."

THE FIRST LADY

Eliza McCardle Johnson was an invalid when Andrew Johnson became President on April 15, 1865. Their daughter, Martha Johnson Patterson, the wife of Senator David Trotter Patterson, acted as White House hostess. Another daughter, Mary Johnson Stover, the wife of Daniel Stover, also acted in this capacity.

U. S. Grant

ULYSSES SIMPSON GRANT

Born—Apr. 27, 1822 (Given name—Hiram Ulysses Grant)

Birthplace—Point Pleasant, Ohio

College attended—U.S. Military Academy, West Point, N.Y.

Date of graduation—July 1, 1843, four-year course

Religion—Methodist

Ancestry—English, Scotch

Occupation—Soldier

Date and place of marriage—Aug. 22, 1848, St. Louis, Mo.

Age at marriage—26 years, 117 days

Years married—36 years, 335 days

Political party—Republican

State represented—Illinois

Term of office—Mar. 4, 1869-Mar. 3, 1877

Term served—8 years

Administration—21st, 22nd

Congresses—41st, 42nd, 43rd, 44th

Age at inauguration—46 years, 311 days

Lived after term—8 years, 141 days

Occupation after term—Traveling and writing

Date of death—July 23, 1885

Age at death—63 years, 87 days

Place of death—Mount McGregor, N.Y.

Burial place—Grant's Tomb, New York, N.Y.

PARENTS

Father—Jesse Root Grant

Born—Jan. 23, 1794, near Greensburgh, Pa.

For additional data see the end of this section and also specific subject headings in the Index.

Married—June 24, 1821, Point Pleasant, Ohio

Occupation—Leather tanner, factory manager

Died—June 29, 1873, Covington, Ky.

Age at death—79 years, 157 days

Mother—Hannah Simpson Grant

Born—Nov. 23, 1798, Montgomery County, Pa.

Died—May 11, 1883, Jersey City, N.J.

Age at death—84 years, 169 days

BROTHERS AND SISTERS

Ulysses Simpson Grant was the oldest child in a family of six.

CHILDREN

Frederick Dent Grant, b. May 30, 1850, St. Louis, Mo.; m. Oct. 20, 1874, Ida Maria Honoré, Chicago, Ill.; d. Apr. 11, 1912, New York, N.Y.

Ulysses Simpson Grant, b. July 22, 1852, Bethel, Ohio; m. Nov. 1, 1880, Fannie Josephine Chaffee, New York, N.Y.; m. July 12, 1913, America (Workman) Wills, San Diego, Calif.; d. Sept. 25, 1929, San Diego, Calif.

Ellen (Nellie) Wrenshall Grant, b. July 4, 1855, Wistonwisch, Mo.; m. May 21, 1874, Algernon Charles Frederick Sartoris at the White House, Washington, D.C.; m. July 4, 1912, Franklin Hatch Jones, Cobourg, Ontario, Canada; d. Aug. 30, 1922, Chicago, Ill.

Jesse Root Grant, b. Feb. 6, 1858, St. Louis, Mo.; m. Sept. 21, 1880, Elizabeth Chapman, San Francisco, Calif.; m. Aug. 26, 1918, Lillian Burns Wilkins, New York, N.Y.; d. June 8, 1934, Los Altos, Calif.

MRS. ULYSSES SIMPSON GRANT

Name—Julia Boggs Dent Grant

Date of birth—Jan. 26, 1826

Birthplace—St. Louis, Mo.

Age at marriage—22 years, 208 days

Children—3 sons, 1 daughter

Mother—Ellen (Wrenshall) Dent

Father—Frederick Dent

His occupation—Judge

Date of death—Dec. 14, 1902

Age at death—76 years, 322 days

Place of death—Washington, D.C.

Burial place—New York, N.Y.

Years younger than the President—3 years, 274 days

Years she survived the President—17 years, 144 days

THE ELECTION OF 1868

NOMINATIONS FOR TERM 1869-1873

Republican Party Convention (4th) (Union-Republican Party)

May 20-21, 1868, Crosby's Opera House, Chicago, Ill.

Nominated for President—Ulysses Simpson Grant, Ill.

Nominated for Vice President—Schuyler Colfax, Ind.

First ballot: Ulysses Simpson Grant, Ill., 650

Nomination made unanimous

Democratic Party Convention (10th)

July 4-9, 1868, Tammany Hall, New York City

Nominated for President—Horatio Seymour, Ind.

Nominated for Vice President—Francis Preston Blair, Jr., Mo.

Forty-seven nominations were made. Seymour was nominated on the twenty-second ballot; the nomination was declared unanimous before the final vote was recorded.

Total number of votes: 317

Number necessary for nomination: 212

ELECTION RESULTS, NOV. 3, 1868—PRESIDENTIAL AND VICE PRESIDENTIAL CANDIDATES

Republican Party (3,012,833 votes)

Ulysses Simpson Grant, Ill.
Schuyler Colfax, Ind.

Democratic Party (2,703,249 votes)

Horatio Seymour, Ind.
Francis Preston Blair, Jr., Mo.

ELECTORAL VOTES (294 —34 states)

Grant received 72.79 per cent (214 votes—26 states) as follows: Ala. 8; Ark. 5; Calif. 5; Conn. 6; Fla. 3; Ill. 16; Ind. 13; Iowa 8; Kan. 3; Me. 7; Mass. 12; Mich. 8; Minn. 4; Mo. 11; Neb. 3; Nev. 3; N.H. 5; N.C. 9; Ohio 21; Pa. 26; R.I. 4; S.C. 6; Tenn. 10; Vt. 5; W.Va. 5; Wis. 8.

Seymour received 27.21 per cent (80 votes—8 states) as follows: Del. 3; Ga. 9; Ky. 11; La. 7; Md. 7; N.J. 7; N.Y. 33; Ore. 3.

Three states with 26 votes were not represented in the balloting: Miss. 10; Tex. 6; Va. 10.

THE ELECTION OF 1872

NOMINATIONS FOR TERM 1873-1877

Republican Party Convention (5th)

June 5-6, 1872, Academy of Music, Philadelphia, Pa.
Nominated for President—Ulysses Simpson Grant, Ill.
Nominated for Vice President—Henry Wilson, Mass.
First ballot: Ulysses Simpson Grant, Ill., 752
Nomination made unanimous

Democratic Party Convention (11th)

July 9-10, 1872, Ford's Opera House, Baltimore, Md.
Nominated for President—Horace Greeley, N.Y.
Nominated for Vice President—Benjamin Gratz Brown, Mo.

Greeley was nominated on the first ballot.

Total number of votes: 725
Blank votes: 7
Nomination made unanimous

ELECTION RESULTS, NOV. 5, 1872—PRESIDENTIAL AND VICE PRESIDENTIAL CANDIDATES

Republican Party (3,597,132 votes)

Ulysses Simpson Grant, Ill.
Henry Wilson, Mass.

Democratic Party and Liberal Republican Party (2,834,079 votes)

Horace Greeley, N.Y.
Benjamin Gratz Brown, Mo.

Straight-Out Democrats (29,-489 votes)

Charles O'Conor, N.Y.
Charles Francis Adams, Mass.

Prohibition Party (5,608 votes)

James Black, Pa.
John Russell, Mich.

ELECTORAL VOTES (352 —35 states)

The returns of two states—Arkansas and Louisiana—were disputed and not counted.

Grant received 81.205 per cent (286 votes—29 states) as follows: Ala. 10; Calif. 6; Conn. 6; Del. 3; Fla. 4; Ill. 21; Ind. 15; Iowa 11; Kan. 5; Me. 7; Mass. 13; Mich. 11; Minn. 5; Miss. 8; Neb. 3; Nev. 3; N.H. 5; N.J. 9; N.Y. 35; N.C. 10; Ohio 22; Ore. 3; Pa. 29; R.I. 4; S.C. 7; Vt. 5; Va. 11; W.Va. 5; Wis. 10.

Greeley died on November 29, 1872, three weeks after the election. The six states he had carried—Georgia, Kentucky, Maryland, Missouri, Tennessee, and Texas—split their electoral votes among the following: Thomas Andrew Hendricks of Illinois, Benjamin Gratz Brown of Missouri, Charles Jones Jenkins of Georgia, and David Davis of Illinois.

Hendricks received 11.93 per cent (42 votes—4 states) as follows: Ky. 8 (of the 12 votes); Md. 8; Mo. 6 (of the 15 votes); Tenn. 12; Tex. 8.

Brown received 5.14 per cent (18 votes—2 states) as follows: Ga. 6 (of the 11 votes); Ky. 4 (of the 12 votes); Mo. 8 (of the 15 votes).

Jenkins received 2 votes (of the 11 Ga. votes).

Davis received 1 vote (of the 15 Mo. votes).

Greeley received 3 votes (of the 11 Ga. votes), but by House resolution they were not counted.

The electoral vote for the vice presidency was divided, as the party lines were not solidly for one candidate. Nine individuals received electoral votes: Henry Wilson of Massachusetts, Benjamin Gratz Brown of Missouri, Alfred Holt Colquitt of Georgia (Democrat), George Washington Julian of Indiana (Liberal Republican), John McCauley Palmer of Illinois (Democrat), Thomas E. Bramlette of Kentucky (Democrat), William Slocum Groesbeck of Ohio (Democrat), Willis Benson Machen of Kentucky (Democrat), and Nathaniel Prentiss Banks of Massachusetts (Liberal Republican).

Wilson received 81.25 per cent (286 votes—29 states) as follows: Ala. 10; Calif. 6; Conn. 6; Del. 3; Fla. 4; Ill. 21; Ind. 15; Iowa 11; Kan. 5; Me. 7; Mass. 13; Mich. 11; Minn. 5; Miss. 8; Neb. 3; Nev. 3; N.H. 5; N.J. 9; N.Y. 35; N.C. 10; Ohio 22; Ore. 3; Pa. 29; R.I. 4; S.C. 7; Vt. 5; Va. 11; W.Va. 5; Wis. 10.

Brown received 13.35 per cent (47 votes—4 states) as follows: Ga. 5 (of the 11 votes); Ky. 8

(of the 12 votes); Md. 8; Mo. 6 (of the 15 votes); Tenn. 12; Tex. 8.

Colquitt received 5 votes (of the 11 Ga. votes).

Julian received 5 votes (of the 15 Mo. votes).

Palmer received 3 votes (of the 15 Mo. votes).

Bramlette received 3 votes (of the 12 Ky. votes).

Groesbeck received 1 vote (of the 15 Mo. votes).

Machen received 1 vote (of the 12 Ky. votes).

Banks received 1 vote (of the 11 Ga. votes).

APPOINTMENTS TO THE SUPREME COURT

Chief Justice

Morrison Remick Waite, Ohio, Jan. 21, 1874

Associate Justices

Edwin McMasters Stanton, Pa., Dec. 20, 1869 (did not serve)

William Strong, Pa., Feb. 18, 1870

Joseph Philo Bradley, N.J., Mar. 21, 1870

Ward Hunt, N.Y., Dec. 11, 1872

ADMINISTRATION— IMPORTANT DATES

Apr. 13, 1869, George Westinghouse received patent on air brake

May 10, 1869, ceremonies at Promontory, Utah, to celebrate junction of Pacific railroads and start of transcontinental service

Sept. 24, 1869, Black Friday financial panic

Dec. 9, 1869, Knights of Labor formed at Philadelphia, Pa.

Mar. 30, 1870, Fifteenth Amendment to the Constitution ratified

June 22, 1870, Department of Justice created

May 8, 1871, Treaty of Washington signed with Great Britain to provide for settlement of boundary and fishery disputes and *Alabama* claims

Dec. 14, 1871, Chicago fire; 200 killed, 70,000 homeless

1872, revelation of Crédit Mobilier stock scandal involving several members of Congress

Jan. 1, 1872, Civil Service Act became effective

Aug. 25, 1872, international commission, in Geneva Award, directed Great Britain to pay United States $15.5 million to compensate for damages caused by Confederate *Alabama,* built in England despite British neutrality

Feb. 1873, Congress demonetized silver, causing a drop in the value of silver

Sept. 18, 1873, start of financial panic of 1873

Nov. 18, 1874, National

Woman's Christian Temperance Union organized at Cleveland, Ohio

Mar. 10, 1876, Bell transmitted sound of the human voice on telephone

May 10, 1876, International Centennial Exposition opened, Philadelphia, Pa. (to Nov. 10) .

June 25, 1876, General Custer's command destroyed by Indians under Sitting Bull at Little Big Horn River, Mont.

Aug. 1, 1876, Colorado admitted as the 38th state

IMPORTANT DATES IN HIS LIFE

1829-1839, worked on his father's farm

July 1, 1839-July 1, 1843, U.S. Military Academy

July 1, 1843, brevet second lieutenant, 4th Infantry

1846, served under Generals Zachary Taylor and Winfield Scott in Mexican War

Sept. 8, 1847, brevet first lieutenant for gallant and meritorious conduct in Battle of Molino del Rey

Sept. 13, 1847, brevet captain for gallant conduct in the Battle of Chapultepec

Sept. 16, 1847, commissioned first lieutenant

Aug. 5, 1853, commissioned captain

July 31, 1854, resigned from army

1854, farming and real estate business, St. Louis, Mo.

1860, worked in his father's hardware and leather store, Galena, Ill.

1861, drilled volunteers during Civil War

May 17, 1861, brigadier general of volunteers

June 17, 1861, commissioned by Governor Yates of Illinois as colonel of the 21st Illinois Infantry Regiment

Feb. 16, 1862, major general of volunteers

July 4, 1863, captured .Vicksburg; major general, U.S. Army

Nov. 24-25, 1863, Battle of Chattanooga

Mar. 9, 1864, lieutenant general, U.S. Army

June 8, 1864, unsuccessful candidate for the presidential nomination on the Republican ticket

Apr. 9, 1865, received General Lee's surrender at Appomattox, Va.

July 25, 1866, commissioned general of the army by Congress

Aug. 12, 1867-Jan. 13, 1868, secretary of war, ad interim

Mar. 4, 1869-Mar. 3, 1873, President (first term)

Mar. 4, 1873-Mar. 3, 1877, President (second term)

1877-1879, toured the world; left

Philadelphia, Pa., on S.S. *Indiana* on May 17, 1877

1880, visited the South, Cuba, and Mexico

1880, unsuccessful candidate for the presidential nomination on the Republican ticket

Dec. 24, 1883, injured hip in fall; afterwards always walked with cane

1884, failure of Grant and Ward, New York bankers, wiped out his fortune

1885, wrote his *Memoirs,* which were completed four days before he died; family derived about $500,000 from royalties

Apr. 2, 1885, baptized a Methodist by the Reverend John Philip Newman

ULYSSES SIMPSON GRANT

——was the first President born in Ohio.

——was the seventh President elected from a state other than his native state.

——was the only President whose parents were both alive when he was inaugurated.

GRANT'S VICE PRESIDENTS

FIRST TERM

Vice President—Schuyler Colfax (17th V.P.)

Date of birth—Mar. 23, 1823

Birthplace—New York, N.Y.

Political party—Republican

State represented—Indiana

Term of office—Mar. 4, 1869- Mar. 3, 1873

Age at inauguration—45 years, 346 days

Occupation after term—Retired; lecturer

Date of death—Jan. 13, 1885

Place of death—Mankato, Minn.

Age at death—61 years, 296 days

Burial place—South Bend, Ind.

SECOND TERM

Vice President—Henry Wilson (18th V.P.)

Date of birth—Feb. 16, 1812

Birthplace—Farmington, N.H.

Political party—Republican

State represented—Massachusetts

Term of office—Mar. 4, 1873- Nov. 22, 1875

Age at inauguration—61 years, 16 days

Occupation after term—Died in office

Date of death—Nov. 22, 1875

Place of death—Washington, D.C.

Age at death—63 years, 279 days

Burial place—Natick, Mass.

ADDITIONAL DATA ON GRANT

GRANT CHANGED HIS NAME

Ulysses Simpson Grant was given the name Hiram Ulysses Grant when he was born. He transposed it to Ulysses Hiram Grant. When he applied to Representative Thomas Lyon Hamer in 1839 for an appointment to West Point, the congressman made an error and listed Grant as Ulysses Simpson Grant. Grant accepted his accidental change in his name.

GRANT RECEIVED CIGARS

General Grant is reputed to have smoked twenty cigars daily. The cigar habit was acquired after the battle of Fort Donelson, Tenn., February 13-16, 1862. It is reported that General Grant gave the following explanation to General Horace Porter:

I had been a light smoker previous to the attack on Donelson. . . . In the accounts published in the papers, I was represented as smoking a cigar in the midst of the conflict; and many persons, thinking, no doubt, that tobacco was my chief solace, sent me boxes of the choicest brands. . . . As many as ten thousand were soon received. I gave away all I could get rid of, but having such a quantity on hand I naturally smoked more than I would have done under ordinary circumstances, and I have continued the habit ever since.

GRANT ACQUIRED NICKNAME

General Grant's letter to Confederate General Simon Bolivar Buckner dated February 16, 1862, dictating the terms for the surrender of Fort Donelson, earned him the nickname "Unconditional Surrender" Grant. Grant wrote:

Yours of this date proposing armistice, and appointment of commissioners to settle terms of capitulation is just received. No terms except an unconditional and immediate surrender can be accepted. I propose to move immediately upon your works.

LINCOLN PROMOTED GRANT

On March 9, 1864, President Lincoln in the presence of the

entire cabinet in the cabinet chamber at the Executive Mansion presented Grant, then a major general, with his commission as lieutenant general in command of all the Union armies. Lincoln spoke briefly and Grant replied with a short prepared speech.

On July 25, 1866, Grant was appointed a general with four stars, a rank he relinquished when he became President.

SURRENDER OF LEE ANNOUNCED BY GRANT

On April 9, 1865, the surrender of General Lee was announced in the following terse communication to the Secretary of War by General Grant:

Hon. E. M. Stanton,
Secretary of War,
Washington.

General Lee surrendered the Army of Northern Virginia this afternoon on terms proposed by myself. The accompanying additional correspondence will show the conditions fully.

U. S. Grant, Lt. Gen.

GRANT'S RELUCTANT OPPONENT

Horatio Seymour, the Democratic presidential nominee in 1868, was perhaps the most reluctant candidate ever nominated. He knew that the standard bearer of the party would be blamed for the Civil War and that the opposition candidate was Grant, the most popular hero of the war. Seymour refused to be a candidate, but on the twenty-second ballot he was unanimously chosen. He received 80 electoral votes compared with 214 for Grant.

FIRST INAUGURATION

Ulysses Simpson Grant took the oath of office on Thursday, March 4, 1869, on the east portico of the Capitol. Eight full divisions of troops participated in the parade, the most impressive inauguration that had yet been seen.

Retiring President Johnson refused to attend the inauguration. He stayed with his cabinet until noon and then left the city.

The inaugural ball was held in a newly finished section of the Treasury Building. Errors in the checking room caused guests to wait hours to reclaim their possessions. It was reported that costly jewels were stolen.

COLFAX PRESIDED OVER BOTH HOUSES

The first officer to preside over both houses of Congress

was Schuyler Colfax of Indiana, who served as Speaker of the House of Representatives in the 38th, 39th, and 40th Congresses (December 7, 1863-November 10, 1868). As Vice President under President Grant he presided over the Senate from March 4, 1869 to March 3, 1873.

WOMAN PRESIDENTIAL CANDIDATE

The first woman presidential candidate was Victoria Claflin Woodhull, who was nominated May 10, 1872, at a convention held at Apollo Hall, New York City, by a group of seceders and unauthorized delegates attending the National Woman Suffrage Association convention at Steinway Hall, New York City. The group adopted the name Equal Rights Party. Judge Carter of Cincinnati, Ohio, nominated Mrs. Woodhull.

Members of the group were known as People's Party and also as the National Radical Reformers. About five hundred delegates, representing twenty-six states and four territories, were present at the convention.

NEGRO VICE PRESIDENTIAL CANDIDATE

The first Negro vice presidential candidate was Frederick Douglass, who was nominated with Victoria Claflin Woodhull at the Equal Rights Party convention held May 10, 1872, at Apollo Hall, New York City.

CATHOLIC NOMINATED FOR PRESIDENCY

Charles O'Conor of New York, a Catholic, was nominated for the presidency at the Democratic convention at Louisville, Ky., by a wing of the Democrats who refused to accept the nomination of Horace Greeley made at Baltimore, Md. O'Conor declined the nomination on August 31, 1872, but his name, nevertheless, was listed as a candidate and he received approximately thirty thousand votes from twenty-three states.

SECOND INAUGURATION

Ulysses Simpson Grant took the oath of office for his second term on Tuesday, March 4, 1873. The oath was administered by Chief Justice Chase. The parade was marred by a near-blizzard. The thermometer registered zero causing marchers great discomfort, and several West Point cadets lost consciousness because of the cold. The inaugural ball was held at Judiciary Square in a temporary building so cold that the guests wore their coats while dancing. The valves on the musicians' instruments froze and the violinists had difficulty manipulating their violins. The ice cream and the champagne were frozen solid.

GRANT RECEIVED HAWAIIAN KING

The first reigning king to visit the United States was David Kalakaua, king of the Sandwich Islands (Hawaii), who was received by President Ulysses Simpson Grant at the White House on December 15, 1874. Congress tendered him a reception on December 18, 1874. Grant arranged for a treaty of reciprocity, which was concluded January 30, 1875, with ratification being effected at Washington, D.C., on June 3, 1875. The king came to the United States on the U.S.S. *Benicia* and returned on the U.S.S. *Pensacola*.

GRANT REINSTATED AS GENERAL

General Grant suffered great financial reverses after his term of office and was almost destitute. To relieve this situation, Congress passed legislation restoring former President Grant to his old military status as general. On March 3, 1885, Congress passed an act (23 Stat.L.-

434) to authorize an additional appointment on the retired list of the Army—from among those who had been generals commanding the armies of the United States or generals-in-chief of said army—of one person with the rank and full pay of general.

GRANT WROTE "BEST SELLER"

One of the best-paying books of its time and still high on the all-time list was President Grant's *Memoirs*. Royalties amounted to an estimated $500,000. He never saw his book in type, as he died four days after he had completed the manuscript. The book was published in 1885.

WANT OF MUSICAL KNOWLEDGE

President Grant claimed that he knew only two tunes. One was "Yankee Doodle" and the other wasn't.

THE FIRST LADY

Julia Dent Grant, wife of President Grant, was very much admired as a White House hostess.

RUTHERFORD BIRCHARD HAYES

RUTHERFORD BIRCHARD HAYES

Born—Oct. 4, 1822

Birthplace—Delaware, Ohio

College attended—Kenyon College, Gambier, Ohio

Date of graduation—Aug. 3, 1842, Bachelor of Arts

Religion—Attended Methodist Church

Ancestry—Scotch

Occupation—Lawyer

Date and place of marriage—Dec. 30, 1852, Cincinnati, Ohio

Age at marriage—30 years, 87 days

Years married—40 years, 18 days

Political party—Republican

State represented—Ohio

Term of office—Mar. 4, 1877-Mar. 3, 1881

Term served—4 years

Administration—23rd

Congresses—45th, 46th

Age at inauguration—54 years, 151 days

Lived after term—11 years, 319 days

Occupation after term—Philanthropic activities

Date of death—Jan. 17, 1893

Age at death—70 years, 105 days

Place of death—Fremont, Ohio

Burial place—Spiegel Grove State Park, Fremont, Ohio

PARENTS

Father—Rutherford Hayes

Born—Jan. 4, 1787, Brattleboro, Vt.

For additional data see the end of this section and also specific subject headings in the Index.

Married—Sept. 13, 1813

Occupation—Storekeeper

Died—July 20, 1822, Delaware, Ohio

Age at death—35 years, 197 days

Mother—Sophia Birchard Hayes

Born—Apr. 15, 1792, Wilmington, Vt.

Died—Oct. 30, 1866, Columbus, Ohio

Age at death—74 years, 198 days

BROTHERS AND SISTERS

Rutherford Birchard Hayes was the fifth child in a family of five

CHILDREN

Birchard Austin Hayes, b. Nov. 4, 1853, Cincinnati, Ohio; m. Dec. 30, 1886, Mary Nancy Sherman, Norwalk, Ohio; d. Jan. 24, 1926, Toledo, Ohio

James Webb Cook Hayes, b. Mar. 20, 1856, Cincinnati, Ohio; m. Sept. 30, 1912, Mary Otis Miller, Fremont, Ohio; d. July 26, 1934, Fremont, Ohio

Rutherford Platt Hayes, b. June 24, 1858, Cincinnati, Ohio; m. Oct. 24, 1894, Lucy Hayes Platt, Columbus, Ohio; d. July 31, 1927, Tampa, Fla.

Joseph Thompson Hayes, b. Dec. 21, 1861, Cincinnati, Ohio; d. June 24, 1863, near Charleston, W.Va.

George Crook Hayes, b. Sept. 29, 1864, Chillicothe, Ohio; d. May 24, 1866, Chillicothe, Ohio

Fanny Hayes, b. Sept. 2, 1867, Cincinnati, Ohio; m. Sept. 1, 1897, Harry Eaton Smith, Fremont, Ohio; d. Mar. 18, 1950, Lewiston, Me.

Scott Russell Hayes, b. Feb. 8, 1871, Columbus, Ohio; m. Sept. 1912, Maude Anderson; d. May 6, 1923, Croton-on-the-Hudson, N.Y.

Manning Force Hayes, b. Aug. 1, 1873, Fremont, Ohio; d. Aug. 28, 1874, Fremont, Ohio

MRS. RUTHERFORD BIRCHARD HAYES

Name—Lucy Ware Webb Hayes

Date of birth—Aug. 28, 1831

Birthplace—Chillicothe, Ohio

Age at marriage—21 years, 124 days

Children—7 sons, 1 daughter

Mother—Maria Cook Webb

Father—James Webb

His occupation—Physician

Date of death—June 25, 1889

Age at death—57 years, 301 days

Place of death—Fremont, Ohio

Burial place—Fremont, Ohio

Years younger than the President—8 years, 328 days

Years the President survived her—3 years, 206 days

THE ELECTION OF 1876

NOMINATIONS FOR TERM 1877-1881

Republican Party Convention (6th)

June 14-16, 1876, Exposition Hall, Cincinnati, Ohio

Nominated for President—Rutherford Birchard Hayes, Ohio

Nominated for Vice President—William Almon Wheeler, N.Y.

Hayes was nominated on the seventh ballot.

Total number of votes: first ballot, 754; seventh ballot, 756

Number necessary for nomination: 379

Democratic Party Convention (12th)

June 27-29, 1876, Merchant's Exchange, St. Louis, Mo.

Nominated for President—Samuel Jones Tilden, N.Y.

Nominated for Vice President —Thomas Andrews Hendricks, Ind.

Tilden was nominated on the second ballot.

Total number of votes: 738

Number necessary for nomination: 492

ELECTION RESULTS, NOV. 7, 1876—PRESIDENTIAL AND VICE PRESIDENTIAL CANDIDATES

Republican Party (4,036,298 votes)

Rutherford Birchard Hayes, Ohio

William Almon Wheeler, N.Y.

Democratic Party (4,300,590 votes)

Samuel Jones Tilden, N.Y.

Thomas Andrews Hendricks, Ind.

Greenback Party (81,737 votes)

Peter Cooper, N.Y.

Samuel Fenton Cary, Ohio

Prohibition Party (9,522 votes)

Green Clay Smith, Ky.

Gideon Tabor Stewart, Ohio

American Party (2,636 votes)

James B. Walker, Ill.

Donald Kirkpatrick, N.Y.

DISPUTED ELECTION DECIDED BY ELECTORAL COMMISSION

It was not until March 2, 1877, that the nation knew who would be inaugurated President of the United States on Monday, March 5, 1877.

Tilden had won a majority of the popular votes, but neither candidate had the requisite 185 electoral votes—Tilden had 184 and Hayes had 165. Twenty votes were in dispute: the votes of three southern states with "carpetbag" governments (Florida, Louisiana, and South Carolina) were claimed by both parties, and an elector of a fourth state (Oregon) was found ineligible. When the electoral college met in December 1876 there was a conflict as to which electors should be certified. The Constitution provided that the votes should be counted in the presence of both houses of Congress. But the Republican-controlled Senate and the Democratic-controlled House could not agree on how the votes were to be counted. To end the deadlock congressional leaders suggested a compromise: decision by a bipartisan electoral commission consisting of seven Republicans, seven Democrats, and one independent. Unexpectedly, the independent (Supreme Court Justice David Davis) retired, and a Republican (Justice Bradley) was substituted.

The count, begun on February 1, was not completed until March 2. The commission, which voted strictly on partisan lines (eight to seven in favor of all Hayes electors), consisted of the following members:

Justices of the Supreme Court

Nathan Clifford (President of the Commission) Me., Democrat; Samuel Freeman Miller, Iowa, Republican; Stephen Johnson Field, Calif., Democrat; William Strong, Pa., Republican; Joseph Philo Bradley, N.J., Republican

U.S. Senators (appointed by the Vice President)

George Franklin Edmunds, Vt., Republican; Oliver Hazard Perry Throckmorton, Ind., Republican; Frederick Theodore Frelinghuysen, N.J., Republican; Thomas Francis Bayard, Del., Democrat; Allen Granberry Thurman, Ohio, Democrat

U.S. Representatives (appointed by the Speaker)

Henry B. Payne, Ohio, Democrat; Eppa Hunton, Va., Democrat; Josiah Gardner Abbott, Mass., Democrat; James Abram Garfield, Ohio, Republican;

George Frisbie Hoar, Mass., Republican

According to most historians, the Democrats agreed to accept the decision of the electoral commission only in return for a promise that all troops would be withdrawn from the carpetbag states, thereby ending the Reconstruction governments and giving the Democrats control in the South.

ELECTORAL VOTES (369 —38 states)

Hayes received 50.14 per cent (185 votes—21 states) as follows: Calif. 6; Colo. 3; Fla. 4; Ill. 21; Iowa 11; Kans. 5; La. 8; Me. 7; Mass. 13; Mich. 11; Minn. 5; Neb. 3; Nev. 3; N.H. 5; Ohio 22; Ore. 3; Pa. 29; R.I. 4; S.C. 7; Vt. 5; Wis. 10.

Tilden received 49.86 per cent (184 votes—17 states) as follows: Ala. 10; Ark. 6; Conn. 6; Del. 3; Ga. 11; Ind. 15; Ky. 12; Md. 8; Miss. 8; Mo. 15; N.J. 9; N.Y. 35; N.C. 10; Tenn. 12; Tex. 8; Va. 11; W.Va. 5.

APPOINTMENTS TO THE SUPREME COURT

Associate Justices

John Marshall Harlan, Ky., Nov. 29, 1877

William Burnham Woods, Ga., Dec. 21, 1880

ADMINISTRATION— IMPORTANT DATES

Feb. 12, 1877, first news dispatch telephoned to Boston *Globe*

Apr. 24, 1877, President Hayes withdrew federal troops from New Orleans

May 10, 1877, opening ceremonies of the Permanent Exhibition, Philadelphia, Pa.

July 21, 1877, troops from Philadelphia, Pa., attacked by railroad strikers at Pittsburgh, Pa.

Oct. 4, 1877, surrender of Chief Joseph ended war with Idaho Indians

Feb. 19, 1878, Edison obtained phonograph patent

Feb. 21, 1878, first telephone directory issued at New Haven, Conn.

Feb. 28, 1878, Bland-Allison Act passed over presidential veto permitting limited coinage of silver

Oct. 4, 1878, first Chinese embassy officials received by President Hayes

Jan. 1, 1879, resumption of specie payment—redemption of paper money in coin

Feb. 15, 1879, act passed to permit women to practice before U.S. Supreme Court

Mar. 3, 1879, Belva Ann Lockwood, first woman admitted to practice before U.S. Supreme Court

Mar. 3, 1879, office of U.S. Geological Survey director authorized

Oct. 21, 1879, first electric incandescent lamp of practical value invented by Thomas Alva Edison

Nov. 1, 1879, Indian school opened at Carlisle, Pa.

Nov. 4, 1879, James and John Ritty granted patent on the cash register

1880, New York City (not including Brooklyn) the first city with population of a million (1,206,299 shown in the 1880 census report)

Mar. 10, 1880, first Salvation Army services held by Commissioner George Scott Railton and seven women at New York City

July 20, 1880, Egyptian obelisk, "Cleopatra's Needle," arrived at New York City

IMPORTANT DATES IN HIS LIFE

18——, attended elementary schools, the Methodist Academy at Norwalk, Ohio, and the Webb Preparatory School, Middletown, Conn.

1842, graduated from Kenyon College

1845, graduated from Harvard Law School; admitted to the bar; practiced in Sandusky (now Fremont), Ohio

1849, moved to Cincinnati; practiced law

1857-1859, city solicitor of Cincinnati

June 27, 1861, commissioned major, 23rd Regiment, Ohio Volunteer Infantry

Sept. 19, 1861, appointed judge advocate general

Oct. 24, 1861, lieutenant colonel

Sept. 14, 1862, wounded in left arm at South Mountain

1862, detailed to act as brigadier general in command of Kanawhe division

July 1863, checked Confederate raid led by John Morgan

1864, commanded brigade under General Crook

July 1864, with Colonel Milligan ordered to charge superior force; Milligan fell and Hayes conducted retreat

Sept. 1864, second Battle of Winchester

Sept. 22, 1864, routed enemy at Fisher's Hill

Oct. 9, 1864, brigadier general of volunteers

Oct. 19, 1864, Battle of Cedar Creek; badly stunned when his horse was killed

Mar. 3, 1865, breveted major general of volunteers "for gallant and distinguished services during the campaign of 1864 in West Virginia and particularly at the battles of Fisher's Hill"

Mar. 4, 1865-July 20, 1867, U.S. House of Representatives (from Ohio)

June 8, 1865, resigned from Army

Jan. 13, 1868, governor of Ohio

1872, unsuccessful candidate for election to Congress; declined appointment as U.S. treasurer at Cincinnati

Jan. 10, 1876-Mar. 2, 1877, governor of Ohio

Mar. 4, 1877-Mar. 3, 1881, President

1880, declined to run for a second term

RUTHERFORD BIRCHARD HAYES

——was the second President born in Ohio.

——was the first President sworn in on March 3 in a private ceremony at the White House.

——was the third President inaugurated on March 5.

HAYES' VICE PRESIDENT

Vice President—William Almon Wheeler (19th V.P.)

Date of birth—June 30, 1819

Birthplace—Malone, N.Y.

Political party—Republican

State represented—New York

Term of office—Mar. 4, 1877-Mar. 3, 1881

Age at inauguration—57 years, 247 days

Occupation after term—Lawyer

Date of death—June 4, 1887

Place of death—Malone, N.Y.

Age at death—67 years, 339 days

Burial place—Malone, N.Y.

ADDITIONAL DATA ON HAYES

INAUGURATION

Rutherford Birchard Hayes took the oath of office on Monday, March 5, 1877, the oath being administered by Chief Justice Morrison Remick Waite at the east end of the Capitol.

As March 4 for the third time in the history of the republic fell on a Sunday, and as this was the most disputed election in history, Hayes took the oath of office privately on Saturday, March 3, in the Red Room of the White House. This was the first time that a President-elect had taken the oath in the White House.

A torchlight parade was held Monday night and a reception followed at the Willard Hotel, Washington, D.C. No inaugural parade or inaugural ball was held.

SILVER WEDDING AN-NIVERSARY HELD AT WHITE HOUSE

President Hayes celebrated his silver wedding anniversary on December 31, 1877, in the White House. Reverend Dr. Lorenzo Dow McCabe of Ohio Wesleyan University, who had united Lucy Webb and Rutherford Birchard Hayes on December 30, 1852, reenacted the ceremony at their silver wedding.

ABOLITION OF SEX DIS-CRIMINATION IN LAW PRACTICE BEFORE SUPREME COURT

President Hayes on February 15, 1879, signed "an act to relieve certain legal disabilities of women." It provided that any woman member of the bar of good moral character who had practiced for three years before a state Supreme Court was eligible for admittance to practice before the Supreme Court of the United States. The first woman admitted to practice before the Supreme Court was Belva Ann Bennett Lockwood.

HAYES VISITED THE WEST COAST

The first President in office to visit the west coast was Hayes. He attended a reunion of the Twenty-third Ohio Regiment on September 1, 1880, at the Opera House, Canton, Ohio, and left from there for the west coast. On September 8, 1880, he arrived at San Francisco, Calif. He stopped at the Palace Hotel in the same suite occupied by former President Grant on September 20, 1879, on his return from his world tour.

HAYES GLAD TO RETIRE

President Hayes wrote a letter to Guy Bryan on January 1, 1881, in which he said, "Nobody ever left the Presidency with less regret, less disappointment, fewer heartburnings, or more general content with the result of his term (in his own heart, I mean) than I do." (Guy Bryan of Texas, a descendant of Stephen F. Austin, had been a classmate of Hayes at Kenyon College.)

HAYES ESCAPED INJURY

After President Garfield's inauguration on March 4, 1881, former President Hayes left Washington on a special train of the Baltimore and Potomac Railroad. A few miles out of Baltimore, Md., his train collided with another and the former President was thrown several feet out of his chair. Two people were killed and twenty were seriously injured in the collision. The train was delayed twenty-four hours. Hayes was with a party of friends in the fifth car. The three preceding cars contained the Cleveland City Troop, which had marched in the inaugural parade.

THE FIRST LADY

Lucy Ware Webb, the wife of President Hayes, acquired the nickname "Lemonade Lucy" while she was first lady of the land because of her habit of serving lemonade and other soft drinks instead of liquor at White House receptions. Both the President and his wife were total abstainers.

JAMES ABRAM GARFIELD

Born—Nov. 19, 1831

Birthplace—Orange, Ohio

College attended—Williams College, Williamstown, Mass.

Date of graduation—Aug. 6, 1856, four-year course

Religious denomination—Disciples of Christ

Ancestry—English

Occupation—Teacher

Date and place of marriage—Nov. 11, 1858, Hiram, Ohio

Age at marriage—26 years, 357 days

Years married—22 years, 312 days

Political party—Republican

State represented—Ohio

Term of office—Mar. 4, 1881-Sept. 19, 1881

Term served—199 days

Administration—24th

Congress—47th

Age at inauguration—49 years, 105 days

Lived after term—Died in office

Date of death—Sept. 19, 1881

Age at death—49 years, 304 days

Place of death—Elberon, N.J.

Burial place—Lake View Cemetery, Cleveland, Ohio

PARENTS

Father—Abram Garfield

Born—Dec. 28, 1799

Married—Feb. 3, 1820, Zanesville, Ohio

Occupation—Farmer, canal constructor

For additional data see the end of this section and also specific subject headings in the Index.

Died—May 8, 1833, Otsego County, Ohio

Age at death—33 years, 126 days

Mother—Eliza Ballou Garfield

Born—Sept. 21, 1801, Richmond, N.H.

Died—Jan. 21, 1888, Mentor, Ohio

Age at death—86 years, 122 days

BROTHERS AND SISTERS

James Abram Garfield was the fifth child in a family of five.

CHILDREN

Eliza Arabella Garfield, b. July 3, 1860, Hiram, Ohio; d. Dec. 3, 1863, Hiram, Ohio

Harry Augustus Garfield, b. Oct. 11, 1863, Hiram, Ohio; m. June 14, 1888, Belle Hartford Mason, Williamstown, Mass.; d. Dec. 12, 1942, Williamstown, Mass.

James Rudolph Garfield, b. Oct. 17, 1865, Hiram, Ohio; m. Dec. 30, 1890, Helen Newell, Chicago, Ill.; d. Mar. 24, 1950, Cleveland, Ohio

Mary ("Molly") Garfield, b. Jan. 16, 1867, Washington, D.C.; m. June 14, 1888, Joseph Stanley-Brown, Mentor,

Ohio; d. Dec. 30, 1947, Pasadena, Calif.

Irvin McDowell Garfield, b. Aug. 3, 1870, Hiram, Ohio; m. Oct. 16, 1906, Susan Emmons, Falmouth, Mass.; d. July 18, 1951, Boston, Mass.

Abram Garfield, b. Nov. 21, 1872, Washington, D.C.; m. Oct. 14, 1897, Sarah Granger Williams, Cleveland, Ohio; m. Apr. 12, 1947, Helen Grannis Matthews, Cleveland, Ohio; d. Oct. 16, 1958, Cleveland, Ohio

Edward Garfield, b. Dec. 25, 1874, Hiram, Ohio; d. Oct. 25, 1876, Washington, D.C.

MRS. JAMES ABRAM GARFIELD

Name—Lucretia Rudolph Garfield

Date of birth—Apr. 19, 1832

Birthplace—Hiram, Ohio

Age at marriage—26 years, 206 days

Children—5 sons, 2 daughters

Mother— ——— Green Mason Rudolph

Father—Zebulon Rudolph

His occupation—Farmer

Date of death—Mar. 14, 1918

Age at death—85 years, 329 days

Place of death—Pasadena, Calif.

Burial place—Cleveland, Ohio

Years younger than the President—151 days

Years she survived the President—36 years, 176 days

THE ELECTION OF 1880

NOMINATIONS FOR TERM 1881-1885

Republican Party Convention (7th)

June 2-5, 7-8, 1880, Exposition Hall, Chicago, Ill.
Nominated for President—James Abram Garfield, Ohio
Nominated for Vice President—Chester Alan Arthur, N.Y.

Garfield was nominated on the thirty-sixth ballot.

Total number of votes: 755
Number necessary for nomination: 378

Democratic Party Convention (13th)

June 22-24, 1880, Music Hall, Cincinnati, Ohio
Nominated for President—Winfield Scott Hancock, Pa.
Nominated for Vice President—William Hayden English, Ind.

Hancock was nominated on the second ballot.

Total number of votes: first ballot, 726½; second ballot, 738

Number necessary for nomination: 492

ELECTION RESULTS, NOV. 2, 1880—PRESIDENTIAL AND VICE PRESIDENTIAL CANDIDATES

Republican Party (4,454,416 votes)

James Abram Garfield, Ohio
Chester Alan Arthur, N.Y.

Democratic Party (4,444,952 votes)

Winfield Scott Hancock, Pa.
William Hayden English, Ind.

Greenback Labor Party (National Party) (308,578 votes)

James Baird Weaver, Iowa
Benjamin J. Chambers, Tex.

Prohibition Party (10,305 votes)

Neal Dow, Me.
Henry Adams Thompson, Ohio

American Party (700 votes)

John Wolcott Phelps, Vt.
Samuel Clarke Pomeroy, Kan.

ELECTORAL VOTES (369 —38 states)

Garfield received 57.99 per cent (214 votes—19 states) as follows: Calif. 1 (of the 6

votes) ; Colo. 3; Conn. 6; Ill.
21; Ind. 15; Iowa 11; Kan. 5;
Me. 7; Mass. 13; Mich. 11;
Minn. 5; Neb. 3; N.H. 5; N.Y.
35; Ohio 22; Ore. 3; Pa. 29;
R.I. 4; Vt. 5; Wis. 10.

Hancock received 42.01 per
cent (155 votes—19 states) as
follows: Ala. 10; Ark. 6; Calif.
5 (of the 6 votes) ; Del. 3; Fla.
4; Ga. 11; Ky. 12; La. 8; Md.
8; Miss. 8; Mo. 15; Nev. 3;
N.J. 9; N.C. 10; S.C. 7; Tenn.
12; Tex. 8; Va. 11; W.Va. 5.

APPOINTMENTS TO THE SUPREME COURT

Associate Justice

Stanley Matthews, Ohio, May
12, 1881

ADMINISTRATION— IMPORTANT DATES

Apr. 9, 1881, Post Office Department discovery of fraudulent payments for mail services caused several resignations

May 16, 1881, Senators Roscoe Conkling and Thomas Collier Platt of New York resigned because of a disagreement with President Garfield over federal appointments in New York

May 21, 1881, American Red Cross organized

IMPORTANT DATES IN HIS LIFE

1841, worked on farm; supported widowed mother

18——, attended district school three months every winter

1848, driver, helmsman, carpenter on Ohio canals

Mar. 6, 1849, entered Geauga Seminary, Chester, Ohio

1849, taught in district school

1851, attended Western Reserve Eclectic Institute, Hiram, Ohio

18——, professor of ancient languages and literature, Hiram College, Hiram, Ohio

1857-1861, president of Eclectic Institute of Hiram College; taught Latin, Greek, higher mathematics, history, philosophy, English literature and English rhetoric

1859, Ohio Senate

1860, admitted to the bar

Aug. 21, 1861, commissioned lieutenant colonel of 42nd Regiment, Ohio Volunteer Infantry

Nov. 27, 1861, promoted to colonel

Dec. 14, 1861, ordered into field at Big Sandy Valley (in charge of 18th Brigade)

Jan. 10, 1862, defeated Confederate forces under General Marshall at Paintville, Ky.

Jan. 11, 1862, promoted to brigadier general of volunteers

1862, commanded brigade at Shiloh but was not ordered into fighting until the second day, when the battle was over

1862, developed camp fever; relieved of command and given leave to recuperate

Feb. 1863, appointed chief of staff under General Rosecrans

Mar. 4, 1863-Nov. 8, 1880, U.S. House of Representatives (from Ohio) (elected in 1862 while in military service)

Sept. 19, 1863, promoted to major general of volunteers

Dec. 5, 1863, resigned from army to take seat in House of Representatives

1877, member of the Electoral Commission created by act of Congress approved Jan. 29, 1877, to decide the contests in the various states in the disputed election of 1876

Jan. 13, 1880, elected by Ohio legislature to U.S. Senate for term beginning Mar. 4, 1881

June 8, 1880, nominated for the presidency at the Republican convention at·Chicago

Nov. 4, 1880, elected President

Nov. 8, 1880, resigned from House of Representatives

Dec. 23, 1880, declined senatorial election, having been elected President

Mar. 4, 1881-Sept. 19, 1881, President

July 2, 1881, shot by Charles J. Guiteau while passing through the railroad depot, Washington, D.C.

Sept. 19, 1881, died from effects of the wound at Elberon, N.J.

JAMES ABRAM GARFIELD

——was the third President born in Ohio.

——was the first President whose mother was present at his inauguration.

——was the fourth President to die in office.

——was the second President assassinated.

——was the sixth President whose mother was alive when he was inaugurated.

——was the first President to review an inaugural parade from a stand in front of the White House.

——was the second President who was survived by his mother.

——was the first left-handed President.

GARFIELD'S VICE PRESIDENT

Vice President—Chester Alan Arthur (20th V.P.)

For biographical information see Chester Alan Arthur, 21st President.

ADDITIONAL DATA ON GARFIELD

GARFIELD DISPERSED HECKLERS

In 1863 General James Abram Garfield, speaking in favor of abolition at Chestertown, Md., was besieged by a barrage of eggs thrown by a rebel sympathizer. Garfield stopped his speech and said, "I have just come from fighting brave rebels at Chickamauga; I shall not flinch before cowardly rebels." He continued his speech and his opponents dispersed.

GARFIELD CALMED THE MOB

Fifty thousand angry citizens answered a call to assemble at the Custom House, New York City, on April 15, 1865, ready to take the law into their own hands to avenge the death of President Lincoln. Two men in the crowd who expressed sentiments against the martyred President were attacked; one was killed, the other severely injured. About ten thousand people prepared to march to the office of the New York *World* crying "Vengeance!" A telegram that arrived from Washington stating "Seward is dying" stopped the march for a

moment. Garfield, then visiting New York as a member of Congress, lifted his arm and in a loud voice addressed the mob:

Fellow-citizens! Clouds and darkness are round about Him! His pavilion is dark waters and thick clouds of the skies! Justice and judgment are the establishment of His throne! Mercy and truth shall go before His face! Fellow-citizens! God reigns and the Government at Washington still lives!

The crowd was deeply moved by Garfield's words and the threatened riot never occurred.

NOMINATION OF GARFIELD

At the Republican Convention of 1880, on the first ballot, not one vote was cast for Garfield. On the second, third, fourth, and fifth ballots, a delegate from Pennsylvania cast his vote for Garfield. A delegate from Alabama joined him on the sixth and seventh ballots. On the eighth ballot, Garfield lost the Alabama vote. The ninth, tenth and eleventh ballots saw delegates from Massachusetts and one from Pennsylvania casting their votes for Garfield. The Massachusetts delegate did not vote for Garfield on the twelfth and thirteenth ballots but the

Pennsylvania delegate still voted for Garfield. The next five ballots saw Garfield dropped from the running. He did not receive a single vote in the fourteenth, fifteenth, sixteenth, seventeenth, and eighteenth ballots.

The delegate from Pennsylvania brought Garfield back into the running, casting one vote for him in the nineteenth, twentieth, twenty-first, and twenty-second ballots. The next eight ballots, the twenty-third to the thirtieth, saw Garfield's strength double. Instead of one vote from Pennsylvania, he received two. The next three ballots, the thirty-first to the thirty-third, witnessed a drop in Garfield's strength. He managed to keep only one vote, that from Pennsylvania.

The thirty-fourth vote showed that the persistent delegate from Pennsylvania was a great strategist, because Wisconsin added sixteen votes to his, giving Garfield seventeen votes. The next ballot, the thirty-fifth, showed Garfield with fifty votes; on the next ballot he received 399 of the 756 votes, which gave him the Republican nomination for the presidency. This was the largest number of ballots cast at a Republican convention up to that time.

Garfield was the only presidential nominee who was present in the convention hall to see himself nominated. Garfield was the leader of the Ohio delegation, which originally supported Secretary of the Treasury John Sherman for the presidency.

GARFIELD CAMPAIGNED IN GERMAN AS WELL AS IN ENGLISH

Garfield studied Latin and Greek at Williams College and took up German as an elective study. The latter language was of great help to him in his campaign for the German-American vote. On October 18, 1880, a delegation of about five hundred German-Americans from Cleveland, Ohio, visited General Garfield at Mentor, Ohio. He welcomed them in German, "Wilkommen alle," and often used the German language in campaigning.

TEN THOUSAND VOTES DETERMINED THE PRESIDENCY

A plurality of about one tenth of one percent of the popular vote enabled Garfield to become President of the United States. Garfield received 4,454,416 votes; Hancock, the Democratic candidate, received 4,444,952 votes. With a plurality of 9,464 votes Garfield won 214 of the electoral votes, as compared with 155 for Hancock.

GARFIELD QUALIFIED FOR THREE FEDERAL POSITIONS AT THE SAME TIME

On November 2, 1880, Garfield qualified for three federal positions. He was a congressman from Ohio, having taken office in the House of Representatives on March 4, 1863, and having served in the 38th Congress and the eight succeeding Congresses. On January 13, 1880, while he was serving in the House of Representatives, he was elected by the legislature of Ohio to serve in the United States Senate for the term beginning March 4, 1881. On November 2, 1880, Garfield was elected President of the United States. On that date, he was President-elect, senator-elect, and a member of the House of Representatives.

As the senatorial and presidential terms began on the same day, Garfield surrendered his seat and never sat in the Senate. (John Sherman served in his place.) On November 8, 1880, Garfield resigned from the House and on March 4, 1881, he was inaugurated President of the United States.

INAUGURATION

James Abram Garfield took the oath of office on Friday, March 4, 1881. Chief Justice Morrison Remick Waite administered the oath.

A heavy snowstorm, accompanied by strong winds, and the damp, penetrating cold kept the crowds down to a minimum. Despite the weather, about fifteen to twenty thousand people were in the two-and-a-half-hour parade. In the evening, a fireworks display thrilled the city.

The inaugural ball was held in the Hall of the Smithsonian Institution. An electric lamp, which was a great attraction to many of the guests, hung over the main entrance. The music was supplied by 150 musicians, members of the German Orchestra of Philadelphia under the direction of William Stoll, Jr., and the United States Marine Band under John Philip Sousa.

Those who attended the inaugural ball for President Garfield held at the Smithsonian Institution paid five dollars for tickets. Those who paid one dollar extra were entitled to a supper, which was served in a temporary building. The bill of fare consisted of pickled oysters, chicken salad, roast turkey, roast ham, roast beef, beef tongues, ice cream, water ices, assorted cakes, jellies, rolls, bread and butter, tea, coffee, lemonade, fruits, and relishes.

The caterers prepared 50 hams, 1,500 pounds of turkey, 100 gallons of oysters, 200 gallons of chicken salad, 150 gallons of ice cream, 50 gallons of water ices, 50 gallons of jelly, 350 pounds of butter, 15,000 cakes, 200 gallons of coffee and 2,000 biscuits.

GARFIELD'S MOTHER WITNESSED INAUGURATION

Mrs. Elizabeth Ballou Garfield was the first mother of a President to witness the inauguration of her son. The first act of President Garfield after his inauguration was to kiss his mother. Mrs. Garfield was also the first mother of a President to live at the White House.

GARFIELD JUDGES GARFIELD

Garfield said:

I do not care what others say and think about me. But there is one man's opinion which I very much value, and that is the opinion of James Garfield. Others I need not think about. I can get away from them, but I have to be with him all the time. He is with me when I rise up and when I lie down; when I eat and talk; when I go out and come in. It makes a great difference whether he thinks well of me or not.

GARFIELD ASSASSINATED

Garfield was shot on July 2, 1881, at the Baltimore and Potomac Railway Depot, Washington, D.C., by Charles Julius Guiteau, a disappointed office-seeker who had wanted to be appointed United States consul at Paris. The President survived eighty days, during which time his only official act was the signing of an extradition paper. On September 6, 1881, Garfield was taken to Elberon, N.J., to recuperate, but he died there of blood poisoning on September 19, 1881. He had three funerals, one at Elberon, N.J., another at Washington, D.C., where his body rested in state for three days, and the third at Cleveland, Ohio, where he was buried.

Guiteau was tried on November 14, 1881. The verdict was rendered on January 25, 1882 and he was hanged at the jail at Washington, D.C., on June 30, 1882.

PRESIDENT GARFIELD'S LAST LETTER

August 11, 1881

Dear Mother:

Don't be disturbed by conflicting reports about my condition. It is true I am still weak and on my back, but I am gaining every day and need only time and patience to bring me through. Give my love to all the relatives and friends and especially to sisters Hetty and Mary.

Your loving son,

JAMES ABRAM GARFIELD

Mrs. Eliza Garfield,
Hiram, Ohio

THE FIRST LADY

Lucretia ("Crete") Rudolph Garfield was first lady of the land for less than seven months, her husband meeting an untimely death at the hand of the assassin Guiteau.

CHESTER ALAN ARTHUR

Chester A Arthur

CHESTER ALAN ARTHUR

Born—Oct. 5, 1830

Birthplace—Fairfield, Vt.

College attended—Union College, Schenectady, N.Y.

Date of graduation—July 1848

Religion—Episcopalian

Ancestry—Scotch-Irish

Occupation—Lawyer

Date and place of marriage—Oct. 25, 1859, New York, N.Y.

Age at marriage—29 years, 20 days

Years married—20 years, 79 days

Political party—Republican

State represented—New York

Term of office—Sept. 20, 1881-Mar. 3, 1885 (Arthur succeeded to the presidency on the death of James Abram Garfield.)

Term served—3 years, 166 days

Administration—24th

Congresses—47th, 48th

Age at inauguration—50 years, 350 days

Lived after term—1 year, 260 days

Occupation after term—Lawyer

Date of death—Nov. 18, 1886

Age at death—56 years, 44 days

Place of death—New York, N.Y.

Burial place—Rural Cemetery, Albany, N.Y.

PARENTS

Father—William Arthur

Born—Dec. 5, 1796, Antrim County, Ireland

For additional data see the end of this section and also specific subject headings in the Index.

Married—Apr. 12, 1821, Dunham, Quebec

Occupation—Baptist clergyman

Died—Oct. 27, 1875, Newtonville, N.Y.

Age at death—78 years, 326 days

Mother—Malvina Stone Arthur

Born—Apr. 29, 1802, Berkshire, Vt.

Died—Jan. 16, 1869, Newtonville, N.Y.

Age at death—66 years, 262 days

BROTHERS AND SISTERS

Chester Alan Arthur was the fifth child and the oldest son in a family of nine.

CHILDREN

William Lewis Herndon Arthur, b. Dec. 10, 1860, New York, N.Y.; d. July 7, 1863, Englewood, N.J.

Chester Alan Arthur, b. July 25, 1864, New York, N.Y.; m. May 8, 1900, Myra Townsend Fithian Andrews, Montreux, Switzerland; m. Nov. 3, 1934, Mrs. Rowena Dashwood Graves, Colorado Springs, Colo.; d. July 17, 1937, Colorado Springs, Colo.

Ellen Herndon Arthur, b. Nov. 21, 1871; m. Charles Pinkerton; d. Sept. 6, 1915, Mount Kisco, N.Y.

MRS. CHESTER ALAN ARTHUR

Name—Ellen Lewis Herndon Arthur

Date of birth—Aug. 30, 1837

Birthplace—Fredericksburg, Va.

Age at marriage—22 years, 56 days

Children—2 sons, 1 daughter

Mother—Frances Elizabeth Hansbrough Herndon

Father—William Lewis Herndon

His occupation—Captain, U.S. Navy

Date of death—Jan. 12, 1880

Age at death—42 years, 135 days

Place of death—New York, N.Y.

Burial place—Albany, N.Y.

Years younger than the President—6 years, 329 days

Years the President survived her—6 years, 310 days

APPOINTMENTS TO THE SUPREME COURT

Associate Justices

Horace Gray, Mass., Dec. 20, 1881

Roscoe Conklin, N.Y., Feb. 1882
(declined appointment)

Samuel Blatchford, N.Y., Mar. 22, 1882

ADMINISTRATION—IMPORTANT DATES

May 22, 1882, treaty of peace, amity, commerce, and navigation signed with Korea

Aug. 5, 1882, exclusion act passed restricting Chinese immigration

Mar. 9, 1883, Civil Service Commission organized

Nov. 18, 1883, standard time adopted

1884, United States granted exclusive right to establish coaling and repair station at Pearl Harbor, Oahu, Hawaii, by Hawaiian king

May 17, 1884, establishment of territorial government in Alaska (formed from territory ceded to the United States by Russia by treaty of March 30, 1867)

Dec. 1884, treaty with Nicaragua for construction of a canal

Dec. 16, 1884, President Arthur pressed a button at Washington, D.C., to open the World's Industrial and Cotton Centennial Exposition at New Orleans, La.

Feb. 21, 1885, Washington Monument dedicated, Washington, D.C.

IMPORTANT DATES IN HIS LIFE

18——, attended public schools

18——, taught penmanship at Pownal, Vt., to earn tuition

1848, graduated from Union College

1851, principal of academy in North Pownal, Vt.

1848-1853, taught school, studied law

1854, admitted to the bar; practiced at New York, N.Y.

1857, judge advocate of Second Brigade, New York State Militia

1860, appointed engineer-in-chief on the staff of Governor Morgan with the rank of brigadier-general, New York State Militia

July 10-Dec. 31, 1862, quartermaster-general with the rank of brigadier-general

1863, resumed practice of law at New York, N.Y.

Nov. 24, 1871-July 11, 1878, collector of the Port of New York (appointed by President Grant)

July 11, 1878, removed as collector by executive order issued by President Hayes

1878, resumed practice of law at New York, N.Y.

1880, delegate from New York to Republican National Convention at Chicago to name Grant for a third term

Nov. 5, 1880, nominated for the vice presidency

Mar. 4, 1881, inaugurated Vice President

Sept. 20, 1881-Mar. 3, 1885, President (succeeded to the presidency on the death of James Abram Garfield)

June 1884, unsuccessful candidate for the presidency on the Republican ticket

CHESTER ALAN ARTHUR

——was the first President born in Vermont.

——was the eighth President elected from a state other than his native state.

——was the fourth widower inaugurated President.

ADDITIONAL DATA ON ARTHUR

THREE PRESIDENTS IN ONE YEAR

In 1881, for the second time in American history, there were three Presidents in one year. Rutherford Birchard Hayes concluded his term on March 3, 1881. On March 4, 1881, James Abram Garfield was inaugurated President. Garfield died September 19, 1881, on which date Chester Alan Arthur, his Vice President, became President.

In 1841, the three Presidents of the United States had been Martin Van Buren, William Henry Harrison, and John Tyler.

OATH OF OFFICE

Chester Alan Arthur, who succeeded to the presidency upon the death of President Garfield, took the oath of office at his residence, 123 Lexington Avenue, New York, N.Y., at 2 A.M. on September 20, 1881. (Garfield had died at 10:30 P.M. on September 19.) The oath was administered by New York Supreme Court Justice John R. Brady.

The oath was repeated on Thursday, September 22, 1881, in the Vice President's room at the Capitol, where it was administered by Chief Justice Morrison Remick Waite in the presence of former Presidents Hayes and Grant.

HOSTESS AT THE WHITE HOUSE

President Arthur's wife, Ellen Herndon Arthur, died on January 12, 1880, before her husband succeeded to the presidency. As Arthur's only daughter, Ellen, was only ten years of age, the duties of mistress of the White House were assumed by Mary Arthur McElroy (Mrs. John McElroy) of Albany, the President's sister.

GROVER CLEVELAND

GROVER CLEVELAND

Born—Mar. 18, 1837 (Given name—Stephen Grover Cleveland)

Birthplace—Caldwell, N.J.

College attended—None

Religion—Presbyterian

Ancestry—English-Irish

Occupation—Lawyer, sheriff

Date and place of marriage— June 2, 1886, Washington, D.C.

Age at marriage—49 years, 76 days

Years married—22 years, 22 days

Political party—Democratic

State represented—New York

Term of office—Mar. 4, 1885- Mar. 3, 1889

Term served—4 years

Administration—25th

Congresses—49th, 50th

Age at inauguration—47 years, 351 days

Lived after term—19 years, 112 days

Occupation after term—Re- elected President in 1892

Date of death—June 24, 1908

Age at death—71 years, 98 days

Place of death—Princeton, N.J.

Burial place—Princeton, N.J.

PARENTS

Father—Richard Falley Cleveland

Born—June 19, 1804, Norwich, Conn.

Married—Sept. 10, 1829, Baltimore, Md.

Occupation—Congregational minister

For additional data see the end of this section, the section on Grover Cleveland, 24th President, and also specific subject headings in the Index.

Died—Oct. 1, 1853, Holland Patent, N.Y.

Age at death—49 years, 104 days

Mother—Anne Neal Cleveland

Born—Feb. 4, 1806, Baltimore, Md.

Died—July 19, 1882, Holland Patent, N.Y.

Age at death—76 years, 165 days

BROTHERS AND SISTERS

Grover Cleveland was the fifth child in a family of nine.

CHILDREN

Ruth Cleveland, b. Oct. 3, 1891, New York, N.Y.; d. Jan. 7, 1904, Princeton, N.J.

Esther Cleveland, b. Sept. 9, 1893, in White House, Washington, D.C.; m. Mar. 14, 1918, William Sydney Bence Bosanquet, London, England

Marion Cleveland, b. July 7, 1895, Buzzards Bay, Mass.; m. Nov. 28, 1917, William Stanley Dell, Princeton, N.J.; . m. July 25, 1926, John Harlan Amen, Tamworth, N.H.

Richard Folsom Cleveland, b. Oct. 28, 1897, Princeton, N.J.; m. June 20, 1923, Ellen Douglas Gailor, Memphis, Tenn.

Francis Grover Cleveland, b. July 18, 1903, Buzzards Bay, Mass; m. June 20, 1925, Alice Erdman, Princeton, N.J.

MRS. GROVER CLEVELAND

Name—Frances Folsom Cleveland

Date of birth—July 21, 1864

Birthplace—Buffalo, N.Y.

Age at marriage—21 years, 316 days

Children—3 daughters, 2 sons

Mother—Emma Cornelia Harmon Folsom

Father—Oscar Folsom

His occupation—Lawyer

Date of death—Oct. 29, 1947

Age at death—83 years, 100 days

Place of death—Baltimore, Md.

Burial place—Princeton, N.J.

Years younger than the President—27 years, 125 days

Years she survived the President—39 years, 137 days

THE ELECTION OF 1884

NOMINATIONS FOR TERM 1885-1889

Democratic Party Convention (14th)

July 8-11, 1884, Exposition Hall, Chicago, Ill.

Nominated for President—
Grover Cleveland, N.Y.

Nominated for Vice President—
Thomas Andrew Hendricks,
Ind.

Cleveland was nominated on
the second ballot.

Total number of votes: 820
Number necessary for nomination: 547

**Republican Party Convention
(8th)**

June 3-6, 1884, Exposition Hall,
Chicago, Ill.

Nominated for President—James
Gillespie Blaine, Me.

Nominated for Vice President—
John Alexander Logan, Ill.

Blaine was nominated on the
fourth ballot.

Total number of votes: first ballot, 818; fourth ballot, 813
Number necessary for nomination: 411

**ELECTION RESULTS,
NOV. 4, 1884—PRESI-
DENTIAL AND VICE
PRESIDENTIAL
CANDIDATES**

Democratic Party (4,874,986
votes)

Grover Cleveland, N.Y.
Thomas Andrews Hendricks,
Ind.

Republican Party (4,851,981
votes)

James Gillespie Blaine, Me.
John Alexander Logan, Ill.

**Greenback Party and Anti-
Monopoly Party** (175,370
votes)

Benjamin Franklin Butler,
Mass.
Absolom Madden West, Miss.

Prohibition Party (150,369
votes)

John Pierce St. John, Kan.
William Daniel, Md.

ELECTORAL VOTES (401
—38 states)

Cleveland received 54.61 per
cent (219 votes—20 states) as
follows: Ala. 10; Ark. 7; Conn.
6; Del. 3; Fla. 4; Ga. 12; Ind.
15; Ky. 13; La. 8; Md. 8; Miss.
9; Mo. 16; N.J. 9; N.Y. 36;
N.C. 11; S.C. 9; Tenn. 12; Tex.
13; Va. 12; W.Va. 6.

Blaine received 45.39 per cent
(182 votes—18 states) as follows: Calif. 8; Colo. 3; Ill. 22;
Iowa 13; Kan. 9; Me. 6;
Mass. 14; Mich. 13; Minn. 7;
Neb. 5; Nev. 3; N.H. 4; Ohio
23; Ore. 3; Pa. 30; R.I. 4; Vt.
4; Wis. 11.

**APPOINTMENTS TO
THE SUPREME COURT**

Chief Justice

Melville Weston Fuller, Ill.,
July 20, 1888

Associate Justice

Lucius Quintus Cincinnatus Lamar, Miss., Jan. 16, 1888

ADMINISTRATION—
IMPORTANT DATES

Apr. 8, 1885, U.S. Marines
landed at Panama

May 17, 1885, Apache chief
Geronimo on warpath in Arizona and New Mexico

Sept. 3, 1885, Naval War College opened at Newport, R.I.

Jan. 19, 1886, Presidential Succession Act approved

Mar. 22, 1886, first Interstate
Commerce Commission ap-
pointed

May 17, 1886, act passed providing for commissioning of
graduates of U.S. Military
Academy as second lieuten-
ants

Oct. 28, 1886, dedication of the
Statue of Liberty

Dec. 1886, American Federation
of Labor organized

Feb. 4, 1887, Interstate Commerce Act approved

Feb. 23, 1887, importation of
opium from China prohibited

Aug. 9, 1887, Colorado troops
battled Ute Indians

May 30, 1888, Massachusetts
first state to adopt the Aus-
tralian ballot

IMPORTANT DATES IN
HIS LIFE

18——, clerk at store, Clinton,
N.Y.

Oct. 5, 1853, assistant teacher,
New York Institution for the
Blind

Aug. 1855, clerk and copyist for
a Buffalo, N.Y., law firm, at
no salary, then at $4 a week

1858, salary raised to $500 a
year

1859, admitted to the bar

1861, helped edit a book about
cattle

Nov. 1862, elected ward super-
visor, Buffalo

1863-1865, assistant district attorney of Erie County, N.Y.

1865, unsuccessful candidate for
district attorney

1871-1873, sheriff of Erie
County

1882, mayor of Buffalo

Jan. 1, 1883-Jan. 6, 1885, governor of New York

July 11, 1884, nominated for the
presidency by the Democratic
convention at Chicago, Ill.

Mar. 4, 1885-Mar. 3, 1889,
President (first term)

June 5, 1888, nominated for the
presidency by the Democratic
convention at St. Louis, Mo.

Nov. 6, 1888, defeated in election
by Republican candidate, Benjamin Harrison

Mar. 4, 1889, returned to law
practice

June 2, 1892, nominated for the
presidency by the Democratic
convention at Chicago, Ill.

Mar. 4, 1893-Mar. 3, 1897, President (second term)

Oct. 15, 1901, trustee of Princeton University

GROVER CLEVELAND

——was the only President born
in New Jersey.

——was the only President who
was defeated for reelec-
tion and later reelected,
thus serving two noncon-
secutive terms (March 4,
1885-March 3, 1889, and
March 4, 1893-March 3,
1897).

——was the only President married in the White House.

——was the ninth President
elected from a state other
than his native state.

——was the seventh President
whose mother was alive
when he was inaugurated.

——was the first President
elected after the Civil
War who had not taken
an active part in the conflict.

——was the first Democratic
President elected after the
Civil War.

CLEVELAND'S
VICE PRESIDENT

Vice President—Thomas Andrews Hendricks (21st V.P.)

Date of birth—Sept. 7, 1819

Birthplace—Muskingum
County, Ohio

Political party—Democratic

State represented—Indiana

Term of office—Mar. 4, 1885-
Nov. 25, 1885

Age at inauguration—65 years,
178 days

Occupation after term—Died
in office

Date of death—Nov. 25, 1885

Age at death—66 years, 79
days

Place of death—Indianapolis,
Ind.

Burial place—Indianapolis, Ind.

ADDITIONAL DATA ON
CLEVELAND

CLEVELAND CHANGED
NAME

Grover Cleveland was originally named Stephen Grover
Cleveland, for Stephen Grover,
the minister of the First Presbyterian Church at Caldwell, N.J.,
from 1787 to 1837. This was the
position to which Cleveland's
father was appointed. Cleveland
dropped his first name, Stephen,
in his youth.

CLEVELAND HANGED CRIMINALS

On January 1, 1871, Grover Cleveland took office as sheriff of Erie County, Buffalo, N.Y. Instead of delegating disagreeable tasks, such as hangings, to others, he personally carried out the duties of his office. On September 6, 1872, he superintended the hanging of Patrick Morrissey, convicted of stabbing his mother.

The Buffalo *Express* on September 7, 1872, reported that "the sheriff [Cleveland] stood at the gallows with his right hand on the rod attached to the trap bolt, and at fourteen minutes past twelve, Mr. Emerick gave the signal."

On February 14, 1873, Cleveland took charge also of the hanging of Jack Gaffney, a gambler, convicted of shooting and killing a man during a card game at Buffalo.

TWO OF CLEVELAND'S BROTHERS PERISHED IN FIRE AT SEA

On October 22, 1872, the S.S. *Missouri* of the Atlantic Mail Line bound from New York City to Havana, Cuba, burned at sea. Over eighty lives were lost, including two of Cleveland's brothers: Richard Cecil Cleveland, aged 37, and Lewis Frederick Cleveland, aged 31. Grover Cleveland at that time was sheriff of Erie County.

RELIGIOUS ISSUE IN THE CAMPAIGN OF 1884

A few days before the election, on October 29, 1884, a delegation of Protestant clergymen met the Republican candidate at the Fifth Avenue Hotel in New York City. One of the ministers, Dr. Samuel Dickinson Burchard, made a speech in which he referred to the Democrats as the party of "rum, Romanism, and rebellion." In his reply, Blaine failed to disavow this insult to the Catholic Church and the Democratic party, and his subsequent denials of anti-Catholic bigotry came too late. As a result Blaine lost many votes in New York, which had been expected to vote Republican, and he failed to carry that key state. Since a few hundred more votes would have carried the state for Blaine—Cleveland's New York plurality was under twelve hundred—the religious issue played a significant part in the election.

FIRST INAUGURATION

Grover Cleveland took the oath of office on his mother's Bible on Wednesday, March 4,

1885, on the east portico of the Capitol. The oath was administered by Chief Justice Morrison Remick Waite. The President reviewed the parade from the White House.

PRESIDENT MARRIED IN WHITE HOUSE

James Buchanan and Grover Cleveland were the only bachelors elected President. Buchanan remained a bachelor but Cleveland married his ward, Frances Folsom (the daughter of his deceased law partner), on June 2, 1886, in a ceremony performed in the White House. Before his marriage the President's sister, Rose Elizabeth Cleveland, acted as White House hostess.

Benj Harrison

BENJAMIN HARRISON

Born—Aug. 20, 1833

Birthplace—North Bend, Ohio

College attended—Miami University, Oxford, Ohio

Date of graduation—June 24, 1852, two-year course, Bachelor of Arts

Religious denomination—Presbyterian

Ancestry—English

Occupation—Lawyer

Date of first marriage—Oct. 20, 1853

Age at marriage—20 years, 61 days

Years married—39 years, 5 days

Date and place of second marriage—Apr. 6, 1896, New York, N.Y.

Age at second marriage—62 years, 229 days

Years married—4 years, 341 days

Political party—Republican

State represented—Indiana

Term of office—Mar. 4, 1889-Mar. 3, 1893

Term served—4 years

Administration—26th

Congresses—51st, 52nd

Age at inauguration—55 years, 196 days

Lived after term—8 years, 9 days

Occupation after term—Lawyer, teacher

Date of death—Mar. 13, 1901

Age at death—67 years, 205 days

Place of death—Indianapolis, Ind.

For additional data see the end of this section and also specific subject headings in the Index.

Burial place—Crown Hill Cemetery, Indianapolis, Ind.

PARENTS

Father—John Scott Harrison

Born—Oct. 4, 1804, Vincennes, Ind.

Married (1)—Lucretia Knapp Johnson

Married (2)—Elizabeth Ramsey Irwin

Occupation—Farmer, U.S. congressman

Died—May 25, 1878, North Bend, Ohio

Age at death—73 years, 233 days

First wife of father—Lucretia Knapp Johnson Harrison

Born—Sept. 16, 1804

Married—1824

Died—Feb. 6, 1830

Age at death—25 years, 143 days

Mother—Elizabeth Ramsey Irwin Harrison

Born—July 18, 1810, Mercersburg, Pa.

Married—Aug. 12, 1831

Died—Aug. 15, 1850

Age at death—40 years, 28 days

BROTHERS AND SISTERS

Benjamin Harrison was the fifth of his father's thirteen children, the second of ten children of a second marriage.

CHILDREN

By first wife, Caroline Lavinia Scott Harrison

Russell Benjamin Harrison, b. Aug. 12, 1854, Oxford, Ohio; m. Jan. 9, 1884, Mary Angeline Saunders, Omaha, Neb.; d. Dec. 13, 1936, Indianapolis, Ind.

Mary Scott Harrison, b. Apr. 3, 1858; m. Nov. 5, 1884, James Robert McKee, Indianapolis, Ind.; d. Oct. 28, 1930, Greenwich, Conn.

By second wife, Mary Scott Lord Dimmick Harrison

Elizabeth Harrison, b. Feb. 21, 1897, Indianapolis, Ind.; m. Apr. 6, 1921, James Blaine Walker, New York, N.Y.

MRS. BENJAMIN HARRISON (first wife)

Name—Caroline Lavinia Scott Harrison

Born—Oct. 1, 1832

Birthplace—Oxford, Ohio

Age at marriage—21 years, 19 days

Children—1 son, 1 daughter

Mother—Mary Potts Neal Scott

Father—John Witherspoon Scott

His occupation—Presbyterian minister

Date of death—Oct. 25, 1892

Age at death—60 years, 24 days

Place of death—Washington, D.C.

Burial place—Indianapolis, Ind.

Years older than the President —323 days

Years the President survived her—8 years, 139 days

MRS. BENJAMIN HARRISON (second wife)

Name—Mary Scott Lord Dimmick Harrison

Born—Apr. 30, 1858

Birthplace—Honesdale, Pa.

Age at marriage—37 years, 341 days

Children—1 daughter

Mother—Elizabeth Scott Lord

Father—Russell Farnham Lord

His occupation—Engineer and manager, Delaware and Hudson Canal Co.

Date of death—Jan. 5, 1948

Age at death—89 years, 250 days

Place of death—New York, N.Y.

Burial place—Indianapolis, Ind.

Years younger than the President—24 years, 253 days

Years she survived the President—46 years, 298 days

The second Mrs. Harrison was the widow of Walter Erskine Dimmick, who died Jan. 14, 1882. She married Benjamin Harrison after the expiration of his term as President.

THE ELECTION OF 1888

NOMINATIONS FOR TERM 1889-1893

Republican Party Convention (9th)

June 19-23, 25, 1888, Civic Auditorium, Chicago, Ill.
Nominated for President—Benjamin Harrison, Ind.
Nominated for Vice President— Levi Parsons Morton, N.Y.

Harrison was nominated on the eighth ballot.

Total number of votes: first ballot, 831; eighth ballot, 830
Number necessary for nomination: 416

Democratic Party Convention (15th)

June 5-7, 1888, Exposition Building, St. Louis, Mo.
Nominated for president— Grover Cleveland, N.Y.
Nominated for vice president— Allen Granberry Thurman, Ohio

First ballot: 822, Grover Cleveland, N.Y.; nominated by acclamation

ELECTION RESULTS, NOV. 6, 1888—PRESIDENTIAL AND VICE PRESIDENTIAL CANDIDATES

Democratic Party (5,540,309 votes)

Grover Cleveland, N.Y.
Allen Granberry Thurman, Ohio

Republican Party (5,444,337 votes)

Benjamin Harrison, Ind.
Levi Parsons Morton, N.Y.

Prohibition Party (249,506 votes)

Clinton Bowen Fisk, N.J.
John Anderson Brooks, Mo.

Union Labor Party (146,935 votes)

Alson Jenness Streeter, Ill.
Charles E. Cunningham, Ark.

United Labor Party (2,818 votes)

Robert Hall Cowdrey, Ill.
William H. T. Wakefield, Kan.

American Party (1,612 votes)

James Langdon Curtis, N.Y.
Peter Dinwiddie Wigginton, Calif.

Equal Rights Party

Belva Ann Lockwood, D.C.
Charles Stuart Wells

ELECTORAL VOTES (401 —38 states)

Harrison received 58.10 per cent (233 votes—20 states) as follows: Calif. 8; Colo. 3; Ill. 22; Ind. 15; Iowa 13; Kan. 9; Me. 6; Mass. 14; Mich. 13; Minn. 7; Neb. 5; Nev. 3; N.H. 4; N.Y. 36; Ohio 23; Ore. 3; Pa. 30; R.I. 4; Vt. 4; Wis. 11.

Cleveland received 41.90 per cent (168 votes—18 states) as follows: Ala. 10; Ark. 7; Conn. 6; Del. 3; Fla. 4; Ga. 12; Ky. 13; La. 8; Md. 8; Miss. 9; Mo. 16; N.J. 9; N.C. 11; S.C. 9; Tenn. 12; Tex. 13; Va. 12; W.Va. 6.

APPOINTMENTS TO THE SUPREME COURT

Associate Justices

David Josiah Brewer, Kan., Dec. 18, 1889
Henry Billings Brown, Mich., Dec. 29, 1890
George Shiras, Jr., Pa., July 26, 1892
Howell Edmunds Jackson, Tenn., Feb. 18, 1893

ADMINISTRATION— IMPORTANT DATES

Apr. 22, 1889, Oklahoma opened to settlers

May 31, 1889, Johnstown flood

Oct. 2, 1889, Pan-American Conference

Nov. 2, 1889, North Dakota admitted as the 39th state

Nov. 2, 1889, South Dakota admitted as the 40th state

Nov. 8, 1889, Montana admitted as the 41st state

Nov. 11, 1889, Washington admitted as the 42nd state

July 2, 1890, Sherman Anti-Trust Act enacted

July 3, 1890, Idaho admitted as the 43rd state

July 10, 1890, Wyoming admitted as the 44th state

July 14, 1890, Sherman Silver Purchase Act passed

IMPORTANT DATES IN HIS LIFE

1853, admitted to the bar, practiced at Cincinnati, Ohio

1854, moved to Indiana

1855, received A.M. degree

1860, reporter of decisions, Indiana Supreme Court

July 14, 1862, commissioned second lieutenant of Indiana Volunteers

July 1862-June 1865, formed Company A of the 70th Regiment, Indiana Volunteer Infantry, and was made captain; at the organization of the regiment was commissioned colonel; went with regiment to Kentucky and served until June 1865

1864-1868, served as reporter of Indiana Supreme Court while still in military service

Jan. 23, 1865, breveted brigadier general

June 8, 1865, honorable discharge from army

1876, unsuccessful candidate for governor of Indiana

1879, member, Mississippi River Commission

Mar. 4, 1881-Mar. 3, 1887, U.S. Senate (from Indiana)

Mar. 4, 1889-Mar. 3, 1893, President

1892, unsuccessful candidate for a second term—defeated by Cleveland

1900, practiced law, served in Paris as chief attorney for the Republic of Venezuela in the Venezuela-Great Britain boundary dispute

BENJAMIN HARRISON

——was the fourth President born in Ohio.

——was the tenth President elected from a state other than his native state.

——was the third President to remarry.

——was the fifth President to marry a widow.

——was the second President whose wife died while he was in office.

HARRISON'S VICE PRESIDENT

Vice President—Levi Parsons Morton (22nd V.P.)

Born—May 16, 1824

Birthplace—Shoreham, Vt.

Political party—Republican

State represented—New York

Term of office—Mar. 4, 1889-Mar. 3, 1893

Age at inauguration—64 years, 292 days

Occupation after term—Governor of New York, 1895-1897

Date of death—May 16, 1920

Place of death—Rhinebeck, N.Y.

Age at death—96 years

Burial place—Rhinebeck, N.Y.

ADDITIONAL DATA ON HARRISON

GRANDSON OF A PRESIDENT

Benjamin Harrison was the only grandson of a President to become President. The twenty-third President was a grandson of William Henry Harrison, our ninth President, who took office on March 4, 1841, and died on April 4, 1841.

INAUGURATION

Benjamin Harrison took the oath of office on Monday, March 4, 1889. The oath was administered by Chief Justice Melville Weston Fuller on the east portico of the Capitol. Despite the torrential rains and strong winds, Harrison rode to the Capitol in an open carriage and delivered his inaugural address.

A parade that continued after dark was marred by the inclement weather.

The inaugural ball, attended by more than 12,000 persons, was held in the Pension Office, 5th and F Streets, Washington, D.C. An orchestra of one hundred provided the music. The menu included blue points in ice. The hot foods consisted of bouillon in cups, steamed oysters, oysters à la poulette, chicken croquettes, sweetbread pâté à la reine, and terrapin, Philadelphia style. The cold foods were assorted roll sandwiches, mayonnaise of chicken, lobster salad, cold tongue en Bellevue, cold ham à la Montmorency, boned turkey à la Américaine, bread of quail à la Cicéron, pâté de foie gras à la Harrison, terrine of game à la Morton. The desserts were assorted ice cream, orange water ice, Roman punch, pyramid of nougat renaissance, beehive of bon-bons Republican, Pavilion Rustic, and assorted fancy cakes. Fruits, other desserts, and coffee were also available.

A one-hour fireworks display was held on the Monument grounds, the concluding display being a set piece representing the Capitol and the White House.

HARRISON PRECEDED AND FOLLOWED BY CLEVELAND

Benjamin Harrison was the only President who was preceded and succeeded by the same man. When Grover Cleveland retired from office on March 4, 1889, Harrison was sworn in and when Harrison retired on March 4, 1893, Grover Cleveland took the oath of office for a second time.

TWO CABINET SECRETARIES WITH SAME NAME

Benjamin Harrison was the only President who had two secretaries in his cabinet with the same last name. For a period of eight months, from June 29, 1892 to February 23, 1893, he had two secretaries named Foster. One was Charles Foster of Ohio, secretary of the treasury from February 24, 1891 to March 3, 1893; the other was

John Watson Foster of Indiana, secretary of state from June 29, 1892 to February 23, 1893.

SIX STATES ADMITTED

More states were admitted into the United States during Benjamin Harrison's administration than in any other. The states were (39) South Dakota, November 2, 1889; (40) North Dakota, November 2, 1889; (41) Montana, November 8, 1889; (42) Washington, November 11, 1889; (43) Idaho, July 3, 1890, and (44) Wyoming, July 10, 1890.

HARRISON HAD FIRST BILLION-DOLLAR CONGRESS

The first Congress to appropriate a billion dollars was the 52nd Congress (March 4, 1891 to March 3, 1893) which appropriated $507,376,397.52 in the first session for the fiscal year 1893, and $519,535,293.31 in the second session for the fiscal year 1894. The appropriations included the postal service items payable from postal revenues and estimated permanent annual appropriations including sinking-fund requirements.

HARRISON'S FIRST WIFE

Caroline Scott Harrison was the first President General of the National Society of the Daughters of the American Revolution. The society was organized on October 11, 1890 and incorporated on June 8, 1891.

HARRISON'S SECOND WIFE

Mary Scott Lord Dimmick Harrison, the second wife of Benjamin Harrison, never was mistress of the White House in her own right, although she lived at the White House two years. She was a niece of Caroline Scott Harrison, the President's first wife. She lived at the White House for two years, taking charge of the social functions as Mrs. Harrison had become an invalid. She married the President after completion of his term of office. They were married at St. Thomas's Protestant Episcopal Church, New York City, by the Reverend J. Wesley Brown.

HARRISON'S DAUGHTER WAS YOUNGER THAN HIS GRANDCHILDREN

On February 21, 1897, Mary Scott Lord Dimmick Harrison, Harrison's second wife, bore a baby daughter to her husband. The child was younger than Harrison's four grandchildren. Harrison's son, Russell Benjamin Harrison, had two children: Marthena, born January 18, 1888 and William Henry, born August 10, 1896. His daughter, Mary Scott Harrison McKee, had two children: Benjamin Harrison McKee, born in 1887, and Mary Lodge McKee, born in 1888.

GROVER CLEVELAND

GROVER CLEVELAND

Term of office—Mar. 4, 1893-
Mar. 3, 1897
Administration—27th
Congresses—53rd, 54th
Age at inauguration—55 years,
351 days
Lived after term—11 years, 112
days

THE ELECTION OF 1892

NOMINATIONS FOR
TERM 1893-1897

**Democratic Party Convention
(16th)**

June 21-23, 1892, in specially
constructed building, Chicago,
Ill.
Nominated for President—
Grover Cleveland, N.Y.
Nominated for Vice President—
Adlai Ewing Stevenson, Ill.

Cleveland was nominated on
the first ballot.

Total number of votes: 909½
Number necessary for nomina-
tion: 607
Nomination made unanimous

**Republican Party Convention
(10th)**

June 7-10, 1892, Industrial Exposition Building, Minneapolis, Minn.
Nominated for President—Benjamin Harrison, Ind.
Nominated for Vice President
—Whitelaw Reid, N.Y.

Harrison was nominated on
the first ballot.

Total number of votes: 904⅛
Number necessary for nomination: 453

* See also Grover Cleveland, 22nd President.

ELECTION RESULTS, NOV. 8, 1892—PRESIDENTIAL AND VICE PRESIDENTIAL CANDIDATES

Democratic Party (5,556,918 votes)

Grover Cleveland, N.Y.
Adlai Ewing Stevenson, Ill.

Republican Party (5,176,108 votes)

Benjamin Harrison, Ind.
Whitelaw Reid, N.Y.

People's Party (Populists) (1,041,028 votes)

James Baird Weaver, Iowa
James Gaven Field, Va.

Prohibition Party (264,138 votes)

John Bidwell, Calif.
James Britton Cranfill, Tex.

Socialist Labor Party (21,512 votes)

Simon Wing, Mass.
Charles Horatio Matchett, N.Y.

ELECTORAL VOTES (444 —44 states)

Cleveland received 62.39 per cent (277 votes—23 states) as follows: Ala. 11; Ark. 8; Calif. 8 (of the 9 votes); Conn. 6; Del. 3; Fla. 4; Ga. 13; Ill. 24; Ind. 15; Ky. 13; La. 8; Md. 8; Mich. 5 (of the 14 votes); Miss. 9; Mo. 17; N.J. 10; N.Y. 36; N.C. 11; N.D. 1 (of the 3 votes); Ohio 1 (of the 23 votes); S.C. 9; Tenn. 12; Tex. 15; Va. 12; W.Va. 6; Wis. 12.

Harrison received 32.66 per cent (145 votes—16 states) as follows: Calif. 1 (of the 9 votes); Iowa 13; Me. 6; Mass. 15; Mich. 9 (of the 14 votes); Minn. 9; Mont. 3; Neb. 8; N.H. 4; N.D. 1 (of the 3 votes); Ohio 22 (of the 23 votes); Ore. 3 (of the 4 votes); Pa. 32; R.I. 4; S.D. 4; Vt. 4; Wash. 4; Wyo. 3.

Weaver received 4.95 per cent (22 votes—4 states) as follows: Colo. 4; Idaho 3; Kan. 10; Nev. 3; N.D. 1 (of the 3 votes); Ore. 1 (of the 4 votes).

The North Dakota vote was divided evenly among the three candidates.

APPOINTMENTS TO THE SUPREME COURT

Associate Justices

Edward Douglass White, La., Feb. 19, 1894
Rufus William Peckham, N.Y., Dec. 9, 1895

ADMINISTRATION— IMPORTANT DATES

1893, financial panic
May 1, 1893, World's Columbian

Exposition (Chicago World's Fair) opened by President Cleveland

Oct. 30, 1893, Sherman Silver Purchase Act repealed

May 1894, President Cleveland sent federal troops to Chicago to stop obstruction of mails by Pullman Company strikers

July 4, 1894, Hawaii made a republic

Aug. 18, 1894, Carey Act passed, providing for land reclamation by irrigation

Feb. 24, 1895, Cuban revolt began

May 20, 1895, income tax declared unconstitutional

Dec. 17, 1895, Cleveland's message to Congress denounced Great Britain's refusal to arbitrate with Venezuela in territorial dispute between Venezuela and British Guinea

Jan. 4, 1896, Utah admitted as the 45th state

CLEVELAND'S VICE PRESIDENT

Vice President—Adlai Ewing Stevenson (23rd V.P.)

Date of birth—Oct. 25, 1835

Birthplace—Christian County, Ky.

Political party—Democratic

State represented—Illinois

Term of office—Mar. 4, 1893-Mar. 3, 1897

Age at inauguration—57 years, 132 days

Occupation after term—Politics

Date of death—June 14, 1914

Place of death—Chicago, Ill.

Age at death—78 years, 234 days

Burial place—Bloomington, Ill.

ADDITIONAL DATA ON CLEVELAND

CLEVELAND STAGED COMEBACK

Grover Cleveland was inaugurated on March 4, 1885, as the twenty-second President. He was a candidate for reelection in 1888 for the 1889-1893 term but was defeated by Benjamin Harrison, who received 233 of the 401 electoral votes. In 1892 Harrison was a candidate for reelection for the 1893-1897 term but he was defeated by Cleveland, who received 277 of the 444 electoral votes. Cleveland was inaugurated on March 4, 1893. As Cleveland served two nonconsecutive terms, he is referred to by most authorities as the twenty-second and the twenty-fourth President.

CLEVELAND RECEIVED PLURALITY VOTE THREE TIMES

In the 1884 election Cleveland received 4,874,986 votes while

Blaine received 4,851,981. In 1888 Cleveland received 5,540,-309 votes, about 100,000 more than Harrison, but Cleveland was not elected as the electoral vote was in Harrison's favor. In 1892 Cleveland received the popular vote plurality for the third time—5,556,918 votes compared with 5,176,108 for Harrison. As he also received the greater electoral vote he was elected President for the second time.

SECOND INAUGURATION

Grover Cleveland took the oath of office on Saturday, March 4, 1893, on the east portico of the Capitol. Chief Justice Melville Weston Fuller administered the oath. The inaugural parade lasted about six hours, although there was much rain and snow.

CLEVELAND AND THE GEORGE WASHINGTONS

When Grover Cleveland looked over the roster of the 53rd Congress, which took office with him on March 4, 1893, he found that George Washington was the Christian name of eight congressmen:

George Washington Smith, Murphysboro, Ill.

George Washington Fithian, Newton, Ill.

George Washington Ray, Norwich, N.Y.

George Washington Houk, Dayton, Ohio

George Washington Hulick, Batavia, Ohio

George Washington Wilson, London, Ohio

George Washington Shell, Laurens, S.C.

George Washington Murray, Sumter, S.C.

SURGERY PERFORMED ON CLEVELAND

In 1893 President Cleveland was afflicted with cancer of the mouth, the growth necessitating the removal of his upper left jaw. The operation was performed without any publicity on July 1, 1893, aboard Commodore E. C. Benedict's yacht *Oneida* on Long Island Sound. Dr. Joseph Decatur Bryant was the chief surgeon. In a second secret operation, on July 17, other parts of the growth were removed and the President was fitted with an artificial jaw of vulcanized rubber. By August 7 he had recovered sufficiently to address Congress.

PRESIDENT'S DAUGHTER BORN IN WHITE HOUSE

The first child of a President to be born in the White House was Esther Cleveland, the second child of President and Mrs. Grover Cleveland. She was born on September 9, 1893.

FEDERAL TROOPS DISPATCHED TO MAINTAIN ORDER

Without the request of Governor John Peter Altgeld of Illinois, President Cleveland dispatched federal troops from Fort Sheridan to Chicago, Ill., on July 4, 1894, to maintain order and insure the transportation of mail during the strike of the employees of the Pullman Palace Car Company and the sympathetic strike of railway workers.

FIRST LADY

When Grover Cleveland was reelected for a second, nonconsecutive term, Frances Folsom Cleveland, with an experienced hand, took over the duties of first lady of the land.

FIRST PRESIDENT'S WIFE TO REMARRY

On February 10, 1913, President Cleveland's widow, Frances Folsom Cleveland, married Thomas Jex Preston, Jr., a professor of archeology at Princeton University. (Grover Cleveland had died on June 24, 1908.)

WILLIAM McKINLEY

Born—Jan. 29, 1843

Birthplace—Niles, Ohio

College attended—Allegheny College, Meadville, Pa.

Date of graduation—Left before graduation

Religion—Methodist

Ancestry—Scotch-Irish

Occupation—Lawyer

Date and place of marriage— Jan. 25, 1871, Canton, Ohio

Age at marriage—27 years, 361 days

Years married—30 years, 232 days

Political party—Republican

State represented—Ohio

Term of office—Mar. 4, 1897- Sept. 14, 1901

Term served—4 years, 194 days

Administration—28th, 29th

Congresses—55th, 56th, 57th

Age at inauguration—54 years, 34 days

Lived after term—Died in office

Date of death—Sept. 14, 1901

Age at death—58 years, 228 days

Place of death—Buffalo, N.Y.

Burial place—Adjacent to Westlawn Cemetery, Canton, Ohio

PARENTS

Father—William McKinley

Born—Nov. 15, 1807, Pine Township, Pa.

Married—Jan. 6, 1829

Occupation—Iron manufacturer

Died—Nov. 24, 1892, Canton, Ohio

Age at death—85 years, 9 days

For additional data see the end of this section and also specific subject headings in the Index.

Mother—Nancy Campbell Allison McKinley

Born—Apr. 22, 1809, near Lisbon, Ohio

Died—Dec. 12, 1897, Canton, Ohio

Age at death—88 years, 234 days

BROTHERS AND SISTERS

William McKinley was the seventh child in a family of nine.

CHILDREN

Katherine McKinley, b. Jan. 25, 1872, d. July 25, 1875

Ida McKinley, b. Mar. 31, 1873, d. Aug. 22, 1873

MRS. WILLIAM McKINLEY

Name—Ida Saxton McKinley

Date of birth—June 8, 1847

Birthplace—Canton, Ohio

Age at marriage—23 years, 231 days

Children—2 daughters

Mother—Catherine Dewalt Saxton

Father—James Asbury Saxton

His occupation—Banker

Date of death—May 26, 1907

Age at death—59 years, 352 days

Place of death—Canton, Ohio

Burial place—Canton, Ohio

Years younger than the President—4 years, 130 days

Years she survived the President—5 years, 254 days

THE ELECTION OF 1896

NOMINATIONS FOR TERM 1897-1901

Republican Party Convention (11th)

June 16-18, 1896, at a specially built auditorium, St. Louis, Mo.

Nominated for President—William McKinley, Ohio

Nominated for Vice President—Garret Augustus Hobart, N.J.

McKinley was nominated on the first ballot.

Total number of votes: 907

Nomination made unanimous

Democratic Party Convention (17th)

July 7-11, 1896, the Coliseum, Chicago, Ill.

Nominated for President—William Jennings Bryan, Neb.

Nominated for Vice President—Arthur Sewall, Me.

Bryan was nominated on the fifth ballot.

Total number of votes: first ballot, 752; fifth ballot, 768
Number necessary for nomination: 512
Nominated by acclamation

ELECTION RESULTS, NOV. 3, 1896—PRESIDENTIAL AND VICE PRESIDENTIAL CANDIDATES

Republican Party (7,104,779 votes)

William McKinley, Ohio
Garret Augustus Hobart, N.J.

Democratic Party (6,502,925 votes)

William Jennings Bryan, Neb.
Arthur Sewall, Me.

Populist Party (People's Party) (222,583 votes)

William Jennings Bryan, Neb.
Thomas Edward Watson, Ga.

National Democratic Party (133,148 votes)

John McAuley Palmer, Ill.
Simon Bolivar Buckner, Ky.

Prohibition Party (132,007 votes)

Joshua Levering, Md.
Hale Johnson, Ill.

Socialist Labor Party (36,274 votes)

Charles Horatio Matchett, N.Y.
Matthew Maguire, N.J.

National Party (13,969 votes)

Charles Eugene Bentley, Neb.
James Haywood Southgate, N.C.

ELECTORAL VOTES (447 —45 states)

McKinley received 60.63 per cent (271 votes—23 states) as follows: Calif. 8 (of the 9 votes); Conn. 6; Del. 3; Ill. 24; Ind. 15; Iowa 13; Ky. 12 (of the 13 votes); Me. 6; Md. 8; Mass. 15; Mich. 14; Minn. 9; N.H. 4; N.J. 10; N.Y. 36; N.D. 3; Ohio 23; Ore. 4; Pa. 32; R.I. 4; Vt. 4; W.Va. 6; Wis. 12.

Bryan received 39.37 per cent (176 votes—22 states) as follows: Ala. 11; Ark. 8; Calif. 1 (of the 9 votes); Colo. 4; Fla. 4; Ga. 13; Idaho 3; Kan. 10; Ky. 1 (of the 13 votes); La. 8; Miss. 9; Mo. 17; Mont. 3; Neb. 8; Nev. 3; N.C. 11; S.C. 9; S.D. 4; Tenn. 12; Tex. 15; Utah 3; Va. 12; Wash. 4; Wyo. 3.

For the vice presidency the electoral votes were divided as follows:

Hobart, McKinley's Republican running-mate, received 271 votes.

Sewall, Bryan's Democratic running-mate, received 149 votes.

Watson, Bryan's Populist running-mate, received 27 votes.

THE ELECTION OF 1900

NOMINATIONS FOR TERM 1901-1905

Republican Party Convention (12th)

June 19-21, 1900, Exposition Auditorium, Philadelphia, Pa.

Nominated for President—William McKinley, Ohio

Nominated for Vice President—Theodore Roosevelt, N.Y.

First ballot: William McKinley, Ohio, 926

Nomination made unanimous

Democratic Party Convention (18th)

July 4-6, 1900, Convention Hall, Kansas City, Mo.

Nominated for President—William Jennings Bryan, Neb.

Nominated for Vice President—Adlai Ewing Stevenson, Ill.

First ballot: William Jennings Bryan, Neb., 936

Nomination made unanimous

ELECTION RESULTS, NOV. 6, 1900—PRESIDENTIAL AND VICE PRESIDENTIAL CANDIDATES

Republican Party (7,207,923 votes)

William McKinley, Ohio
Theodore Roosevelt, N.Y.

Democratic Party (6,358,138 votes)

William Jennings Bryan, Neb.
Adlai Ewing Stevenson, Ill.

Prohibition Party (208,914 votes)

John Granville Woolley, Ill.
Henry Brewer Metcalf, Ohio

Social-Democratic Party (87,814 votes)

Eugene Victor Debs, Ind.
Job Harriman, Calif.

People's Party (Populists—Middle-of-the-Road, Anti-Fusionist faction) (50,373 votes)

Wharton Barker, Pa.
Ignatius Donnelly, Minn.

Socialist Labor Party (39,739 votes)

Joseph Francis Malloney, Mass.
Valentine Remmel, Pa.

Union Reform Party (5,700 votes)

Seth Hockett Ellis, Ohio
Samuel T. Nicholson, Pa.

United Christian Party (5,500 votes)

Jonah Fitz Randolph Leonard, Iowa
David H. Martin, Pa.

ELECTORAL VOTES (447 —45 states)

McKinley received 65.33 per cent (292 votes—28 states) as follows: Calif. 9; Conn. 6; Del. 3; Ill. 24; Ind. 15; Iowa 13; Kan. 10; Me. 6; Md. 8; Mass. 15; Mich. 14; Minn. 9; Neb. 8; N.H. 4; N.J. 10; N.Y. 36; N.D. 3; Ohio 23; Ore. 4; Pa. 32; R.I. 4; S.D. 4; Utah 3; Vt. 4; Wash. 4; W.Va. 6; Wis. 12; Wyo. 3.

Bryan received 34.67 per cent (155 votes—17 states) as follows: Ala. 11; Ark. 8; Colo. 4; Fla. 4; Ga. 13; Idaho 3; Ky. 13; La. 8; Miss. 9; Mo. 17; Mont. 3; Nev. 3; N.C. 11; S.C. 9; Tenn. 12; Tex. 15; Va. 12.

APPOINTMENTS TO THE SUPREME COURT

Associate Justice
Joseph McKenna, Calif., Jan. 21, 1898

ADMINISTRATION— IMPORTANT DATES

Feb. 15, 1898, battleship U.S.S. *Maine* blown up in Havana harbor

Apr. 23, 1898, President McKinley issued call for 125,000 volunteers to serve two years

Apr. 25, 1898, United States declared war against Spain

May 1, 1898, Commodore Dewey, commander of Asiatic squadron, destroyed Spanish fleet at Manila Bay in the Philippines

July 1, 1898, United States Expeditionary Force at Manila

July 1, 1898, first balloon destroyed by enemy gunfire, Santiago, Cuba

July 7, 1898, Hawaii annexed to the United States by act of Congress

Aug. 12, 1898, peace protocol signed

Nov. 8, 1898, South Dakota voters approved initiative and referendum

Dec. 10, 1898, Treaty of Paris signed: Spain freed Cuba and ceded Puerto Rico, Guam, and the Philippines to the United States, receiving $20 million in payment for the Philippines; the United States established as a world power

Feb. 4, 1899, Filipino insurgents started unsuccessful guerrilla war against United States to gain recognition of independence

Mar. 3, 1899, George Dewey made Admiral of the Navy

Apr. 11, 1899, Philippines, Puerto Rico, and Guam formally acquired by the United States

Dec. 2, 1899, American Samoa acquired by treaty

Sept. 8, 1900, Galveston tornado

Nov. 3-10, 1900, first automobile show, New York City

IMPORTANT DATES IN HIS LIFE

18——, attended public schools, Poland Academy, and Allegheny College

1859, taught school near Poland, Ohio

June 11, 1861, enlisted as a private in the 23rd Regiment, Ohio Volunteer Infantry

Sept. 10, 1861, Battle of Carnifax Ferry, his first engagement

Apr. 15, 1862, promoted to commissary sergeant

Sept. 17, 1862, Battle of Antietam

Sept. 24, 1862, commissioned second lieutenant

Feb. 7, 1863, promoted to first lieutenant

July 25, 1864, promoted to captain

Mar. 13, 1865, brevet major of volunteers for gallant and

meritorious services at battles of Opequan, Fisher's Hill, and Cedar Creek

July 26, 1865, honorable discharge with rank of captain

1865-1867, studied law

1867, admitted to the bar; practiced at Canton County, Ohio

1869-1871, prosecuting attorney, Stark County, Ohio

Mar. 4, 1877-Mar. 3, 1883, U.S. House of Representatives (from Ohio)

Mar. 4, 1883, presented credentials as a member-elect to the 48th Congress (served to May 27, 1884, when he was succeeded by Jonathan Hasson Wallace, who contested his election)

Mar. 4, 1885-Mar. 3, 1891, U.S. House of Representatives (from Ohio)

June 1888, received two complimentary votes for nomination to the presidency on the Republican ticket

1890, unsuccessful candidate for reelection to Congress

Jan. 11, 1892-Jan. 13, 1896, governor of Ohio

June 1892, unsuccessful candidate for Republican nomination for the presidency

Nov. 1896, nominated as presidential candidate on Republican ticket

Mar. 4, 1897-Mar. 3, 1900, President (first term)

Mar. 4, 1901, inaugurated President (second term)

Sept. 6, 1901, shot by anarchist while attending Pan-American Exposition, Buffalo, N.Y.

Sept. 14, 1901, died from wounds

WILLIAM McKINLEY

——was the fifth President born in Ohio.

——was the fifth President to die in office.

——was the third President assassinated.

——was the second Ohio-born President to be assassinated.

——was the fifth Ohio-born President elected within twenty-eight years.

McKINLEY'S VICE PRESIDENTS

FIRST TERM

Vice President—Garret Augustus Hobart (24th V.P.)

Date of birth—June 3, 1844

Birthplace—Long Branch, N.J.

Political party—Republican

State represented—New Jersey

Term of office—Mar. 4, 1897-Nov. 21, 1899

Age at inauguration—52 years, 274 days

Occupation after term—Died in office

Date of death—Nov. 21, 1899

Place of death—Paterson, N.J.

Age at death—55 years, 171 days

Burial place—Paterson, N.J.

SECOND TERM

Vice President—Theodore Roosevelt (25th V.P.)

For biographical information see Theodore Roosevelt, 26th President.

ADDITIONAL DATA ON McKINLEY

McKINLEY CAMPAIGNED BY TELEPHONE

William McKinley was the first President to use the telephone for campaign purposes. In 1896 he telephoned thirty-eight of his campaign managers in as many states from his residence at Canton, Ohio, on matters pertaining to his campaign.

FIRST INAUGURATION

William McKinley took the oath of office on Thursday, March 4, 1897, on the east portico of the Capitol. The oath was administered by Chief Justice Melville Weston Fuller. The ceremonies were climaxed by an impressive parade.

SECOND INAUGURA-
TION

President McKinley took his second oath of office on Monday, March 4, 1901, on the east portico of the Capitol. Chief Justice Melville Weston Fuller administered the oath. The inaugural parade was even larger than the one held during his first inauguration.

Drenched by showers, many spectators left to avoid the downpour. The fireworks scheduled for the evening were postponed because of the rain.

McKINLEY ASSASSI-
NATED

President McKinley was shot on September 6, 1901, at the Pan-American Exposition, Buffalo, N.Y., by Leon Czolgosz, a factory worker who was an anarchist. Czolgosz fired two shots from a pistol hidden in his handkerchief. McKinley died on September 14, 1901. Czolgosz was tried in the Supreme Court of New York and was convicted. He was electrocuted on October 29, 1901, at Auburn State Prison, Auburn, N.Y.

THE FIRST LADY

Ida Saxton McKinley had been an invalid for many years before coming to the White House. She was an epileptic and had a seizure at the second inaugural ball. The President was noted for his tender affection for and great devotion to his ailing wife.

THEODORE ROOSEVELT

Theodore Roosevelt.

THEODORE ROOSEVELT

Born—Oct. 27, 1858

Birthplace—New York, N.Y.

College attended—Harvard University, Cambridge, Mass.

Date of graduation—June 30, 1880, four-year course, Bachelor of Arts

Religious denomination—Dutch Reformed Church

Ancestry—Dutch

Occupation—Rancher, lawyer, political official

Date and place of first marriage—Oct. 27, 1880, Brookline, Mass.

Age at marriage—22 years

Years married—3 years, 110 days

Date and place of second marriage—Dec. 2, 1886, London, England

Age at second marriage—28 years, 36 days

Years married—32 years, 35 days

Political party—Republican

State represented—New York

Term of office—Sept. 14, 1901-Mar. 3, 1909 (Roosevelt succeeded to the presidency on the death of William McKinley.)

Term served—7 years, 171 days

Administration—29th, 30th

Congresses—57th, 58th, 59th, 60th

Age at inauguration—42 years, 322 days

Lived after term—9 years, 309 days

Occupation after term—Writer, big-game hunter, political leader

For additional data see the end of this section and also specific subject headings in the Index.

Date of death—Jan. 6, 1919

Age at death—60 years, 71 days

Place of death—Oyster Bay, N.Y.

Burial place—Young's Memorial Cemetery, Oyster Bay, N.Y.

PARENTS

Father—Theodore Roosevelt

Born—Sept. 22, 1831, New York, N.Y.

Married—Dec. 22, 1853, Roswell, Ga.

Occupation—Glass importer, Collector of the Port, merchant

Died—Feb. 9, 1878, New York, N.Y.

Age at death—46 years, 140 days

Mother—Martha Bulloch Roosevelt

Born—July 8, 1834, Hartford, Conn.

Died—Feb. 14, 1884, New York, N.Y.

Age at death—49 years, 221 days

BROTHERS AND SISTERS

Theodore Roosevelt was the second of four children.

CHILDREN

By first wife, Alice Lee Roosevelt

Alice Lee Roosevelt, b. Feb. 12, 1884, New York, N.Y.; m. Feb. 17, 1906, Nicholas Longworth, at the White House, Washington, D.C.

By second wife, Edith Kermit Carow Roosevelt

Theodore Roosevelt, b. Sept. 13, 1887, Oyster Bay, N.Y.; m. June 20, 1910, Eleanor Butler Alexander, New York, N.Y.; d. July 12, 1944, Normandy, France

Kermit Roosevelt, b. Oct. 10, 1889, Oyster Bay, N.Y.; m. June 11, 1914, Belle Wyatt Willard, Madrid, Spain; d. June 4, 1943, on active military duty in Alaska

Ethel Carow Roosevelt, b. Aug. 13, 1891, Oyster Bay, N.Y.; m. Apr. 4, 1913, Dr. Richard Derby, Oyster Bay, N.Y.

Archibald Bulloch Roosevelt, b. Apr. 9, 1894, Washington, D.C.; m. Apr. 14, 1917, Grace Stackpole Lockwood, Boston, Mass.

Quentin Roosevelt, b. Nov. 19, 1897, Washington, D.C.; d. July 14, 1918, shot down in aerial combat in France

MRS. THEODORE ROOSEVELT (first wife)

Name—Alice Hathaway Lee Roosevelt

Date of birth—July 29, 1861

Birthplace—Chestnut Hill, Mass.

Age at marriage—19 years, 82 days

Children—1 daughter

Mother—Caroline Haskell Lee

Father—George Cabot Lee

Date of death—Feb. 14, 1884

Age at death—22 years, 192 days

Place of death—New York, N.Y.

Burial place—Cambridge, Mass.

Years younger than the President—2 years, 283 days

Years the President survived her—34 years, 326 days

MRS. THEODORE ROOSEVELT (second wife)

Name—Edith Kermit Carow Roosevelt

Date of birth—Aug. 6, 1861

Birthplace—Norwich, Conn.

Age at marriage—25 years, 118 days

Children—4 sons, 1 daughter

Mother—Gertrude Elizabeth Tyler Carow

Father—Charles Carow

Date of death—Sept. 30, 1948

Age at death—87 years, 45 days

Place of death—Oyster Bay, N.Y.

Burial place—Oyster Bay, N.Y.

Years younger than the President—2 years, 293 days

Years she survived the President—29 years, 267 days

THE ELECTION OF 1904

NOMINATIONS FOR TERM 1905-1909

Republican Party Convention (13th)

June 21-23, 1904, the Coliseum, Chicago, Ill.

Nominated for President—Theodore Roosevelt, N.Y.

Nominated for Vice President—Charles Warren Fairbanks, Ind.

First ballot: Theodore Roosevelt, N.Y., 994

Nomination made unanimous

Democratic Party Convention (19th)

July 6-9, 1904, the Coliseum, St. Louis, Mo.

Nominated for President—Alton Brooks Parker, N.Y.

Nominated for Vice President—Henry Gassaway Davis, W.Va.

Parker was nominated on the first ballot.

Total number of votes: 1,000
Number necessary for nomination: 667
Nomination made unanimous

ELECTION RESULTS, NOV. 8, 1904—PRESIDENTIAL AND VICE PRESIDENTIAL CANDIDATES

Republican Party (7,623,486 votes)

Theodore Roosevelt, N.Y.
Charles Warren Fairbanks, Ind.

Democratic Party (5,077,911 votes)

Alton Brooks Parker, N.Y.
Henry Gassaway Davis, W.Va.

Socialist Party (402,283 votes)

Eugene Victor Debs, Ind.
Benjamin Hanford, N.Y.

Prohibition Party (258,536 votes)

Silas Comfort Swallow, Pa.
George W. Carroll, Tex.

People's Party (117,183 votes)

Thomas Edward Watson, Ga.
Thomas Henry Tibbles, Neb.

Socialist Labor Party (31,249 votes)

Charles Hunter Corregan, N.Y.
William Wesley Cox, Ill.

Continental Party (1,000 votes)

Austin Holcomb, Ga.
A. King, Mo.

ELECTORAL VOTES (476 —45 states)

Roosevelt received 70.60 per cent (336 votes—32 states) as follows: Calif. 10; Colo. 5; Conn. 7; Del. 3; Idaho 3; Ill. 27; Ind. 15; Iowa 13; Kan. 10; Me. 6; Md. 1 (of the 8 votes); Mass. 16; Mich. 14; Minn. 11; Mo. 18; Mont. 3; Neb. 8; Nev. 3; N.H. 4; N.J. 12; N.Y. 39; N.D. 4; Ohio 23; Ore. 4; Pa. 34; R.I. 4; S.D. 4; Utah 3; Vt. 4; Wash. 5; W.Va. 7; Wis. 13; Wyo. 13.

Parker received 29.40 per cent (140 votes—13 states) as follows: Ala. 11; Ark. 9; Fla. 5; Ga. 13; Ky. 13; La. 9; Md. 7 (of the 8 votes); Miss. 10; N.C. 12; S.C. 9; Tenn. 12; Tex. 18; Va. 12.

APPOINTMENTS TO THE SUPREME COURT

Associate Justices

Oliver Wendell Holmes, Mass., Dec. 4, 1902
William Rufus Day, Ohio, Feb. 23, 1903
William Henry Moody, Mass., Dec. 12, 1906

ADMINISTRATION—IMPORTANT DATES

Sept. 18, 1901, commission form of government adopted, Galveston, Tex.

Dec. 11, 1901, first wireless signal received from Europe

May 12, 1902, Pennsylvania coal strike begun

May 20, 1902, Cuban republic inaugurated

June 17, 1902, Newlands conservation act passed

Dec. 14, 1902, laying of Pacific cable began at San Francisco, Calif.

Dec. 19, 1902, U.S. intervention in Venezuelan dispute with European nations

Feb. 14, 1903, Department of Commerce and Labor created

Mar. 19, 1903, reciprocity treaty with Cuba ratified

Oct. 17, 1903, Alaska boundary award made

Nov. 6, 1903, Republic of Panama recognized

Nov. 18, 1903, Isthmian Canal Convention; Panama ceded Canal Zone strip ten miles wide through lease and sale to United States

Dec. 17, 1903, Wright brothers' airplane flight, Kitty Hawk, N.C.

Feb. 26, 1904, Panama Canal Zone formally acquired by the United States

Dec. 2, 1904, President Roosevelt issued corollary to the Monroe Doctrine, defending American intervention in Latin America to stop European aggression

Sept. 5, 1905, Russo-Japanese peace treaty signed, Portsmouth, N.H.

Apr. 18-20, 1906, San Francisco earthquake; about 500 deaths and damage estimated at $1 billion

June 30, 1906, federal Pure Food and Drugs Act passed

1907, financial panic

Oct. 18, 1907, Fourth Hague Convention signed by 32 nations

Nov. 16, 1907, Oklahoma admitted as the 46th state

Dec. 16, 1907, American battleships left on around-the-world cruise

1907-1908, "gentleman's agreement" with Japan—Japanese declared they would issue no passports to laborers wishing to emigrate to the United States

Feb. 9, 1909, first narcotics prohibition act passed

IMPORTANT DATES IN HIS LIFE

18——, attended public schools

1880, graduated from Harvard

1880-1881, studied law

1882-1884, New York State Assembly

1884-1886, at his North Dakota ranch

1886, returned to New York City; unsuccessful candidate for mayor

May 13, 1889-1895, U.S. Civil Service Commission (appointed by President Harrison)

May 6, 1895, president of New York City Board of Police Commissioners

Apr. 19, 1897, appointed assistant secretary of the Navy

1898, resigned Navy post; organized First Regiment U.S. Volunteers Cavalry, known as "Roosevelt's Rough Riders"

May 6, 1898, lieutenant colonel

July 11, 1898, colonel

Sept. 15, 1898, mustered out of service

1899-1901, governor of New York

1900, nominated as vice presidential candidate on Republican ticket

Mar. 4, 1901, inaugurated Vice President

Sept. 14, 1901, succeeded to the presidency on the death of President McKinley; took oath of office at Buffalo, N.Y.

1904, nominated for another term as President on the Republican ticket

Mar. 4, 1905-Mar. 3, 1909, President (second term)

June 1908, received three complimentary votes at Republican nominating convention

1910, left for Africa on a big-game hunting and scientific expedition outfitted by the Smithsonian Institution

1910, special ambassador from the United States at the funeral of King Edward VII of England

June 1912, unsuccessful candidate for Republican nomination for the presidency

Aug. 1912, organized Progressive ("Bull Moose") Party; nominated as presidential candidate

1913, headed exploring party to South America

1916, declined nomination from the Progressive Party as presidential candidate

1916-1919, engaged in literary pursuits

THEODORE ROOSEVELT

——was the third President born in New York.

——was the second President married on his birthday.

——was the fourth President to remarry.

——was the first President to win a Nobel Peace Prize.

——was the youngest President.

ROOSEVELT'S VICE PRESIDENT

Vice President—Charles Warren Fairbanks (26th V.P.)

Date of birth—May 11, 1852

Birthplace—Unionville Center, Ohio

Political party—Republican

State represented—Indiana

Term of office—Mar. 4, 1905-Mar. 3, 1909

Age at inauguration—52 years, 297 days

Occupation after term—Lawyer

Date of death—June 4, 1918

Place of death—Indianapolis, Ind.

Age at death—66 years, 24 days

Burial place—Indianapolis, Ind.

ADDITIONAL DATA ON ROOSEVELT

DOUBLE TRAGEDY IN THE ROOSEVELT FAMILY

Thursday, February 14, 1884, was a day of tragedy for Assemblyman Theodore Roosevelt. On that day, at Roosevelt's home in New York City, his mother died of typhoid fever and his wife, Alice, died of Bright's disease.

FIRST OATH OF OFFICE

After the death of President McKinley, Theodore Roosevelt took the oath of office on Saturday, September 14, 1901, at 3:32 P.M., at the residence of Ansley Wilcox at Buffalo, N.Y. The oath was administered by Judge John R. Hazel of the United States District Court.

THE YOUNGEST PRESIDENT

Theodore Roosevelt was the youngest man to take the oath of office as Chief Executive. He was a little over forty-two years and ten months old when sworn in.

ROOSEVELT RODE IN AUTOMOBILE AND AIRPLANE

The first President to ride in an automobile was Theodore Roosevelt who was a passenger in a purple-lined Columbia Electric Victoria in a trip through Hartford, Conn., on August 22, 1902. Twenty carriages followed the presidential automobile during its tour of the city.

After his term of office, Roosevelt again pioneered when he took a ride in an airplane on October 11, 1910, at St. Louis, Mo. He was a passenger in an airplane piloted by "Archie"

Hoxsey. Roosevelt was the first of the Presidents to fly in an airplane.

ROOSEVELT APPOINTED COMMERCE AND LABOR SECRETARY

On February 16, 1903, Theodore Roosevelt appointed George B. Cortelyou secretary of commerce and labor, the first man to hold that office.

INAUGURATION IN 1905

Theodore Roosevelt took the oath of office Saturday, March 4, 1905, on the east portico of the Capitol. Chief Justice Melville Weston Fuller administered the oath. A spectacular parade was witnessed by more than 200,000 visitors.

ROOSEVELT VISITED A FOREIGN COUNTRY .

Theodore Roosevelt was the first President to visit a foreign country during his term of office. He traveled to Panama on the U.S.S. *Louisiana*. After visiting Panama from November 14 to 17, 1906, he went to Puerto Rico.

PEACE PRIZE TO ROOSEVELT

The first American recipient of a Nobel Prize was Theodore Roosevelt, to whom the $40,000 prize was awarded in 1906 for his services in concluding the treaty of peace between Russia and Japan at the end of the Russo-Japanese War.

ASSASSINATION OF ROOSEVELT ATTEMPTED

When President Roosevelt was leaving the Hotel Gilpatrick in Milwaukee, Wis., on October 14, 1912, during a presidential campaign, John Nepomuk Schrank, a saloon keeper, attempted to assassinate him. Roosevelt was shot in the chest. The assassin was opposed to Roosevelt's attempt to capture a third term.

Five alienists decided Schrank was suffering from insane delusions, and on November 13, 1912, he was declared insane. He was committed to the Northern State Hospital for the Insane at Oshkosh, Wis., and died September 15, 1943, at Central State Hospital, Waupun, Wis.

THE PRESIDENT'S FAMILY

When Theodore Roosevelt succeeded to the presidency, Edith Kermit Carow, Roosevelt's second wife, became the first lady of the land. The White

House was a lively place because of the activities of the President's children—four sons and two daughters. During Roosevelt's administration, Alice Lee Roosevelt, the daughter of the President by his first wife, Alice Lee, was married to Nicholas Longworth at the White House.

WILLIAM HOWARD TAFT

Born—Sept. 15, 1857

Birthplace—Cincinnati, Ohio

College attended—Yale

Date of graduation—June 27, 1878

Religion—Unitarian

Ancestry—English

Occupation—Lawyer

Date and place of marriage—June 19, 1886, Cincinnati, Ohio

Age at marriage—28 years, 277 days

Years married—43 years, 262 days

Political party—Republican

State represented—Ohio

Term of office—Mar. 4, 1909-Mar. 3, 1913

Term served—4 years

Administration—31st

Congresses—61st, 62nd

Age at inauguration—51 years, 170 days

Lived after term—17 years, 4 days

Occupation after term—Chief Justice, United States

Date of death—Mar. 8, 1930

Age at death—72 years, 174 days

Place of death—Washington, D.C.

Burial place—Arlington National Cemetery, Arlington, Va.

PARENTS

Father—Alphonso Taft

Born—Nov. 5, 1810, East Townshend, Vt.

For additional data see the end of this section and also specific subject headings in the Index.

Married (1)—Fanny Phelps

Married (2)—Louise Maria Torrey

Occupation—Lawyer, U.S. Secretary of War

Died—May 21, 1891, San Diego, Calif.

Age at death—80 years, 197 days

First wife of father—Fanny Phelps Taft

Born—Mar. 28, 1823, West Townshend, Vt.

Married—Aug. 29, 1841, Townshend, Vt.

Died—June 2, 1852, Cincinnati, Ohio

Age at death—29 years, 66 days

Mother—Louise Maria Torrey Taft

Born—Sept. 11, 1827, Boston, Mass.

Married—Dec. 26, 1853, Millbury, Mass.

Died—Dec. 8, 1907, Millbury, Mass.

Age at death—80 years, 88 days

BROTHERS AND SISTERS

William Howard Taft was the seventh of his father's ten children, the second of five children of a second marriage.

CHILDREN

Robert Alphonso Taft, b. Sept. 8, 1889, Cincinnati, Ohio; m. Oct. 17, 1914, Martha Wheaton Bowers, Washington, D.C.; d. July 31, 1953, New York, N.Y.

Helen Herron Taft, b. Aug. 1, 1891, Cincinnati, Ohio; m. July 19, 1920, Frederick Johnson Manning, Murray Bay, Canada

Charles Phelps Taft, b. Sept. 20, 1897, Cincinnati, Ohio; m. Oct. 6, 1917, Eleanor Kellogg Chase, Waterbury, Conn.

MRS. WILLIAM HOWARD TAFT

Name—Helen Herron Taft

Date of birth—Jan. 2, 1861

Birthplace—Cincinnati, Ohio

Age at marriage—25 years, 168 days

Children—2 sons, 1 daughter

Mother—Harriet Collins Herron

Father—John Williamson Herron

His occupation—Judge

Date of death—May 22, 1943

Age at death—82 years, 140 days

Place of death—Washington, D.C.

Burial place—Arlington National Cemetery, Arlington, Va.

Years younger than the President—3 years, 109 days

Years she survived the President—13 years, 75 days

THE ELECTION OF 1908

NOMINATIONS FOR TERM 1909-1913

Republican Party Convention (14th)

June 16-19, 1908, the Coliseum, Chicago, Ill.
Nominated for President—William Howard Taft, Ohio
Nominated for Vice President—James Schoolcraft Sherman, N.Y.

Taft was nominated on the first ballot.

Total number of votes: 979
Nomination made unanimous

Democratic Party Convention (20th)

July 8-10, 1908, Civic Auditorium, Denver, Colo.
Nominated for President—William Jennings Bryan, Neb.
Nominated for Vice President—John Worth Kern, Ind.

Bryan was nominated on the first ballot.

Total number of votes: 993

ELECTION RESULTS, NOV. 3, 1908—PRESIDENTIAL AND VICE PRESIDENTIAL CANDIDATES

Republican Party (7,678,908 votes)

William Howard Taft, Ohio
James Schoolcraft Sherman, N.Y.

Democratic Party (6,409,104 votes)

William Jennings Bryan, Neb.
John Worth Kern, Ind.

Socialist Party (420,793 votes)

Eugene Victor Debs, Ind.
Benjamin Hanford, N.Y.

Prohibition Party (253,840 votes)

Eugene Wilder Chafin, Ill.
Aaron Sherman Watkins, Ohio

Independence Party (82,872 votes)

Thomas Louis Hisgen, Mass.
John Temple Graves, Ga.

People's Party (Populist Party) (29,100 votes)

Thomas Edward Watkins, Ga.
Samuel Williams, Ind.

Socialist Labor Party (14,021 votes)

August Gillhaus, N.Y.
Donald L. Munro, Va.

United Christian Party

Daniel Braxton Turney, Ill.

Lorenzo S. Coffin, Iowa

ELECTORAL VOTES (483 —46 states)

Taft received 66.46 per cent (321 votes—29 states) as follows: Calif. 10; Conn. 7; Del. 3; Idaho 3; Ill. 27; Ind. 15; Iowa 13; Kan. 10; Me. 6; Md. 2 (of the 8 votes); Mass. 16; Mich. 14; Minn. 11; Mo. 18; Mont. 3; N.H. 4; N.J. 12; N.Y. 39; N.D. 4; Ohio 23; Ore. 4; Pa. 34; R.I. 4; S.D. 4; Utah 3; Vt. 4; Wash. 5; W.Va. 7; Wis. 13; Wyo. 3.

Bryan received 33.54 per cent (162 votes—17 states) as follows: Ala. 11; Ark. 9; Colo. 5; Fla. 5; Ga. 13; Ky. 13; La. 9; Md. 6 (of the 8 votes); Miss. 10; Neb. 8; Nev. 3; N.C. 12; Okla. 7; S.C. 9; Tenn. 12; Tex. 18; Va. 12.

APPOINTMENTS TO THE SUPREME COURT

Chief Justice

Edward Douglass White, La., Dec. 19, 1910 (served as Associate Justice, 1894-1910)

Associate Justices

Horace Harmon Lurton, Tenn., Dec. 20, 1909

Charles Evans Hughes, N.Y., May 2, 1910

Willis Van Devanter, Wyo., Dec. 16, 1910

Joseph Rucker Lamar, Ga., Dec. 17, 1910

Mahlon Pitney, N.J., Mar. 13, 1912

ADMINISTRATION— IMPORTANT DATES

Apr. 6, 1909, Peary discovered the North Pole

July 30, 1909, army officer, B. D. Foulois, made first transcontinental flight

Aug. 2, 1909, U.S. government purchased its first airplane

Aug. 11, 1909, first radio SOS from an American ship

Feb. 8, 1910, Boy Scouts of America incorporated

June 1, 1910, Atlantic fisheries dispute settled by The Hague

June 25, 1910, postal savings bank authorized

Jan 3, 1911, postal banks established

Jan. 6, 1911, "Flying Fish," first successful hydroplane, flown

Feb. 15, 1911, U.S. Commerce Court opened

Oct. 18, 1911, keel of *Jupiter,* first electrically propelled vessel of U.S. Navy, laid

Jan. 6, 1912, New Mexico admitted as the 47th state

Feb. 14, 1912, Arizona admitted as the 48th state

Aug. 24, 1912, parcel post service authorized

Nov. 25, 1912, American College of Surgeons incorporated

Jan. 1, 1913, parcel post service began

Feb. 25, 1913, Sixteenth Amendment to the Constitution ratified, giving Congress the power to collect taxes on income

IMPORTANT DATES IN HIS LIFE

June 5, 1874, graduated from Woodward High School, Cincinnati, Ohio

June 27, 1878, graduated from Yale University

May 1, 1880, graduated from Cincinnati Law School

May 5, 1880, admitted to the bar

1880-1881, law reporter on Cincinnati newspapers

1881-1882, assistant prosecuting attorney, Cincinnati, Ohio

1887, assistant city solicitor, Cincinnati

Mar. 7, 1887-Feb. 1890, judge, Superior Court of Cincinnati

Feb. 4, 1890-1892, U.S. Solicitor General

Mar. 17, 1892-1900, U.S. Federal Circuit Court

1896-1900, dean, University of Cincinnati Law School

Mar. 13, 1900-1901, president of Philippines Commission

July 4, 1901, appointed governor-general of Philippine Islands

1902, arranged with Pope Leo XIII for the purchase of Roman Catholic lands in the Philippines

Feb. 1, 1904-June 1908, secretary of war under President Theodore Roosevelt

1907, government mission to Cuba, Panama, and Philippine Islands

1907, provisional governor of Cuba

Mar. 4, 1909-Mar. 3, 1913, President

Apr. 1, 1913-1921, professor of law, Yale University

June 30, 1921-Feb. 3, 1930, chief justice, U.S. Supreme Court

WILLIAM HOWARD TAFT

——was the sixth President born in Ohio.

——was the first President to become chief justice of the United States.

——was the first President who had been a member of a cabinet after the Civil War.

——was the first cabinet member other than a secretary of state to become President.

TAFT'S VICE PRESIDENT

Vice President—James Schoolcraft Sherman (27th V.P.)

Date of birth—Oct. 24, 1855

Birthplace—Utica, N.Y.

Political party—Republican

State represented—New York

Term of office—Mar. 4, 1909-Oct. 30, 1912

Age at inauguration—53 years, 131 days

Occupation after term—Died in office

Date of death—Oct. 30, 1912

Place of death—Utica, N.Y.

Age at death—57 years, 6 days

Burial place—Utica, N.Y.

ADDITIONAL DATA ON TAFT

TAFT AT YALE

William Howard Taft stood second in scholarship in the Yale class of 1878, which consisted of 132 graduates. On graduation day, he was 20 years and 285 days old. He was 5 feet 10¾ inches tall and weighed 225 pounds. The average weight of his classmates was 151 pounds.

INAUGURATION

William Howard Taft took the oath of office on Thursday, March 4, 1909, in the Senate Chamber. The oath was to have been administered on the east portico of the Capitol, but as a blizzard was raging the ceremonies were held indoors. The oath was administered by Chief Justice Melville Weston Fuller. It was the sixth time Justice Fuller officiated in this capacity.

Ice forming on trees cracked branches and made transportation so hazardous that incoming trains were prevented from entering the city. Most of the inaugural parade was disbanded; only a small part of the planned parade was held. Mrs. Taft set a precedent by riding to the White House with her husband.

Instead of riding back to the White House with the new President, former President Roosevelt went directly to the railroad station from which he left the city.

JAPANESE CHERRY TREES PLANTED

In 1909 Mrs. Taft was instrumental in securing eighty Japanese cherry trees from various nurseries, all that were available at that time. These were planted along the banks of the Potomac River in West Potomac Park.

On December 10, 1909, a shipment of two thousand additional trees, the gift of the City of

Tokyo to the City of Washington, reached Seattle, Washington. They were transported to Washington, D.C., where they were destroyed by burning after inspection by the United States Department of Agriculture showed them to be infested with insect pests and fungus diseases. A second consignment of three thousand trees replaced them. The first of these trees was planted by Mrs. Taft on March 27, 1912, the second by Viscountess Chinda, the wife of the Japanese ambassador. The trees were planted around the Tidal Basin and along Riverside Drive in East and West Potomac Parks.

TAFT OPENED BASE-BALL SEASON

William Howard Taft was the first President to pitch a ball to open the baseball season. On April 14, 1910, he tossed the baseball which opened the American League game between Washington and Philadelphia. A crowd of 12,226 broke all previous attendance records.

SILVER WEDDING CELEBRATION

President and Mrs. Taft celebrated their silver wedding anniversary at the White House with a night garden party on June 19, 1911, for about five thousand guests. The members of the House of Representatives presented them with a $1,700 solid-silver service and the members of the Senate gave them compote dishes.

FIRST PRESIDENT OF FORTY-EIGHT STATES

The forty-eighth state admitted to the United States was Arizona, which became a state on February 14, 1912, during the Taft administration. President Taft thus became the first President of the forty-eight states which comprised the Union until 1959.

VICE PRESIDENT RE-NOMINATED BUT DIED BEFORE ELECTION

James Schoolcraft Sherman of New York was elected Vice President to serve with President Taft from March 4, 1909 to March 3, 1913. In 1912 he was renominated by the Republicans for a second term, but he died on October 30, 1912, six days before the election. The eight electoral votes which would have been cast for him had he lived were transferred to Nicholas Murray Butler, nominated by the Republican National Committee.

THE FIRST LADY

As Helen Herron Taft was ill during part of Taft's administration, her sister, Mrs. Louis More, often acted as White House hostess.

PRESIDENT BECAME CHIEF JUSTICE

President Taft was the first and only President of the United States to become chief justice of the United States. Taft was appointed by President Warren G. Harding on June 30, 1921, and he resigned on February 3, 1930, a few weeks before his death.

TAFT BURIED IN ARLINGTON CEMETERY

The only President buried in the National Cemetery at Arlington, Va., is William Howard Taft, interred March 11, 1930.

WOODROW WILSON

Woodrow Wilson

WOODROW WILSON

Born—Dec. 28, 1856 (Given name—Thomas Woodrow Wilson)

Birthplace—Staunton, Va.

College attended—Princeton University, Princeton, N.J.

Date of graduation—June 18, 1879, four-year course, Bachelor of Arts

Religion—Presbyterian

Ancestry—Scotch-Irish

Occupation—Teacher, governor

Date and place of first marriage—June 24, 1885, Savannah, Ga.

Age at marriage—28 years, 178 days

Years married—29 years, 43 days

Date and place of second marriage—Dec. 18, 1915, Washington, D.C.

Age at second marriage—58 years, 355 days

Years married—8 years, 47 days

Political party—Democratic

State represented—New Jersey

Term of office—Mar. 4, 1913-Mar. 3, 1921

Term served—8 years

Administration—32nd, 33rd

Congresses—63rd, 64th, 65th, 66th

Age at inauguration—56 years, 66 days

Lived after term—2 years, 337 days

Occupation after term—Lawyer

Date of death—Feb. 3, 1924

Age at death—67 years, 37 days

For additional data see the end of this section and also specific subject headings in the Index.

Place of death—Washington, D.C.

Burial place—National Cathedral, Washington, D.C.

PARENTS

Father—Joseph Ruggles Wilson

Born—Feb. 28, 1822, Steubenville, Ohio

Married—June 7, 1849, Chillicothe, Ohio

Occupation—Presbyterian minister

Died—Jan. 21, 1903, Princeton, N.J.

Age at death—80 years, 327 days

Mother—Jessie Janet Woodrow Wilson

Born—Dec. 20, 1826, Carlisle, England

Died—Apr. 15, 1888, Clarksville, Tenn.

Age at death—61 years, 116 days

BROTHERS AND SISTERS

Woodrow Wilson was the third child in a family of four.

CHILDREN

By first wife, Ellen Louise Axson Wilson

Margaret Woodrow Wilson, b.

Apr. 30, 1886, Gainesville, Ga.; d. Feb. 12, 1944, Pondicherry, India

Jessie Woodrow Wilson, b. Aug. 28, 1887, Gainesville, Ga.; m. Nov. 25, 1913, Francis Bowes Sayre, at the White House, Washington, D.C.; d. Jan. 15, 1933, Cambridge, Mass.

Eleanor Randolph Wilson, b. Oct. 16, 1889, Middletown, Conn.; m. May 7, 1914, William Gibbs McAdoo, at the White House, Washington, D.C.

By second wife, Edith Bolling Galt

None

MRS. WOODROW WILSON (first wife)

Name—Ellen Louise Axson Wilson

Date of birth—May 15, 1860

Birthplace—Savannah, Ga.

Age at marriage—25 years, 40 days

Children—3 daughters

Mother—Margaret Hoyt Axson

Father—Samuel Edward Axson

His occupation—Presbyterian minister

Date of death—Aug. 6, 1914

Age at death—54 years, 83 days

Place of death—Washington, D.C.

Burial place—Rome, Ga.

Years younger than the President—3 years, 138 days

Years the President survived her—9 years, 181 days

MRS. WOODROW WILSON (second wife)

Name—Edith Bolling Galt Wilson

Date of birth—Oct. 15, 1872

Birthplace—Wytheville, Va.

Age at marriage—43 years, 64 days

Children—None

Mother—Sallie White Bolling

Father—William Holcombe Bolling

His occupation—Judge

Years younger than the President—15 years, 291 days

At the time of her marriage to President Wilson she was the widow of Norman Galt, whom she had married at Wytheville, Va., on April 30, 1896, and who had died on January 28, 1908.

THE ELECTION OF 1912

NOMINATIONS FOR TERM 1913-1917

Democratic Party Convention (21st)

June 25-29, July 1-2, 1912, Fifth Maryland Regiment Armory, Baltimore, Md.

Nominated for President—Woodrow Wilson, N.J.

Nominated for Vice President—Thomas Riley Marshall, Ind.

Wilson was nominated on the forty-sixth ballot.

Total number of votes: 1,086

Number necessary for nomination: 545

Republican Party Convention (15th)

June 18-22, 1912, the Coliseum, Chicago, Ill.

Nominated for President—William Howard Taft, Ohio

Nominated for Vice President—James Schoolcraft Sherman, N.Y.

Taft was nominated on the first ballot.

Total number of votes: 728

Of the 1,078 delegates present, 344 did not vote.

ELECTION RESULTS, NOV. 5, 1912—PRESIDENTIAL AND VICE PRESIDENTIAL CANDIDATES

Democratic Party (6,293,454 votes)

Woodrow Wilson, N.J.
Thomas Riley Marshall, Ind.

Progressive Party (4,119,538 votes)

Theodore Roosevelt, N.Y.
Hiram Warren Johnson, Calif.

Republican Party (3,484,980 votes)

William Howard Taft, Ohio
James Schoolcraft Sherman, N.Y. (votes transferred to Nicholas Murray Butler, N.Y., after the death of Sherman on Oct. 30, 1912)

Socialist Party (900,672 votes)

Eugene Victor Debs, Ind.
Emil Seidel, Wis.

Prohibition Party (206,275 votes)

Eugene Wilder Chafin, Ill.
Aaron Sherman Watkins, Ohio

Socialist Labor Party (28,750 votes)

Arthur E. Reimer, Mass.
August Gillhaus, N.Y.

ELECTORAL VOTES (531 —48 states)

Wilson received 81.92 per cent (435 votes—40 states) as follows: Ala. 12; Ariz. 3; Ark. 9; Calif. 2 (of the 13 votes); Colo. 6; Conn. 7; Del. 3; Fla. 6; Ga. 14; Idaho 4; Ill. 29; Ind. 15; Iowa 13; Kan. 10; Ky. 13; La. 10; Me. 6; Md. 8; Mass. 18;

Miss. 10; Mo. 18; Mont. 4; Neb. 8; Nev. 3; N.H. 4; N.J. 14; N.M. 3; N.Y. 45; N.C. 12; N.D. 5; Ohio 24; Okla. 10; Ore. 5; R.I. 5; S.C. 9; Tenn. 12; Texas 20; Va. 12; W.Va. 8; Wis. 13; Wyo. 3.

Roosevelt received 16.57 per cent (88 votes—6 states) as follows: Calif. 11 (of the 13 votes); Mich. 15; Minn. 12; Pa. 38; S.D. 5; Wash. 7.

Taft received 1.51 per cent (8 votes—2 states) as follows: Utah 4; Vt. 4.

The Republican electoral votes for the vice presidency were transferred to Butler after the death of Sherman.

THE ELECTION OF 1916

NOMINATIONS FOR TERM 1917-1921

Democratic Party Convention (22nd)

June 14-16, 1916, the Coliseum, St. Louis, Mo.
Nominated for President— Woodrow Wilson, N.J.
Nominated for Vice President— Thomas Riley Marshall, Ind.
First ballot: Woodrow Wilson, N.J. 1,093
Nominated by acclamation

Republican Party Convention (16th)

June 7-10, 1916, the Coliseum, Chicago, Ill.

Nominated for President—
Charles Evans Hughes, N.Y.
Nominated for Vice President—
Charles Warren Fairbanks,
Ind.

Hughes was nominated on the
third ballot.

Total number of votes: first ballot, 984½; third ballot, 986

ELECTION RESULTS, NOV. 7, 1916—PRESIDENTIAL AND VICE PRESIDENTIAL CANDIDATES

Democratic Party (9,129,606 votes)

Woodrow Wilson, N.J.
Thomas Riley Marshall, Ind.

Republican Party (8,538,221 votes)

Charles Evans Hughes, N.Y.
Charles Warren Fairbanks, Ind.

Socialist Party (585,113 votes)

Allan Louis Benson, N.Y.
George Ross Kirkpatrick, N.J.

Prohibition Party (220,506 votes)

James Franklin Hanly, Ind.
Ira Landrith, Mass.

Socialist Labor Party (13,403 votes)

Arthur E. Reimer, Mass.
Caleb Harrison, Ill.

ELECTORAL VOTES (531 —48 states)

Wilson received 52.17 per cent (277 votes—30 states) as follows: Ala. 12; Ariz. 3; Ark. 9; Calif. 13; Colo. 6; Fla. 6; Ga. 14; Idaho 4; Kan. 10; Ky. 13; La. 10; Md. 8; Miss. 10; Mo. 18; Mont. 4; Neb. 8; Nev. 3; N.H. 4; N.M. 3; N.C. 12; N.D. 5; Ohio 24; Okla. 10; S.C. 9; Tenn. 12; Tex. 20; Utah 4; Va. 12; Wash. 7; W.Va. 1 (of the 8 votes); Wyo. 3.

Hughes received 47.83 per cent (254 votes—18 states) as follows: Conn. 7; Del. 3; Ill. 29; Ind. 15; Iowa 13; Me. 6; Mass. 18; Mich. 15; Minn. 12; N.J. 14; N.Y. 45; Ore. 5; Pa. 38; R.I. 5; S.D. 4; Vt. 4; W.Va. 7 (of the 8 votes); Wis. 13.

APPOINTMENTS TO THE SUPREME COURT

Associate Justices

James Clark McReynolds, Tenn., Aug. 29, 1914
Louis Dembitz Brandeis, Mass., June 1, 1916
John Hessin Clarke, Ohio, July 24, 1916

ADMINISTRATION— IMPORTANT DATES

May 31, 1913, Seventeenth Amendment to the Constitution ratified (direct election of senators)

Dec. 23, 1913, Federal Reserve Act

Apr. 22, 1914, Vera Cruz taken by U.S. Navy

Aug. 15, 1914, Panama Canal admitted commercial traffic

Sept. 26, 1914, Federal Trade Commission established

Oct. 15, 1914, Clayton Anti-Trust Act passed

Nov. 23, 1914, U.S. troops withdrawn from Vera Cruz

Jan. 25, 1915, New York to San Francisco transcontinental telephone demonstration

Feb. 20, 1915, Panama-Pacific Exposition opened, San Francisco, Calif.

May 7, 1915, sinking of *Lusitania* by German submarine

Oct. 19, 1915, United States recognized de facto government of Carranza in Mexico

Feb. 28, 1916, treaty signed with Haitian government for United States to assume protectorate over Haiti

Mar. 1916, General Pershing with 6,000 troops sent to Mexico in pursuit of revolutionary bandit Francisco ("Pancho") Villa

July 17, 1916, Federal Farm Loan Act signed

Sept. 1, 1916, Keating-Owen Child Labor Act signed

Sept. 3, 1916, Adamson Act established eight-hour-day on railroads

Sept. 7, 1916, Senate ratified treaty to purchase Danish West Indies (Virgin Islands)

Nov. 1916, Jeannette Rankin of Montana elected as first congresswoman

Mar. 3, 1917, Virgin Islands purchased from Denmark for $25 million

Apr. 6, 1917, United States declared war against Germany

June 8, 1917, advance unit of American Expeditionary Force landed at Liverpool, England

July 28, 1917, War Industries Board created

Dec. 7, 1917, United States declared war against Austria-Hungary

Dec. 26, 1917, railroads placed under government operation

Jan. 8, 1918, Wilson outlined his "fourteen points" to Congress

Nov. 11, 1918, armistice signed at 11 A.M.

Jan. 29, 1919, Eighteenth Amendment to the Constitution ratified (prohibition of liquor manufacture, sale, and transportation)

June 28, 1919, Treaty of Versailles signed

Nov. 19, 1919, Treaty of Versailles rejected by the Senate

Jan. 13, 1920, first meeting of

League of Nations called; United States not represented

June 10, 1920, Federal Water Power Act approved

Aug. 26, 1920, Nineteenth Amendment to the Constitution ratified (woman suffrage)

Feb. 22, 1921, first transcontinental airmail flight from San Francisco to New York

IMPORTANT DATES IN HIS LIFE

1856, family moved to Augusta, Ga.

1870, family moved to Columbia, S.C.

1873, entered Davidson College, Davidson, N.C.

1874, withdrew from college because of ill health

Sept. 1875, entered the College of New Jersey (now Princeton)

June 18, 1879, graduated from Princeton

Oct. 2, 1879, entered University of Virginia Law School

1880, left school because of ill health

June 30, 1881, graduated from law school

1882, admitted to the bar

1882-1883, practiced law at Atlanta, Ga., with partner, Edward I. Renick

1885, taught history and political science at Bryn Mawr College, Bryn Mawr, Pa.

June 1886, received Ph.D. degree in political science from Johns Hopkins University

1888-1890, taught at Wesleyan University, Middletown, Conn.

1890-1902, professor of jurisprudence and political economy, Princeton University

June 9, 1902, unanimously elected president of Princeton University

Oct. 25, 1902-Oct. 23, 1910, president of Princeton University

Sept. 15, 1910, nominated by the Democrats as candidate for governor of New Jersey

Jan. 7, 1911-Mar. 1, 1913, governor of New Jersey

July 2, 1912, nominated by the Democrats for the presidency

Nov. 5, 1912, elected President of the United States

Mar. 4, 1913-Mar. 3, 1921, President

Dec. 8, 1915, married Edith Bolling Galt at Washington, D.C.

Dec. 4, 1918, sailed for Europe to attend Peace Conference at Paris

Jan. 18, 1919, addressed opening session of Paris Peace Conference

Feb. 1919, returned to United States

Mar. 1919, sailed for Europe

June 28, 1919, signed peace

treaty with Germany at Versailles, France

July 8, 1919, returned to United States

Sept. 26, 1919, collapsed; suffered paralytic stroke at Pueblo, Colo.

Oct. 2, 1919, stroke paralyzed his left arm and leg

Oct. 4, 1919, complete physical breakdown

Dec. 10, 1920, awarded Nobel Peace Prize

Mar. 4, 1921, after inauguration of his successor retired to his Washington, D.C., residence, where his health continued to deteriorate

WOODROW WILSON

——was the eighth President born in Virginia.

——was the second Democratic President since the Civil War.

——was the first President who majored in history and government at college.

——was the first President who had been president of a major university.

——was the fourth President inaugurated on March 5 (March 4 was a Sunday).

——was the eleventh President elected from a state other than his native state.

——was the third President whose wife died while he was in office.

——was the fifth President to remarry.

——was the sixth President to marry a widow.

WILSON'S VICE PRESIDENT

Vice President—Thomas Riley Marshall (28th V.P.)

Date of birth—Mar. 14, 1854

Birthplace—North Manchester, Ind.

Political party—Democratic

State represented—Indiana

Term of office—Mar. 4, 1913- Mar. 3, 1921

Age at inauguration—58 years, 355 days

Occupation after term—Lawyer and writer

Date of death—June 1, 1925

Place of death—Washington, D.C.

Age at death—71 years, 79 days

Burial place—Indianapolis, Ind.

ADDITIONAL DATA ON WILSON

EXTRAORDINARY POLITICAL RISE OF WILSON

Within two years and 170 days, Woodrow Wilson rose

from a citizen who had never held public office to President of the United States. Wilson had never been a candidate for political office until September 15, 1910, when the Democrats nominated him for governor of New Jersey. He took office on January 17, 1911, and served two years. On July 2, 1912, he was nominated as the Democratic candidate for the presidency; on November 5, 1912, he was elected; and on March 4, 1913, he took office as President.

THREE PRESIDENTIAL RIVALS

The three men who served as Presidents of the United States from September 14, 1901, to March 3, 1921, were all candidates for the presidency on November 5, 1912, each representing a different political party. The candidates were Theodore Roosevelt, Progressive, who served from September 14, 1901, to March 3, 1909; William Howard Taft, Republican, who served from March 4, 1909, to March 3, 1913; and Woodrow Wilson, Democrat, who was to serve from March 4, 1913, to March 3, 1921.

Taft received 3,484,980 popular votes, and Roosevelt received 4,119,538 votes; their combined total was 7,604,518 votes. Wilson, who had 6,293,454 votes, had a plurality. He was elected with 435 electoral votes to Roosevelt's 88 votes and Taft's 8 votes. Wilson was the only President who simultaneously defeated two other Presidents in one election.

FIRST INAUGURATION

Woodrow Wilson took the oath of office on Tuesday, March 4, 1913, on the east portico of the Capitol. The oath was administered by Chief Justice Edward Douglass White. The day was cold and disagreeable.

WILSON APPOINTED NAMESAKE TO CABINET

Woodrow Wilson was the only President who had a cabinet member with the same last name as his own—Secretary of Labor William Bauchop Wilson of Pennsylvania, who took office on March 5, 1913.

WILSON APPOINTED FIRST SECRETARY OF LABOR

The work of secretary of commerce and labor was divided into two separate departments with the passing of a law on March 4, 1913. On March 5,

1913, President Wilson appointed William C. Redfield as secretary of commerce and William Bauchop Wilson as secretary of labor.

WILSON HELD FIRST PRESS CONFERENCE

The first presidential press conference was held on March 15, 1913, eleven days after his inauguration, by President Wilson at the Executive Offices in the White House. Newsmen who covered White House news were invited, and about 125 attended. The meeting was suggested by Joseph Patrick Tumulty, Wilson's private secretary. Previously news conferences had been limited to selected and favored newsmen.

WILSON EARNED DOCTORATE

Woodrow Wilson was the first President who had earned a doctoral degree. His thesis, *Congressional Government, a Study in American Politics,* earned him his doctorate from Johns Hopkins University in 1886. The work contained 333 pages and was published October 7, 1884, by the Houghton Mifflin Company, Boston, Mass. It ran into fifteen editions.

WILSON APPOINTED BRANDEIS

The first Jewish associate justice of the Supreme Court was Louis Dembitz Brandeis, appointed on January 28, 1916, by President Woodrow Wilson. The nomination was confirmed by the Senate on June 1, 1916, and Brandeis was sworn in on June 3, 1916. He served until February 13, 1939.

WILSON INTENDED TO RESIGN

Wilson wrote to Secretary of State Robert Lansing on November 5, 1916, two days prior to his reelection:

What would it be my duty to do were Mr. [Charles Evans] Hughes to be elected? Four months would elapse before he could take charge of the affairs of the government, and during those four months I would be without such moral backing from the nation as would be necessary to steady and control our relations with other governments. I would be known to be the rejected, not the accredited, spokesman of the country; and yet the accredited spokesman would be without legal authority to speak for the nation. Such a situation would be fraught with the gravest dangers. The direction of the foreign policy of the government would in effect have been taken out of my hands and yet its new definition would be impossible until March.

I feel that it would be my duty to relieve the country of the perils of such a situation at once. The course I have in mind is dependent upon the consent and cooperation of the Vice President; but if I could gain his consent to the plan, I would ask your permission to invite Mr. Hughes to become Secretary of State and would then join the Vice President in resigning, and thus open to Mr. Hughes the immediate succession to the presidency.

The election of Woodrow Wilson and Thomas Riley Marshall for a second term made this drastic action unnecessary.

FINAL COUNT CHANGED RESULTS

The early returns of the election of November 7, 1916, indicated that Wilson had been defeated and that Charles Evans Hughes had been elected President. Many newspapers carried the news of Wilson's defeat. When the votes of California were finally tabulated, Hughes lost the state by approximately 4,000 votes—a loss which insured the election of Wilson.

SECOND INAUGURATION

Woodrow Wilson took the oath of office Monday, March 5, 1917, as March 4 fell on Sunday for the fifth time during an inaugural year in the history of the country. Chief Justice Edward Douglass White again administered the oath to him.

WILSON'S FOURTEEN POINTS

The fourteen points which President Wilson announced to Congress in January 1918 as necessary for world peace were the following:

1. Open treaties openly arrived at through international diplomacy
2. Freedom of the seas
3. Free international trade
4. Reduction of national armaments
5. Impartial adjustment of colonial claims
6. Evacuation of Russian territory
7. Evacuation of Belgium
8. Evacuation of French territory and return of Alsace-Lorraine to France
9. Readjustment of Italian frontiers
10. Autonomy for Austria and Hungary

11. Evacuation of Rumania, Serbia, and Montenegro, and security for the Balkan states

12. Self-determination for the peoples of the Turkish empire

13. Independence for Poland

14. Formation of a "general association of nations"

WILSON VISITED EUROPE

Woodrow Wilson was the first President of the United States to cross the Atlantic while in office. He left Washington, D.C., December 4, 1918, and sailed on the transport S.S. *George Washington* from Hoboken, N.J. He arrived at Brest, France, on December 13, 1918. He left there on February 15, 1919, and landed at Boston, Mass., on February 24, 1919.

Wilson made a second trip, leaving Hoboken, N.J., on March 5, 1919, arriving March 13, 1919, at Brest, from which city he sailed on June 29, 1919, returning to Hoboken on July 8, 1919.

The trips were made to further the peace negotiations after the World War.

CABINET MEETINGS NOT CALLED

After his paralytic stroke on September 26, 1919, Wilson issued no calls for cabinet meetings. The first cabinet meeting he held after September 2, 1919, was called on April 13, 1920. It took place in the President's study in the White House instead of the cabinet room. The cabinet, however, met unofficially without call.

WILSON APPOINTED WOMAN AS SUB-CABINET MEMBER

Wilson created a precedent when he appointed a woman as a sub-cabinet member. On June 26, 1920, he appointed Annette Abbott Adams as assistant attorney general, a post which she held until August 15, 1921.

ELECTION RETURNS BROADCAST

Election returns were broadcast for the first time on August 31, 1920, when WWJ of Detroit, Mich., broadcast the results of congressional and county primaries.

WILSON THE SECOND PRESIDENT TO RECEIVE NOBEL PRIZE

Woodrow Wilson was the second President to receive the Nobel Prize for Peace, the first having been awarded to President Theodore Roosevelt. On December 10, 1920, at Christiania, Norway, the 1919 prize was presented to President Wilson and received by Albert Schmedeman, the American minister to Norway. The prize carried with it a gift of 150,000 kroner, then worth about $29,100.

THE FIRST LADIES

Ellen Louise Axson Wilson died on August 6, 1914, having served only seventeen months as first lady of the land. A daughter, Margaret, took over the functions as hostess of the White House, serving until December 18, 1915, when President Wilson married Edith Bolling Galt. After Wilson suffered a paralytic attack on September 26, 1919, social activities at the White House were suspended for the balance of his term.

WILSON BURIED IN WASHINGTON, D.C.

The only President buried in Washington, D.C., is Woodrow Wilson, interred February 5, 1924, in the National Cathedral (the Protestant Episcopal Cathedral of Saints Peter and Paul).

W.G. Harding

WARREN GAMALIEL HARDING

Born—Nov. 2, 1865

Birthplace—Corsica, Ohio

College attended—Ohio Central College, Iberia, Ohio

Years attended—1879-1882

Religion—Baptist

Ancestry—Scotch-Irish, English

Occupation—Editor

Date and place of marriage— July 8, 1891, Marion, Ohio

Age at marriage—25 years, 248 days

Years married—32 years, 25 days

Political party—Republican

State represented—Ohio

Term of office—Mar. 4, 1921- Aug. 2, 1923

Term served—2 years, 151 days

Administration—34th

Congress—67th

Age at inauguration—55 years, 122 days

Lived after term—Died in office

Date of death—Aug. 2, 1923

Age at death—57 years, 273 days

Place of death—San Francisco, Calif.

Burial place—Marion, Ohio

PARENTS

Father—George Tryon Harding

Born—June 12, 1843, Blooming Grove (now Corsica), Ohio

For additional data see the end of this section and also specific subject headings in the Index.

Married (1)—Phoebe Elizabeth Dickerson

Married (2)—Eudora Adella Kelley Luvisi

Married (3)—Alice Severns

Occupation—Physician

Died—Nov. 19, 1928, Santa Ana, Calif.

Age at death—84 years, 160 days

Mother—Phoebe Elizabeth Dickerson Harding

Born—Dec. 21, 1843, near Blooming Grove, Ohio

Married—May 7, 1864, Galion, Ohio

Died—May 20, 1910

Age at death—66 years, 159 days

Second wife of father—Eudora Adella Kelley Luvisi Harding

Born—Sept. 25, 1868, near Bartonia, Ind.

Married—Nov. 23, 1911, Anderson, Ind.

Divorced—1916

Died—July 24, 1955, Union City, Ind.

Third wife of father—Alice Severns Harding

Born—1869

Married—Aug. 11, 1921, Monroe, Mich.

Died—July 25, 1955, Union City, Ind.

BROTHERS AND SISTERS

Warren Gamaliel Harding was the oldest of eight children.

CHILDREN

None

MRS. WARREN GAMALIEL HARDING

Name—Florence Kling De Wolfe Harding

Date of birth—Aug. 15, 1860

Birthplace—Marion, Ohio

Age at marriage—30 years, 327 days

Mother—Louisa M. Bouton Kling

Father—Amos H. Kling

His occupation—Banker, merchant

Date of death—Nov. 21, 1924

Age at death—64 years, 98 days

Place of death—Marion, Ohio

Burial place—Marion, Ohio

Years older than the President—5 years, 79 days

Years she survived the President—1 year, 111 days

Florence Kling De Wolfe was divorced from Henry De Wolfe. They had one son, Marshall Eugene De Wolfe.

THE ELECTION OF 1920

NOMINATIONS FOR TERM 1921-1925

Republican Party Convention (17th)

June 8-12, 1920, the Coliseum, Chicago, Ill.

Nominated for President— Warren Gamaliel Harding, Ohio

Nominated for Vice President— Calvin Coolidge, Mass.

Harding was nominated on the tenth ballot.

Total number of votes: 984
Nomination made unanimous

Democratic Party Convention (23rd)

June 28-30, July 1-3, 5-6, 1920, Civic Auditorium, San Francisco, Calif.

Nominated for President— James Middleton Cox, Ohio

Nominated for Vice President— Franklin Delano Roosevelt, N.Y.

Cox was nominated on the forty-fourth ballot.

Total number of votes: 1094
Number necessary for nomination: 729

On the forty-fourth ballot the rules were suspended and Cox was declared nominated unanimously.

ELECTION RESULTS, NOV. 2, 1920—PRESIDENTIAL AND VICE PRESIDENTIAL CANDIDATES

Republican Party (16,152,200 votes)

Warren Gamaliel Harding, Ohio
Calvin Coolidge, Mass.

Democratic Party (9,147,353 votes)

James Middleton Cox, Ohio
Franklin Delano Roosevelt, N.Y.

Socialist Party (919,799 votes)

Eugene Victor Debs, Ind.
Seymour Stedman, Ill.

Farmer Labor Party (265,411 votes)

Parley Parker Christensen, Utah
Maximilian Sebastian Hayes, Ohio

Prohibition Party (189,408 votes)

Aaron Sherman Watkins, Ohio
David Leigh Colvin, N.Y.

Socialist Labor Party (31,715 votes)

William Wesley Cox, Mo.
August Gillhaus, N.Y.

Single Tax Party (5,837 votes)

Robert C. Macauley
R. G. Barnum

ELECTORAL VOTES (531 —48 states)

Harding received 76.08 per cent (404 votes—37 states) as follows: Ariz. 3; Calif. 13; Colo. 6; Conn. 7; Del. 3; Idaho 4; Ill. 29; Ind. 15; Iowa 13; Kan. 10; Me. 6; Md. 8; Mass. 18; Mich. 15; Minn. 12; Mo. 18; Mont. 4; Neb. 8; Nev. 3; N.H. 4; N.J. 14; N.M. 3; N.Y. 45; N.D. 5; Ohio 24; Okla. 10; Ore. 5; Pa. 38; R.I. 5; S.D. 5; Tenn. 12; Utah 4; Vt. 4; Wash. 7; W.Va. 8; Wis. 13; Wyo. 3.
Cox received 23.92 per cent (127 votes—11 states) as follows: Ala. 12; Ark. 9; Fla. 6; Ga. 14; Ky. 13; La. 10; Miss. 10; N.C. 12; S.C. 9; Tex. 20; Va. 12.

APPOINTMENTS TO THE SUPREME COURT

Chief Justice

William Howard Taft, Ohio, June 30, 1921

Associate Justices

George Sutherland, Utah, Sept. 5, 1922

Pierce Butler, Minn., Dec. 21, 1922

Edward Terry Sanford, Tenn., Jan. 29, 1923

ADMINISTRATION— IMPORTANT DATES

Mar. 28, 1921, Nevada first state to authorize executions by lethal gas

Apr. 11, 1921, Iowa enacted first state cigarette tax

May 3, 1921, West Virginia approved first state sales tax

May 19, 1921, first immigration quota act passed

June 10, 1921, U.S. Budget Bureau created

June 20, 1921, first congresswoman to preside over the House of Representatives, Mrs. Alice M. Robertson of Oklahoma, announced the vote on an appropriation

June 27, 1921, U.S. Comptroller General appointed

July 21, 1921, battleship sunk by an airplane in demonstration at Hampton Roads, Va.

Nov. 11, 1921, dedication of the Tomb of the Unknown Soldier at Arlington, Va.

Nov. 12, 1921, conference on the Limitation of Armaments at Washington, D.C.; nine nations represented

Mar. 29, 1922, Five-power Limitation on Naval Armaments Treaty (France, Great Britain, Italy, Japan, United States)

June 16, 1922, helicopter flight by H. A. Berliner demonstrated to U.S. Bureau of Aeronautics

Oct. 3, 1922, first woman senator, Rebecca L. Felton of Georgia, appointed

Oct. 27, 1922, Navy Day celebrated for the first time as an annual holiday

Jan. 23, 1923, first woman elected to Congress to serve in the place of her husband, Mrs. Mae Ella Nolan of California, took office

IMPORTANT DATES IN HIS LIFE

1879-1882, attended Ohio Central College (originally Iberia College) Iberia, Ohio

18——, studied law

18——, taught school

18——, in insurance business

Nov. 26, 1884, with two others purchased Marion, Ohio, *Star* for $300

1895, county auditor, Marion, Ohio (his first political office)

1899-1903, Ohio Senate

1904-1905, lieutenant-governor of Ohio

1910, unsuccessful Republican candidate for governor of Ohio

Mar. 4, 1915-Jan. 13, 1921, U.S. Senate (from Ohio)

Mar. 4, 1921-Aug. 2, 1923, President

WARREN GAMALIEL HARDING

——was the seventh President born in Ohio.

——was the sixth President elected from Ohio.

——was the second President elected while a senator.

——was the sixth President to die in office.

——was the fourth Ohioan to die in office.

——was the first newspaper publisher elected to the presidency.

——was the second President to marry a woman who had been divorced.

——was the fourth President whose father was alive when he was inaugurated.

——was the only President who was survived by his father.

——was the first President to ride to his inauguration in an automobile.

HARDING'S VICE PRESIDENT

Vice President—Calvin Coolidge (29th V.P.)

For biographical information see Calvin Coolidge, 30th President.

HARDING AND THE SMOKE-FILLED ROOM

The 1920 Republican convention in Chicago was unable to decide upon a candidate after the first day of balloting (June 11, 1920), and it did not seem likely that an amicable decision would be reached by the contenders and their adherents. On June 12, 1920, Senator Harding received 692⅕ votes on the tenth ballot, a total which won him the nomination.

On Sunday, June 13, 1920, the New York *Times* carried the headline "Prophesied How Harding Would Win—Daugherty, His Campaign Manager, Said Fifteen Tired Men Would Put Him Over." The story stated that Harry Micajah Daugherty, the Ohio lawyer and politician who managed Harding's campaign, had said shortly before the presidential primaries in Ohio:

> At the proper time after the Republican National Convention meets, some fifteen men, bleary-eyed with loss of sleep and perspiring profusely with the excessive heat, will sit down in seclusion around a big table. I will be with them and will present the name of Senator Harding to them, and before we get through they will put him over.

In the early hours of the morning of June 12 a group of senators and party leaders met in a room at the Blackstone Hotel. Daugherty's prediction had come true.

THREE NEWSPAPER-MEN PRESIDENTIAL NOMINEES IN 1920

Three of the presidential candidates in 1920 were active newspapermen. Warren Gamaliel Harding, the Republican candidate, was the editor and publisher of the Marion, Ohio, *Star*. James Middleton Cox, the Democratic candidate, became the owner and publisher of the Dayton, Ohio, *Daily News* in 1898 and later acquired other newspapers. Robert C. Macauley, the candidate of the Single Tax Party, was a reporter on the Philadelphia *Inquirer*.

PRESIDENTIAL ELECTION RETURNS BROADCAST

Presidential election returns were communicated by radio for the first time on November 2, 1920, when Leo H. Rosenberg of station KDKA, Pittsburgh, Pa., broadcast the results of the Harding-Cox election.

INAUGURATION

Warren Gamaliel Harding took the oath of office on Friday, March 4, 1921, on the east portico of the Capitol. Chief Justice Edward Douglass White administered the oath.

Accompanied by outgoing President Woodrow Wilson, he rode to the Capitol in an automobile, the first President to ride thus to his inaugural. This inauguration was also the first one described over radio. Another innovation was the use of an amplifying public-address system so that the assembled crowds could hear the proceedings.

HARDING BROADCAST SPEECH

The first President to broadcast over the radio was Warren Gamaliel Harding, whose speech at the dedication of the Francis Scott Key Memorial at Fort McHenry, Baltimore, Md., on June 14, 1922, was transmitted by WEAR (now WFBR), Baltimore, Md. His voice was carried over telephone wires to the studio from which it was broadcast. President Harding's World Court speech on June 21, 1923, at St. Louis, Mo., was transmitted over KSD, St. Louis,

Mo., and WEAF, New York, N.Y.

On November 5, 1921, a message from President Harding had been broadcast from Washington, D.C., to twenty-eight countries. It was sent in code over the RCA 25,000-volt station at Rocky Point, N.Y.

HARDING VISITED ALASKA AND CANADA

President Harding was the first President to visit Alaska and Canada during his term of office. He sailed on the U.S.S. *Henderson,* a naval transport, and visited Metlakahtla, Alaska, on July 8, 1923, and Vancouver, British Columbia, on July 26, 1923.

CABINET MEMBER CONVICTED OF CRIME

The first cabinet member convicted of a crime was Albert Bacon Fall, secretary of the interior during the Harding administration. On October 25, 1929, after a trial in the District of Columbia Supreme Court, Fall was found guilty by Justice William Hitz of having received and accepted a bribe of $100,000 from Edward Laurence Doheny in connection with the Elk Hills

Naval Oil Reserve in California. The bribe had been given with a view to influencing Fall to grant valuable oil leases to Doheny's Pan-American Petroleum and Transport Company. Also involved were the Teapot Dome oil reserves in Wyoming, which Fall had secretly leased to Harry F. Sinclair. On November 1, 1929, Fall was sentenced to one year in prison and a $100,000 fine.

THE FIRST LADY

Although not in good health, Florence Kling Harding went to the West Coast, Canada, and Alaska with her husband, who died in San Francisco on the return trip.

CALVIN COOLIDGE

CALVIN COOLIDGE

Born—July 4, 1872 (Given name—John Calvin Coolidge)

Birthplace—Plymouth, Vt.

College attended—Amherst College, Amherst, Mass.

Date of graduation—June 26, 1895, four-year course, Bachelor of Arts

Religion—Congregationalist

Ancestry—English

Occupation—Governor, lawyer

Date and place of marriage—Oct. 4, 1905, Burlington, Vt.

Age at marriage—33 years, 92 days

Years married—27 years, 93 days

Political party—Republican

State represented—Massachusetts

Term of office—Aug. 3, 1923-Mar. 3, 1929 (Coolidge succeeded to the presidency on the death of Warren Gamaliel Harding.)

Term served—5 years, 214 days

Administration—34th, 35th

Congresses—68th, 69th, 70th

Age at inauguration—51 years, 30 days

Lived after term—3 years, 307 days

Occupation after term—Writer, columnist

Date of death—Jan. 5, 1933

Age at death—60 years, 185 days

Place of death—Northampton, Mass.

Burial place—Plymouth, Vt.

For additional data see the end of this section and also specific subject headings in the Index.

PARENTS

Father—John Calvin Coolidge

Born—Mar. 31, 1845, Plymouth, Vt.

Married (1)—Victoria Josephine Moor

Married (2)—Caroline A. Brown

Occupation—Farmer, storekeeper, notary public

Died—Mar. 18, 1926, Plymouth, Vt.

Age at death—80 years, 352 days

Mother—Victoria Josephine Moor Coolidge

Born—Mar. 14, 1846, Pinney Hollow, Vt.

Married—May 6, 1868, Plymouth, Vt.

Died—Mar. 14, 1885, Plymouth, Vt.

Age at death—39 years

Second wife of father—Caroline A. Brown Coolidge

Born—Jan. 22, 1857

Married—Sept. 9, 1891

Died—May 18, 1920, Plymouth, Vt.

Age at death—63 years, 116 days

BROTHERS AND SISTERS

Calvin Coolidge was the older of two children of his father's first marriage.

CHILDREN

John Coolidge, b. Sept. 7, 1906, Northampton, Mass.; m. Sept. 23, 1929, Florence Trumbull, Plainville, Conn.

Calvin Coolidge, b. Apr. 13, 1908, Northampton, Mass.; d. July 7, 1924, Washington, D.C.

MRS. CALVIN COOLIDGE

Name—Grace Anna Goodhue Coolidge

Date of birth—Jan. 3, 1879

Birthplace—Burlington, Vt.

Age at marriage—26 years, 274 days

Children—2 sons

Mother—Lemira Barnett Goodhue

Father—Andrew Issachar Goodhue

Date of death—July 8, 1957

Age at death—78 years, 186 days

Place of death—Northampton, Mass.

Burial place—Plymouth, Vt.

Years younger than the President—6 years, 183 days

Years she survived the President—24 years, 184 days

THE ELECTION OF 1924

NOMINATIONS FOR TERM 1925-1929

Republican Party Convention (18th)

June 10-12, 1924, Municipal Auditorium, Cleveland, Ohio
Nominated for President—Calvin Coolidge, Mass.
Nominated for Vice President—Charles Gates Dawes, Ill.

Coolidge was nominated on the first ballot.

Total number of votes: 1109
Nomination made unanimous

Democratic Party Convention (24th)

June 24-28, 30, July 1-5, 7-9, 1924, Madison Square Garden, New York, N.Y.
Nominated for President—John William Davis, W.Va.
Nominated for Vice President—Charles Wayland Bryan, Neb.

Davis was nominated on the one hundred and third ballot.

Total number of votes: first ballot, 1096; one hundred and third ballot, 1090
Number necessary for nomination: 731

This was the longest nominating convention of a major political party. Sixty candidates were nominated for the presidency.

ELECTION RESULTS, NOV. 4, 1924—PRESIDENTIAL AND VICE PRESIDENTIAL CANDIDATES

Republican Party (15,725,016 votes)

Calvin Coolidge, Mass.
Charles Gates Dawes, Ill.

Democratic Party (8,386,503 votes)

John William Davis, W.Va.
Charles Wayland Bryan, Neb.

Progressive Party (4,822,856 votes)

Robert Marion La Follette, Wis.
Burton Kendall Wheeler, Mont.

Prohibition Party (57,520 votes)

Herman Preston Faris, Mo.
Marie Caroline Brehm, Calif.

Socialist Labor Party (36,428 votes)

Frank T. Johns, Ore.
Verne L. Reynolds, N.Y.

Communist Party (Workers Party) (36,386 votes)

William Zebulon Foster, Ill.
Benjamin Gitlow, N.Y.

American Party (23,967 votes)

Gilbert Owen Nations, D.C.
Charles Hiram Randall, Calif.

Commonwealth Land Party
(1,582 votes)

William J. Wallace, N.J.
John Cromwell Lincoln, Ohio

ELECTORAL VOTES (531 —48 states)

Coolidge received 71.94 per cent (382 votes—35 states) as follows: Ariz. 3; Calif. 13; Colo. 6; Conn. 7; Del. 3; Idaho 4; Ill. 29; Ind. 15; Iowa 13; Kan. 10; Ky. 13; Me. 6; Md. 8; Mass. 18; Mich. 15; Minn. 12; Mo. 18; Mont. 4; Neb. 8; Nev. 3; N.H. 4; N.J. 14; N.M. 3; N.Y. 45; N.D. 5; Ohio 24; Ore. 5; Pa. 38; R.I. 5; S.D. 5; Utah 4; Vt. 4; Wash. 7; W.Va. 8; Wyo. 3.

Davis received 25.61 per cent (136 votes—12 states) as follows: Ala. 12; Ark. 9; Fla. 6; Ga. 14; La. 10; Miss. 10; N.C. 12; Okla. 10; S.C. 9; Tenn. 12; Tex. 20; Va. 12.

La Follette received 2.45 per cent (1 state): Wis. 13.

APPOINTMENT TO THE SUPREME COURT

Associate Justice
Harlan Fiske Stone, N.Y., Feb. 5, 1925

ADMINISTRATION— IMPORTANT DATES

1923-1924, Teapot Dome oil scandal of Harding administration revealed in Senate investigations

May 15, 1924, soldier bonus bill vetoed, later passed over veto by both houses of Congress

May 26, 1924, immigration bill signed reducing quotas established in 1921

June 2, 1924, citizenship granted to non-citizen American Indians born in the United States

July 1, 1924, transcontinental airmail regular service established

July 1, 1924, U.S. Foreign Service created

Dec. 17, 1924, diesel electric locomotive placed in service

Jan. 5, 1925, first woman governor, Nellie Tayloe Ross, took office in Wyoming

Mar. 23, 1925, Tennessee enacted law making it unlawful to teach theory of evolution

Mar. 16, 1926, liquid fuel rocket flown

Apr. 6, 1926, Tacna-Arica Conference between Chile and Peru held at Washington, D.C.

May 9, 1926, Richard E. Byrd and Floyd Bennett made first flight over North Pole

May 31, 1926, Sesquicentennial Exposition opened, Philadelphia, Pa.

June 14, 1926, Board of Mediation appointed to succeed Railroad Labor Board

July 2, 1926, Distinguished Flying Cross authorized

Feb. 23, 1927, U.S. Radio Commission created

May 20, 1927, Lindbergh's transatlantic solo flight

Jan. 15, 1929, Kellogg-Briand peace pact ratified by U.S. Senate

IMPORTANT DATES IN HIS LIFE

1895, graduated from Amherst College

July 2, 1897, admitted to the bar; practiced in Northampton, Mass.

1899, member of City Council, Northampton, Mass.

1900-1901, city solicitor, Northampton, Mass.

June 1903-Jan. 1, 1904, clerk of the courts, Hampshire County, Northampton, Mass.

1907-1908, Massachusetts House of Representatives

1909, resumed law practice, Northampton, Mass.

1910-1911, mayor, Northampton, Mass.

1912-1915, Massachusetts Senate

1914-1915, president of Massachusetts Senate

1916-1918, lieutenant governor of Massachusetts

1919-1920, governor of Massachusetts

1919, settled Boston police strike

Mar. 4, 1921, inaugurated Vice President

Aug. 3, 1923, succeeded to the presidency on the death of President Harding

Nov. 1924, nominated for another term as President on the Republican ticket

Mar. 4, 1925-Mar. 3, 1929, President (second term)

1928, declined to be a candidate for renomination

19——, chairman of Nonpartisan Railroad Commission

19——, honorary president, Foundation for the Blind

1929, published his *Autobiography*

1930, conducted syndicated newspaper column

CALVIN COOLIDGE

——was the second President born in Vermont.

——was the twelfth President elected from a state other than his native state.

——was the fifth President whose father was alive when he was inaugurated.

——was the first President sworn in by his father.

——was the first President whose inaugural ceremonies were broadcast.

——was the first President sworn in by a former President.

COOLIDGE'S VICE PRESIDENT

Vice President—Charles Gates Dawes (30th V.P.)

Date of birth—Aug. 27, 1865

Birthplace—Marietta, Ohio

Political party—Republican

State represented—Illinois

Term of office—Mar. 4, 1925-Mar. 3, 1929

Age at inauguration—59 years, 189 days

Occupation after term—Banker

Date of death—Apr. 23, 1951

Place of death—Evanston, Ill.

Age at death—85 years, 239 days

Burial place—Chicago, Ill.

ADDITIONAL DATA ON COOLIDGE

COOLIDGE BORN ON INDEPENDENCE DAY

Calvin Coolidge was born on July 4, 1872, at Plymouth, Vt., on the ninety-sixth anniversary of the Declaration of Independence.

FIRST OATH OF OFFICE

Calvin Coolidge, who succeeded to the presidency on the death of President Harding, took the oath of office as President at the family homestead at Plymouth, Vt., at 2:47 A.M. on August 3, 1923. The oath was administered to him by his father, Colonel John Calvin Coolidge, a notary public and justice of the peace. The ceremony, which took place in the sitting room by the light of a kerosene lamp, was witnessed by Mrs. Coolidge, Senator Dale Porter Hinman, and Coolidge's stenographer and chauffeur.

The oath was repeated on Tuesday, August 21, 1923, by Calvin Coolidge in his suite at the Willard Hotel, Washington, D.C. It was administered by Justice Adolph August Hoehling of the District of Columbia Supreme Court.

PRESIDENTIAL CANDIDATES POSED FOR NEWSREELS

The first films of presidential candidates were seen by movie spectators in September 1924. On August 11, 1924, Theodore W. Case and Lee de Forest took motion pictures on the grounds of the White House of President Calvin Coolidge, Republican candidate for reelection. On the same day they photographed Senator Robert Marion La Follette, Progressive Party candidate, who posed on the steps of the Capitol. Later, movies were taken of John William Davis, Democratic presidential nominee, at Locust Valley, N.Y.

INAUGURATION IN 1925

Calvin Coolidge took the oath of office on Wednesday, March 4, 1925, on the east portico of the Capitol. The oath was administered by Chief Justice William Howard Taft. This was the first time that a former President administered the oath to a President-elect.

The forty-one minute inaugural speech was broadcast by twenty-five radio stations and heard by an audience estimated at 22,800,000.

THE PRESIDENT'S FAMILY

Mrs. Grace Goodhue Coolidge was not given to much social entertainment. During the Coolidges' residence at the White House, their son Calvin Coolidge, Jr., died. President Coolidge's father also died less than two years later, with the result that White House social functions were greatly curtailed.

LIKENESS OF COOLIDGE ON COINS

The first coin bearing the likeness of a living President was the 1926 Sesquicentennial half dollar, the obverse of which bore the heads of Presidents George Washington and Calvin Coolidge. The reverse depicted the Liberty Bell. The net coinage was 141,120 pieces struck at the mint at Philadelphia, Pa.

Herbert Hoover

HERBERT CLARK HOOVER

Born—Aug. 10, 1874

Birthplace—West Branch, Iowa

College attended—Stanford University, Stanford, Calif.

Date of graduation—May 29, 1895, four-year course, Bachelor of Arts

Religious denomination—Society of Friends (Quaker)

Ancestry—Swiss-German

Occupation—Engineer

Date and place of marriage—Feb. 10, 1899, Monterey, Calif.

Age at marriage—24 years, 184 days

Years married—44 years, 331 days

Political party—Republican

State represented—California

Term of office—Mar. 4, 1929-Mar. 3, 1933

Term served—4 years

Administration—36th

Congresses—71st, 72nd

Age at inauguration—54 years, 206 days

Occupations after term—Special reorganization commissions, writing

PARENTS

Father—Jesse Clark Hoover

Born—Sept. 2, 1846, West Milton, Ohio

Married—Mar. 12, 1870

Occupation—Blacksmith, farm implement business

Died—Dec. 10, 1880, West Branch, Iowa

Age at death—34 years, 99 days

Mother—Hulda Randall Minthorn Hoover

For additional data see the end of this section and also specific subject headings in the Index.

Born—May 4, 1848, Burgersville, Ontario, Canada

Died—Feb. 24, 1883, West Branch, Iowa

Age at death—34 years, 296 days

BROTHERS AND SISTERS

Herbert Clark Hoover was the second child in a family of three.

CHILDREN

Herbert Clark Hoover, b. Aug. 4, 1903, London, England; m. June 25, 1925, Margaret E. Watson, Palo Alto, Calif.

Allan Henry Hoover, b. July 17, 1907, London, England; m. Mar. 17, 1937, Margaret Coberly, Los Angeles, Calif.

MRS. HERBERT CLARK HOOVER

Name—Lou Henry Hoover

Date of birth—Mar. 29, 1875

Birthplace—Waterloo, Iowa

Age at marriage—23 years, 318 days

Children—2 sons

Mother—Florence Weed Henry

Father—Charles Delano Henry

His occupation—Banker

Date of death—Jan. 7, 1944

Age at death—68 years, 284 days

Place of death—New York, N.Y.

Burial place—Palo Alto, Calif.

Years younger than the President—231 days

THE ELECTION OF 1928

NOMINATIONS FOR TERM 1929-1933

Republican Party Convention (19th)

June 12-15, 1928, Civic Auditorium, Kansas City, Mo.
Nominated for President—Herbert Clark Hoover, Calif.
Nominated for Vice President—Charles Curtis, Kan.

Hoover was nominated on the first ballot.

Total number of votes: 1,089
Nomination made unanimous

Democratic Party Convention (25th)

June 26-29, 1928, Sam Houston Hall, Houston, Texas
Nominated for President—Alfred Emanuel Smith, N.Y.
Nominated for Vice President—Joseph Taylor Robinson, Ark.

Smith was nominated on the first ballot.

Total number of votes: 1,097½
Number necessary for nomination: 733
Nomination made unanimous

ELECTION RESULTS, NOV. 6, 1928—PRESIDENTIAL AND VICE PRESIDENTIAL CANDIDATES

Republican Party (21,391,381 votes)

Herbert Clark Hoover, Calif.
Charles Curtis, Kan.

Democratic Party (15,016,443 votes)

Alfred Emanuel Smith, N.Y.
Joseph Taylor Robinson, Ark.

Socialist Party (267,895 votes)

Norman Thomas, N.Y.
James Hudson Maurer, Pa.

Communist Party (Workers Party) (21,181 votes)

William Zebulon Foster, Ill.
Benjamin Gitlow, N.Y.

Socialist Labor Party (21,608 votes)

Verne L. Reynolds, N.Y.
Jeremiah D. Crowley, N.Y.

Prohibition Party (20,106 votes)

William Frederick Varney, N.Y.
James Arthur Edgerton, Va.

Farmer Labor Party (6,390 votes)

Frank Elbridge Webb, Calif.
Will Vereen, Ga.

ELECTORAL VOTES (531 —48 states)

Hoover received 83.62 per cent (444 votes—40 states) as follows: Ariz. 3; Calif. 13; Colo. 6; Conn. 7; Del. 3; Fla. 6; Idaho 4; Ill. 29; Ind. 15; Iowa 13; Kan. 10; Ky. 13; Me. 6; Md. 8; Mich. 15; Minn. 12; Mo. 18; Mont. 4; Neb. 8; Nev. 3; N.H. 4; N.J. 14; N.M. 3; N.Y. 45; N.C. 12; N.D. 5; Ohio 24; Okla. 10; Ore. 5; Pa. 38; S.D. 5; Tenn. 12; Tex. 20; Utah 4; Vt. 4; Va. 12; Wash. 7; W.Va. 8; Wis. 13; Wyo. 3.

Smith received 16.38 per cent (87 votes—8 states) as follows: Ala. 12; Ark. 9; Ga. 14; La. 10; Mass. 18; Miss. 10; R.I. 5; S.C. 9.

APPOINTMENTS TO THE SUPREME COURT

Chief Justice

Charles Evans Hughes, N.Y., Feb. 13, 1930

Associate Justices

Owen Josephus Roberts, Pa., May 20, 1930
Benjamin Nathan Cardozo, N.Y., Mar. 2, 1932

ADMINISTRATION— IMPORTANT DATES

Mar. 16, 1929, Indiana taxed chain stores

May 16, 1929, first Motion Picture Academy "Oscars" awarded

June 15, 1929, Agricultural Marketing Act established Farm Board to encourage cooperatives and dispose of surpluses

July 10, 1929, new small-size dollar bills issued

Oct. 25, 1929, former cabinet member A. B. Fall convicted

Oct. 29, 1929, stock market panic preceding depression

Nov. 19-27, 1929, White House conference on depression

Nov. 28, 1929, Richard Byrd made South Pole flight

Feb. 10, 1930, Grain Stabilization Corporation authorized

Mar. 26, 1930, Inter-American highway appropriation bill enacted

July 1, 1930, streamlined submarine *Nautilus* commissioned

July 21, 1930, Veterans Administration created

Feb. 14, 1931, Airmail Flyers' Medal of Honor authorized

Mar. 3, 1931, "Star-Spangled Banner" adopted as national anthem

June 1931, Hoover moratorium on German debts arranged

July 1, 1931, Harold Gatty and Wiley Post completed airplane flight around the world

Sept. 26, 1931, keel laid for the *Ranger,* first aircraft carrier

Dec. 15, 1931, Maria Norton of New Jersey appointed chairman of House committee (first woman to head congressional committee)

Jan. 12, 1932, Hattie Caraway of Arkansas elected senator (first woman to hold Senate office by election rather than appointment)

Jan. 22, 1932, Reconstruction Finance Corporation created

May 21, 1932, Amelia Earhart Putnam completed first transatlantic solo flight by a woman

July 1932, bonus army march on Washington, D.C., by unemployed veterans

Feb. 6, 1933, Twentieth ("Lame Duck") Amendment to the Constitution ratified

IMPORTANT DATES IN HIS LIFE

1884, moved to Newberg, Ore.

1891, enrolled at Leland Stanford University

1895, graduated from Leland Stanford University

1895-1913, mining engineer, consultant in North America,

Europe, Asia, Africa, and Australia

1899, went to China with his bride

1900, took part in defense of Tientsin in Boxer outbreak

1914-1915, chairman of American Relief Committee in London

1915-1918, chairman of Commission for Relief in Belgium

Aug. 1917-June 1919, U.S. food administrator

1919, chairman of Supreme Economic Conference, Paris

1920, chairman of European Relief Council

1921-1928, secretary of commerce under Presidents Harding and Coolidge

June 14, 1928, nominated for the presidency by the Republican convention at Kansas City, Mo.

Mar. 4, 1929-Mar. 3, 1933, President

Nov. 8, 1932, defeated for reelection by Democratic candidate, Franklin Delano Roosevelt

1946, appointed coordinator of European food program by President Truman

1947-1949, 1953-1955, chairman of Commission on Organization of the Executive Branch of the Government (Hoover Commission on administrative reform)

HERBERT CLARK HOOVER

——was the first President born in Iowa.

——was the thirteenth President elected from a state other than his native state.

——was the first President to have served in a cabinet other than as secretary of state or war.

——was the last President whose term of office ended on March 3.

HOOVER'S VICE PRESIDENT

Vice President—Charles Curtis (31st V.P.)

Date of birth—Jan. 25, 1860

Birthplace—Topeka, Kan.

Political party—Republican

State represented—Kansas

Term of office—Mar. 4, 1929-Mar. 3, 1933

Age at inauguration—69 years, 38 days

Occupation after term—Lawyer

Date of death—Feb. 8, 1936

Place of death—Washington, D.C.

Age at death—76 years, 14 days

Burial place—Topeka, Kan.

ADDITIONAL DATA ON HOOVER

FIRST PRESIDENT BORN WEST OF THE MISSISSIPPI

Herbert Clark Hoover, born August 10, 1874, at West Branch, Iowa, was the first President born west of the Mississippi River. His wife, Lou Henry Hoover, born March 29, 1875, at Waterloo, Iowa, was the first President's wife born west of the Mississippi.

ASTEROID NAMED FOR HOOVER

The first asteroid named for an American President was Hooveria. It was discovered in March 1920 by Professor Johann Palisan of the University of Vienna, Austria, and named for Herbert Hoover. At that time, Hoover was not yet President; he was engaged in providing food for the distressed European peoples.

NOTIFICATION OF NOMINATION TELEVISED

Presidential nomination notification ceremonies were televised for the first time on Wednesday, August 22, 1928, at the Assembly Chamber, Albany, N.Y., when Democratic candidate Alfred Emanuel Smith was notified of his nomination. The pictures were transmitted by television to Schenectady, N.Y., and sent out by short wave over 2XAF and 2XAD by the General Electric Company.

INAUGURATION

Herbert Clark Hoover took his oath of office on Monday, March 4, 1929, on the east portico of the Capitol. A crowd of about fifty thousand witnessed the ceremony.

At 1:08 P.M. Chief Justice William Howard Taft administered the oath of office. Twenty years before, on March 4, 1909, the same oath had been administered to Taft by Chief Justice Edward Douglass White.

The *Los Angeles* and four other blimps and thirty airplanes flew over the city. Rain fell in the afternoon. At 8 P.M. a fireworks display thrilled the crowds. At 9 P.M. the largest inaugural ball up to that time was held at the Washington Auditorium. The ball was opened by an Indian orchestra from Tulsa, Okla. The reigning woman at the ball was Mrs. Gann, sister of Vice President Curtis.

HUGHES REAPPOINTED TO SUPREME COURT

President Hoover established a precedent when he appointed as chief justice of the United States Charles Evans Hughes, who served February 13, 1930, to July 1, 1941. This was Hughes' second appointment to the Court, a distinction accorded no other person. He was appointed an associate justice of the Supreme Court by President Taft, serving from May 2, 1910, to June 10, 1916 when he resigned. He became the Republican nominee for President in 1916 and was defeated by Woodrow Wilson. Afterward he served as secretary of state (1921-1925), a member of The Hague Tribunal (1926-1930), and a judge on the Permanent Court of International Justice (1928-1930).

ABSOLUTE MONARCH VISITED HOOVER

The first absolute monarch to visit the United States was King Prajadhipok of Siam. He arrived in New York City April 1931, accompanied by his wife, Queen Rambai Barni, and the royal entourage. President Hoover received them on April 29, 1931. They crossed into the United States on April 19, 1931, at Portal, N.D., from Canada. This was not, however, the King's first visit to the United States. As a prince he had arrived at New York City from England on September 22, 1924, for a short visit.

THE FIRST LADY

Lou Henry Hoover lived in Washington while Herbert Hoover was secretary of commerce under Presidents Harding and Coolidge from 1921 to 1928. She had numerous personal friends in the city when they moved into the White House, and as a result social functions were more friendly than formal.

HOOVER HONORED

President Hoover has been one of the most honored Presidents in our history. He has received over fifty honorary degrees from American universities, over twenty-five honorary degrees from foreign universities, the freedom of more than a dozen cities, and over seventy medals and awards, in addition to about a hundred miscellaneous honors.

On January 13, 1958, General Mark Wayne Clark, president of the Citadel, South Carolina State Military College, bestowed the honorary degree of doctor of laws on the former President at the Citadel. It was the eighty-third degree that he had received, one for each year of his life. He was honored as "engineer, humanitarian and statesman."

On April 25, 1958, the University of the State of New York, at the 89th convocation of the Board of Regents, awarded him an honorary degree, which he received in absentia as he was recovering from a gall-bladder operation.

FRANKLIN DELANO ROOSEVELT

FRANKLIN DELANO ROOSEVELT

Born—Jan. 30, 1882

Birthplace—Hyde Park, N.Y.

College attended—Harvard College, Cambridge, Mass.

Date of graduation—June 24, 1903, four-year course, Bachelor of Arts

Religion—Episcopalian

Ancestry—Dutch

Occupation—Governor, lawyer

Date and place of marriage—Mar. 17, 1905, New York, N.Y.

Age at marriage—23 years, 46 days

Years married—40 years, 26 days

Political party—Democratic

State represented—New York

Term of office—Mar. 4, 1933-Apr. 12, 1945

Term served—12 years, 39 days

Administration—37th, 38th, 39th, 40th

Congresses—73rd, 74th, 75th, 76th, 77th 78th, 79th

Age at inauguration—51 years, 33 days

Lived after term—Died in office

Date of death—Apr. 12, 1945

Age at death—63 years, 72 days

Place of death—Warm Springs, Ga.

Burial place—Family plot, Hyde Park, N.Y.

PARENTS

Father—James Roosevelt

Born—July 16, 1828, Hyde Park, N.Y.

For additional data see the end of this section and also specific subject headings in the Index.

Married (1)—Rebecca Brien Howland

Married (2)—Sara Delano

Occupation—Vice president of Delaware and Hudson Railroad, lawyer, financier

Died—Dec. 8, 1900, New York, N.Y.

Age at death—72 years, 145 days

First wife of father—Rebecca Brien Howland Roosevelt

Born—Jan. 15, 1831

Married—1853

Died—Aug. 21, 1876

Age at death—45 years, 218 days

Mother—Sara Delano Roosevelt

Born—Sept. 21, 1854, Newburgh, N.Y.

Married—Oct. 7, 1880, Hyde Park, N.Y.

Died—Sept. 7, 1941, Hyde Park, N.Y.

Age at death—86 years, 351 days

BROTHER

Franklin Delano Roosevelt was a second son, the only child of his father's second marriage.

CHILDREN

Anna Eleanor Roosevelt, b. May 3, 1906, New York, N.Y.; m. June 5, 1926, Curtis Bean Dall, Hyde Park, N.Y.; m. Jan. 18, 1935, John Boettiger, New York, N.Y.; m. Nov. 11, 1952, James Addison Halsted, Malibu, Calif.

James Roosevelt, b. Dec. 23, 1907, New York, N.Y.; m. June 4, 1930, Betsy Cushing, Brookline, Mass.; m. Apr. 14, 1941, Romelle Theresa Schneider, Beverly Hills, Calif.; m. July 1, 1956, Gladys Irene Owens, Los Angeles, Calif.

Franklin Roosevelt, b. 1908, d. 1909

Elliott Roosevelt, b. Sept. 23, 1910, New York, N.Y.; m. Jan. 16, 1932, Elizabeth Browning Donner, Bryn Mawr, Pa.; m. July 22, 1933, Ruth Josephine Googins, Burlington, Iowa; m. Dec. 3, 1944, Faye Emerson, Grand Canyon, Ariz.; m. Mar. 15, 1951, Minnewa Bell Ross, Miami Beach, Fla.

Franklin Delano Roosevelt, b. Aug. 17, 1914, Campobello, New Brunswick, Canada; m. June 30, 1937, Ethel Du Pont, Wilmington, Del.; m. Aug. 31, 1949, Suzanne Perrin, New York, N.Y.

John Aspinwall Roosevelt, b. Mar. 2, 1916; m. June 18, 1938, Anne Lindsay Clark, Nahant, Mass.

MRS. FRANKLIN DELANO ROOSEVELT

Name—Anna Eleanor Roosevelt

Date of birth—Oct. 11, 1884

Birthplace—New York, N.Y.

Age at marriage—20 years, 157 days

Children—5 sons, 1 daughter

Mother—Anna Livingston Hall Roosevelt

Father—Elliott Roosevelt

Years younger than the President—2 years, 254 days

THE ELECTION OF 1932

NOMINATIONS FOR TERM 1933-1937

Democratic Party Convention (26th)

June 27-29, 1932, Chicago Stadium, Chicago, Ill.
Nominated for President—Franklin Delano Roosevelt, N.Y.
Nominated for Vice President—John Nance Garner, Tex.

Roosevelt was nominated on the fourth ballot.

Total number of votes: first ballot, 1,154; fourth ballot, 1,148½
Number necessary for nomination: 766

Republican Party Convention (20th)

June 14-16, 1932, Chicago Stadium, Chicago, Ill.
Nominated for President—Herbert Clark Hoover, Calif.
Nominated for Vice President—Charles Curtis, Kan.

Hoover was nominated on the first ballot.

Total number of votes: 1,150
Nomination made unanimous

ELECTION RESULTS, NOV. 8, 1932—PRESIDENTIAL AND VICE PRESIDENTIAL CANDIDATES

Democratic Party (22,821,857 votes)

Franklin Delano Roosevelt, N.Y.
John Nance Garner, Tex

Republican Party (15,761,845 votes)

Herbert Clark Hoover, Calif.
Charles Curtis, Kan.

Socialist Party (881,951 votes)

Norman Thomas, N.Y.
James Hudson Maurer, Pa.

Communist Party (102,785 votes)

William Zebulon Foster, Ill.
James William Ford, N.Y.

Prohibition Party (81,869 votes)

William David Upshaw, Ga.
Frank Stewart Regan, Ill.

Liberty Party (53,425 votes)

William Hope Harvey, Ark.
Frank B. Hemenway, Wash.

Socialist Labor Party (33,276 votes)

Verne L. Reynolds, N.Y.
John W. Aiken, Mass.

Farmer Labor Party (7,309 votes)

Jacob Sechler Coxey, Ohio
Julius J. Reiter, Minn.

ELECTORAL VOTES (531 —48 states)

Roosevelt received 88.89 per cent (472 votes—42 states) as follows: Ala. 11; Ariz. 3; Ark. 9; Cal. 22; Colo. 6; Fla. 7; Ga. 12; Idaho 4; Ill. 29; Ind. 14; Iowa 11; Kan. 9; Ky. 11; La. 10; Md. 8; Mass. 17; Mich. 19; Minn. 11; Miss. 9; Mo. 15; Mont. 4; Neb. 7; Nev. 3; N.J. 16; N.M. 3; N.Y. 47; N.C. 13; N.D. 4; Ohio 26; Okla. 11; Ore. 5; R.I. 4; S.C. 8; S.D. 4; Tenn. 11; Tex. 23; Utah 4; Va. 11;

Wash 8; W.Va. 8; Wis. 12; Wyo. 3.

Hoover received 11.11 per cent (59 votes—6 states) as follows: Conn. 8; Del. 3; Me. 5; N.H. 4; Pa. 36; Vt. 3.

THE ELECTION OF 1936

NOMINATIONS FOR TERM 1937-1941

Democratic Party Convention (27th)

June 23-27, 1936, Convention Hall, Philadelphia, Pa.
Nominated for President—Franklin Delano Roosevelt, N.Y.
Nominated for Vice President—John Nance Garner, Tex.

Franklin Delano Roosevelt was renominated by acclamation and no vote was taken.

Republican Party Convention (21st)

June 9-12, 1936, Municipal Auditorium, Cleveland, Ohio
Nominated for President—Alfred Mossman Landon, Kan.
Nominated for Vice President—Frank Knox, Ill.

Landon was nominated on the first ballot.

Total number of votes: **1,003**
Number necessary for nomination: **502**

ELECTION RESULTS, NOV. 3, 1936—PRESIDENTIAL AND VICE PRESIDENTIAL CANDIDATES

Democratic Party (24,751,597 votes)

Franklin Delano Roosevelt, N.Y.
John Nance Garner, Tex.

Republican Party (16,679,853 votes)

Alfred Mossman Landon, Kan.
Frank Knox, Ill.

Union Party (892,793 votes)

William Lemke, N.D.
Thomas Charles O'Brien, Mass.

Socialist Party (187,720 votes)

Norman Thomas, N.Y.
George A. Nelson, Wis.

Communist Party (80,159 votes)

Earl Russell Browder, Kan.
James William Ford, N.Y.

Prohibition Party (37,847 votes)

David Leigh Colvin, N.Y.
Claude A. Watson, Calif.

Socialist Labor Party (12,777 votes)

John W. Aiken, Mass.
Emil F. Teichert, N.Y.

ELECTORAL VOTES (531 —48 states)

Roosevelt received 98.49 per cent (523 votes—46 states—all states except Maine and Vermont).

Landon received 1.51 per cent (8 votes—2 states) as follows: Me. 5; Vt. 3.

THE ELECTION OF 1940

NOMINATIONS FOR TERM 1941-1945

Democratic Party Convention (28th)

July 15-18, 1940, Chicago Stadium, Chicago, Ill.
Nominated for President— Franklin Delano Roosevelt, N.Y.
Nominated for Vice President— Henry Agard Wallace, Iowa

Roosevelt was nominated on the first ballot.

Number necessary for nomination: 551
Roosevelt nominated by acclamation

Republican Party Convention (22nd)

June 24-28, 1940, Convention Hall, Philadelphia, Pa.

Nominated for President—
Wendell Lewis Willkie, Ind.
Nominated for Vice President—
Charles Linza McNary, Ore.

Willkie was nominated unanimously on the sixth ballot.

Total number of votes: first ballot, 1,000; sixth ballot, 998
Number necessary for nomination: 501

ELECTION RESULTS, NOV. 5, 1940—PRESIDENTIAL AND VICE PRESIDENTIAL CANDIDATES AND OTHER PARTY VOTES

Democratic Party (27,243,466 votes)

Franklin Delano Roosevelt, N.Y.
Henry Agard Wallace, Iowa

Republican Party (22,304,755 votes)

Wendell Lewis Willkie, Ind.
Charles Linza McNary, Ore.

Socialist Party (99,557 votes)

Norman Thomas, N.Y.
Maynard C. Krueger, Ill.

Prohibition Party (57,812 votes)

Roger Ward Babson, Mass.
Edgar V. Moorman, Ill.

Communist Party (Workers' Party) (46,251 votes)

Earl Russell Browder, Kan.
James William Ford, N.Y.

Socialist Labor Party (9,458 votes)

John W. Aiken, Mass.
Aaron M. Orange, N.Y.

Other Parties

Georgia, Independent Democrats, 22,428
California, Progressives, 16,506
Mississippi, Independent Republicans, 4,550
Minnesota, Industrial, 2,553
Pennsylvania, Independent Government, 1,518
Maryland, Labor Party of Maryland, 657
Miscellaneous, 5,701

ELECTORAL VOTES (531 —48 states)

Roosevelt received 84.56 per cent (449 votes—38 states) as follows: Ala. 11; Ariz. 3; Ark. 9; Calif. 22; Conn. 8; Del. 3; Fla. 7; Ga. 12; Idaho 4; Ill. 29; Ky. 11; La. 10; Md. 8; Mass. 17; Minn. 11; Miss. 9; Mo. 15; Mont. 4; Nev. 3; N.H. 4; N.J. 16; N.M. 3; N.Y. 47; N.C. 13; Ohio 26; Okla. 11; Ore. 5; Pa. 36; R.I. 4; S.C. 8; Tenn. 11; Tex. 23; Utah 4; Va. 11; Wash. 8; W.Va. 8; Wis. 12; Wyo. 3.

Willkie received 15.44 per cent (82 votes—10 states) as follows: Colo. 6; Ind. 14; Iowa 11; Kan. 9; Me. 5; Mich. 19; Neb. 7; N.D. 4; S.D. 4; Vt. 3.

THE ELECTION OF 1944

NOMINATIONS FOR TERM 1945-1949

Democratic Party Convention (29th)

July 19-21, 1944, Chicago Stadium, Chicago, Ill.

Nominated for President— Franklin Delano Roosevelt, N.Y.

Nominated for Vice President— Harry S Truman, Mo.

Roosevelt was nominated on the first ballot.

Total number of votes: 1,176
Number necessary for nomination: 589

Republican Party Convention (23rd)

June 26-28, 1944, Chicago Stadium, Chicago, Ill.

Nominated for President— Thomas Edmund Dewey, N.Y.

Nominated for Vice President— John William Bricker, Ohio

Dewey was nominated on the first ballot.

Total number of votes: 1,057
Number necessary for nomination: 529

ELECTION RESULTS, NOV. 7, 1944—PRESIDENTIAL AND VICE PRESIDENTIAL CANDIDATES AND OTHER PARTY VOTES

Democratic Party (25,602,505 votes)

Franklin Delano Roosevelt, N.Y.
Harry S Truman, Mo.

Republican Party (22,006,278 votes)

Thomas Edmund Dewey, N.Y.
John William Bricker, Ohio

Socialist Party (80,518 votes)

Norman Thomas, N.Y.
Darlington Hoopes, Pa.

Prohibition Party (74,758 votes)

Claude A. Watson, Calif.
Andrew Johnson, Ky.

Socialist Labor Party (45,336 votes)

Edward A. Teichert, Pa.
Arla A. Albaugh, Ohio

Other Parties

Texas, Texas Regulars, 135,439
Massachusetts, blanks, 49,328
Mississippi, Regular Democrats, 9,964
Mississippi, Independent Republicans, 7,859

South Carolina, Southern Democrats, 7,799

Georgia, Independent Democrats, 3,373

Miscellaneous, 2,527

ELECTORAL VOTES (531 —48 states)

Roosevelt received 81.36 per cent (432 votes—36 states) as follows: Ala. 11; Ariz. 4; Ark. 9; Calif. 25; Conn. 8; Del. 3; Fla. 8; Ga. 12; Idaho 4; Ill. 28; Ky. 11; La. 10; Md. 8; Mass. 16; Mich. 19; Minn. 11; Miss. 9; Mo. 15; Mont. 4; Nev. 3; N.H. 4; N.J. 16; N.M. 4; N.Y. 47; N.C. 14; Okla. 10; Ore. 6; Pa. 35; R.I. 4; S.C. 8; Tenn. 12; Tex. 23; Utah 4; Va. 11; Wash. 8; W.Va. 8.

Dewey received 18.64 per cent (99 votes—12 states) as follows: Colo. 6; Ind. 13; Iowa 10; Kan. 8; Me. 5; Neb. 6; N. D. 4; Ohio 25; S.D. 4; Vt. 3; Wis. 12; Wyo. 3.

APPOINTMENTS TO THE SUPREME COURT

Chief Justice

Harlan Fiske Stone, N.Y., July 3, 1941

Associate Justices

Hugo LaFayette Black, Ala., Oct. 4, 1937

Stanley Forman Reed, Ky., Jan. 27, 1938

Felix Frankfurter, Mass., Jan. 20, 1939

William Orville Douglas, Conn., Apr. 15, 1939

Frank Murphy, Mich., Jan. 18, 1940

James Francis Byrnes, S.C., July 8, 1941

Robert Houghwout Jackson, N.Y., July 11, 1941

William Blount Rutledge, Iowa, Feb. 15, 1943

ADMINISTRATION— IMPORTANT DATES

Mar. 4, 1933, Good Neighbor policy in Latin American relations announced

Mar. 5-13, 1933, bank holiday

Mar. 9-June 16, 1933, "Hundred Days" congressional session in which New Deal recovery measures were enacted

Mar. 31, 1933, Civilian Conservation Corps created

May 12, 1933, Agricultural Adjustment Act passed

May 12, 1933, Federal Emergency Relief Act approved

May 18, 1933, Tennessee Valley Authority established

May 27, 1933, opening of Century of Progress Exposition, Chicago

June 5, 1933, gold repeal joint resolution canceled clauses in debts, taking United States completely off gold standard

June 13, 1933, Home Owners Loan Corporation created

June 16, 1933, Federal Deposit Insurance Corporation created

June 16, 1933, Farm Credit Administration authorized

June 16, 1933, National Recovery Administration and Public Works Administration created by National Industrial Recovery Act

July 1933, Wiley Post made solo world flight

Nov. 16, 1933, United States recognized U.S.S.R.

Dec. 5, 1933, Twenty-first Amendment to the Constitution ratified (repeal of Prohibition)

Jan. 30, 1934, Gold Reserve Act devalued the dollar

Mar. 24, 1934, Philippine Independence Act, providing for independence in 1946

May 31, 1934, Platt Amendment repealed with ratification of Cuban treaty

June 6, 1934, Securities and Exchange Commission authorized

June 12, 1934, Reciprocal Tariff Act passed

June 19, 1934, Federal Communications Commission created

June 27, 1934, Railway Pension Act passed

June 28, 1934, Federal Housing Administration authorized

Apr. 8, 1935, Works Progress Administration established

May 27, 1935, National Industrial Recovery Act declared unconstitutional

July 5, 1935, Wagner Labor Relations Act passed

Aug. 1935, Neutrality Act passed

Aug. 14, 1935, Social Security Act passed

Aug. 26, 1935, Federal Power Commission established under Public Utility Holding Act

Jan. 6, 1936, Agricultural Adjustment Act declared unconstitutional

Feb. 29, 1936, Soil Conservation and Domestic Allotment Act passed

June 26, 1936, Merchant Marine Act passed, providing for Maritime Commission and ship subsidies

Dec. 1936, Inter-American Conference, Buenos Aires, Argentina

Jan.-June 1937, CIO sit-down strikes

Feb. 5, 1937, Supreme Court controversy started with Roosevelt's "court packing" recommendations

Sept. 2, 1937, Wagner-Steagall Housing Act passed

Oct.-Nov. 1937, business recession

Feb. 16, 1938, second Agricultural Adjustment Act passed

June 24, 1938, Food, Drug and Cosmetic Act passed

June 25, 1938, Fair Labor Standards Act passed

July 1938, Howard Hughes made world flight in three days, nineteen hours

Dec. 1938, Pan-American Conference on hemispheric solidarity, Lima, Peru

Feb. 18, 1939, opening of Golden Gate International Exposition, San Francisco, Calif.

Apr. 3, 1939, Administrative Reorganization Act passed

Apr. 30, 1939, opening of New York World's Fair

June 1939, visit of King George VI and Queen Elizabeth

Sept. 1, 1939, Germany invaded Poland

Sept. 3, 1939, Britain and France declared war on Germany; World War II begun

Sept. 5, 1939, United States proclaimed its neutrality in European war

May 10, 1940, Churchill became Prime Minister of England

May 28, 1940, King Leopold surrendered Belgian army

June 28, 1940, Alien Registration Act passed

Sept. 3, 1940, Roosevelt announced trade of fifty over-age destroyers to Great Britain in exchange for air bases in New World

Sept. 16, 1940, Selective Training and Service Act approved

Oct. 16, 1940, registration for selective service, ages 21 to 35

Oct. 28, 1940, Italy invaded Greece

Jan. 6, 1941, "Four Freedoms" enunciated

Mar. 11, 1941, Lend-Lease Act passed

June 22, 1941, Germany invaded Russia

July 7, 1941, Roosevelt announced occupation of Iceland by U.S. troops on invitation of Icelandic government

July 26, 1941, General MacArthur appointed commander of U.S. forces in the Philippines

July 30, 1941, United States recognized Czechoslovak government-in-exile located in London and headed by Dr. Eduard Beneš

Aug. 9, 1941, Roosevelt and Churchill held three-day conference off Newfoundland Coast

Aug. 14, 1941, Atlantic Charter —eight-point statement of principles for peace—issued jointly by United States and Great Britain

Sept. 29, 1941, three-power Moscow conference; United States and Great Britain agreed to send U.S.S.R. large supplies of war material

Dec. 7, 1941, Japan attacked Hawaii, Guam, and the Philippines

Dec. 8, 1941, United States declared war against Japan

Dec. 11, 1941, Germany and Italy declared war against the United States

Dec. 12, 1941, Guam captured (first American possession to fall into enemy hands)

Dec. 17, 1941, Rear Admiral Nimitz replaced Admiral Kimmel as commander-in-chief of U.S. Pacific fleet

Dec. 20, 1941, Admiral King designated commander-in-chief of U.S. naval forces

Dec. 22, 1941, Churchill arrived in the United States on a battleship; returned by airplane Jan. 14, 1942

Jan. 1, 1942, United Nations declaration signed by twenty-six nations at Washington, D.C., affirming principles of Atlantic Charter

Jan. 2, 1942, fall of Manila, P.I.

Jan. 26, 1942, first American Expeditionary Force landed in Ulster, Northern Ireland

Mar. 17, 1942, General MacArthur in command of Allied forces in Australia and the southwest Pacific

Apr. 9, 1942, fall of Bataan, P.I.

Apr. 18, 1942, Kobe, Nagoya, Tokyo, and Yokohama bombed by American airplanes from carrier *Hornet*

May 14, 1942, Women's Auxiliary Army Corps authorized

June 18, 1942, Churchill conferred with Roosevelt at Washington, D.C.

Oct.-Dec. 1942, Allied invasion of North Africa

Nov. 3, 1942, United States severed relations with Vichy government

Nov. 13, 1942, American naval victory at Guadalcanal

Dec. 2, 1942, self-sustained nuclear chain reaction demonstration, Chicago, Ill.

Jan. 14-24, 1943, Churchill and Roosevelt conferred in North Africa

Jan. 28, 1943, Roosevelt and President Vargas of Brazil conferred at Natal, Brazil

May-June 1943, United Nations Conference on Food and Agriculture, Hot Springs, Va., established United Nations Food and Agriculture Organization

Sept.-Dec. 1943, invasion of Italy

Nov. 9, 1943, United Nations Relief and Rehabilitation Administration established with signing of agreement by forty-four nations at Washington, D.C.

Nov. 28-Dec. 1, 1943, Churchill, Stalin, and Roosevelt conferred at Teheran, Iran

Dec. 8, 1943, American carriers raided the Marshall Islands

Mar. 4, 1944, first American bomber attacked Berlin

June 6, 1944, D-Day invasion of France by Allies

June 22, 1944, Servicemen's Readjustment Act (G.I. Bill of Rights) approved

July 1944, United Nations Monetary and Financial Conference, Bretton Woods, N.H.

Aug.-Oct. 1944, Dumbarton Oaks conference on a postwar international organization; proposals served as basis for United Nations charter

Feb. 4-11, 1945, Churchill, Stalin, and Roosevelt conferred at Yalta in the Crimea

IMPORTANT DATES IN HIS LIFE

1896-1900, student at Groton School, Groton, Mass.

1900-1904, student at Harvard

1904-1907, student at Columbia Law School

1907, admitted to the bar

1907-1910, practiced in New York City with firm of Carter, Ledyard, and Milburn

Jan. 1, 1911-Mar. 17, 1913, first public office—New York State Senate (from Dutchess County)

1913-1920, assistant secretary of the Navy

1914, unsuccessful in Democratic primaries for U.S. Senate (from New York)

July-Sept. 1918, in Europe on army inspection

Jan. 1919, in Europe in charge of demobilization

July 1920, received Democratic nomination for the vice presidency at San Francisco convention as running mate of James M. Cox

Nov. 1920, defeated for the vice presidency

1920, returned to New York law practice with firm of Emmet, Marvin and Roosevelt

1920-1928, vice president of Fidelity and Deposit Company

Aug. 1921, stricken with infantile paralysis at summer home, Campobello, New Brunswick, Canada

1924, member of law firm of Roosevelt and O'Connor

1929-1933, governor of New York

Mar. 4, 1933-Jan. 19, 1937, President (first term)

Jan. 20, 1937-Jan. 19, 1941, President (second term) (first President to take office on the new date specified by the Twentieth Amendment)

Jan. 20, 1941-Jan. 19, 1945, President (third term)

Jan. 20, 1945-Apr. 12, 1945, President (fourth term)

FRANKLIN DELANO ROOSEVELT

——was the fourth President born in New York.

——was the seventh President to die in office.

——was the eighth President whose mother was alive when he was inaugurated.

——was the first President whose mother could have voted for him for the presidency.

——was the third Democratic President since the Civil War.

——was the fourth President to die a natural death in office.

——was the first President elected for a third term (and also a fourth term).

ROOSEVELT'S VICE PRESIDENTS

FIRST AND SECOND TERMS

Vice President—John Nance Garner (32nd V.P.)

Date of birth—Nov. 22, 1868

Birthplace—Near Detroit, Red River County, Tex.

Political party—Democratic

State represented—Texas

Term of office—Mar. 4, 1933- Jan. 19, 1941

Age at inauguration—64 years, 102 days

Occupation after term—Retired, farmer

THIRD TERM

Vice President—Henry Agard Wallace (33rd V.P.)

Date of birth—Oct. 7, 1888

Birthplace—Adair County, Iowa

Political party—Democratic

State represented—Iowa

Term of office—Jan. 20, 1941- Jan. 19, 1945

Age at inauguration—52 years, 105 days

Occupation after term—Editor, plant breeder

FOURTH TERM

Vice President—Harry S Truman (34th V.P.)

For biographical information see Harry S Truman, 34th President.

ADDITIONAL DATA ON ROOSEVELT

F.D.R. RELATED TO ELEVEN FORMER PRESIDENTS

Genealogists have shown that President Franklin Delano Roosevelt was related by blood or through marriage to eleven former Presidents: Washington, John Adams, Madison, John

Quincy Adams, Van Buren, William Henry Harrison, Taylor, Grant, Benjamin Harrison, Theodore Roosevelt, and Taft.

ROOSEVELT FLEW TO ACCEPT NOMINATION AT CONVENTION

The first nominating convention at which a presidential nominee made a speech of acceptance was the Democratic convention held at Chicago, Ill., July 1932, when Governor Franklin Delano Roosevelt of New York accepted the nomination and addressed the delegates.

Roosevelt was also the first presidential candidate to fly to a political convention to make his acceptance speech. He chartered a ten-passenger tri-motor airplane for himself and his party and flew from Albany, N.Y., to Chicago on July 2.

GARNER ELECTED TO TWO OFFICES

On November 8, 1932, John Nance Garner was elected as a representative to the 73rd Congress and as Vice President under President Roosevelt. Garner had been elected as a Democrat to the 58th Congress and the fifteen succeeding Congresses and served from March

4, 1903, to March 3, 1933. He resigned from the 73rd Congress on March 3, 1933, the day before his inauguration as Vice President.

ASSASSINATION OF ROOSEVELT ATTEMPTED

An attempt on the life of President Roosevelt was made on February 15, 1933, at Miami, Fla. by Giuseppe Zangara, a bricklayer, whose shot killed Anton J. Cermak, Mayor of Chicago, Ill., who was with the President. Cermak died on March 6, 1933. Zangara's shots wounded five other persons.

FIRST INAUGURATION

Franklin Delano Roosevelt took the oath of office on Saturday, March 4, 1933, on the east portico of the Capitol. Chief Justice Charles Evans Hughes administered the oath.

A reception was held for about fifty diplomatic missions and a stand-up luncheon for about two thousand persons. The inaugural ball was held at the Washington Auditorium, Washington, D.C. Rosa Ponselle sang "The Star-Spangled Banner." The ball was attended by Mrs. Roosevelt but not by the President.

ELECTORS INVITED TO INAUGURAL

Presidential electors generally become forgotten people after they cast their ballots. The 531 electors, of whom all but 59 were Democrats, were invited by President-elect Roosevelt to attend his inaugural at Washington, D.C. on March 4, 1933. This was the first time the Electoral College was invited to witness an inaugural.

WOMAN APPOINTED TO CABINET

Roosevelt established a precedent when he appointed a woman to the presidential cabinet. He appointed Frances Perkins (Mrs. Paul Wilson) secretary of labor. She served from March 4, 1933, to June 30, 1945. Prior to the appointment Frances Perkins had been industrial commissioner for New York.

ROOSEVELT APPOINTED WOMAN MINISTER

On April 12, 1933, President Roosevelt appointed the first woman to represent the United States as a minister to a foreign country. The appointee was Ruth Bryan Owen, the eldest daughter of William Jennings Bryan, who was appointed envoy extraordinary and minister plenipotentiary to Denmark and Iceland. Her nomination was confirmed by the Senate without even the customary formality of reference to a committee.

U.S.S.R. RECOGNIZED

Recognition of the Union of Soviet Socialist Republics was effected November 16, 1933, between President Roosevelt and Maksim Maksimovich Litvinov, the Soviet People's Commissar for Foreign Affairs. The first Soviet representative to the United States was Alexander Antonovich Troyanovsky, who was accredited as Russian ambassador from January 8, 1934, to June 22, 1938. The first ambassador from the United States to the Union of Soviet Socialist Republics was William Christian Bullitt, who was appointed by President Roosevelt and who served from November 21, 1933, until August 25, 1936.

TWENTY-FIRST AMENDMENT ENACTED

The Twenty-first Amendment was the first amendment ratified by conventions in the several states. The first twenty amendments were ratified by state legislatures.

This amendment, which repealed the eighteenth, was proposed by the 72nd Congress on February 20, 1933. Ratification was completed on December 5, 1933, when the thirty-sixth state, Utah, approved the amendment. On this date the secretary of state announced that it had been adopted by the necessary number of states.

PRESIDENT ROOSEVELT RECORD TRAVELER

Franklin Delano Roosevelt established numerous precedents in the field of traveling while he was President of the United States.

He was the first President to visit South America while in office. On July 10, 1934, he stopped at Cartagena, Colombia. Prior to this visit, President Enrique Olaya Herrera of Colombia had visited President Roosevelt on board the cruiser U.S.S. *Houston*.

He was also the first President to go through the Panama Canal, passing through it on July 11, 1934, on the U.S.S. *Houston*. He was greeted at Balboa, Panama, by President Harmodio Arias and Foreign Secretary Arosemena of Panama.

Roosevelt was also the first President to visit Hawaii. He landed on July 25, 1934, at Hilo, Hawaii, where he was greeted by Governor Joseph Poindexter.

These three "firsts" took place while Roosevelt was President. Other Presidents had made similar trips either before or after their terms of office.

ROOSEVELT BROADCAST FROM A FOREIGN COUNTRY

The first President to broadcast from a foreign country was Franklin Delano Roosevelt, whose speech on July 10, 1934, from Cartagena, Colombia, South America, was relayed to New York and transmitted over the combined WEAF, WJZ, and WABC networks.

PRESIDENT AND VICE PRESIDENT OUT OF THE COUNTRY

While President Roosevelt was aboard the U.S.S. *Houston* on his vacation, Vice President John Nance Garner sailed for Japan from Seattle, Wash., on October 16, 1936, on the *President Grant*. This was the first time that both President and Vice President were simultaneously out of the country. Under the act of succession of January 19, 1886, Cordell Hull, secretary of state, acted as President. Technically, President Roosevelt was on United States soil as he was on a United States naval ship.

VETO READ TO CONGRESS

The first veto message read directly by a President was the Patman bonus bill veto, read May 22, 1935, by President Roosevelt to a joint session of Congress. The bill provided for the immediate payment to veterans of the payable 1945 face value of their adjusted service certificates. Within an hour after the veto, the House voted 322 to 98 to override it. The original vote on the measure had been 318 to 90. The following day the Senate voted 54 to 40 to override the veto. The original vote had been 55 to 33. This was short of the two-thirds vote needed to override the veto.

OFFICIAL FLAG FOR VICE PRESIDENT

The first flag for a Vice President was established February 7, 1936, by Executive Order No. 7,285, signed by President Roosevelt. The flag was designed with the seal of the United States and a blue star in each corner on a field of white. The Navy had previously created a flag for the Vice President, but its use by other governmental departments was optional.

PENSIONS TO PRIVATE WORKERS

The first pension payments by the United States Government to workers in private industry were mailed on July 13, 1936, when checks totaling $901.56 were sent to eighteen retired railroad employees, in accordance with the Railroad Retirement Act of August 29, 1935 (49 Stat.L.967), which appropriated $46,685,000 "to establish a retirement system for employees of carriers subject to the Interstate Commerce Act, and for other purposes."

WORST REPUBLICAN DEFEAT

The worst defeat in recent times was suffered in 1936 by the Republican candidate, Alfred Mossman Landon of Kansas, who carried only two states, Maine and Vermont. He received 8 electoral votes. Franklin Delano Roosevelt carried forty-six states, receiving 523 electoral votes.

In 1912, William Howard Taft received only 8 electoral votes. The other 523 electoral votes were divided between Woodrow Wilson (435 votes) and Theodore Roosevelt (88 votes).

SECOND INAUGURATION

Franklin Delano Roosevelt took his second oath of office on Wednesday, January 20, 1937. The oath was administered by Chief Justice Charles Evans Hughes. This was the first inauguration held on January 20. The day was seasonably cold. Electric pads were used to keep the President and the chief justice warm.

ROOSEVELT RODE ON DIESEL

President Roosevelt was the first President to ride on a Diesel train. On October 23, 1937, he rode on a Diesel train on the Baltimore and Ohio Railroad from Washington, D.C., to New York City. He was en route to his home at Hyde Park, N.Y.

ROOSEVELT HONORED BY POSTAGE STAMP

Although the United States Postal Laws and Regulations forbid placing the picture of a living President on postage stamps, these laws do not apply outside the United States. In 1938, Guatemala issued a souvenir sheet of four stamps to commemorate the second term of President Jorge Ubico. One of the stamps, a four-cent carmine-and-sepia stamp, bore a picture of Franklin Delano Roosevelt.

ROOSEVELT ON TELEVISION

The first President to appear on television was Franklin Delano Roosevelt, who spoke on April 30, 1939, at the opening ceremonies of the New York World's Fair from the Federal Building on the Exposition Grounds overlooking the Court of Peace. The proceedings were telecast by the National Broadcasting Company.

ROOSEVELT RECEIVED KING AND QUEEN OF ENGLAND

The first King and Queen of England to visit the United States were King George VI and Queen Elizabeth, who arrived by way of Canada, crossing the international border on the night of June 7, 1939, at the Suspension Bridge Station, Niagara Falls, N.Y. At an outdoor picnic arranged by President Roosevelt, the King and Queen were served hot dogs. They visited New York City and Washington, D.C., and recrossed the border on the morning of June 12, 1939, bound for Halifax, Nova Scotia, whence they sailed on June 15, 1939.

FIRST THIRD-TERM PRESIDENT

Franklin Delano Roosevelt was the first and only President to be elected for a third term. He received 27,243,466 of the 49,815,312 votes cast on November 5, 1940, carrying 38 of the 48 states and winning 449 of the 531 electoral votes. His opponent, Wendell Lewis Willkie, the Republican candidate, received 22,304,755 votes and 82 electoral votes.

Roosevelt was reelected for a fourth term in 1944, definitely shattering the two-term tradition of all former Presidents. The ratification of the Twenty-second Amendment in 1951, however, limited the office of President to two terms.

THIRD INAUGURATION

Franklin Delano Roosevelt took his third oath of office on Monday, January 20, 1941. The oath was administered by Chief Justice Charles Evans Hughes. A buffet luncheon was served to invited guests. Despite the cold weather, there was an impressive parade.

Mrs. Sara Delano Roosevelt, who had been the first mother of a President to witness her son's second inauguration, also witnessed the third. Because of the two-term limitation set by the Twenty-second Amendment, no other mother will have that distinction.

ROOSEVELT GODFATHER TO PRINCE GEORGE

The first President to become a godfather to a member of the English royal family was President Roosevelt. On August 4, 1942, the Duke of Kent, youngest brother of King George VI, served as proxy for President Roosevelt at the christening of his son, Michael George Charles Franklin, Prince George of Kent, who was born July 4, 1942.

ROOSEVELT BROADCAST IN FRENCH

Franklin Delano Roosevelt was the first President to broadcast in a foreign language. On November 7, 1942, he addressed the French people in their own language from Washington, D.C., at the same time that the American Army was taking part in the invasion of French territorial possessions in Africa.

ROOSEVELT LEFT THE UNITED STATES IN WARTIME

President Roosevelt was the first President to leave the confines of the United States in wartime. His itinerary on a 16,965-mile trip follows: January 9, 1943, left Washington, D.C., by train; January 10, 1943, arrived at Miami, Fla., and flew to Trinidad, B.W.I.; January 11, flew from Trinidad to Belem, Brazil; January 12-13, flew to Bathurst, Gambia; January 14, arrived at Casablanca; January 21, drove to Rabat and Port Lyautey and back to Casablanca; January 24, drove from Casablanca to Marrakech; January 25, flew from Marrakech to Bathurst; January 27, flew from Bathurst to Roberts Field, Liberia, and back to Bathurst before taking off for Brazil; January 28, arrived at Natal; January 29, flew from Natal to Trinidad; January 30, flew from Trinidad to Miami; left Miami by train and arrived at Washington, D.C., January 31, 1943.

PRESIDENTS OF NEGRO COUNTRIES VISITED THE UNITED STATES

The first president of a Negro country to visit the United States was President Edwin Barclay of Liberia, who addressed the United States Senate on May 27, 1943, the day following his arrival.

On October 14, 1943, President Elie Lescot of Haiti, former Minister to the United States, arrived for a brief visit.

ROOSEVELT PRESENTED MEDAL

On June 21, 1943, President Roosevelt presented the first Medal of Honor to a soldier who had already received a Distinguished Service Cross in World War II. It was awarded to Gerry Kisters of Bloomington, Ind., for heroism in the Sicily campaign. In May 1943 General George Catlett Marshall had awarded him the Distinguished Service Cross for bravery in Africa.

CABINET MEMBER ADDRESSED CONGRESS

Secretary of State Cordell Hull, who reported to President Roosevelt on the tripartite conference at Moscow for the maintenance of peace and security in the postwar world, established a precedent by making a further report to Congress on November 18, 1943. The two houses of Congress, being in recess, assembled to hear him. Technically, it was not a joint session.

DEMOCRATIC VICTORIES

Franklin Delano Roosevelt won four consecutive elections, as many as the Democrats had won between the time of Abraham Lincoln and Herbert Hoover.

In 1884 Grover Cleveland defeated James Gillespie Blaine.

In 1892 Grover Cleveland defeated Benjamin Harrison.

In 1912 Woodrow Wilson defeated William Howard Taft.

In 1916 Woodrow Wilson defeated Charles Evans Hughes.

FOURTH INAUGURATION

Franklin Delano Roosevelt took his fourth oath of office on Saturday, January 20, 1945. The oath was administered by Chief Justice Harlan Fiske Stone on the south portico of the White House, a location used for the third time since 1829. President Roosevelt, bareheaded and without an overcoat, delivered a six-minute address.

A light snow had fallen on the night preceding the inauguration; and on inauguration day the thermometer registered one degree above freezing. The sky was overcast and one of the smallest crowds in recent times witnessed the ceremonies. A canvas mat was spread on the lawn for the diplomats, high government officials and the press. A crowd of about 2,000 spectators gathered beyond the south fence. Roosevelt's thirteen grandchildren were present.

ENTIRE DIVISION CITED

The first presidential citation to an entire division was made on March 15, 1945, to the 101st Airborne Division, the heroes of Bastogne, by General Dwight David Eisenhower. From December 18 to 27 the men had withstood overwhelming odds.

THE FIRST LADY

Mrs. Franklin Delano Roosevelt, born Anna Eleanor Roosevelt, daughter of Elliot Roosevelt, President Theodore Roosevelt's younger brother, has always been active in civic affairs. As a young girl she worked as a volunteer in a settlement house, and after her marriage she assisted her husband in his rising political career.

During her husband's administration she established a precedent as a first lady famous in her own right, though not without subjecting herself to much controversy and criticism. Engaging actively in public life, she traveled considerably, making numerous speeches and reporting her observations in the press.

Since the death of her husband, Eleanor Roosevelt has continued to travel widely at home and abroad, to write about her experiences, and to devote herself to humanitarian interests both national and international. From 1949 to 1952 she served as a United States delegate to the United Nations General Assembly. Known almost as well in foreign countries as in her own, she has often been referred to as "the first lady of the world."

HARRY S TRUMAN

HARRY S TRUMAN

Born—May 8, 1884

Birthplace—Lamar, Mo.

College attended—None

Religion—Baptist

Ancestry — English-Scotch-Irish

Occupation—Lawyer, senator, Vice President

Date and place of marriage—June 28, 1919, Independence, Mo.

Age at marriage—35 years, 51 days

Political party—Democratic

State represented—Missouri

Term of office—Apr. 12, 1945-Jan. 20, 1953 (Truman succeeded to the presidency on the death of Franklin Delano Roosevelt.)

Term served—7 years, 283 days

Administration—40th, 41st

Congresses—79th, 80th, 81st, 82nd

Age at inauguration—60 years, 339 days

Occupation after term—Writing

PARENTS

Father—John Anderson Truman

Born—Dec. 5, 1851, Jackson County, Mo.

Married—Dec. 28, 1881, Grandview, Mo.

Occupation—Farmer, livestock dealer

Died—Nov. 3, 1914, Kansas City, Mo.

Age at death—62 years, 333 days

For additional data see the end of this section and also specific subject headings in the Index.

Mother—Martha Ellen Young Truman

Born—Nov. 25, 1852, Jackson County, Mo.

Died—July 26, 1947, Grandview, Mo.

Age at death—94 years, 243 days

BROTHERS AND SISTERS

Harry S Truman is the oldest of three children.

CHILDREN

(Mary) Margaret Truman, b. Feb. 17, 1924, Independence, Mo.; m. Apr. 21, 1956, Clifton Daniel, Independence, Mo.

MRS. HARRY S TRUMAN

Name—Bess (Elizabeth Virginia) Wallace Truman

Date of birth—Feb. 13, 1885

Birthplace—Independence, Mo.

Age at marriage—34 years, 135 days

Children—1 daughter

Mother—Madge Gates Wallace

Father—David Willock Wallace

His occupation—Farmer

Years younger than the President—281 days

THE ELECTION OF 1948

NOMINATIONS FOR TERM 1949-1953

Democratic Party Convention (30th)

July 12-14, 1948, Convention Hall, Philadelphia, Pa.

Nominated for President—Harry S Truman, Mo.

Nominated for Vice President—Alben William Barkley, Ky.

Truman was nominated on the first ballot.

Total number of votes: 1,211

Number necessary for nomination: 606

Republican Party Convention (24th)

June 21-25, 1948, Convention Hall, Philadelphia, Pa.

Nominated for President—Thomas Edmund Dewey, N.Y.

Nominated for Vice President—Earl Warren, Calif.

Dewey was nominated unanimously on the third ballot.

Total number of votes: 1,091

Number necessary for nomination: 548

ELECTION RESULTS, NOV. 2, 1948—PRESIDENTIAL AND VICE PRESIDENTIAL CANDIDATES

Democratic Party (24,105,695 votes)

Harry S Truman, Mo.

Alben William Barkley, Ky.

Republican Party (21,969,170 votes)

Thomas Edmund Dewey, N.Y.
Earl Warren, Calif.

States' Rights Democratic Party ("Dixiecrat" Party) (1,169,021 votes)

James Strom Thurmond, S.C.
Fielding Lewis Wright, Miss.

Progressive Party (1,156,103 votes)

Henry Agard Wallace, Iowa
Glen Hearst Taylor, Idaho

Socialist Party (139,009 votes)

Norman Thomas, N.Y.
Tucker P. Smith, Mich.

Prohibition Party (103,216 votes)

Claude A. Watson, Calif.
Dale Learn, Pa.

Socialist Labor Party (29,061 votes)

Edward A. Teichert, Pa.
Stephen Emery, N.Y.

Socialist Workers Party (13,-613 votes)

Farrell Dobbs, N.Y.
Grace Carlson, Minn.

ELECTORAL VOTES (531 —48 states)

Truman received 57.06 per cent (303 votes—28 states) as follows: Ariz. 4; Ark. 9; Calif. 25; Colo. 6; Fla. 8; Ga. 12; Idaho 4; Ill. 28; Iowa 10; Ky. 11; Mass. 16; Minn. 11; Mo. 15; Mont. 4; Nev. 3; N.M. 4; N.C. 14; Ohio 25; Okla. 10; R.I. 4; Tenn. 11 (of the 12 votes); Tex. 23; Utah 4; Va. 11; Wash. 8; W.Va. 8; Wis. 12; Wyo. 3.

Dewey received 35.59 per cent (189 votes—16 states) as follows: Conn. 8; Del. 3; Ind. 13; Kan. 8; Me. 5; Md. 8; Mich. 19; Neb. 6; N.H. 4; N.J. 16; N.Y. 47; N.D. 4; Ore. 6; Penn. 35; S.D. 4; Vt. 3.

Thurmond received 7.35 per cent (39 votes—4 states) as follows: Ala. 11; La. 10; Miss. 9; S.C. 8; Tenn. 1 (of the 12 votes).

APPOINTMENTS TO THE SUPREME COURT

Chief Justice

Frederick Moore Vinson, Ky., June 21, 1946

Associate Justices

Harold Hitz Burton, Ohio, Oct. 1, 1945

Thomas Campbell Clark, Tex., Aug. 24, 1949

Sherman Minton, Ind., Oct. 12, 1949

ADMINISTRATION—
IMPORTANT DATES

May 7, 1945, V-E Day—Germans unconditionally surrendered to Allied forces

June 26, 1945, United Nations charter signed at San Francisco

July 16, 1945, first atomic bomb detonated, Alamogordo, N.M.

July 17-Aug. 2, 1945, Truman attended tripartite conference near Potsdam, Germany, establishing a Council of Foreign Ministers representing the United States, France, Great Britain, China and the U.S.S.R.

July 28, 1945, United Nations charter ratified

Aug. 6, 1945, first atomic bomb dropped, killing 80,000 persons in Hiroshima, Japan

Aug. 9, 1945, atomic bomb dropped on Nagasaki, Japan

Aug. 14, 1945, Japan surrendered

Sept. 2, 1945, V-J Day—Japanese accepted surrender terms aboard U.S.S. *Missouri*

July 4, 1946, Philippine Republic established

Aug. 1, 1946, Atomic Energy Commission created

Aug. 2, 1946, Legislative Reorganization Act passed

Dec. 31, 1946, cessation of World War II hostilities proclaimed

Feb. 10, 1947, Big Four treaty signed after New York meeting of foreign ministers, Dec. 1946

Mar. 4-6, 1947, Truman three-day good-will visit to Mexico City

Apr. 12, 1947, United Nations granted United States trusteeship of Pacific Islands formerly held by Japan

May 15, 1947, Congress approved "Truman Doctrine"—aid to Greece and Turkey to combat communism

May-June 1947, Congress passed Labor-Management Relations Act (Taft-Hartley Law) and overrode presidential veto

June 10-12, 1947, Truman in Ottawa as guest of Governor General Viscount Alexander of Tunis (first state visit to Canada by any President)

June 14, 1947, peace treaties with Bulgaria, Hungary, Italy, and Rumania ratified by the Senate

July 18, 1947, Presidential Succession Act passed

July 26, 1947, National Military Establishment created, with services integrated under secretary of defense

Sept. 2-19, 1947, Truman flew to closing session of the Inter-American Defense Conference at Petrópolis, Brazil, and the signing of the hemispheric mutual defense treaty

Feb. 21-25, 1948, Truman visited Puerto Rico, the Virgin Islands, and U.S. naval base at Guantánamo, Cuba

Apr. 1, 1948, Soviets began Berlin blockade; United States and Great Britain set up airlift of food and coal to West Berlin

Apr. 2, 1948, Congress passed foreign-aid bill establishing Economic Cooperation Administration (known as European Recovery Program or Marshall Plan)

May 25, 1948, first union contract with sliding wage scale negotiated by General Motors and United Auto Workers

Jan. 19, 1949, President's salary raised to $100,000

Apr. 4, 1949, North Atlantic Treaty signed by twelve nations, Washington, D.C.

Apr. 8, 1949, United States, Great Britain, and France agreed to establish West German republic

Apr. 20, 1949, discovery of cortisone announced

Sept. 30, 1949, Berlin blockade ended

Oct. 26, 1949, minimum-wage bill raised salaries to 75 cents an hour

Jan. 31, 1950, Truman announced plans for production of hydrogen bomb

June 25, 1950, North Korean Communists crossed 38th Parallel, invading Republic of Korea; United Nations requested support for South Korea

July 1, 1950, first U.S. ground troops in Korea

July 3, 1950, U.S. troops and North Koreans in battle

July 8, 1950, General MacArthur named commander of U.S. troops in Korea

Aug. 27, 1950, Army seized railroads to prevent strike

Oct. 7, 1950, U.S. First Cavalry made first crossing of the 38th Parallel

Nov. 1, 1950, attempted assassination of Truman by two Puerto Rican nationalists

Nov. 26, 1950, Red Chinese entered Korean War; forced U.S. troops back

Dec. 8, 1950, United States banned shipments to Communist China

Dec. 16, 1950, Truman proclaimed state of national emergency

Feb. 26, 1951, Twenty-second Amendment ratified (limiting Presidents to two terms)

Apr. 2, 1951, General Eisenhower opened Supreme Headquarters Allied Powers, Europe (SHAPE) in Paris

Apr. 11, 1951, General MacArthur relieved of Far Eastern command because of failure to heed presidential directives

Sept. 1, 1951, Tripartite Security Treaty signed at San Francisco, Calif. (United States, Australia, and New Zealand)

Sept. 4, 1951, first transcontinental television broadcast

Sept. 8, 1951, Japanese peace treaty signed, San Francisco, Calif.

Oct. 19, 1951, war between United States and Germany formally ended

Dec. 31, 1951, Mutual Security Administration established to replace Economic Cooperation Administration

Mar. 30, 1952, Japanese peace treaty ratified by the Senate

Apr. 8, 1952, Truman ordered seizure of steel mills to prevent a strike

May 23, 1952, railroads under army control since Aug. 27, 1950, restored to owners after signing of union contract

May 25, 1952, atomic artillery shell fired in Nevada

May 26, 1952, peace contract signed in Bonn by United States, Great Britain, France, and West Germany

June 2, 1952, seizure of steel mills declared illegal by Supreme Court

July 3, 1952, Puerto Rico made a commonwealth

Nov. 16, 1952, Atomic Energy Commission announced hydrogen bomb tests in Pacific

IMPORTANT DATES IN HIS LIFE

1886, moved to Harrisonville, Mo.

1888, moved to farm at Grandview, Mo.

Dec. 28, 1890, moved to Independence, Mo.

1892, attended public school, Independence, Mo.

1895, worked at Clinton Drug Store, earning three dollars a week

1901, graduated from high school

1901, worked in mail room of Kansas City *Star*

1902, timekeeper for contractor working for Santa Fe Railroad

1903-1905, worked at National Bank of Commerce, Kansas City, Mo.

1905, worked at Union National Bank, Kansas City, Mo.

June 14, 1905, joined National Guard of Missouri as charter member of Battery B

1906-1917, worked as partner on his father's farm

1917, helped organize 2nd Missouri Field Artillery, and later 129th Field Artillery, 35th Division

June 22, 1917, commissioned a first lieutenant

Sept. 26, 1917, first lieutenant, Field Artillery

1917, went to School of Fire; did regular battery duty and ran the regimental canteen

Mar. 1918, recommended for promotion

Mar. 30, 1918, overseas with the Division School Detail; sailed on *George Washington*

Apr. 20-June 18, 1918, Second Corps Artillery School at Chantillon-sur-Seine

June 1918, rejoined regiment as a captain; made adjutant, Second Battalion

July 5, 1918, regiment sent to Artillery School at Coëtquidan

July 11, 1918, ordered to command Battery D 129th Field Artillery

Aug. 15, 1918, ordered to front

Aug. 18, 1918, arrived in Vosges Mountains in Alsace

Sept. 12-16, 1918, at St. Mihiel

Sept. 26-Oct. 3, 1918, at Meuse-Argonne

Oct. 8-Nov. 7, 1918, at Sommedieu

Nov. 7-11, 1918, at second phase of Meuse-Argonne offensive

Apr. 20, 1919, returned to New York

May 6, 1919, discharged, as major

1919-1921, haberdashery business, Kansas City, Mo.

1922-1924, judge, County Court, Jackson County, Mo. (administrative, not judicial, position)

1923-1925, studied law at Kansas City Law School

1924, unsuccessful candidate for reelection as judge

1926-1934, presiding judge, County Court, Jackson County, Mo.

Jan. 3, 1935-Jan. 17, 1945, U.S. Senate (from Missouri)

1941-1944, chairman of Special Senate Committee to Investigate the National Defense Program ("Truman Committee")

Nov. 1944, nominated as vice presidential candidate on Democratic ticket

Jan. 20, 1945, inaugurated Vice President

Apr. 12, 1945, succeeded to the presidency on the death of President Roosevelt

July 1948, nominated for another term as President on Democratic ticket

Nov. 1948, won election, upsetting all polls predicting certain Republican victory

Jan. 20, 1949-Jan. 19, 1953, President (second term)

HARRY S TRUMAN

——was the first President born in Missouri.

——was the ninth President whose mother was alive when he was inaugurated.

——was the fourth Democratic President since the Civil War.

TRUMAN'S VICE PRESIDENT

Vice President—Alben William Barkley (35th V.P.)

Date of birth—Nov. 24, 1877

Birthplace—near Lowes, Graves County, Ky.

Political party—Democratic

State represented—Kentucky

Term of office—Jan. 20, 1949-Jan. 20, 1953

Age at inauguration—71 years, 57 days

Occupation after term—Senator

Date of death—Apr. 30, 1956

Place of death—Lexington, Va.

Age at death—78 years, 157 days

Burial place—Paducah, Ky.

ADDITIONAL DATA ON TRUMAN

HARRY "S" TRUMAN

The initial "S" in President Harry S Truman's name has no special significance and is not an abbreviation of any name. It is said to have been chosen by his parents to avoid a display of favoritism, since his paternal grandfather's name was Shippe (Anderson Shippe Truman) and his maternal grandfather's name was Solomon Young.

FIRST OATH OF OFFICE

Harry S Truman took the oath of office on Thursday, April 12, 1945, at 7:09 P.M., in the Cabinet Room at the White House. The oath was administered by Chief Justice Harlan Fiske Stone.

TRUMAN PRESENTED MEDAL TO CONSCIENTIOUS OBJECTOR

A unique medal presentation ceremony was held on October 12, 1945, when President Truman presented a medal of honor to a conscientious objector, the first time such an award was made. The recipient was Private Desmond T. Doss of Lynchburg, Va., whose acts of heroism and outstanding bravery as a medical corpsman on Okinawa between April 29 and May 21, 1943, earned him this signal distinction.

TRUMAN TRAVELED IN SUBMARINE

President Truman was the first President to travel underwater in a modern submarine. He embarked at Key West, Fla., on November 21, 1946, in the U-2513, a captured German submarine. The submarine submerged off Key West during naval exercises.

President Theodore Roosevelt went aboard the *Plunger,* which submerged and remained underwater for almost an hour on August 25, 1905, off Oyster Bay, N.Y.

TRUMAN TELECAST ADDRESS FROM WHITE HOUSE

The first presidential address telecast from the White House was delivered on October 5, 1947, by President Truman. He spoke about food conservation and the world food crisis, proposing meatless Tuesdays and eggless and poultryless Thursdays. The speech was relayed to New York City, Schenectady, and Philadelphia.

INAUGURATION IN 1949

Harry S Truman took the oath of office on Thursday, January 20, 1949. It was administered by Chief Justice Frederick Moore Vinson.

There was a brilliant and cloudless sky and the air was clear and crisp. The thermometer hovered between 30° and 40°.

About 44,000 persons in the specially constructed grandstand witnessed the three-hour parade, which was seven and a half miles long. The ceremonies and parade were viewed by about a million persons in Washington and by about ten million on television. The honor guard was Battery D, the regiment in which Truman had served during World War I. Over seven hundred airplanes, led by five B-36's, participated in a display of aerial power.

A reception was held at the National Gallery of Art for 7,500 to 10,000 guests, and an inaugural ball was held at the National Guard Armory.

As the White House was undergoing repairs, the President temporarily occupied Blair House.

ASSASSINATION ATTEMPT MADE ON TRUMAN

President Truman escaped assassination on November 1, 1950, when at 2:15 P.M. Oscar Collazo and Griselio Torresola, two Puerto Rican nationalists, tried to shoot their way into Blair House. Leslie Coffelt of Arlington, Va., a White House guard, was killed and two others wounded. Torresola was killed and Collazo was wounded.

One hour after the shooting, President Truman dedicated a memorial to British Field Marshal Sir John Dill at the Arlington National Cemetery.

On July 24, 1952, Collazo was sentenced to die on August 1, 1952, but his sentence was commuted to life imprisonment.

TRUMAN RECEIVED FIRST WOMAN AMBASSADOR

President Truman was the first President to receive officially a woman ambassador from a foreign country. On May 12, 1952, he received the letter of credence from Her Excellency Shrimati Vijaya Lakshmi Pandit, ambassador of India.

THE FIRST LADY

During her husband's administration Bess Wallace Truman, in contrast to her predecessor, was very retiring and endeavored to keep out of the public eye as much as possible. Mrs. Truman was well known to an intimate group of friends in Washington, however, as she had been her husband's secretary while he was a senator. The Trumans' daughter, Margaret, made frequent appearances as a concert singer and a television performer.

DWIGHT DAVID
EISENHOWER

Dwight D. Eisenhower

DWIGHT DAVID EISENHOWER

Born—Oct. 14, 1890 (Given name—David Dwight Eisenhower)

Birthplace—Denison, Tex.

College attended—United States Military Academy, West Point, N.Y.

Date of graduation—June 12, 1915, four-year course

Religion—Presbyterian

Ancestry—Swiss-German

Occupation—Army officer

Date and place of marriage—July 1, 1916, Denver, Colo.

Age at marriage—25 years, 260 days

Political party—Republican

State represented—New York

Term of office—Elected to serve Jan. 20, 1953-Jan. 20, 1961

Administration—42nd, 43rd

Congresses—83rd, 84th, 85th, 86th

Age at inauguration—62 years, 98 days

PARENTS

Father—David Jacob Eisenhower

Born—Sept. 23, 1863, Elizabethville, Pa.

Married—Sept. 23, 1885, Hope, Kan.

Occupation—Mechanic, manager of gas company

Died—Mar. 10, 1942, Abilene, Kan.

Age at death—79 years, 168 days

Mother—Ida Elizabeth Stoever (or Stover) Eisenhower

For additional data see the end of this section and also specific subject headings in the Index.

Born—May 1, 1862, Mount Sidney, Va.

Died—Sept. 11, 1946, Abilene, Kan.

Age at death—84 years, 133 days

BROTHERS

Dwight David Eisenhower was the third of seven sons.

CHILDREN

David Dwight Eisenhower, b. Sept. 24, 1917, Denver, Colo.; d. Jan. 2, 1921, Camp Meade, Md.

John Sheldon Doud Eisenhower, b. Aug. 3, 1923, Denver, Colo.; m. June 10, 1947, Barbara Jean Thompson, Fort Monroe, Va.

MRS. DWIGHT DAVID EISENHOWER

Name—Mary (Mamie) Geneva Doud Eisenhower

Born—Nov. 14, 1896

Birthplace—Boone, Iowa

Age at marriage—19 years, 229 days

Children—2 sons

Mother—Elivera Carlson Doud

Father—John Sheldon Doud

His occupation—Meat packer

Years younger than the President—6 years, 30 days

THE ELECTION OF 1952

NOMINATIONS FOR TERM 1953-1957

Republican Party Convention (25th)

July 7-11, 1952, International Amphitheatre, Chicago, Ill.

Nominated for President—Dwight David Eisenhower, N.Y.

Nominated for Vice President—Richard Milhous Nixon, Calif.

Eisenhower was nominated on the first ballot.

Total number of votes: 1,206

Number necessary for nomination: 604

Nomination made unanimous

Democratic Party Convention (31st)

July 21-26, 1952, International Amphitheatre, Chicago, Ill.

Nominated for President—Adlai Ewing Stevenson, Ill.

Nominated for Vice President—John Jackson Sparkman, Ala.

Stevenson was nominated on the third ballot.

Total number of votes: first ballot, 1,229; third ballot, 1,228

Number necessary for nomination: 616

Nomination made unanimous

ELECTION RESULTS, NOV. 4, 1952—PRESIDENTIAL AND VICE PRESIDENTIAL CANDIDATES AND OTHER PARTY VOTES

Republican Party (33,778,963 votes)

Dwight David Eisenhower, N.Y.
Richard Milhous Nixon, Calif.

Democratic Party (27,314,992 votes)

Adlai Ewing Stevenson, Ill.
John Jackson Sparkman, Ala.

Progressive Party (135,007 votes)

Vincent William Hallinan, Calif.
Charlotta A. Bass, N.Y.

Prohibition Party (72,769 votes)

Stuart Hamblen, Calif.
Dr. Enoch Arden Holtwick, Ill.

Socialist Labor Party (30,376 votes)

Eric Hass, N.Y.
Stephen Emery, N.Y.

Socialist Party (19,685 votes)

Darlington Hoopes, Pa.
Samuel Herman Friedman, N.Y.

Socialist Workers Party (10,-306 votes)

Farrell Dobbs, N.Y.
Myra Tanner Weiss, N.Y.

Other Parties

South Carolina Republicans (separate set of electors), 158,289
Christian Nationalists, 13,883
Poor Man's Party, 4,203
Oregon Independent votes, 3,665
Constitution Party, 3,089
People's Party of Connecticut, 1,466
Social Democrats, 504
America First Party, 233
Scattering, 4,489
Total: 189,821

ELECTORAL VOTES (531 —48 states)

Eisenhower received 83.24 per cent (442 votes—39 states) as follows: Ariz. 4; Calif. 32; Colo. 6; Conn. 8; Del. 3; Fla. 10; Idaho 4; Ill. 27; Ind. 13; Iowa 10; Kan. 8; Me. 5; Md. 9; Mass. 16; Mich. 20; Minn. 11; Mo. 13; Mont. 4; Neb. 6; Nev. 3; N.H. 4; N.J. 16; N.M. 4; N.Y. 45; N.D. 4; Ohio 25; Okla. 8; Ore. 6; Pa. 32; R.I. 4; S.D. 4; Tenn. 11; Tex. 24;

Utah 4; Vt. 3; Va. 12; Wash. 9; Wis. 12; Wyo. 3.

Stevenson received 16.76 per cent (89 votes—9 states) as follows: Ala. 11; Ark. 8; Ga. 12; Ky. 10; La. 10; Miss. 8; N.C. 14; S.C. 8; W.Va. 8.

THE ELECTION OF 1956

NOMINATIONS FOR TERM 1957-1961

Republican Party Convention (26th)

Aug. 20-23, 1956, the Cow Palace, San Francisco, Calif.
Nominated for President—
Dwight David Eisenhower, N.Y.
Nominated for Vice President—
Richard Milhous Nixon, Calif.

Eisenhower was nominated by acclamation on the first ballot.

Democratic Party Convention (32nd)

Aug. 13-16, 1956, International Amphitheatre, Chicago, Ill.
Nominated for President—Adlai Ewing Stevenson, Ill.
Nominated for Vice President—
Estes Kefauver, Tenn.

Stevenson was nominated on the first ballot.

Total number of votes: 1,372

Number necessary for nomination: 686½

ELECTION RESULTS, NOV. 6, 1956—PRESIDENTIAL AND VICE PRESIDENTIAL CANDIDATES

Republican Party (35,581,003 votes)

Dwight David Eisenhower, N.Y.
Richard Milhous Nixon, Calif.

Democratic Party (25,738,765 votes)

Adlai Ewing Stevenson, Ill.
Estes Kefauver, Tenn.

Liberal Party (292,557 votes)

Adlai Ewing Stevenson, Ill.
Estes Kefauver, Tenn.

States' Rights Party (109,961 votes)

Thomas Coleman Andrews, Va.
Thomas Harold Werdel, Calif.

Prohibition Party (41,937 votes)

Dr. Enoch Arden Holtwick, Ill.
Edward M. Cooper, Calif.

Socialist Labor Party (41,159 votes)

Eric Hass, N.Y.
Georgia Cozzini, Wis.

Texas Constitution Party
(30,999 votes)

William Ezra Jenner, Ind.
Joseph Bracken Lee, Utah

Socialist Workers Party (5,549
votes)

Farrell Dobbs, N.Y.
Myra Tanner Weiss, N.Y.

American Third Party (1,829
votes)

Henry Krajewski, N.J.
Ann Marie Yezo, N.J.

Socialist Party (846 votes)

Darlington Hoopes, Pa.
Samuel Herman Friedman,
N.Y.

Other Parties

Conservative Party (N.J.),
5,317
Black and Tan Grand Old
Party (Miss.), 4,313
Industrial Government (N.Y.),
2,080
Militant Workers (Pa.), 2,035
American Party, 483
Virginia Social Democrats, 444
New Party (N.M.), 364

ELECTORAL VOTES (531 —48 states)

Eisenhower received 86.06 per
cent (457 votes—41 states) as
follows: Ariz. 4; Calif. 32;
Colo. 6; Conn. 8; Del. 3; Fla.
10; Idaho 4; Ill. 27; Ind. 13;
Iowa 10; Kan. 8; Ky. 10; La.
10; Me. 5; Md. 9; Mass. 16;
Mich. 20; Minn. 11; Mont. 4;
Neb. 6; Nev. 3; N.H. 4; N.J.
16; N.M. 4; N.Y. 45; N.D. 4;
Ohio 25; Okla. 8; Ore. 6; Pa.
32; R.I. 4; S.D. 4; Tenn. 11;
Tex. 24; Utah 4; Vt. 3; Va.
12; Wash. 9; W.Va. 8; Wis.
12; Wyo. 3.

Stevenson did not receive all
74 Democratic votes; one vote
went to Walter Burgwyn Jones
of Alabama.

Stevenson received 13.75 per
cent (73 votes—7 states) as follows: Ala. 10 (of the 11 votes);
Ark. 8; Ga. 12; Miss. 8; Mo.
13; N.C. 14; S.C. 8.

Jones received 00.19 per cent
(1 of the 11 Ala. votes).

APPOINTMENTS TO THE SUPREME COURT

Chief Justice

Earl Warren, Calif., Oct. 5,
1953

Associate Justices

John Marshall Harlan, N.Y.,
Mar. 28, 1955
William Joseph Brennan, Jr.,
N.J., Oct. 16, 1956
Charles Evans Whittaker, Mo.,
Mar. 25, 1957
Potter Stewart, Ohio, Oct. 14,
1958

ADMINISTRATION— IMPORTANT DATES

Jan. 1953, neutralization of Formosa by Seventh Fleet ended

Apr. 22, 1953, states given title to offshore oil

July 27, 1953, Korean war ended with signing of armistice calling for demilitarized zone and voluntary repatriation of prisoners

Aug.-Sept. 1953, American prisoners of war in Korea repatriated

Dec. 4-8, 1953, Eisenhower conferred at Bermuda with prime ministers of Britain and France on exchange of atomic information

Jan. 21, 1954, first atomic submarine, *Nautilus,* launched, Groton, Conn.

Mar. 1, 1954, five representatives wounded in House of Representatives by shots fired by Puerto Rican nationalists

May 13, 1954, St. Lawrence Seaway bill authorized joint construction by the United States and Canada

May 17, 1954, Supreme Court decreed racial segregation in schools unconstitutional

June 25-29, 1954, Eisenhower and Prime Minister Churchill conferred at Washington, D.C., on world peace

Aug. 24, 1954, Communist party outlawed, but party membership not made a crime

Sept. 1, 1954, social security coverage extended to ten million additional persons (farmers, professional people, etc.)

Sept. 8, 1954, Southeast Asia defense treaty (SEATO) signed

Oct. 25, 1954, first telecast of a cabinet meeting

Jan. 28, 1955, Congress approved presidential request to allow U.S. forces to defend Formosa against Communist aggression

Feb. 7, 1955, U.S. Seventh Fleet helped evacuation of Communist-threatened Tachen Islands, near Formosa

Mar. 16, 1955, secret Yalta Conference papers released by State Department

Apr. 12, 1955, Salk vaccine declared "safe, effective, and potent"

Apr. 21, 1955, U.S. occupation of Germany ended; troops remained on contractual basis

May 15, 1955, Big Four foreign ministers signed treaty restoring sovereignty to Austria

May 31, 1955, Supreme Court reaffirmed principle of school integration, ordering gradual compliance by local authorities

July 18-23, 1955, Geneva summit conference of Big Four heads of state

Sept. 24, 1955, Eisenhower suffered heart attack

Oct. 27, 1955, Geneva meeting of Big Four foreign ministers

Dec. 5, 1955, AFL-CIO merger

Jan. 30, 1956, British Prime Minister Eden conferred with Eisenhower at Washington, D.C.

Mar. 12, 1956, manifesto issued by southern senators and representatives pledging use of all legal means to reverse Supreme Court integration ruling

June 9, 1956, Eisenhower underwent emergency ileitis operation

July 19, 1956, United States withdrew offers to finance construction of Aswan Dam in Egypt, precipitating Egyptian seizure of Suez Canal

Oct. 31, 1956, Eisenhower, deploring Anglo-French-Israeli attack on Egypt, promised that United States would not be involved

Nov. 8, 1956, United States offered to admit Hungarian refugees of anti-Soviet revolt

Mar. 9, 1957, Eisenhower Doctrine bill signed, authorizing use of U.S. forces to assist Middle East nations threatened by Communist aggression

May 14, 1957, United States resumed military aid to Yugoslavia, halted during Tito's reconciliation with U.S.S.R.

June 1957, controversial Supreme Court decisions on civil rights, limiting powers of legislative and executive branches of government

June 1957, Prime Minister Kishi of Japan visited Washington, D.C.; joint American-Japanese communiqué issued announcing withdrawal of American ground combat forces in Japan

July 1957, United States proposed ban on nuclear tests after establishment of inspection system

July 29, 1957, United States ratified International Atomic Energy Agency (proposed by Eisenhower in 1953) to pool atomic resources for peaceful use

Sept. 9, 1957, Congress approved establishment of Civil Rights Commission

Sept. 19, 1957, first underground nuclear explosion, Nevada proving grounds

Sept. 24, 1957, Eisenhower sent federal troops to scene of violence at Little Rock, Ark., high school to enforce integration of Negro students who had been barred by national guardsmen ordered by governor

Oct. 4, 1957, launching of first Soviet Sputnik set off demand

...ter American efforts
...nse and technology

N... ...-5, 1957, Eisenhower suffered mild stroke, but recovered rapidly

1957-1958, business recession; over 5 million unemployed before reversal of downward trend

Jan. 31, 1958, launching of Explorer I, first American satellite

May 1958, Vice President Nixon, on Latin American tour, attacked by anti-U.S. demonstrators

July-Oct. 1958, U.S. troops in Lebanon at request of Lebanese government threatened by United Arab Republic infiltration

July-Aug. 1958, polar voyages of atomic submarines *Nautilus* and *Skate*

July 29, 1958, Eisenhower signed bill establishing National Aeronautics and Space Administration

Sept. 1958, closing of schools in which integration had been ordered in Arkansas and Virginia

Jan. 3, 1959, Alaska proclaimed the 49th state

Mar. 18, 1959, Eisenhower signed act admitting Hawaii as the 50th state

IMPORTANT DATES IN HIS LIFE

1909, graduated from Abilene High School, Abilene, Kan.

1911, entered U.S. Military Academy

1915, graduated from U.S. Military Academy (61st in class of 164, 95th in deportment); commissioned second lieutenant of infantry; assigned to 19th Infantry, San Antonio, Tex.

1918, commanded 6,000 men at Tank Training Center at Camp Colt, near Gettysburg, Pa.; served at army training posts in World War I, but did not go overseas

Nov. 1918, lieutenant colonel (temporary rank) in Tank Corps

1922-1924, executive officer, Camp Gaillard, Panama Canal Zone

1925-1926, Command and General Staff School, Fort Leavenworth, Kan.; graduated first in class of 275

1928, Army War College, Washington, D.C.

1929-1933, assistant executive, Office of Assistant Secretary of War

1933, Army Industrial college

1935-1939, major; assistant to General MacArthur in the Philippines

1940, returned to the United

States; joined Fifteenth Infantry

1941, chief of staff, Third Army; brigadier general (temporary rank)

Feb. 1942, chief, War Plans Division of War Department General Staff

Apr. 1942, assistant chief of staff in charge of Operations Division of War Department General Staff; major general (temporary rank)

June 25, 1942, appointed commanding general, European Theatre of Operations

July 1942, lieutenant general (temporary rank); in London for strategy discussions with British

Nov. 8, 1942, appointed commander in chief of Allied forces in North Africa

Feb. 1943, full general (temporary rank)

July-Dec. 1943, directed invasions of Sicily and Italy

Dec. 24, 1943, appointed supreme commander, Allied Expeditionary Forces

June 6, 1944, led D-Day invasion of Normandy

Dec. 20, 1944, General of the Army (temporary rank)

May 7, 1945, accepted surrender of German Army at Rheims (V-E Day)

May-Nov. 1945, commander of U.S. occupation forces in Europe

Nov. 19, 1945-Feb. 7, 1948, chief of staff, U.S. Army; first chief of staff under unification of armed services in 1947

Feb. 7, 1948, retired from active duty in the army

June 7, 1948, appointed president of Columbia University

July 1948, declined to run for the presidency of the United States

Dec. 19, 1950, granted indefinite leave of absence from Columbia University to serve as commander of NATO forces in Europe

Jan. 1952, name entered in first Republican presidential primaries

May 30, 1952, turned over command of Allied forces in Europe to General Ridgway

June 1952, resigned from the army

July 1952, received Republican presidential nomination

Nov. 4, 1952, elected President

Nov. 17, 1952, resigned from Columbia University, effective Jan. 19, 1953

Dec. 1952, made 22,000-mile preinauguration air trip to Korea to fulfill campaign pledge

Jan. 20, 1953-Jan. 20, 1957, President (first term)

Sept. 24, 1955, suffered heart attack at Denver, Colo.

Feb. 29, 1956, announced his availability for second term

1956, underwent emer-
[g]leitis operation

[Ju]... 56, renominated by Republicans

Nov. 6, 1956, elected President
for second term

Jan. 21, 1957, inaugurated for
second term (took oath of
office in private ceremony on
Sunday, Jan. 20)

Nov. 25, 1957, suffered mild
stroke, but recovered rapidly

DWIGHT DAVID EISENHOWER

——was the first President born
in Texas.

——was the fourteenth President elected from a state
other than his native
state.

——was the first President to
serve a constitutionally
limited presidential term
(under the provisions of
the Twenty-second
Amendment).

——was the first Republican in
the twentieth century to
win two successive presi-
dential elections.

——was the first President of
forty-nine (and later
fifty) states.

——was the first President to
serve with three Con-
gresses in which both
chambers were controlled
by an opposing political
party.

EISENHOWER'S VICE PRESIDENT

Vice President—Richard Milhous Nixon (36th V.P.)

Date of birth—Jan. 9, 1913

Birthplace—Yorba Linda, Calif.

Political party—Republican

State represented—California

Terms of office—Elected to
serve Jan. 20, 1953-Jan. 20,
1961

Age at inauguration—40 years,
11 days

ADDITIONAL DATA ON EISENHOWER

EISENHOWER CHANGED NAME

The Eisenhower family Bible
records the birth of President
Eisenhower's mother and father
and his two brothers, Arthur
and Edgar. The entry for a
third son is "D. Dwight Eisenhower," the "D" an abbreviation
for David. Later, David Dwight
Eisenhower reversed his Christian names.

EISENHOWER WON HIS WINGS

President Eisenhower learned
to pilot an airplane when he was
a lieutenant colonel in the Philippines on the staff of General
Douglas MacArthur. His first

solo flight was made on May 19, 1937. On November 30, 1939, he received pilot's license number 93,258. He was the first President licensed to pilot an airplane.

EISENHOWER RESIGNED AS GENERAL

On July 18, 1952, about a week after his nomination as the presidential candidate on the Republican ticket, General Eisenhower resigned as General of the Army, forfeiting an annual pension of $19,542 (later increased to $22,943), an office at government expense, and a staff of eight aides including a colonel, a lieutenant colonel, a major, and five enlisted men.

FIRST INAUGURATION

Dwight David Eisenhower took the oath of office on Tuesday, January 20, 1953. The oath was administered by Chief Justice Frederick Moore Vinson.

Before delivering his inaugural address, the President offered a prayer, the text of which follows:

My friends, before I begin the expression of those thoughts that I deem appropriate to this moment, would you permit me the privilege of uttering a little private prayer of my own. And I ask that you bow your heads.

Almighty God, as we stand here at this moment my future associates in the Executive branch of Government join me in beseeching that Thou will make full and complete our dedication to the service of the people in this throng, and their fellow citizens everywhere.

Give us, we pray, the power to discern clearly right from wrong, and allow all our words and actions to be governed thereby, and by the laws of this land. Especially we pray that our concern shall be for all the people regardless of station, race or calling.

May cooperation be permitted and be the mutual aim of those who, under the concepts of our Constitution, hold to differing political faiths; so that all may work for the good of our beloved country and Thy glory. Amen.

The two-and-a-half-hour inaugural parade was witnessed by an estimated 1 million persons, of whom 60,000 were in the grandstand in seats ranging in price from $3 to $15, according to location. About 22,000 service men and women and

5,000 civilians were in the parade, which included 50 state and organization floats costing $100,000. There were also 65 musical units, 350 horses, 3 elephants, an Alaskan dog team, and the 280-millimeter atomic cannon. It was the most elaborate inaugural pageant ever held.

In addition to a governors' reception for 3,000 invited guests, there were two inaugural festivals, one at the Uline Arena for 11,000 persons, and one at the Capitol Theater for 3,500 persons. Tickets ranged in price from $3 to $12. Forty stars of stage, screen, and TV participated in the celebration.

In the evening two inaugural balls were held, one at the National Guard Armory and the other at the gymnasium of Mc-Donough Hall at Georgetown University.

INCOMING STAFF ATTENDED CHURCH SERVICE

The first time an entire official family attended church services with an incoming President was on January 20, 1953, when President-elect Eisenhower and his staff attended a pre-inaugural service at the National Presbyterian Church on Connecticut Avenue, Washington, D.C. The Reverend Edward

L. R. Elson, pastor of the church, conducted the service.

EISENHOWER BECAME COMMUNICANT

President Eisenhower was the first President to take the complete action from baptism to confirmation and full communicant membership in a church subsequent to his inauguration.

The President was received into the membership of the National Presbyterian Church of Washington, D.C., by baptism and confession of faith before the session of the church early on Sunday morning February 1, 1953, and thereafter on the same day participated as a church member in the service of Holy Communion.

EISENHOWER APPOINTED GRANDSONS TO POSITIONS HELD BY THEIR GRANDFATHERS

John Foster Dulles of New York, who served as secretary of state under President Eisenhower from January 21, 1953, until April 1959, was the grandson of John Watson Foster of Indiana, who served as secretary of state under Benjamin Harrison from June 29, 1892 to February 22, 1893.

John Marshall Harlan, who took office on March 28, 1955, as an associate justice of the Supreme Court, is a grandson of John Marshall Harlan, who served in the same capacity from November 29, 1877 to October 14, 1911.

PRESIDENTIAL NEWS CONFERENCE TELEVISED

The first presidential news conference to be recorded by both newsreels and television was held January 19, 1955, when reporters questioned President Eisenhower about Red China and Formosa, national security, the imprisonment of American fliers, trade with the Communists, and other subjects. The conference was filmed by Fox Movietone News and the National Broadcasting Company, which pooled the telecast with the other networks. The program was held until officially released.

PAY OF VICE PRESIDENT AND OTHER OFFICIALS INCREASED

On March 2, 1955, President Eisenhower signed the congressional-judicial pay bill granting federal employees the highest salaries ever paid to government officials. The pay of congressmen was increased from $15,000 to $22,500 a year, and the pay of the Vice President and Speaker of the House from $30,000 to $35,000.

The salary of the chief justice was raised from $25,500 to $35,000; associate justices, from $25,000 to $35,000; higher court judges, from $17,500 to $25,000; lower court judges, from $15,000 to $22,500; deputy attorney generals, from $17,500 to $21,000; solicitor general, from $17,500 to $20,500 a year, etc.

EISENHOWER STRICKEN WITH HEART ATTACK AND OTHER ILLNESSES

The first presidential candidate who had suffered a heart attack was President Eisenhower. The attack occurred on September 24, 1955 while the President was on vacation at Denver, Colo. His first steps after the illness were taken on October 25, 1955 at the Fitzsimons Army Hospital at Denver. On February 29, 1956, he announced that he would be available for a second term.

During his administration, President Eisenhower was also operated on for ileitis and suffered a very slight stroke.

EISENHOWER WON GREATEST POPULAR VOTE

The greatest popular vote in United States history was recorded on November 6, 1956, when 62,027,040 cast their ballots at the polls. Dwight Eisenhower, the Republican candidate, received 35,581,003 votes or over 57 per cent. His Democratic opponent was Adlai Stevenson, who received 26,031,322 votes or almost 42 per cent. The combined total of votes cast for all the other candidates was 414,715 votes or less than .7 per cent.

SECOND INAUGURATION

As January 20, 1957 fell on a Sunday, President Eisenhower took the oath of office in a private White House ceremony.

On Monday, January 21, 1957, he repeated the oath at the inaugural ceremonies held on the east portico of the White House. The oath was administered by Chief Justice Earl Warren.

In the afternoon 750,000 spectators watched a three-and-a-half-hour parade over a three-mile route. Marching in the parade were 17,000 people, including 11,757 in military service. There were 47 marching units, 52 bands, and 10 drum and bugle corps. The highlight of the parade was a mammoth float—408 feet long and mounted on 164 wheels—which introduced the theme "Liberty and Strength Through Consent of the Governed."

Four inaugural balls were held in the evening—at the Armory, the Mayflower Hotel, the Statler Hotel, and the Sheraton-Park Hotel.

EISENHOWER SUBMERGED IN ATOMIC SUBMARINE

President Eisenhower was the first President to submerge in an atomic-powered submarine. He was aboard the *Seawolf* on September 26, 1957, when the submarine submerged five miles southwest of Brentons Reef, off Newport, R.I., and remained sixty feet below the surface for about fifteen minutes. (Eisenhower had submerged twice before in a submarine—at Panama after World War I.)

THE FIRST LADY

Mary (Mamie) Geneva Doud Eisenhower is reserved, dignified, and unassuming, avoiding unnecessary publicity. Before her husband's administration, as an army wife for thirty-seven years, she grew accustomed to meeting groups of influential people.

Part II

COMPARATIVE DATA

THE PRESIDENTS

Family History and Names

THE PRESIDENTS OF CHARLES CITY COUNTY

Charles City County, Va., is noted as the birthplace of two men who were simultaneously elected President and Vice President of the United States. They were William Henry Harrison and John Tyler, elected November 3, 1840, and inaugurated March 3, 1841.

The careers of the two men who became the ninth and the tenth Presidents had much in common. Both had been members of the Virginia legislature and both had been state governors, Harrison of Indiana and Tyler of Virginia. Each had served in the House of Representatives and the Senate.

PRESIDENTS WHO WERE RELATED

John Adams and John Quincy Adams, father and son, were the most closely related Presidents.

William Henry Harrison was the grandfather of Benjamin Harrison.

James Madison and Zachary Taylor were second cousins.

Franklin Delano Roosevelt, genealogists have shown, was remotely related to eleven former Presidents, five by blood and six by marriage. He was a fifth cousin of Theodore Roosevelt.

OCCUPATIONS OF PRESIDENTS' FATHERS

Nineteen of the thirty-three Presidents of the United States were descended from fathers who made their living from the soil as farmers or planters.

Eight of the fathers were members of the learned professions: four lawyers, three clergymen, and one physician.

Only two Presidents were descended from statesmen of national prominence: William Henry Harrison, whose father was one of the signers of the Declaration of Independence, and John Quincy Adams, whose father, a lawyer, had been a President of the United States.

Six Presidents were descended from fathers who were salaried or engaged in their own business.

THREE MINISTERS' SONS ELECTED TO THE PRESIDENCY

The fathers of Chester Alan Arthur, Grover Cleveland, and Woodrow Wilson were ministers. William Arthur was a Baptist clergyman; Richard Falley Cleveland was a Congregational clergyman; and Joseph Ruggles Wilson was a Presbyterian clergyman.

THREE GOVERNORS' SONS ELECTED TO THE PRESIDENCY

The fathers of three Presidents had served their respective states as governors.

William Henry Harrison's father, Benjamin Harrison, served as governor of Virginia from November 30, 1781, to November 30, 1784.

John Tyler's father, John Tyler, also served as governor of Virginia. He served from December 12, 1808, to January 15, 1811.

Franklin Pierce's father, Benjamin Pierce, served two terms as the constitutional executive of New Hampshire, 1827 to 1828 and 1829 to 1830.

NUMBER OF CHILDREN IN THE PRESIDENTS' FAMILIES

No President was an only child; most came from large families.

Eighteen Presidents came from families of 6 or more children:

Seven came from families of 10 or more children: Madison (12), Benjamin Harrison (12), Buchanan (11), Washington (10), Jefferson (10), Polk (10), and Taft (10).

Six came from families of 9 children: Taylor, Fillmore, Pierce, Arthur, Cleveland, and McKinley.

Two came from families of 8 children: Tyler and Harding.

Two came from families of

7 children: William Henry Harrison and Eisenhower.

One came from a family of 6 children: Grant.

Five Presidents came from families of 5 children: Monroe, John Quincy Adams, Van Buren, Hayes, and Garfield.

Two Presidents came from families of 4 children: Theodore Roosevelt and Wilson.

Five Presidents came from families of 3 children: John Adams, Jackson, Lincoln, Hoover, and Truman.

Three Presidents came from families of 2 children: Johnson, Coolidge, and Franklin Delano Roosevelt.

Summing up, the parents of the thirty-three Presidents had a total of 219 children.

PRESIDENTS SURVIVED BY PARENTS

The only President survived by his father was Warren Gamaliel Harding.

The mothers of two Presidents, Polk and Garfield, survived their sons.

PARENTS OF PRESIDENTS ALIVE AT SONS' INAUGURATIONS

Both parents at inauguration

The only President whose parents were both living when he took office was Ulysses Simpson Grant.

Fathers at inaugurations

Five fathers lived to see their sons take office as President:

John Quincy Adams was inaugurated March 4, 1825; his father, John Adams, died on July 4, 1826.

Millard Fillmore took office on July 10, 1850; his father, Nathaniel Fillmore, died on May 2, 1863.

Ulysses Simpson Grant was inaugurated March 4, 1869; his father, Jesse Root Grant, died on June 29, 1873.

Warren Gamaliel Harding was inaugurated March 4, 1921; his father, George Tryon Harding, died on November 19, 1928.

Calvin Coolidge took office on August 3, 1923; his father, John Calvin Coolidge, died on March 18, 1926.

Mothers at inaugurations

Nine mothers lived to see their sons take office as President:

George Washington was inaugurated April 30, 1789; his mother, Mary Ball Washington, died on August 25, 1789.

John Adams was inaugurated March 4, 1797; his mother, Susanna Boylston Adams, died on April 17, 1797.

James Madison was inaugurated on March 4, 1809; his mother, Eleanor Rose Conway Madison, died on February 11, 1829.

James Knox Polk was inaugurated on March 4, 1845; his mother, Jane Knox Polk, died on January 11, 1852.

Ulysses Simpson Grant was inaugurated on March 4, 1869; his mother, Hannah Simpson Grant, died on May 11, 1883.

James Abram Garfield was inaugurated on March 4, 1881; his mother, Eliza Ballou Garfield, died on January 21, 1888.

William McKinley was inaugurated on March 4, 1897; his mother, Nancy Allison McKinley, died on December 12, 1897.

Franklin Delano Roosevelt was inaugurated on March 4, 1933; his mother, Sara Delano Roosevelt, died on September 7, 1941.

Harry S Truman took office on April 12, 1945; his mother, Martha Ellen Young Truman, died on July 25, 1947.

NINE PRESIDENTS' FATHERS REMARRIED

The fathers of nine Presidents remarried. Four of them remarried after the birth of their President-sons.

Millard Fillmore was 31 years and 114 days old when his mother, Phoebe Millard Fillmore, died on May 2, 1831. His father married Eunice Love on May 2, 1834.

Abraham Lincoln was 9 years and 235 days old when his mother, Nancy Hanks Lincoln, died on October 5, 1818. His father married Sarah Bush Johnston on December 2, 1819.

Warren Gamaliel Harding was 44 years and 198 days old when his mother, Phoebe Elizabeth Dickerson Harding, died on May 29, 1910. His father married Aline Severns on August 11, 1921.

Calvin Coolidge was 12 years and 253 days old when his mother, Victoria Josephine Moor Coolidge, died on March 14, 1885. His father married Caroline A. Brown on September 9, 1891.

Five Presidents were the sons of their fathers' second marriages. They were George Washington, Franklin Pierce, Benjamin Harrison, William Howard Taft, and Franklin Delano Roosevelt.

FIVE PRESIDENTS MARRIED MINISTERS' DAUGHTERS

Five Presidents married the daughters of ministers. They were John Adams, Millard Fillmore, Franklin Pierce, Benjamin Harrison, and Woodrow Wilson.

John Adams married Abigail Smith, daughter of William Smith, a Congregational minister, who was ordained a minister of the gospel on November 4, 1829, at Norwich, Conn.

Millard Fillmore married Abigail Powers, daughter of Lemuel Powers, a Baptist clergyman.

Franklin Pierce married Jane Means Appleton, daughter of Jesse Appleton, a Congregational minister.

Benjamin Harrison married Caroline Scott, daughter of John Witherspoon Scott, ordained a clergyman in 1830 in the Presbyterian church. Scott was also a professor and served at Washington College, Miami University, and Oxford Female College.

Woodrow Wilson married Ellen Louise Axson, daughter of Samuel Edward Axson, a Presbyterian minister.

MARRIAGE TO WIDOWS

Six Presidents married widows, including three of the first four Presidents.

George Washington married Martha Dandridge Custis, the widow of Colonel Daniel Parke Custis, on January 6, 1759. In June 1749, at the age of seventeen, she had married Custis, who was twenty years her senior. He died in 1757 of tuberculosis and she became a widow at the age of twenty-five.

Thomas Jefferson married Martha Wayles Skelton, widow of Bathurst Skelton, on January 1, 1772. She had married Skelton on November 20, 1766. He died on September 30, 1768.

James Madison married Dorothea (Dolley) Payne Todd, widow of John Todd, Sr., on September 15, 1794. She had married Todd on January 7, 1790, in the Friends Meeting House, Pine Street, Philadelphia, Pa.

The other three Presidents who married widows were widowers: Millard Fillmore married Caroline Carmichael McIntosh, the widow of Ezekiel C. McIntosh.

Benjamin Harrison married Mary Scott Lord Dimmick, the widow of Walter Erskine Dimmick, a New York lawyer.

Woodrow Wilson married Edith Bolling Galt, the widow of Norman Galt, a Washington, D.C., jeweler. She had married Galt on April 30, 1896. Galt died on January 28, 1908.

MARRIAGE TO DIVORCEES

Andrew Jackson married Rachel Donelson Robards, who

had been married to Captain Lewis Robards. Robards had sued for divorce, but technically the status of the divorce was in question—a fact the Jacksons were not aware of at the time of their marriage. Jackson had a second wedding ceremony performed three years after the first to eliminate all possible doubts concerning the legality of his marriage.

Warren Gamaliel Harding married Florence Kling De Wolfe, who had been married to Henry De Wolfe. Her marriage to Harding took place after the death of her former husband.

WIVES WITH CHILDREN BY FORMER HUSBANDS

Martha Washington was the mother of four children by her marriage to Daniel Parke Custis. The children were Patsy and Jackey Custis, who had died in infancy; Martha Parke Custis, who died in 1774 at the age of sixteen; and John Parke Custis, who died in 1781 at the age of twenty-five, leaving two children.

Martha Jefferson was the mother of one son by her marriage to Bathurst Skelton, who had died before she was twenty. Her son, John Skelton, born November 7, 1767, had died June 10, 1771.

Dolley Madison was the mother of two sons by her marriage to John Todd. Her sons were John Payne Todd, born February 29, 1792, and William Payne Todd, who had died in infancy in 1793.

Florence Harding was the mother of one son by her marriage to Henry De Wolfe, a marriage which had taken place in 1880 and which had ended in divorce. Her son, Marshall Eugene De Wolfe, died of tuberculosis.

LIFE SPAN OF PRESIDENTS' WIVES

Five wives died before their husbands became President:

Martha Jefferson
Rachel Jackson
Hannah Van Buren
Ellen Arthur
Alice Roosevelt (1st wife)

Three wives died while their husbands were in office:

Letitia Tyler (1st wife)
Caroline Harrison (1st wife)
Ellen Wilson (1st wife)

Twenty-five wives died after their husbands' terms:

Martha Washington
Abigail Adams
Dolley Madison

Elizabeth Monroe
Louisa Adams
Anna Harrison
Julia Tyler (2nd wife)
Sarah Polk
Margaret Taylor
Abigail Fillmore (1st wife)
Caroline Fillmore (2nd wife)
Jane Pierce
Mary Lincoln
Eliza Johnson
Julia Grant
Lucy Hayes
Lucretia Garfield
Frances Cleveland
Mary Harrison (2nd wife)
Ida McKinley
Edith Roosevelt (2nd wife)
Helen Taft
Florence Harding
Grace Coolidge
Lou Hoover

LONGEVITY OF THE PRESIDENTS' WIVES

Of the thirty-seven Presidents' wives, four are living: Mrs. Wilson (second wife), Mrs. Franklin Delano Roosevelt, Mrs. Truman, and Mrs. Eisenhower.

Eight of the thirty-three wives no longer living were 81 years of age or older when they died: Mrs. Madison, Mrs. William Henry Harrison, Mrs. Polk, Mrs. Garfield, Mrs. Cleveland, Mrs. Benjamin Harrison (second wife), Mrs. Theodore Roo-

sevelt (second wife), and Mrs. Taft.

Thirteen of the thirty-three were 70 or older when they died. In addition to the eight mentioned above, they were Mrs. Washington, Mrs. John Adams, Mrs. John Quincy Adams, Mrs. Grant, and Mrs. Coolidge.

Twenty-four of the thirty-three were 60 or older when they died.

Twenty-nine of the thirty-three were 50 or older when they died.

The wife who died at the most advanced age was the second wife of Benjamin Harrison, who was 89 years and 250 days old when she died.

The wife who died at the earliest age was the first wife of Theodore Roosevelt, who was only 22 years and 192 days old when she died.

WIDOWS OF PRESIDENTS GRANTED FREE USE OF THE MAILS

An act of Congress of April 3, 1800—"an act to extend the privilege of franking letters and packages to Martha Washington" (2 Stat.L.19)—granted the widow of George Washington the free use of the mails for her natural life. Other presidential widows to whom the franking privilege was extended by acts of Congress were the following:

Dolley Madison, July 2, 1836

Anna Harrison, September 9, 1841

Louisa Adams, March 9, 1848

Sarah Polk, January 10, 1850

Margaret Taylor, July 18, 1850

Mary Lincoln, February 10, 1866

Lucretia Garfield, December 20, 1881

Julia Grant, June 28, 1886

Ida McKinley, January 22, 1902

Mary Harrison, February 1, 1909

Frances Cleveland, February 1, 1909

Edith Roosevelt, October 27, 1919

Florence Harding, January 25, 1924

Edith Wilson, March 4, 1924

Helen Taft, June 14, 1930

Grace Coolidge, June 16, 1934

Eleanor Roosevelt, May 7, 1945

PENSIONS TO PRESIDENTIAL WIDOWS

Pensions of varying amounts were paid to presidential widows by specific acts of Congress. The first to receive a pension was Anna Harrison (Mrs. William Henry Harrison). On June 30, 1841, Congress passed "an act for the relief of Mrs. Harrison, widow of the late President of the United States." She was granted $25,000, equivalent to a year's salary for a President.

A similar award of $25,000 was made to Mary Lincoln on February 21, 1865, and on July 14, 1870, Congress passed "an act granting a pension to Mary Lincoln" which provided "that the secretary of the interior be, and is hereby authorized to place the name of Mary Lincoln, widow of Abraham Lincoln, deceased, late President of the United States, on the pension roll." It authorized a pension of $3,000 a year. An act of February 2, 1882, awarded her an annual pension of $5,000.

An act of March 31, 1882—"an act granting pensions to Lucretia R. Garfield, Sarah Childress Polk and Julia Gardiner Tyler"—directed the secretary of the interior to place their names "on the pension roll and pay each of them a pension during their respective natural lives at the rate of $5,000 a year from and after the 19th day of September 1881." It also specified that the pension of $5,000 granted by this act to Julia Tyler should be in lieu of the pension previously granted her by Congress.

On July 27, 1882, Congress passed an act awarding Lucretia Garfield the sum of $50,000.

Annual pensions of $5,000 were also awarded the following:

Ida McKinley, April 17, 1902

Edith Roosevelt, February 25, 1919

Edith Wilson, February 18, 1929

Grace Coolidge, January 14, 1937

Helen Taft, May 22, 1937

Mary Harrison, May 24, 1938

Frances Cleveland Preston, November 25, 1940 (Mrs. Cleveland had remarried in 1913.)

In 1958 Congress passed an act granting annual pensions of $10,000 to the widows of Presidents.

"FIRST LADY"

The term "first lady" as a synonym for the wife of a President is believed to have been used for the first time in 1877 by Mary Clemmer Ames in an article in the *Independent* describing the inauguration of President Rutherford Birchard Hayes on Monday, March 5, 1877.

The term became popular when a comedy about Dolley Madison by Charles Nirdlinger entitled *The First Lady in the Land* was produced by Henry B.

Harris at the Gaiety Theatre, New York City, on December 4, 1911. It featured Elsie Ferguson, Clarence Handyside, Luke Martin, David Todd, and Beatrice Noyes.

MARRIAGE STATISTICS

Thirty-two of the thirty-three Presidents married. (James Buchanan was the only President who did not marry.) Five Presidents remarried after the death of their first wives.

The President who married at the earliest age was Andrew Johnson, who married Eliza McCardle when he was 18 years and 127 days old.

The President who married for the first time at the most advanced age was Grover Cleveland, who married Frances Folsom when he was 49 years and 76 days old.

Benjamin Harrison was married for a second time when he was 62 years and 229 days old, a little more than three years after he retired from the presidency.

The youngest of the five Presidents to remarry was Theodore Roosevelt, who married Edith Kermit Carow when he was 28 years and 36 days.

The greatest age difference between a President and his wife was that of John Tyler, who was 54 years and 89 days old at marriage, and his second wife, Julia Gardiner, who was 24 years and 53 days old.

The next greatest age difference between a President and his wife was that of Grover Cleveland, who was 49 years and 76 days old at marriage, and Frances Folsom, who was 21 years and 316 days old.

The President who was married the longest was John Adams who was married 54 years and 3 days.

The only Presidents to celebrate golden wedding anniversaries were John Adams and his son, John Quincy Adams. The father was married 54 years and 3 days and the son 50 years and 112 days.

The shortest marriage was that of Theodore Roosevelt and his first wife, Alice Hathaway Lee, who had been married only 3 years and 110 days when she died.

The wife who married at the earliest age was Eliza Mc-Cardle, who married Andrew Johnson when she was 16 years and 213 days old.

The oldest to marry a President was Caroline Carmichael McIntosh, who married Millard Fillmore, her second husband, when she was 44 years and 112 days old.

The oldest to marry for the first time was Bess Wallace, who married Harry S Truman when she was 34 years and 135 days.

Four Presidents married women older than they: Washington, Harding, Fillmore, and Benjamin Harrison. Washington was 246 days younger than his wife, and Harding was 5 years and 79 days younger. Both Mrs. Washington and Mrs. Harding survived their husbands. Fillmore and Benjamin Harrison also married slightly older women. Fillmore was 1 year and 300 days younger than his wife, and Harrison was 323 days younger. Both Fillmore and Harrison survived their wives and remarried.

TWO PRESIDENTS MARRIED ON THEIR BIRTHDAYS

Two Presidents were married on their birthdays. John Tyler married Letitia Christian, his first wife, on March 29, 1813, his twenty-third birthday. Theodore Roosevelt married Alice Hathaway Lee, his first wife, on October 27, 1880, his twenty-second birthday.

WIDOWERS IN THE WHITE HOUSE

Two widowers were elected President: Thomas Jefferson, whose wife had died on September 6, 1782, almost nineteen years before his inauguration on March 4, 1801, and Martin Van Buren, whose wife had died on February 5, 1819, more than eighteen years before his inauguration on March 4, 1837.

Andrew Jackson's wife died on December 22, 1828. She lived to see him elected but died before he was inaugurated on March 4, 1829.

Chester Alan Arthur was a widower when he succeeded to the presidency. His wife had died on January 12, 1880, before he was elected Vice President in November 1880.

When Theodore Roosevelt was elected Vice President in 1900, he was married to his second wife, his first wife having died in 1884.

SECOND MARRIAGES

Theodore Roosevelt remarried before he became President. Tyler and Wilson remarried while they were in office. Fillmore and Benjamin Harrison remarried after their terms as President.

With the exception of Theodore Roosevelt, who was 2 years and 293 days older than his second wife, these Presidents married women considerably younger than they were. Fillmore was 13 years and 287 days

older than his wife, Wilson was 15 years and 291 days older, Harrison was 24 years and 253 days older, and Tyler was 30 years and 26 days older.

Three of the five Presidents who remarried had children by both wives: John Tyler, Benjamin Harrison, and Theodore Roosevelt.

Millard Fillmore and Woodrow Wilson had children by their first marriages but none by their second.

Three of the five wives, Mrs. Fillmore, Mrs. Harrison, and Mrs. Wilson, were widows when they married.

All of the five wives survived their husbands.

CHILDREN OF THE PRESIDENTS

Six of the thirty-three Presidents had no children. They were Washington, Madison, Jackson, Polk, Harding, and Buchanan, who was a bachelor.

The twenty-seven Presidents who had children had a total of 124 children, 75 boys and 49 girls. Only three of them did not have boys—McKinley, Wilson, and Truman. Six of them had boys and no girls—Van Buren, Pierce, Lincoln, Coolidge, Hoover, and Eisenhower.

The President who had the

greatest number of children was John Tyler, the father of fifteen. He had three sons and five daughters by his first wife, Letitia Christian. He married Julia Gardiner while he was President. After leaving the White House, they had seven children, five sons and two daughters.

The President who had the greatest number of children prior to his election was William Henry Harrison, who had ten children, four of whom were alive when he became President.

CHILDREN BORN IN FOREIGN COUNTRIES

George Washington Adams, the son of John Quincy Adams, was the first child of a President born in a foreign country. He was born April 13, 1801, in Berlin, Germany. His youngest sister, Louisa Catherine Adams, was born ten years later at St. Petersburg, Russia. Their father was serving the United States abroad on diplomatic assignments.

Both of President Hoover's sons were born in London, England. Herbert Clark Hoover, Jr., was born August 4, 1903, and Allan Henry Hoover, July 17, 1907.

Franklin Delano Roosevelt, Jr., was born at Campobello, New Brunswick, Canada, on August 17, 1914.

THE PRESIDENTS' DESCENDANTS

The direct lineage of the Presidents extends to the ninth and tenth generations in the case of John Adams and Jefferson. Jefferson's descendants number over 1,225; Adams' descendants over 735.

The President with the greatest number of children was John Tyler, who had fifteen children by his two wives. William Henry Harrison led with the greatest number of grandchildren and great-grandchildren. He had 48 grandchildren and 106 great-grandchildren.

With the deaths of Presidents Washington, Madison, Polk, Buchanan, and Harding, their respective lines ceased.

THE PRESIDENTS' NAMES

Seven Presidents bore the same given name as their fathers: John Adams, James Madison, Andrew Jackson, John Tyler, James Buchanan, William McKinley, and Theodore Roosevelt.

Seven Presidents had family names ending in *son:* Jefferson, Madison, Jackson, William Henry Harrison, Johnson, Benjamin Harrison, and Wilson.

Three Presidents had the same family name as the three earlier Presidents to whom they were related: John Quincy Adams, son of John Adams; Benjamin Harrison, grandson of William Henry Harrison; and Franklin Delano Roosevelt, a fifth cousin of Theodore Roosevelt.

Seventeen of the thirty-three Presidents were not given a middle initial or name. They were George Washington, John Adams, Thomas Jefferson, James Madison, James Monroe, Andrew Jackson, Martin Van Buren, John Tyler, Zachary Taylor, Millard Fillmore, Franklin Pierce, James Buchanan, Abraham Lincoln, Andrew Johnson, Benjamin Harrison, William McKinley, and Theodore Roosevelt.

Twenty of the thirty-three Presidents were given biblical names. Five were named James —the name most frequently given: Madison, Monroe, Polk, Buchanan, and Garfield (whose middle name, Abram, was also biblical). Four were named John: John Adams, John Quincy Adams, Tyler, and Coolidge (originally John Calvin). Two were named Andrew: Jackson and Johnson. Two were named Thomas: Jefferson and Wilson (originally Thomas Woodrow). One—Lincoln—was named Abraham. One —Harrison—was named Benjamin. Also given biblical names were Harding, whose middle name was Gamaliel; Eisenhower, who transposed his name from David Dwight to Dwight David; Taylor, whose first name, Zachary, was an adaptation of Zachariah; Grant, who dropped his original first name, Hiram; and Cleveland, who dropped his original first name, Stephen.

Five Presidents were given at birth first names that they later changed. Hiram Ulysses Grant became Ulysses Simpson Grant, Stephen Grover Cleveland became Grover Cleveland, Thomas Woodrow Wilson became Woodrow Wilson, John Calvin Coolidge became Calvin Coolidge, and David Dwight Eisenhower became Dwight David Eisenhower.

The last names of five Presidents began with the letter *H:* William Henry Harrison, Rutherford Birchard Hayes, Benjamin Harrison, Warren Gamaliel Harding, and Herbert Clark Hoover.

NICKNAMES AND SOBRIQUETS

Many of the Presidents have been known by nicknames and sobriquets, a few of which are given below. In some instances, malcontents have applied epithets to those whom they disliked, but none of these are worthy of inclusion.

Washington

American Fabius, Atlas of America, Cincinnatus of the West, Deliverer of America, Farmer President, Father of His Country, Father of Pittsburgh, Old Fox, Sage of Mount Vernon, Savior of His Country, Stepfather of His Country, Surveyor President, Sword of the Revolution

J. Adams

Atlas of Independence, Colossus of Debate, Colossus of Independence, Duke of Braintree, Father of American Independence, Father of the American Navy, His Rotundity, Old Sink or Swim, Partisan of Independence

Jefferson

Father of the Declaration of Independence, Father of the University of Virginia, Long Tom, Man of the People, Pen of the Revolution, Philosopher of Democracy, Red Fox, Sage of Monticello, Scribe of the Revolution

Madison

Father of the Constitution, Sage of Montpelier

Monroe

Era of Good Feeling President, Last of the Cocked Hats

J. Q. Adams

Accidental President, Old Man Eloquent, Second John

Jackson

Duel Fighter, Hero of New Orleans, King Andrew the First, Land Hero of 1812, Mischievous Andy, Old Hickory, People's President, Pointed Arrow, Sage of the Hermitage, Sharp Knife

Van Buren

American Talleyrand, Enchanter, Fox, Kinderhook Fox, King Martin the First, Little Magician, Little Van, Machiavellian Belshazzar, Mistletoe Politician, Petticoat Pet, Red Fox of Kinderhook, Sage of Kinderhook, Sage of Lindenwald, Whiskey Van, Wizard of Kinderhook, Wizard of the Albany Regency

W. H. Harrison

Farmer President, Hero of Tippecanoe, Log Cabin President,

Old Granny, Old Tip, Old Tippecanoe, Tippecanoe, Washington of the West

Tyler

Accidental President, His Accidency, Young Hickory

Polk

First Dark Horse, Napoleon of the Stump, Young Hickory

Taylor

Old Buena Vista, Old Rough and Ready, Old Zach

Fillmore

Accidental President, American Louis Philippe, His Accidency, Wool-Carder President

Pierce

Handsome Frank, Purse

Buchanan

Bachelor President, Old Buck, Old Public Functionary, Sage of Wheatland, Ten-cent Jimmy

Lincoln

Ancient, Buffoon, Caesar, Father Abraham, Flatboat Man, Grand Wrestler, Great Emancipator, Honest Abe, Illinois Baboon, Jester, Long 'Un, Man of the People, Martyr President, Railsplitter, Sage of Springfield, Sectional President, Tycoon, Tyrant, Uncle Abe

Johnson

Daddy of the Baby, Father of the Homestead Act, His Accidency, King Andy the First, Old Andy, Old Veto, Sir Veto, Tennessee Tailor, Veto President

Grant

American Caesar, Butcher from Galena, Butcher Grant, Galena Tanner, Great Hammerer, Great Peacemaker, Hero of Appomattox, Hero of Fort Donelson, Old Three Stars, Silent Man, Tanner President, Texas, Uncle Sam, Unconditional Surrender, Union Safeguard, United States, Unprecedented Strategist, Unquestionably Skilled, Useless Grant

Hayes

Dark Horse President, Fraud President, Granny Hayes, Hero of '77, His Fraudulency, Old Eight to Seven, President De Facto

Garfield

Canal Boy, Martyr President, Preacher President, Teacher President

Arthur

America's First Gentleman, Arthur the Gentleman, Dude President, Elegant Arthur, First Gentleman of the Land, His Accidency, Our Chet, Prince Arthur

Cleveland

Buffalo Hangman, Buffalo Sheriff, Claimant, Dumb Prophet, Grover the Good, Hangman of Buffalo, Man of Destiny, Old Grover, Old Veto, People's President, Perpetual Candidate, Pretender, Reform Governor, Sage of Princeton, Stuffed Prophet, Uncle Jumbo, Veto Governor, Veto Mayor, Veto President

B. Harrison

Centennial President, Chinese Harrison, Grandfather's Hat, Grandpa's Grandson, Kid Gloves Harrison, Little Ben, Son of His Grandfather

McKinley

Idol of Ohio, Napoleon of Protection, Prosperity's Advance Agent, Stocking-foot Orator

T. Roosevelt

Bull Moose, Driving Force, Dynamo of Power, Four Eyes, Great White Chief, Happy Warrior, Haroun-al-Roosevelt, Hero of San Juan Hill, Man on Horseback, Meddler, Old Lion, Rough Rider, Telescope Teddy, Trust Buster, Typical American

Wilson

Coiner of Weasel-words, Phrasemaker, Professor, Schoolmaster in Politics

Coolidge

Red, Silent Cal

Hoover

Chief, Friend of Helpless Children, Hermit Author of Palo Alto, Man of Great Heart

F. D. Roosevelt

Boss, F.D.R., Houdini in the White House, Sphinx, Squire of Hyde Park, That Man in the White House

Truman

Give 'Em Hell Harry, High Tax Harry, Man from Missouri, Man of Independence

Eisenhower

General Ike, Ike

Cultural and Vocational Background

PRESIDENTS WHO ATTENDED COLLEGE

The following is a list of Presidents who attended college, the institutions attended, and the dates of graduation:

J. Adams—Harvard, July 16, 1775

Jefferson—William and Mary, Apr. 25, 1762

Madison—Princeton, Sept. 25, 1771

Monroe—William and Mary, 1776

J. Q. Adams—Harvard, July 18, 1787

W. H. Harrison—Hampden-Sydney, left before graduation

Tyler—William and Mary, July 4, 1807

Polk—North Carolina, June 4, 1818

Pierce—Bowdoin, Sept. 1, 1824

Buchanan—Dickinson, Sept. 27, 1809

Grant—U.S. Military Academy, July 1, 1843

Hayes—Kenyon, Aug. 3, 1842

Garfield—Williams, Aug. 6, 1856

Arthur—Union, July 1848

B. Harrison—Miami, June 24, 1852

McKinley—Allegheny, left before graduation

T. Roosevelt—Harvard, June 30, 1880

Taft—Yale, June 27, 1878

Wilson—Princeton, June 18, 1879

Harding—Ohio Central, left before graduation

Coolidge—Amherst, June 26, 1895

Hoover—Stanford, May 29, 1895

F. D. Roosevelt—Harvard, June 24, 1903

Eisenhower—U.S. Military Academy, June 12, 1915

PRESIDENTS WHO DID NOT ATTEND COLLEGE

Washington
Jackson
Van Buren
Taylor
Fillmore
Lincoln
Johnson
Cleveland
Truman

EARLY OCCUPATIONS

Washington—Surveyor, farmer
J. Adams—Lawyer, teacher
Jefferson—Lawyer
Madison—Lawyer
Monroe—Lawyer, soldier
J. Q. Adams—Lawyer, private secretary
Jackson—Lawyer, saddler
Van Buren—Lawyer
W. H. Harrison—Soldier
Tyler—Lawyer
Polk—Lawyer, clerk
Taylor—Farmer, soldier
Fillmore—Lawyer, wool-carder
Pierce—Lawyer

Buchanan—Lawyer
Lincoln—Lawyer, farm worker
Johnson—Tailor, public official
Grant—Farmer, soldier
Hayes—Lawyer
Garfield—Lawyer, canal driver
Arthur—Lawyer, teacher
Cleveland—Clerk, teacher
B. Harrison—Lawyer
McKinley—Lawyer, teacher
T. Roosevelt—Public official
Taft—Lawyer
Wilson—Lawyer, teacher
Harding—Journalist
Coolidge—Lawyer
Hoover—Engineer
F. D. Roosevelt—Lawyer
Truman—Lawyer
Eisenhower—Soldier

OCCUPATIONS OF THE PRESIDENTS

Twenty-four of the thirty-three Presidents were admitted to the bar as attorneys, having fulfilled the legal requirements. However, they were not all graduates of law schools.

The nine Presidents not lawyers were George Washington and William Henry Harrison, who were farmers and soldiers; Warren Gamaliel Harding, who was a publisher and editor;

Herbert Hoover, who was an engineer; Zachary Taylor, Ulysses Simpson Grant, and Dwight David Eisenhower, who were professional soldiers; Andrew Johnson and Theodore Roosevelt, who were public officials.

OCCUPATIONS AFTER TERMS

Three Presidents engaged in governmental activities after completing their terms: John Quincy Adams became a representative, Johnson became a senator, and Hoover was active on various government commissions.

Grant, Truman, and Hoover devoted considerable time to writing. Truman and Hoover have also been active as public speakers.

Adams, Pierce, and Buchanan retired from public life and avoided public appearances.

Five Presidents were actively engaged as farmers or planters: Washington, Jefferson, Madison, Jackson, and Hayes. In addition, Washington was also active as commander-in-chief of the army.

Benjamin Harrison was a professor of international law at Leland Stanford University.

Six Presidents traveled extensively after their terms: Van Buren, Fillmore, Polk, Pierce, Grant, and Theodore Roosevelt.

POLITICAL EXPERIENCE

Presidents who had not demonstrated their administrative ability prior to election or proven their vote-getting power were those who had gained fame for their military exploits, namely Washington, Grant, and Eisenhower. Grant, however, had served in Johnson's cabinet as secretary of war ad interim.

The following is a list of the various capacities in which Presidents served and the number of Presidents who served in each:

Ministers to foreign countries —7

Governors of states—13

Vice Presidents—10

Members of presidential cabinets—9

U.S. representatives—14

U.S. senators—13

Members of both the House and Senate—8

Some Presidents served in more than one capacity.

MINISTERS TO FOREIGN COUNTRIES

J. Adams—Great Britain

Jefferson—France

Monroe—France

J. Q. Adams—The Netherlands, Portugal, Prussia, Russia, Great Britain

Van Buren—Great Britain
W. H. Harrison—Colombia
Buchanan—Great Britain

STATE GOVERNORS

Jefferson—Virginia
Monroe—Virginia
Van Buren—New York
Tyler—Virginia
Polk—Tennessee
Johnson—Tennessee
Hayes—Ohio
Cleveland—New York
McKinley—Ohio
T. Roosevelt—New York
Wilson—New Jersey
Coolidge—Massachusetts
F. D. Roosevelt—New York

TERRITORIAL GOV-
ERNORS

Jackson—Florida
W. H. Harrison—Indiana

PRESIDENTS WHO
SERVED IN PRESI-
DENTIAL CABINETS

Secretary of State

Jefferson (under Washington),
Sept. 26, 1789-Mar. 3, 1797
(entered upon duties Mar. 22,
1790)

Madison (under Jefferson),
Mar. 5, 1801-Mar. 3, 1809
(entered upon duties May 2,
1801)

Monroe (under Madison), Apr.
2, 1811-Mar. 3, 1817 (entered
upon duties Apr. 6, 1811)

J. Q. Adams (under Monroe),
Mar. 5, 1817-Mar. 3, 1825
(entered upon duties Sept. 22,
1817)

Van Buren (under Jackson),
Mar. 6, 1829-May 23, 1831
(entered upon duties Mar. 28,
1829)

Buchanan (under Polk), Mar.
6, 1845-Mar. 3, 1849 (entered
upon duties Mar. 10, 1845)

Buchanan (under Taylor),
Mar. 4, 1849-Mar. 6, 1849

Secretary of War

Monroe (under Madison), ad
interim Jan. 1, 1813-Jan. 13,
1813

Monroe (under Madison), ad
interim Aug. 30, 1814-Mar.
14, 1815

Grant (under Johnson), ad interim Aug. 12, 1867-Jan. 13,
1868

Taft (under T. Roosevelt), Jan.
11, 1904-June 29, 1908 (to
take effect Feb. 1, 1904)

Secretary of Commerce

Hoover (under Harding), Mar.
5, 1921-Aug. 2, 1923

Hoover (under Coolidge), Aug. 3, 1923-Aug. 21, 1928

PRESIDENTS WHO SERVED IN BOTH HOUSES OF CONGRESS (8)

J. Q. Adams	Buchanan
Jackson	Johnson
W. H. Harrison	Garfield
	(elected, but
Tyler	did not
Pierce	serve

PRESIDENTS WHO SERVED ONLY IN THE HOUSE OF REPRESENTATIVES (6)

Madison	Lincoln
Polk	Hayes
Fillmore	McKinley

PRESIDENTS WHO SERVED ONLY IN THE SENATE (5)

Monroe	Harding
Van Buren	Truman
B. Harrison	

PRESIDENTS WHO DID NOT SERVE IN CONGRESS (14)

Washington	Taft
J. Adams	Wilson
Jefferson	Coolidge
Taylor	Hoover
Grant	F. D. Roosevelt
Arthur	
Cleveland	Eisenhower
T. Roosevelt	

MILITARY SERVICE

The Constitution (Article II, section 2) provides that "the President shall be Commander in Chief of the Army and Navy of the United States, and of the Militia of the several states, when called into the actual Service of the United States."

Nineteen of the thirty-three Presidents were in actual military service. They are listed below under the wars in which they served, with an asterisk preceding the name of each of the Presidents who served in two or more wars. The dates of service are listed in the individual biographies in Part I.

Revolutionary War
Washington
Monroe
*Jackson

War of 1812
*Jackson
W. H. Harrison
*Taylor

Black Hawk War
*Taylor
Lincoln

Mexican War
*Taylor
Pierce
Buchanan
*Grant

Civil War
Johnson
*Grant
Hayes
Garfield
Arthur
B. Harrison
McKinley

Spanish American War
T. Roosevelt

World War I	World War II
Truman	
*Eisenhower	*Eisenhower

The following Presidents had no military service:

J. Adams	Taft
Jefferson	Wilson
Madison	Harding
J. Q. Adams	Coolidge
Van Buren	Hoover
Polk	F. D. Roosevelt
Fillmore	
Cleveland	

TWO PRESIDENTS WOUNDED IN BATTLE

Although nineteen Presidents were in military service at some time in their lives, only two were wounded in battle.

James Monroe was wounded in the shoulder at the Battle of Trenton, N.J., on December 26, 1776, in the Revolutionary War.

Rutherford Birchard Hayes was wounded four times while serving in the Union Army. On May 10, 1862, a shell wounded his right knee at Giles Court House, Va. He was wounded in the left arm by a musket ball on September 14, 1862, at the Battle of South Mountain, Md. On September 19, 1864, while at Winchester, Va., he was wounded in his head and shoulder by a musket ball. At the Battle of Cedar Creek, Va., October 19, 1864, he was wounded in the ankle, his horse was shot from under him, and he was erroneously reported dead. The following day, he was promoted to brigadier general.

MEMBERS OF PHI BETA KAPPA— YEAR OF ELECTION, CHAPTER, AND TYPE OF MEMBERSHIP

J. Q. Adams—1787, Harvard, in course

Van Buren—1830, Union, honorary

Pierce—1825, Bowdoin, alumnus

Hayes—1880, Kenyon, alumnus

Garfield—1864, Williams, alumnus

Arthur—1848, Union, in course

Cleveland—1907, Princeton, honorary

T. Roosevelt—1880, Harvard, in course

Wilson—1889, Wesleyan, honorary

Coolidge—1921, Amherst, alumnus

F. D. Roosevelt—1929, Harvard, alumnus; 1929, Hobart, honorary

Members in course are elected from candidates for degrees in liberal arts and sciences, generally from the upper tenth of the graduating class.

Alumni members are elected from the alumni body of the sheltering institution; ordinarily they have been graduated at least ten years and are thought to merit recognition for scholarly accomplishment.

Honorary members are elected from outside the student and alumni bodies of the sheltering institution, and are chosen on substantially the same basis as alumni members. Of honorary members the chapters now elect severally an average of not more than one in each triennium.

PRESIDENTS WHO WERE MASONS

Washington—Aug. 4, 1753, Fredericksburg Lodge No. 4, Fredericksburg, Va.

Monroe—1775, Williamsburg Lodge No. 6, Williamsburg, Va.

Jackson—1800, Harmony Lodge No. 1, Nashville, Tenn.

Polk—Sept. 4, 1820, Columbia Lodge No. 31, Columbia, Tenn.

Buchanan—Jan. 24, 1817, Lodge No. 43, Lancaster, Pa.

Johnson—1851, Greeneville Lodge No. 119, Greeneville, Tenn.

Garfield—Nov. 22, 1864, Magnolia Lodge No. 20, Columbus, Ohio.

McKinley—May 3, 1865, Hiram Lodge No. 21, Winchester, Va.

T. Roosevelt—Apr. 24, 1901, Matinecock Lodge No. 806, Oyster Bay, N.Y.

Taft—Feb. 18, 1909, affiliated with Kilwinning Lodge No. 356, Cincinnati, Ohio.

Harding—Aug. 27, 1920, Marion Lodge No. 70, Marion, Ohio.

F. D. Roosevelt—Nov. 28, 1911, Holland Lodge No. 8, Hyde Park, N.Y.

Truman—Mar. 9, 1909, Belton Lodge No. 450, Belton, Mo.

PRESIDENTS' SPORTS AND HOBBIES

At various times in their lives, the Presidents engaged in different sports and games. Some were real enthusiasts, others participated mildly.

Some favorite sports or games indulged in by Presidents while in office follow:

Billiards—J. Q. Adams, Garfield
Boxing—T. Roosevelt
Bridge—Eisenhower
Croquet—Hayes

Driving—Hayes

Fishing—Washington, Jefferson, Arthur, Cleveland, Coolidge, Hoover, F. D. Roosevelt, Truman, Eisenhower

Golf—Taft, Wilson, Harding, Coolidge, Eisenhower

Hunting—B. Harrison, T. Roosevelt, Eisenhower

Indian clubs—Coolidge

Jujitsu—T. Roosevelt

Mechanical horse—Coolidge

Medicine ball—Hoover

Painting—Eisenhower

Pitching hay—Coolidge

Poker—Harding, Truman

Riding—Washington, Jefferson, Jackson, Van Buren, Taylor, McKinley, T. Roosevelt, Taft, Wilson, Harding

Sailing—F. D. Roosevelt

Shooting—Hayes, T. Roosevelt

Swimming—J. Q. Adams, McKinley, F. D. Roosevelt

Tennis—T. Roosevelt

Walking—J. Q. Adams, Lincoln, McKinley, Wilson, Truman

Wrestling—T. Roosevelt

PRESIDENTS' MUSICAL ACCOMPLISHMENTS

Very few of the Presidents had musical training and few had the ability to play musical instruments. Jefferson and Tyler played the violin, Truman the piano, and Coolidge the harmonica. As a young man, Harding played the alto horn and the cornet.

Residence

PRESIDENTS ELECTED FROM STATES OTHER THAN THEIR BIRTHPLACES

The fourteen Presidents listed below were elected from states other than their native states. The name of each is followed by (1) the state from which he was elected and (2) the state in which he was born.

Jackson—Tennessee, South Carolina

W. H. Harrison—Ohio, Virginia

Polk—Tennessee, North Carolina

Taylor—Louisiana, Virginia

Lincoln—Illinois, Kentucky

Johnson—Tennessee, North Carolina

Grant—Illinois, Ohio

Arthur—New York, Vermont

Cleveland—New York, New Jersey

B. Harrison—Indiana, Ohio

Wilson—New Jersey, Virginia

Coolidge—Massachusetts, Vermont

Hoover—California, Iowa

Eisenhower—New York, Texas

FAMOUS PRESIDENTIAL HOMES

Many of the Presidents were born in or lived in homes which have become famous. Some of the more famous homes or estates follow:

Washington—Mount Vernon, Mount Vernon, Va.

Jefferson—Monticello, Charlottesville, Va.

Madison—Montpelier, Va.

Monroe—Ash Lawn, Oak Hill, Va.

Jackson—The Hermitage, Nashville, Tenn.

Van Buren—Lindenwald, Kinderhook, N.Y.

Tyler—Sherwood Forest, Charles City County, Va.

Buchanan—Wheatland, Pa.

Hayes—Spiegel Grove, near Fremont, Ohio

T. Roosevelt—Sagamore Hill, Oyster Bay, N.Y.

Coolidge—The Beeches, Northampton, Mass.

There are other well-known residences, such as the F. D. Roosevelt Home at Hyde Park, N.Y., and the Eisenhower farm at Gettysburg, Pa., but they are not known by any special names.

Age and Physical Characteristics

AGES OF PRESIDENTS IN OFFICE

Andrew Jackson was 69 years and 354 days old when he completed his eight years as President.

Benjamin Harrison was 69 years and 315 days old when he left office, but he served only four years. He was four years older than Jackson when inaugurated.

The oldest President inaugurated was William Henry Harrison, who was 68 years and 23 days old when he was inaugurated. He served only 31 days before he died.

President Eisenhower was 62 years and 98 days when he was inaugurated. Upon completion of his term of eight years, he will be 70 years and 98 days, 109 days older than Jackson.

PHYSICAL APPEAR-
ANCE

There is much interest in comparing the physical characteristics of the Presidents at the time when they were inaugurated or assumed office.

As contemporary reports vary and as writers interpret according to their own impressions, many conflicting reports exist. The description of a Republican President by a Democrat may differ from one by a Republican, and even without bias due to politics, personal appraisals by different people may vary.

The following is a list of known characteristics:

Washington

Height, 6 feet 2 inches; weight, 175 pounds; brown sandy hair, powdered, under powdered wig; blue eyes; high brow, scar on left cheek, black mole under right ear, pockmarks on nose and cheeks; strongly pointed chin; false teeth; powerful physique; broad sloping shoulders

J. Adams

Height, 5 feet 7 inches; corpulent; bald; expanded eyebrows

Jefferson

Height, 6 feet 2½ inches; sandy, reddish hair; prominent cheek-bones and chin; large hands and feet

Madison

Height, 5 feet 4 inches (smallest President in stature); weight, about 100 pounds; blond hair; blue eyes; weak speaking voice

Monroe

Height, 6 feet; rugged physique; blue-gray eyes, well shaped nose, broad forehead; stooped shoulders

J. Q. Adams

Height, 5 feet 7 inches; bald

Jackson

Height, 6 feet, 1 inch; thin; weight, 140 pounds; bushy iron-gray hair, brushed high above forehead; clear, dark blue eyes; prominent eyebrows

Van Buren

Height, 5 feet 6 inches; small, erect, slender; red and graying hair, bald spot; deep wrinkles

W. H. Harrison
Height, 5 feet 8 inches; long, thin face, irregular features

Tyler
Height, 6 feet; thin; light brown hair; blue eyes; light complexion; high-bridged nose

Polk
Height, 5 feet 8 inches; nearly white hair, worn long; sharp gray eyes; high forehead, thin, angular brow

Taylor
Height, 5 feet 8 inches; weight, 170 pounds; black hair; gray eyes, squint; ruddy complexion; short legs in proportion to body

Fillmore
Height, 5 feet 9 inches; finely proportioned body; thin, grayish hair; blue eyes; light complexion; smooth forehead; well developed chest

Pierce
Height, 5 feet 10 inches; erect bearing; penetrating dark gray eyes; small but strong features; stiff military carriage

Buchanan
Height, 6 feet; imperfect vision; light complexion; protruding chin; short neck; muscular appearance

Lincoln
Height, 6 feet 4 inches (tallest President); weight, 180 pounds; beard; black hair; gray eyes

Johnson
Height, 5 feet 10 inches; stocky; brown hair, worn long; light eyes; high forehead

Grant
Height, 5 feet 8½ inches; beard; square, straight brows; large head; heavy nostrils; firm-set mouth

Garfield
Height, 6 feet; light brown, graying hair, receding hair line; beard; blue eyes; large head, high forehead; strong frame, broad shoulders; left-handed

Arthur
Height, 6 feet 2 inches; full side whiskers and mustache; handsome appearance; well proportioned body

Hayes

Height, 5 feet 8½ inches; weight, 170 pounds; dark brown hair; sandy red beard; deeply set blue eyes; large head, high forehead, straight nose, circling brows; mild but very audible voice

Cleveland

Height, 5 feet 11 inches; weight, 260 pounds, corpulent; graying hair, growing bald; heavy, drooping mustache; short neck

B. Harrison

Height, 5 feet 6 inches; blond, graying hair; full beard; small, bright blue eyes; short neck; short legs

McKinley

Height, 5 feet 7 inches; high forehead, receding hair line; prominent chin; broad forehead

T. Roosevelt

Height, 5 feet 10 inches; pince-nez eyeglasses with thick lenses; prominent teeth; bushy eyebrows; drooping mustache; high voice

Taft

Height, 6 feet; huge frame; weight, 300-332 pounds; deepset eyes; ruddy complexion; turned-up mustache

Wilson

Weight, 179 pounds; eyeglasses; clean-cut, ascetic face

Harding

Height, 6 feet; high forehead; graying hair; bushy eyebrows

Coolidge

Height, 5 feet 10 inches; large, clear forehead; thin nose; tightly set lips

Hoover

Height, 5 feet 11 inches; square-faced; ruddy complexion

F. D. Roosevelt

Height, 6 feet 2 inches; weight, 188 pounds; high forehead; graying hair; occasionally wore eyeglasses; wore braces on his legs

Truman

Height, 5 feet 9 inches; weight, 167 pounds; receding steel-gray hair, parted on left; hazel eyes; eyeglasses with thick lenses

Eisenhower

Height, 5 feet 10½ inches; weight, 168-173 pounds; bald, with fringe of sandy, graying hair; blue eyes; ruddy complexion; engaging smile

Death and Burial

PRESIDENTS' DEATHS

Of the thirty no longer living in 1959, seven died in office and twenty-three survived their terms.

No President died in the month of May.

Seven of the thirty-three Presidents died in July.

Two Presidents, John Adams and Thomas Jefferson, died on the same day, July 4, 1826.

Three Presidents died on July 4, John Adams and Thomas Jefferson in 1826, and James Monroe in 1831.

The Whig Party nominated four presidential candidates; the two who were elected, William Henry Harrison and Zachary Taylor, died in office.

With the exception of President Franklin Delano Roosevelt, who was elected four times, no Democratic President died in office.

PRESIDENTS WHO DIED IN OFFICE

Seven Presidents died in office:

William Henry Harrison— died Apr. 4, 1841, Washington, D.C.; served 1 month; unexpired term of 3 years and 11 months filled by John Tyler

Zachary Taylor—died July 9, 1850, Washington, D.C.; served 1 year, 4 months, and 5 days; unexpired term of 2 years, 7 months, and 26 days filled by Millard Fillmore

Abraham Lincoln—died Apr. 14, 1865, Washington, D.C.; served 1 month and 10 days of second term; unexpired term of 3 years, 10 months, and 20 days filled by Andrew Johnson

James Abram Garfield—died Sept. 19, 1881, Elberon, N.J.; served 6 months and 15 days;

unexpired term of 3 years, 5 months, and 15 days filled by Chester Alan Arthur

William McKinley—died Sept. 14, 1901, Buffalo, N.Y.; served 6 months and 10 days of second term; unexpired term of 3 years, 5 months, and 20 days filled by Theodore Roosevelt

Warren Gamaliel Harding—died Aug. 2, 1923, San Francisco, Calif.; served 2 years, 4 months, and 29 days; unexpired term of 1 year, 7 months, and 2 days filled by Calvin Coolidge

Franklin Delano Roosevelt—died Apr. 12, 1945, Warm Springs, Ga.; served 2 months and 23 days of fourth term; unexpired term of 3 years, 9 months, and 7 days filled by Harry S Truman

The presidency of the United States was held for a total of 22 years and 9 months by men who were not elected to the office but who obtained it through the death of the incumbent.

LENGTH OF LIFE AFTER COMPLETION OF TERM

Of the thirty Presidents who are no longer living, twenty-three survived their terms of office. The following list shows

the number of years lived after retirement from the presidency:

Polk—103 days

Arthur—1 year, 260 days

Washington—2 years, 285 days

Wilson—2 years, 337 days

Coolidge—3 years, 308 days

Monroe—6 years, 122 days

Johnson—6 years, 149 days

Buchanan—7 years, 89 days

B. Harrison—8 years, 9 days

Jackson—8 years, 96 days

Grant—8 years, 141 days

T. Roosevelt—9 years, 309 days

Cleveland—11 years, 112 days (after second term)

Hayes—11 years, 319 days

Pierce—12 years, 218 days

Tyler—16 years, 320 days

Jefferson—17 years, 122 days

Taft—17 years, 4 days

J. Q. Adams—18 years, 356 days

Cleveland—19 years, 112 days (after first term)

Madison—19 years, 116 days

Fillmore—21 years, 4 days

Van Buren—21 years, 142 days

J. Adams—25 years, 122 days

AGE AT DEATH

The average life span of the thirty Presidents who are no longer living was 68 years and

181 days. The following list shows the relative longevity of the Presidents:

J. Adams—90 years, 247 days

Madison—85 years, 104 days

Jefferson—83 years, 82 days

J. Q. Adams—80 years, 227 days

Van Buren—79 years, 231 days

Jackson—78 years, 85 days

Buchanan—77 years, 39 days

Fillmore—74 years, 60 days

Monroe—73 years, 67 days

Taft—72 years, 174 days

Tyler—71 years, 295 days

Cleveland—71 years, 98 days

Hayes—70 years, 105 days

W. H. Harrison—68 years, 54 days

Washington—67 years, 295 days

B. Harrison—67 years, 205 days

Wilson—67 years, 37 days

Johnson—66 years, 214 days

Taylor—65 years, 227 days

Pierce—64 years, 319 days

Grant—63 years, 87 days

F. D. Roosevelt—63 years, 72 days

Coolidge—60 years, 185 days

T. Roosevelt—60 years, 71 days

McKinley—58 years, 228 days

Harding—57 years, 273 days

Lincoln—56 years, 62 days

Arthur—56 years, 44 days

Polk—53 years, 225 days

Garfield—49 years, 304 days

RELATIVE LONGEVITY OF THE PRESIDENTS AND THEIR PARENTS

The ages noted in the following list are (1) the age at death of each President, (2) the age at death of his father, and (3) the age at death of his mother.

Washington

67 years, 295 days; about 49 years; 59 years, 148 days

J. Adams

90 years, 247 days; 70 years, 106 days; 98 years, 43 days

Jefferson

83 years, 82 days; 49 years, 170 days; 56 years, 50 days

Madison

85 years, 104 days; 77 years, 337 days; 98 years, 33 days

Monroe

73 years, 67 days; ——; ——

J. Q. Adams

80 years, 227 days; 90 years, 247 days; 73 years, 351 days

Jackson

78 years, 85 days; ——; ——

Van Buren

79 years, 231 days; 80 years, 40 days; about 70 years

W. H. Harrison

68 years, 54 days; 65 years, 19 days; about 62 years

Tyler

71 years, 295 days; 65 years, 312 days; about 36 years

Polk

53 years, 225 days; 55 years, 123 days; 75 years, 57 days

Taylor

65 years, 227 days; 84 years, 291 days; 61 years, 364 days

Fillmore

74 years, 60 days; 91 years, 343 days; about 51 years

Pierce

64 years, 319 days; 81 years, 97 days; about 70 years

Buchanan

77 years, 39 days; about 60 years; about 66 years

Lincoln

56 years, 62 days; 73 years, 11 days; 34 years, 242 days

Johnson

66 years, 214 days; about 33 years; 72 years, 211 days

Grant

63 years, 87 days; 79 years, 157 days; 84 years, 169 days

Hayes

70 years, 105 days; 35 years, 197 days; 74 years, 198 days

Garfield

49 years, 304 days; 33 years, 126 days; 86 years, 122 days

Arthur

56 years, 44 days; 78 years, 326 days; 66 years, 262 days

Cleveland

71 years, 98 days; 49 years, 104 days; 76 years, 165 days

B. Harrison

67 years, 205 days; 73 years, 233 days; 40 years, 28 days

McKinley

58 years, 228 days; 85 years, 9 days; 88 years, 234 days

T. Roosevelt

60 years, 71 days; 46 years, 140 days; 49 years, 221 days

Taft

72 years, 174 days; 80 years, 197 days; 80 years, 88 days

Wilson

67 years, 37 days; 80 years, 327 days; 61 years, 116 days

Harding

57 years, 273 days; 84 years, 160 days; 66 years, 159 days

Coolidge

60 years, 185 days; 80 years, 352 days; 39 years

F. D. Roosevelt

63 years, 72 days; 72 years, 145 days; 86 years, 351 days

RELATIVE LONGEVITY OF THE PRESIDENTS AND THEIR WIVES

It is often stated that the presidency is a killing job, but over half of the Presidents who are no longer living had greater life spans than their respective wives (though they did not necessarily survive their wives). The following list shows the number of years by which the President's life span exceeded that of his wife:

J. Adams—16 years, 261 days

Jefferson—49 years, 125 days

Madison—4 years, 51 days

Monroe—10 years, 347 days

J. Q. Adams—3 years, 136 days

Jackson—16 years, 260 days

Van Buren—43 years, 262 days

Tyler (first wife)—19 years, 358 days

Tyler (second wife)—2 years, 228 days

Taylor—1 year, 261 days

Fillmore (first wife)—19 years, 43 days

Fillmore (second wife)—6 years, 131 days

Pierce—7 years, 54 days

Johnson—1 year, 111 days

Hayes—12 years, 169 days

Arthur—13 years, 274 days

B. Harrison (first wife)—7 years, 181 days

T. Roosevelt (first wife)—37 years, 244 days

Wilson (first wife)—12 years, 319 days

The following is a list of wives whose life spans were greater than those of their husbands:

Mrs. Washington—3 years, 40 days

Mrs. W. H. Harrison—20 years, 161 days

Mrs. Polk—34 years, 119 days

Mrs. Lincoln—7 years, 153 days

Mrs. Grant—13 years, 235 days

Mrs. Garfield—36 years, 25 days

Mrs. Cleveland—12 years, 12 days

Mrs. B. Harrison (2nd wife)—22 years, 45 days

Mrs. McKinley—1 year, 124 days

Mrs. T. Roosevelt (2nd wife) —26 years, 339 days

Mrs. Taft—9 years, 331 days

Mrs. Harding—3 years, 190 days

Mrs. Coolidge—18 years, 1 day

PRESIDENTS WHO SURVIVED THEIR WIVES

Of the thirty Presidents who are no longer living, thirteen became widowers. The following list shows the number of years each lived after the death of his wife:

J. Adams—7 years, 249 days

Jefferson—43 years, 301 days

Monroe—284 days

Jackson—16 years, 168 days

Van Buren—43 years, 169 days

Tyler (first wife)—19 years, 130 days

Fillmore (first wife)—20 years, 343 days

Pierce—5 years, 310 days

Hayes—3 years, 206 days

Arthur—6 years, 310 days

B. Harrison (first wife)—8 years, 139 days

T. Roosevelt (first wife)—34 years, 326 days

Wilson (first wife)—9 years, 181 days

PRESIDENTS' WIVES WHO SURVIVED THEIR HUSBANDS

Of the wives who are no longer living, nineteen became widows. The following list shows the number of years each lived after the death of her husband:

Mrs. Washington—2 years, 159 days

Mrs. Madison—13 years, 14 days

Mrs. J. Q. Adams—4 years, 80 days

Mrs. W. H. Harrison—22 years, 327 days

Mrs. Tyler (2nd wife)—27 years, 173 days

Mrs. Polk—42 years, 60 days

Mrs. Taylor—2 years, 40 days

Mrs. Fillmore (2nd wife)—7 years, 156 days

Mrs. Lincoln—17 years, 92 days

Mrs. Johnson—168 days

Mrs. Grant—17 years, 144 days

Mrs. Garfield—36 years, 176 days

Mrs. Cleveland—39 years, 127 days

Mrs. B. Harrison (2nd wife) —46 years, 298 days

Mrs. McKinley—5 years, 254 days

Mrs. T. Roosevelt (2nd wife) —29 years, 267 days

Mrs. Taft—13 years, 75 days

Mrs. Harding—1 year, 111 days

Mrs. Coolidge—24 years, 184 days

CAUSES OF DEATH

The exact causes of death of many Presidents are not known, since medical and death certificates were not always filed. Furthermore, in many instances there were complications, and the direct causes of death could not be ascertained. There may also be differences in terminology; in the past, illnesses were grouped under generic headings, whereas today the same illnesses would be described in specific terms.

Washington—Pneumonia

J. Adams—Debility

Jefferson—Diarrhea

Madison—Debility

Monroe—Debility

J. Q. Adams—Paralysis

Jackson—Consumption, dropsy

Van Buren—Asthma

W. H. Harrison—Pleurisy, pneumonia

Tyler—Bilious fever

Polk—Diarrhea

Taylor—Bilious fever, typhoid fever, cholera morbus

Fillmore—Debility, paralysis

Pierce—Stomach inflammation

Buchanan—Rheumatic gout

Lincoln—Assassination

Johnson—Paralysis

Grant—Cancer (carcinoma of the tongue and tonsils)

Hayes—Heart disease

Garfield—Assassination

Arthur—Bright's disease, apoplexy (cerebral hemorrhage)

Cleveland—Debility, coronary sclerosis

B. Harrison—Pneumonia

Cleveland—Debility

McKinley—Assassination

T. Roosevelt—Inflammatory rheumatism

Taft—Debility

Harding—Apoplexy (rupture of brain artery), pneumonia, enlargement of the heart, high blood pressure

Wilson—Apoplexy, paralysis

Coolidge—Heart failure (coronary thrombosis)

F. D. Roosevelt—Cerebral hemorrhage

ASSASSINATIONS AND ATTEMPTED ASSASSINATIONS

Three Presidents, Lincoln, Garfield, and McKinley, were assassinated while in office.

Attempts were made against the lives of Presidents Jackson, Theodore Roosevelt, and Truman. Attempts were made also against Lincoln and Franklin Delano Roosevelt before they assumed the presidency.

Details are given in the respective biographical chapters in Part I.

LAST WORDS

Inasmuch as there is great interest in the last words of famous people, what are purported to be the last words of the Presidents are given. Since emotion and grief are important factors in these final scenes, there is variance in the reported accounts. The generally accepted last words of the Presidents follow:

Washington—"It is well."

J. Adams—"Thomas Jefferson still survives." "Independence forever."

Jefferson—"Is it the fourth? [a reference to the Fourth of July] I resign my spirit to God, my daughter to my country."

Madison—"I always talk better lying down."

J. Q. Adams—"This is the last of earth. I am content."

Jackson—"I hope to meet each of you in heaven. Be good children, all of you, and strive to be ready when the change comes."

Van Buren—"There is but one reliance."

W. H. Harrison—"Sir, I wish you to understand the true principles of government. I wish them carried out. I ask nothing more." (Spoken in delirium to Vice President Tyler)

Tyler—"Doctor, I am going . . . perhaps it is best."

Polk—"I love you, Sarah, for all eternity, I love you."

Taylor—"I am about to die. I expect the summons very soon. I have tried to discharge all my duties faithfully. I regret nothing, but am sorry that I am about to leave my friends."

Fillmore—"The nourishment [food] is palatable."

Buchanan—"O Lord God Almighty, as Thou wilt."

Johnson—"Oh, do not cry. Be good children and we shall all meet in Heaven."

Grant—"Water."

Hayes—"I know that I am going where Lucy [his wife] is."

Garfield—"The people my trust." "Oh, Swaim, there is a pain here . . . oh, oh Swaim." (Spoken to Davi

Gaskill Swaim, his chief of staff)

Cleveland—"I have tried so hard to do right."

B. Harrison—"Are the doctors here?" "Doctor . . . my lungs."

McKinley—"It is God's way. His will be done, not ours." "We are all going, we are all going, we are all going. Oh, dear."

T. Roosevelt—"Please put out the light."

Wilson—"Edith [his wife], I'm a broken machine, but I'm ready."

Harding—"That's good. Go on, read some more." (Spoken to his wife, who was reading to him)

F. D. Roosevelt—"I have a terrific headache."

THE PRESIDENTS' ESTATES

There has always been interest in comparing the estates of Presidents. In order not to obtain an inaccurate impression, there are certain basic facts to consider.

First, there is a variance between the appraisal of the same estate by different people, especially concerning real property and personal possessions. Unless a piece of property is actually sold, values range from high to low according to different appraisers.

When comparing the monetary value of Presidents' estates, one must consider the purchasing power of the dollar in the years under consideration. For example, it might now take about $20 million to acquire Washington's real estate, which was valued at $530,000. (It may be noted that Washington was "land poor." Although his land holdings were worth a great deal, he was sometimes hard pressed for cash.)

Even if the figures given are exact to the penny, they are not always accurate estimates of the Presidents' wealth because many Presidents, while living, made appreciable gifts and donations to their families. Often estates were divided and distributed before death to avoid the imposition of excise and inheritance taxes.

The figures below indicate the total value of the estates, not solely cash and securities. They are estimates and are likely to vary with the final amounts reported by the administrators or filed with the surrogates.

Washington—$530,000 ("land poor")

J. Adams—$30,000

Jefferson—owed $40,000

Madison—value unknown

Monroe—none

J. Q. Adams—$60,000

Jackson—value unknown ("land poor")

Van Buren—value unknown

W. H. Harrison—in debt

Tyler—value unknown

Polk—$100,000 to $150,000

Taylor—$142,000

Fillmore—value unknown

Pierce—$70,000

Buchanan—value unknown

Lincoln—$83,000 (net estate of $83,343 increased by the administrators to $110,974)

Johnson—$50,000

Grant—none (left manuscript of book which brought in approximately $500,000)

Hayes—value unknown

Garfield—value unknown

Arthur—value unknown

Cleveland—$250,000

B. Harrison—$375,000

McKinley—$215,000

T. Roosevelt—$811,000

Taft—$475,000

Harding—$487,000

Wilson—$600,000

Coolidge—$500,000

F. D. Roosevelt—$1,085,500

PERIODS IN WHICH THERE WERE NO FORMER PRESIDENTS LIVING

There were four periods during which no former Presidents of the United States were living.

The first period was December 14, 1799-March 3, 1801, during the administration of John Adams. George Washington, the first and only living former President, died on December 14, 1799.

The second period was July 31, 1875-March 3, 1877, during the administration of Ulysses S. Grant. Andrew Johnson died on July 31, 1875.

The third period was June 24, 1908-March 3, 1909, during the administration of Theodore Roosevelt. Grover Cleveland died on June 24, 1908.

The fourth period was January 5, 1933-March 3, 1933, during the administration of Herbert Hoover. Calvin Coolidge died on January 5, 1933.

Commemoratives

PRESIDENTS DEPICTED ON COINS

The first President depicted on a U.S. coin (excluding commemorative currency) was Abraham Lincoln, shown on the bronze penny commemorating the centennial of his birth. Production of this coin began in June 1909 at the mint at Philadelphia, Pa., and the first delivery of the coins was made June 30, 1909, to the Cashier of the Mint.

The second President depicted on a U.S. coin was George Washington, shown on a twenty-five-cent silver coin, the bicentennial quarter commemorating the bicentennial of his birth. The first coins were struck June 4, 1932, at the Philadelphia mint.

The third President depicted on a U.S. coin was Thomas Jefferson, shown on the five-cent piece of 1938. The first coins were ordered cast on October 1, 1938, and released to the public on November 15, 1938. They were coined at the mints at Philadelphia, Denver, Colo., and San Francisco, Calif.

The fourth President depicted on a U.S. coin was Franklin Delano Roosevelt, shown on a ten-cent silver piece. Production of the coins commenced January 16, 1946. They were coined at Denver and San Francisco and were issued on January 30, 1946, Roosevelt's birthday.

PRESIDENTS DEPICTED ON PAPER CURRENCY

Portraits of Presidents appear on U.S. paper currency on the following denominations: Washington, one dollar; Jefferson, two dollars; Lincoln, five dollars; Jackson, twenty dollars;

Grant, fifty dollars; McKinley, five hundred dollars; Cleveland, one thousand dollars; Madison, five thousand dollars; Wilson, one hundred thousand dollars. The currency in circulation is of four kinds: silver certificates, national bank notes, United States notes, and Federal Reserve notes.

PRESIDENTS DEPICTED ON POSTAGE STAMPS

The Presidents have served as subjects on postage stamps since the first issue in 1847, but it was not until 1938 that one issue depicted all the Presidents.

The 1938 issue of ordinary postage stamps showed likenesses of all the Presidents from Washington to Coolidge arranged in accordance with their tenure of office. The following list names the President, the denomination and color of the stamp, and the date of issue in 1938:

Washington—1 cent green, Apr. 25

J. Adams—2 cent red, June 3

Jefferson—3 cent purple, June 16

Madison—4 cent pink, July 1

Monroe—5 cent blue, July 21

J. Q. Adams—6 cent red orange, July 28

Jackson—7 cent sepia, Aug. 4

Van Buren—8 cent olive, Aug. 11

W. H. Harrison—9 cent pink, Aug. 18

J. Tyler—10 cent salmon, Sept. 2

Polk—11 cent blue, Sept. 8

Taylor—12 cent lavender, Sept. 14

Fillmore—13 cent green, Sept. 22

Pierce—14 cent blue, Oct. 6

Buchanan—15 cent gray, Oct. 13

Lincoln—16 cent black, Oct. 20

Johnson—17 cent crimson, Oct. 27

Grant—18 cent brown, Nov. 3

Hayes—19 cent lilac, Nov. 10

Garfield—20 cent green, Nov. 10

Arthur—21 cent steel blue, Nov. 22

Cleveland—22 cent copper red, Nov. 22

B. Harrison—24 cent gray, Dec. 2

McKinley—25 cent burgundy, Dec. 2

T. Roosevelt—30 cent blue, Dec. 8

Taft—50 cent lavender, Dec. 8

Wilson—$1 lavender and black, Aug. 29

Harding—$2 green and black, Sept. 29

Coolidge—$4 red and black, Nov. 17

THE PRESIDENTIAL MEDALS

The thirty-three Presidents of the United States have been commemorated by bronze medals, three inches in diameter. These medals are sold by the Superintendent, United States Mint, Philadelphia, Pa., for $2.50 each with the understanding that they are not to be resold at a profit.

The Washington medal was designed by DuVivier; the Jefferson and Madison medals by Reich; the Monroe, John Quincy Adams, Jackson and Van Buren medals by Furst; the William Henry Harrison, Lincoln, Hayes, Wilson, and Harding medals by Morgan; the Garfield, Arthur, Benjamin Harrison, McKinley, Theodore Roosevelt, and Taft medals by C. Barber and Morgan; the Fillmore, Pierce, and Buchanan medals by Ellis and Willson; the Johnson medal by Pacquet; the Grant medal by W. Barber; the Cleveland medal by W. Barber; the Coolidge, Hoover, and Franklin Delano Roosevelt medals by Sinnock; the Truman medal by Sinnock and Roberts; the Eisenhower medal by Roberts and Gasparro. The designers of the John Adams, Tyler, Polk, and Taylor medals are unknown.

PRESIDENTS IN THE HALL OF FAME

The Hall of Fame of Great Americans on the New York University campus, New York City, has honored twelve Presidents.

At the first Hall of Fame election in 1900, five Presidents were elected: George Washington, John Adams, Thomas Jefferson, Abraham Lincoln, and Ulysses Simpson Grant.

In 1905, two more Presidents were elected: James Madison and John Quincy Adams.

Five years later, Andrew Jackson was elected. In 1930, James Monroe was elected, and in 1935, Grover Cleveland. Both Woodrow Wilson and Theodore Roosevelt were elected in 1950.

One of the qualifications for election is that twenty-five years must have passed between the death of the nominee and the election.

PRESIDENTS IN STATUARY HALL

Statuary Hall, established by act of July 2, 1864, permits each state to place in Statuary Hall, in the House of Representatives, two statues honoring their distinguished citizens. The statues of three Presidents have been placed in the rotunda: James Abram Garfield by Ohio, Andrew Jackson by Tennessee, and George Washington by Virginia.

PLACES NAMED FOR PRESIDENTS

Only one state, Washington, bears the name of a President. The capital cities of four states were named for Presidents: Jackson, Miss.; Jefferson City, Mo.; Lincoln, Neb.; and Madison, Wis.

General Statistics

PARENTS AND ANCESTORS OF THE PRESIDENTS

18 of 33 were of English ancestry

16 of 33 had fathers who were farmers

3 of 33 had fathers who were lawyers

3 of 33 had fathers who were ministers

3 of 33 had fathers who were state governors

1 of 33 had a father who was a physician

2 of 33 were posthumous children

11 of 33 lost their fathers before they were 21

6 of 33 lost their fathers while in their teens

9 of 33 had fathers who married twice

1 of 33 was survived by his father

5 of 33 had fathers living at their inaugurations

1 of 33 had a father who was President

1 of 33 had a grandfather who was President

2 of 33 were survived by their mothers

9 of 33 had mothers living at their inaugurations

1 of 33 had both parents living at his inauguration

SIBLINGS OF THE PRESIDENTS

7 of 33 had 9 or more brothers and sisters

13 of 33 had 8 or more brothers and sisters

15 of 33 had 7 or more brothers and sisters

17 of 33 had 6 or more brothers and sisters

18 of 33 had 5 or more brothers and sisters

8 of 33 were the first-born in their families

5 of 33 were the second-born, the first sons, in their families

3 of 33 were the second-born, the second sons, in their families

16 of 33 were the first-born sons in their families

29 of 33 had sisters

No President was an only child

MARRIAGES AND WIVES OF THE PRESIDENTS

32 of 33 married

6 of 32 married widows

2 of 32 married divorcees

2 of 32 remarried after leaving the presidency

2 of 32 married on their birthdays

2 of 32 celebrated golden wedding anniversaries

3 of 32 lost their wives before they were inaugurated

3 of 32 lost their wives while in office

5 of 32 remarried

1 of 37 wives was not born in the United States

18 of 37 wives were born in New York, Ohio, or Virginia

4 of 37 wives were college graduates

4 of 37 wives were older than their husbands

4 of 37 wives had children by former husbands

16 of 37 wives lived to be over 70

9 of 37 wives lived to be over 80

1 of 37 wives lived to be over 90

8 of 37 wives died in Washington, D.C.

CHILDREN OF THE PRESIDENTS

6 of 33 were childless

12 of 33 had no daughters

9 of 33 had no sons

1 of 33 had fifteen children

1 of 33 had a son who became President

2 of 33 had sons who became senators

7 of 33 had sons who became representatives

1 of 33 had a son who served in both houses of Congress

LIFE AND DEATH OF THE PRESIDENTS

27 of 33 lived to be over 60

7 of 33 died in July

3 of 33 died on July 4

7 of 33 died in office

3 of 33 were assassinated

CULTURAL, VOCATIONAL, AND GEOGRAPHICAL BACKGROUND OF THE PRESIDENTS

10 of 33 were Episcopalians

23 of 33 were college graduates

12 of 33 were members of Phi Beta Kappa

13 of 33 were Masons

20 of 33 had military service

24 of 33 were lawyers

5 of 33 served as secretaries of state

8 of 33 served in presidential cabinets

10 of 33 served as Vice Presidents

19 of 33 were elected to Congress

13 of 33 served as senators

14 of 33 served as representatives

8 of 33 served in both houses of Congress

7 of 33 served as ambassadors

13 of 33 served as state governors

5 of 33 were residents of Virginia

17 of 33 were residents of New York, Ohio, or Virginia

14 of 33 were residents of states other than their native states

ELECTIONS, TENURE, AND INAUGURATIONS OF THE PRESIDENTS

1 of 33 was elected for a third term

1 of 33 was elected for a fourth term

10 of 33 were elected for second terms

8 of 33 served full second terms

7 of 33 became President by succession

3 of 7 who succeeded to the presidency were subsequently elected in their own right

14 of 33 were elected for only one term

10 of 33 elected for one term completed the term

12 of 33 did not receive a majority of popular votes

28 of 33 were over 50 when inaugurated

17 of 33 were over 60 when inaugurated

7 of 33 were over 70 when inaugurated

THE PRESIDENCY

Elections

NOMINATING CONVENTIONS FIRST HELD BY ANTI-MASONIC PARTY

Until 1832, candidates for the presidency and the vice presidency were selected by caucuses generally held in secret by the various political parties.

The first national nominating convention at which delegates from various states selected their candidates was held by the newly-formed Anti-Masonic Party, which held its first convention at Philadelphia, Pa., in 1830.

The first convention at which national nominating was the feature was held on September 26, 1831, at the Athenaeum, Baltimore, Md. The presiding officer at this convention was John Spencer of New York. Two tellers, Abner Phelps of Massachusetts, and Thaddeus Stevens of Pennsylvania, were appointed. They sat in the center of the hall where the delegates, when their names were called, deposited their ballots in an open box. The first ballot for the presidency showed 111 votes cast, of which 108 were for William Wirt of Maryland, 1 for Richard Rush of Pennsylvania, and two blanks. As only 84 votes were necessary for the choice it was moved that the nomination be made unanimous. This motion was carried, and William Wirt of Maryland became the first presidential candidate nominated by a national nominating committee.

CONVENTIONS OF 1832

In 1832, both the National Republicans and the Democrats

held their first nominating conventions at Baltimore, Md. The Democrats unanimously nominated Andrew Jackson of Tennessee on the first ballot, and the National Republicans unanimously nominated Henry Clay of Kentucky on the first ballot.

THE TWO-THIRDS RULE

The two-thirds rule requiring presidential and vice presidential nominees to obtain two thirds of the vote cast at the nominating convention was first adopted May 22, 1832, at the Democratic National Convention held at Baltimore, Md. The rule stated:

> Resolved: That each state be entitled, in the nomination to be made of a candidate for the vice presidency, to a number of votes equal to the number to which they will be entitled in the electoral college, under the new apportionment, in voting for the President and the Vice President; and that two thirds of the whole number of the votes in the convention shall be necessary to constitute a choice.

PRESIDENTS NOMINATED IN CHURCHES

Two Presidents were nominated by their parties at conventions held in churches. Three unsuccessful presidential candidates were also nominated in churches.

Martin Van Buren was nominated on May 20, 1835, by the Democrats at a convention held in the First Presbyterian Church, Baltimore, Md. William Henry Harrison was nominated on December 4, 1839, by the Whigs at a convention held at the First Lutheran (or Zion) Church, Baltimore, Md.

The three unsuccessful candidates nominated in churches were Henry Clay, nominated on May 1, 1844, by the Whigs in convention at the Universalist Church, Baltimore, Md.; Lewis Cass, nominated on May 22, 1848, by the Democrats at the Universalist Church, Baltimore, Md.; and John Bell, nominated by the Constitutional Union Party on May 9, 1860, in the Presbyterian Church, Baltimore, Md.

CONVENTION CITIES (1856-1956)

The following lists show the number of conventions held in each city. Dates in italics indicate years in which the party was victorious.

Republican Conventions

Chicago, Ill., 13—*1860, 1868, 1880*, 1884, *1888, 1904, 1908,*

1912, 1916, *1920*, 1932, 1944, *1952*

Philadelphia, Pa., 5—1856, *1872, 1900*, 1940, 1948

Cleveland, Ohio, 2—*1924, 1936*

Baltimore, Md., 1—*1864*

Cincinnati, Ohio, 1—*1876*

Kansas City, Mo., 1—*1928*

Minneapolis, Minn., 1—1892

St. Louis, Mo., 1—*1896*

San Francisco, Calif., 1—*1956*

Democratic Conventions

Chicago, Ill., 9—1864, *1884, 1892,* 1896, *1932, 1940, 1944,* 1952, 1956

St. Louis, Mo., 4—1876, 1888, 1904, *1916*

Baltimore, Md., 3—1860, 1872, *1912*

Kansas City, Mo., 1—1900

Cincinnati, Ohio, 2—*1856*, 1880

New York, N.Y., 2—1868, 1924

Philadelphia, Pa., *2—1936, 1948*

Charleston, S.C., 1—1860

Denver, Colo., 1—1908

Houston, Tex., 1—1928

San Francisco, Calif., 1—*1920*

The 1960 Democratic convention is scheduled to be held at Los Angeles, Calif., and the Republican convention at Chicago, Ill.

CONVENTION FAILED TO SELECT NOMINEES

The only nominating convention of a major party which did not decide upon a presidential candidate was the Democratic convention of 1860, which met at the Hall of the South Carolina Institute, Charleston, S.C., on April 23, 1860. After ten days in session, during which 57 indecisive ballots were taken, the convention adjourned to meet at Baltimore, Md., on June 18, 1860. In a six-day session at the Front Street Theatre in Baltimore, Stephen Arnold Douglas of Illinois was nominated on the second ballot.

LONGEST NOMINATING CONVENTION

The Democratic convention of 1924, in session 14 days, required 103 ballots before a presidential nominee was agreed upon. On the first ballot, William Gibbs McAdoo of California had 431½ votes, nearly twice as many as the next highest candidate, Alfred Emanuel Smith of New York, who had 241 votes. As 731 votes were necessary for choice, the balloting continued and 103 ballots were taken before one candidate received the necessary number. John William Davis of West Virginia, who had only 31 votes on the first ballot, won the nomination on the 103rd ballot, receiving 844 votes.

CONVENTION RULES

There is no set rule which governs every convention although there is a more or less standard procedure. Conventions usually open with an invocation. Credentials and committee rules are reported upon. A temporary chairman is selected. The keynote speech is delivered. Accredited delegates vote for a permanent chairman. The reports of committees are voted upon and a platform is adopted. A presidential nominee is chosen. A vice presidential nominee is chosen. Committees are appointed to notify the selected nominees. A new national committee is selected to act for the party and carry on the campaign until the next convention.

CONVENTION NOMINATIONS— 1832-1956

Since the first nominating convention in 1832, there have been 64 conventions held by the major political parties. At these 64 conventions, 37 presidential nominations were made by acclamation or on the first ballot. Of the 37 candidates nominated on the first ballot, 19 were elected—12 Republicans and 7 Democrats; of the 18 losers who were nominated on the first ballot, 9 were Democrats, 6 were Republicans, and 3 were Whigs.

The successful candidate who required the greatest number of ballots at a nominating convention was Franklin Pierce, Democrat, who did not receive the nomination until the 49th ballot. Woodrow Wilson, Democrat, was a runner-up, requiring 46 ballots before he was nominated in 1912. The Republican who required the greatest number of ballots in order to win a nomination was James Abram Garfield, who was nominated on the 36th ballot in 1880.

John William Davis, Democrat, ranks far out in the field of candidates requiring large numbers of ballots for nomination. In 1924 there were 103 ballots before Davis was selected as the Democratic Party's standard-bearer.

PRESIDENTIAL "DARK HORSES"

Numerous dark horses have made spectacular and unbelievable runs to secure nominations. The first dark horse to win was Polk, in 1844. Three other dark horses achieved victories: Pierce in 1852, Garfield in 1880, and Harding in 1920. Two dark horses made valiant attempts but were not elected: Seymour in 1868 and Bryan in 1896.

WOMEN PRESIDENTIAL AND VICE PRESIDENTIAL CANDIDATES

Only the minor political parties have nominated women as presidential or vice presidential candidates. The nominations follow:

1872—Victoria Claflin Woodhull, N.Y., presidential nominee of the People's Party (Equal Rights Party)

1884—Belva Ann Bennett Lockwood, D.C., presidential nominee of the Equal Rights Party

1888—Belva Ann Bennett Lockwood, D.C., presidential nominee of the Equal Rights Party

1924—Marie Caroline Brehm, Calif., vice presidential nominee of the Prohibition Party

1936—Florence Garvin, R.I., vice presidential nominee of the National Greenback Party

1948—Grace Carlson, Minn., vice presidential nominee of the Socialist Workers Party

1952—Charlotta A. Bass, N.Y., vice presidential nominee of the Progressive Party

1952—Myra Tanner Weiss, N.Y., vice presidential nominee of the Socialist Workers Party

1952—Charlotta A. Bass, N.Y., vice presidential nominee of the American Labor Party

1956—Georgia Cozzini, Wis., vice presidential nominee of the Socialist Labor Party

1956—Myra Tanner Weiss, N.Y., vice presidential nominee of the Socialist Workers Party

1956—Ann Marie Yezo, N.J., vice presidential nominee of the American Third Party

GENERALS VERSUS ADMIRALS FOR THE PRESIDENCY

Despite the many sea battles in which United States naval heroes have been engaged, no admiral has been nominated for the presidency. The preference has been entirely in favor of the generals.

The Presidents who had been generals were Washington, Jackson, William Henry Harrison, Taylor, Pierce, Grant, Hayes, Garfield, Benjamin Harrison, and Eisenhower. Johnson and Arthur were military governors with the rank of general.

Nominated by their respective parties but unsuccessful in the contest for the presidency were Generals Winfield Scott, George B. McClellan, John Charles Fremont, and Winfield Scott Hancock.

Although Theodore Roosevelt was not a general, he had served with distinction in the Spanish-American War.

PRESIDENTIAL CANDIDATES FROM THE SAME STATES

Illinois presented two presidential candidates in 1860, Abraham Lincoln and Stephen Arnold Douglas. Lincoln received 180 electoral votes and Douglas 12 electoral votes.

Illinois had two presidential nominees in 1872. Ulysses Simpson Grant received 286 electoral votes and David Davis received 1 electoral vote.

In 1904, Theodore Roosevelt and Alton Brooks Parker were the candidates, both from New York. Roosevelt received 336 electoral votes, and Parker received 140 electoral votes.

Ohio had two candidates for the presidency in 1920, Warren Gamaliel Harding and James Middleton Cox, the former receiving 404 electoral votes, the latter 127 electoral votes.

In 1940, the two presidential candidates were Franklin Delano Roosevelt of New York and Wendell Lewis Willkie of New York. Roosevelt received 449 electoral votes and Willkie received 82 electoral votes.

New York again in 1944 presented two presidential candidates. Franklin Delano Roosevelt received 432 electoral votes

and Thomas Edmund Dewey received 99 electoral votes.

CANDIDATES WHO WERE DIVORCED

Governor James Middleton Cox of Ohio, the Democratic nominee defeated by Warren Gamaliel Harding in 1920, had been divorced and had remarried.

Governor Adlai Ewing Stevenson of Illinois, the Democratic nominee defeated by Dwight David Eisenhower in 1952 and 1956, has been the only other divorced candidate representing a major party.

PERSISTENT PRESIDENTIAL CANDIDATE

The most persistent of the presidential candidates was Norman Thomas, who was nominated six times by the Socialist Party and defeated at each election. In 1928, he received 267,420 votes as a candidate against Herbert Hoover. As a contestant in the elections won by Franklin Delano Roosevelt he received 884,782 votes in 1932, 187,512 votes in 1936, 116,798 votes in 1940, and 74,757 votes in 1944. He was also a candidate in 1948, receiving 95,908 votes in the election won by Harry S Truman.

PRESIDENTIAL CANDIDATES WHO SERVED PRISON TERMS

Eugene Victor Debs of Indiana, the Socialist candidate for the presidency in 1900, 1904, 1908, 1912, and 1920, was in jail when he was nominated on May 13, 1920. Sentenced to ten years in federal prison for violation of the Espionage Act, he had begun his sentence on April 13, 1919, and was in prison when he received over 917,000 votes in the November 2, 1920 election. He was pardoned December 25, 1921.

On August 28, 1952, the American Labor Party nominated as its presidential candidate Vincent Hallinan of California, who had been released from the McNeil Island Federal Penitentiary on August 17, 1952, after serving six months for contempt of court in connection with his defense of Harry Bridges, the labor leader.

PRESIDENTIAL CANDIDATE KILLED IN ATTEMPT TO RESCUE DROWNING BOY

Frank T. Johns, of Portland, Ore., Socialist Labor presidential candidate in 1924 and 1928, was campaigning at Bend, Ore., on the bank of the Deschutes River, on May 21, 1928, when his speech was interrupted by a cry for help. Charles Rhodes, an eleven-year-old, was being drawn into deep water about seventy-five feet from the shore. Johns rushed to the boy's rescue and brought him to about ten feet from the shore when he collapsed and they both drowned. Johns was thirty-nine years of age.

To fill the vacancy caused by the death of Johns, the party nominated Verne L. Reynolds.

PROVISIONS FOR DEATH OF CANDIDATE OR PRESIDENT-ELECT

If a presidential nominee should die before election day, his party would select a new candidate in his place. It could be anyone and would not necessarily be the vice presidential nominee. The Democrats require the choice to be made by the Democratic National Committee, each state having the same number of votes. The person with the majority would be nominated for the presidency. The Republicans allow the choice to be made either by the Republican National Committee (the committee members having the same number of votes as their states at the national convention) or by another convention if time permits.

If the President-elect should die after election day but before the meeting of the electoral college, the electors could vote as they desire. They are not obliged to select the Vice President-elect. If both President-elect and Vice President-elect should die, the electoral college could choose any two persons for the offices, with or without the consent of the political party.

If the President-elect should die after receiving the votes of the electoral college, the Vice President would be sworn in as President. If both the President and the Vice President should die, the rule of succession would be invoked: the speaker of the house, the president pro tempore of the Senate, the secretary of state, the secretary of the treasury, and so forth.

ELECTIONS DEVOLVING UPON THE HOUSE AND SENATE

In the event that a presidential candidate does not receive a majority of the electoral votes, the House of Representatives chooses a President from the three leading contenders. Each state is entitled to one vote, and the winning candidate must receive a majority. Should the House of Representatives fail to choose a President, the Vice President-elect becomes President.

The House was called into action twice, in 1801 and in 1825, when Thomas Jefferson and John Quincy Adams were elected respectively.

If the vice presidential candidate does not receive a majority of the electoral votes, the Senate, voting as individuals, selects the Vice President from the two highest candidates. The only time the Senate was called upon to exercise this privilege was in 1837, when it elected Richard Mentor Johnson.

PRESIDENTS ELECTED WITHOUT A POPULAR MAJORITY

Many Presidents were elected without receiving a majority of the votes cast. Listed below are the twelve elections in which winning candidates failed to receive a popular majority. (For details see the appropriate chapters in Part I.)

1824—John Quincy Adams

1844—James Knox Polk

1848—Zachary Taylor

1856—James Buchanan

1860—Abraham Lincoln

1876—Rutherford Birchard Hayes

1880—James Abram Garfield

1884—Grover Cleveland

1888—Benjamin Harrison

1892—Grover Cleveland

1912—Woodrow Wilson

1916—Woodrow Wilson

1948—Harry S Truman

ROOSEVELT'S ELECTORAL LANDSLIDE

The largest electoral vote received by a candidate was that cast for President Franklin Delano Roosevelt in the election of 1936, when he received 523 of the 531 electoral votes (98.49 per cent). The eight opposition votes (Maine 5, Vermont 3) were cast for the Republican nominee, Alfred Mossman Landon of Kansas.

POPULAR AND ELECTORAL VOTES IN THE ELECTION OF 1956

The largest popular vote was cast November 6, 1956, when 62,027,040 votes were recorded: 35,581,003 for Eisenhower (57.36 per cent), 26,031,322 for Stevenson (41.97 per cent), and 414,715 for other candidates (.67 per cent).

Eisenhower received 457 of the 531 electoral votes (86.064 per cent), and Stevenson received 73 votes (13.747 per cent). One Democratic elector, W. F. Turner of Montgomery, Ala., cast his vote not for Stevenson and Kefauver, who had carried the state of Alabama by 85,060 votes, but for Circuit Judge Walter Burgwyn Jones of Montgomery (President) and Senator-elect Herman Eugene Talmadge of Georgia (Vice President).

"THIRD PARTY" ELECTORAL VOTES

In the twenty-six presidential elections since the organization of the Republican Party in 1856, the two-party system has been dominant. With one exception (the Progressive Party in 1912), the strength of third parties has been of little consequence.

Third parties have won electoral votes in only six elections. In 1856, Millard Fillmore, presidential candidate of the American Party, received 8 of the 296 electoral votes (2.7 per cent). In 1860, John Bell, presidential candidate of the Constitutional Union Party, received 39 of the 303 electoral votes (12.87 per cent). In 1892, James Baird Weaver, presidential candidate of the People's Party, received 22 of the 444 electoral votes (4.95 per cent). In 1912, Theodore Roosevelt, presidential candidate of the Progressive Party, received 88 of the 531 electoral votes (16.57 per cent). In 1924, Robert Marion · La Follette, presidential candidate of the Progressive Party, received 13 of the 531 electoral votes (2.45 per cent). In 1948, James Strom Thurmond, presidential candidate of the States' Rights Democratic Party, received 39 of the 531 electoral votes (7.35 per cent).

DEFEATED CANDIDATES LATER ELECTED TO PRESIDENCY

Many candidates defeated at one election for the presidency or the vice presidency were later elected to the presidency.

In the election of 1792, Thomas Jefferson received 4 electoral votes for the vice presidency. John Adams received 77 electoral votes and was elected Vice President, George Washington being reelected for a second term.

In the election of 1796, Thomas Jefferson received 68 electoral votes and John Adams 71 electoral votes. Adams, who had the highest number of votes, was elected President, and Jefferson, who had the next highest number, was automatically elected Vice President.

In the election of 1808, James Madison was elected President. His Vice President was George Clinton of New York, who received 113 electoral votes. Others who received vice presidential electoral votes were James Monroe and James Madison, each of whom received 3 electoral votes.

In the election of 1820, James Monroe received 231 electoral votes and John Quincy Adams received 1 electoral vote.

In the election of 1824, Andrew Jackson was defeated for the presidency by John Quincy Adams. Jackson received a larger number of electoral votes, but not a majority. The House of Representatives voted by states and elected Adams. In the same year, Jackson also received 13 electoral votes for the vice presidency and Martin Van Buren received 9 electoral votes.

Calhoun was elected Vice President.

In the election of 1836, Martin Van Buren, with 170 electoral votes, was elected President. He defeated William Henry Harrison, who received 73 electoral votes. John Tyler, who received 47 electoral votes, was defeated for the vice presidency by Richard Mentor Johnson.

In the election of 1840, when Harrison won with 234 electoral votes, 1 electoral vote was cast for James Knox Polk.

In the election of 1888 Grover Cleveland was defeated for re-election by Benjamin Harrison. In the election of 1892, however, Cleveland was successful in his attempt to regain the presidency.

In the election of 1920, Calvin Coolidge was elected Vice President under Harding, defeating Franklin Delano Roosevelt, who received 127 electoral votes.

ELECTIONS IN WHICH PRESIDENTS WERE RENOMINATED BUT NOT REELECTED

1797

George Washington (not a candidate for reelection), 2 electoral votes; John Adams elected, 71 electoral votes

1800

John Adams, 65 electoral votes; defeated by Thomas Jefferson, 73 electoral votes (election decided by House of Representatives because of Jefferson-Burr electoral tie)

1828

John Quincy Adams, 83 electoral votes; defeated by Andrew Jackson, 178 electoral votes

1840

Martin Van Buren, 60 electoral votes; defeated by William Henry Harrison, 234 electoral votes

1856

Millard Fillmore, 8 electoral votes; defeated by James Buchanan, 174 electoral votes

1888

Grover Cleveland, 168 electoral votes; defeated by Benjamin Harrison, 233 electoral votes

1892

Benjamin Harrison, 145 electoral votes; defeated by Grover Cleveland, 277 electoral votes

1912

Theodore Roosevelt, 88 electoral votes; William Howard Taft,

8 electoral votes; defeated by Woodrow Wilson, 435 electoral votes

1932

Herbert Clark Hoover, 59 electoral votes; defeated by Franklin Delano Roosevelt, 472 electoral votes

Some Presidents had also been defeated when they ran for office prior to their successful elections.

NOMINATIONS AND ELECTIONS

In the 32 presidential elections from 1832 through 1956, the Republicans (and Whigs) nominated a total of 23 men, of whom 14 were elected in 18 elections (Lincoln, Grant, McKinley, and Eisenhower were elected twice).

In 14 unsuccessful elections, the Republicans and Whigs nominated a total of 9 candidates, 5 of whom were defeated when they were nominated a second time: William Henry Harrison, Benjamin Harrison, Taft, Hoover, and Dewey.

In the 32 elections, the Democrats similarly nominated a total of 23 men of whom 9 were elected in 14 elections (Franklin Delano Roosevelt was elected 4

times, Cleveland and Wilson twice).

In 18 unsuccessful elections, the Democrats nominated a total of 15 candidates (William Jennings Bryan was defeated three times and Adlai Ewing Stevenson twice).

REPUBLICAN VERSUS DEMOCRATIC ADMINISTRATIONS

In the years 1856-1956 (the Republican Party ran John Charles Fremont as its first presidential candidate in 1856) the Republicans have elected 12 Presidents for a total of 16 terms or 64 years.

The Republican administrations have been those of Lincoln (and Johnson), 8 years; Grant, 8 years; Hayes, 4 years; Garfield (and Arthur), 4 years; Benjamin Harrison, 4 years; McKinley (and Theodore Roosevelt), 8 years; Roosevelt, 4 years; Taft, 4 years; Harding (and Coolidge), 4 years; Coolidge, 4 years; Hoover, 4 years; and Eisenhower, 8 years.

Since 1856 the Democrats have elected 5 Presidents for a total of 10 terms or 40 years.

The Democratic administrations have been those of Buchanan, 4 years; Cleveland, 8 years (two non-consecutive terms); Wilson, 8 years; F. D. Roosevelt (and Truman), 16 years; and Truman, 4 years.

ADMINISTRATION CHANGES

In the forty-two presidential elections from 1789 through 1956, only fifteen Presidents have succeeded Presidents of a different political party:

Thomas Jefferson (Dem.-Rep.) followed John Adams (Fed.)

Andrew Jackson (Dem.) followed John Quincy Adams (Dem.-Rep.)

William Henry Harrison (Whig) followed Martin Van Buren (Dem.)

James Knox Polk (Dem.) followed John Tyler (Whig)

Zachary Taylor (Whig) followed James Knox Polk (Dem.)

Franklin Pierce (Dem.) followed Millard Fillmore (Whig)

Abraham Lincoln (Rep.) followed James Buchanan (Dem.)

Grover Cleveland (Dem.) followed Chester Alan Arthur (Rep.)

Benjamin Harrison (Rep.) followed Grover Cleveland (Dem.)

Grover Cleveland (Dem.) followed Benjamin Harrison (Rep.)

William McKinley (Rep.) followed Grover Cleveland (Dem.)

Woodrow Wilson (Dem.) followed William Howard Taft (Rep.)

Warren Gamaliel Harding (Rep.) followed Woodrow Wilson (Dem.)

Franklin Delano Roosevelt (Dem.) followed Herbert Hoover (Rep.)

Dwight David Eisenhower (Rep.) followed Harry S Truman (Dem.)

THE LONGEST POLITICAL REGIME

The Democratic-Republicans, considered the forerunners of the present-day Democrats, had the longest uninterrupted term of office. On March 4, 1801, Thomas Jefferson took office and served 8 years. He was followed by James Madison, who served 8 years; James Monroe, who served 8 years; and John Quincy Adams, who served 4 years. The party had been in power 28 years, from March 4, 1801 to March 4, 1829, when Andrew Jackson (usually considered the first Democrat in the present sense) was inaugurated.

The longest Republican regime began on March 4, 1861,

when Abraham Lincoln was inaugurated. Lincoln was reelected and after his death Andrew Johnson completed the remainder of the term. Grant was elected twice and served 8 years. Rutherford B. Hayes served 4 years. James A. Garfield was elected and after his death Chester A. Arthur completed the remainder of the term. The Republicans were in power 24 years, from March 4, 1861, to March 4, 1885, when Grover Cleveland, a Democrat, was inaugurated.

PRESIDENTS NOT NOTIFIED OF THEIR ELECTION

No provision has ever been made for notifying the President of his election. His first official notification takes place when he and the Vice President-elect enter the Senate chamber. After the notification, the President generally goes to the east portico of the Capitol, where he delivers his inaugural address and then takes the oath as President.

The Office

PRESIDENTIAL OATH OF OFFICE

The following oath of office is prescribed by Article II, section 1 of the Constitution:

I do solemnly swear (or affirm) that I will faithfully execute the Office of President of the United States, and will to the best of my ability, preserve, protect and defend the Constitution of the United States.

SUNDAY INAUGURATION DATES

Only four of the thirty-seven March inaugurations fell on Sunday. As a result, the public ceremonies of 1821, 1849, 1877, and 1917 were postponed until the following day.

James Monroe, the fifth President, postponed taking his oath of office for his second term until Monday, March 5, 1821.

Zachary Taylor, the twelfth President, did not take his oath of office until Monday, March 5, 1849 (a circumstance which has caused many to assert that David Rice Atchison, president pro tempore of the Senate, was President for one day between the outgoing James Knox Polk and the incoming Zachary Taylor).

Rutherford Birchard Hayes, the nineteenth President, came into office following a bitter election dispute. He took the oath of office twice: once on Saturday, March 3, 1877, at a private ceremony, and again on Monday, March 5, at a public ceremony.

Woodrow Wilson, the twenty-eighth President, postponed taking his second oath of office until Monday, March 5, 1917.

Only one of the six January inaugurations has fallen on Sunday. Dwight David Eisenhower, the thirty-fourth President, was inaugurated on Sunday, January 20, 1957, at a private ceremony, and again on Monday, January 21, at a public ceremony.

January 20 will fall on Sunday only three times in the next hundred years: in 1985, 2013, and 2041.

INAUGURAL SITES

Thirty-one of the forty-three inaugurations of the elected Presidents were held on the east portico of the Capitol. The other twelve inaugurations were held at the following places:

Federal Hall, Wall Street, New York, N.Y.

1789—George Washington

Congress Hall, Sixth and Chestnut Streets, Philadelphia, Pa.

1793—George Washington
1797—John Adams

Senate chamber, Washington, D.C.

1801—Thomas Jefferson
1805—Thomas Jefferson
1909—William Howard Taft

House of Representatives, Washington, D.C.

1809—James Madison
1813—James Madison
1821—James Monroe
1825—John Quincy Adams
1833—Andrew Jackson

South portico, White House, Washington, D.C.

1945—Franklin Delano Roosevelt

INAUGURAL WEATHER

Of the 43 presidential inaugurations between 1789 and 1957, there were 26 held in clear weather, 10 in rain, and 7 in snow, the weather reported being the weather at noon.

Contemporary reports on the weather often disagree as the

weather was not always the same during the entire day. For example, when Hayes was inaugurated in 1877, it rained until 7 A.M. on March 5 (inauguration day) but it was clear the rest of the day. On the day Garfield was inaugurated, March 4, 1881, it snowed and rained until 10 A.M., and then it cleared, much of the snow having disappeared by the time of the inaugural parade. When Taft was inaugurated in 1909, temperatures were about freezing; over nine inches of snow had fallen on March 3 and until 12:30 P.M. on March 4, and the afternoon of March 4 was windy and cloudy.

The rainy days were in 1845, 1865, 1869, 1873, 1889, 1901, 1929, 1933, 1937, and 1957.

The snowy days were in 1817, 1821, 1833, 1841, 1853, 1893, and 1909.

Details of the weather at the January 20 inaugurations follow: 1937, raining, 33°; 1941, clear, 29°; 1945, cloudy, 35°; 1949, clear, 38°; 1953, partly cloudy, 49°; 1957, overcast, 43°.

RETIRING PRESIDENTS AT INAUGURATIONS OF SUCCESSORS

All but three retiring Presidents have attended the inaugurations of their successors. John Adams was not present at Thomas Jefferson's inauguration, John Quincy Adams was not present at Andrew Jackson's, and Andrew Johnson was not present at Ulysses Simpson Grant's.

AGE AT INAUGURATION

The average age at which the 34 Presidents were inducted into office was 55 years and 38 days. (Grover Cleveland's nonconsecutive inaugurations are counted separately.)

The oldest at the time of his inauguration was William Henry Harrison, who took office when he was 68 years and 23 days old; the youngest was Theodore Roosevelt, who became President when he was 42 years and 322 days old.

Seven Presidents were over sixty when they took office: William Henry Harrison, James Buchanan, Zachary Taylor, Dwight David Eisenhower, John Adams, and Harry S Truman.

Six Presidents were under fifty when they became chief executive: James Knox Polk, James Abram Garfield, Franklin Pierce, Grover Cleveland (first term), Ulysses Simpson Grant, and Theodore Roosevelt.

INAUGURAL ADDRESSES

George Washington, who was inaugurated for a second term on March 4, 1793, at Philadelphia, Pa., used only 135 words in his inaugural address. The longest inaugural address was delivered during a snowfall by William Henry Harrison, who employed 8,445 words, almost twice as many as any other President. He used the personal pronoun "I" forty-five times, a record use. The only President who did not use "I" in his inaugural address was Theodore Roosevelt. The average number of words in the 43 inaugurals is 2,499, the first-person pronoun being used 16 times, and about once every 156 words.

The following list shows the number of words used by the Presidents in their inaugural addresses:

Washington
1,425 (first)
135 (second)

J. Adams
2,308

Jefferson
1,729 (first)
2,158 (second)

Madison
1,175 (first)
1,209 (second)

Monroe
3,217 (first)
4,467 (second)

J. Q. Adams
2,906

Jackson
1,125 (first)
1,172 (second)

Van Buren
3,838

W. H. Harrison
8,445

Polk
4,776

Taylor
996

Pierce
3,334

Buchanan
2,821

Lincoln
3,634 (first)
698 (second)

Grant
1,128 (first)
1,337 (second)

Hayes
2,480

Garfield
2,978

Cleveland
1,681 (first)

B. Harrison
4,388

Cleveland
2,015 (second)

McKinley
3,967 (first)
2,217 (second)

T. Roosevelt
985

Taft
5,433

Wilson
1,802 (first)
1,526 (second)

Harding
3,318

Coolidge
4,059

Hoover
3,801

F. D. Roosevelt
1,883 (first)
1,807 (second)
1,340 (third)
559 (fourth)

Truman
2,242

Eisenhower
2,446 (first)
2,449 (second)

PRESIDENTIAL REQUIREMENTS

There are no legal requirements for the presidency except for one paragraph in Article II, section 1 of the Constitution:

No Person except a natural born Citizen, or a Citizen of the United States, at the time of the Adoption of this Constitution, shall be eligible to the Office of President; neither shall any Person be eligible to that Office who shall not have attained to the Age of thirty five Years, and been fourteen Years a Resident within the United States.

The Constitution specifies "natural born," which does not mean "native born." The exact meaning of "natural born" has never been determined by the courts, but it has been understood to refer to those persons born on foreign soil of American parents. "Native born" refers to those persons born within the territorial limits of the United States.

PRESIDENTIAL POWERS

The duties and powers of the President are specifically enumerated in the Constitution:

ARTICLE II, SECTION 2. The President shall be Commander in Chief of the Army and Navy of the United States, and of the Militia of the several States, when called into the actual Service of the United States; he may require the Opinion, in writing, of the principal Officer in each of the Executive Departments, upon any Subject relating to the Duties of their respective Offices, and he shall have the Power to grant Reprieves and Pardons for Offences against the United States, except in Cases of Impeachment.

He shall have Power, by and with the Advice and Consent of the Senate, to make Treaties, provided two thirds of the Senators present concur; and he shall nominate, and by and with the Advice and Consent of the Senate, shall appoint Ambassadors, other public Ministers and Consuls, Judges of the Supreme Court, and all other Officers of the United States, whose Appointments are not herein otherwise provided for, and which shall be established by Law; but the Congress may by Law vest the Appointment of such inferior Officers, as they think proper, in the President alone, in the

Courts of Law, or in the Heads of Departments.

The President shall have Power to fill up all Vacancies that may happen during the Recess of the Senate, by granting Commissions which shall expire at the End of their next Session.

SECTION 3. He shall from time to time give to the Congress Information of the State of the Union, and recommend to their Consideration such Measures as he shall judge necessary and expedient; he may, on extraordinary Occasions, convene both Houses, or either of them, and in Case of Disagreement between them, with Respect to the Time of Adjournment, he may adjourn them to such Time as he shall think proper; he shall receive Ambassadors and other public Ministers; he shall take Care that the Laws be faithfully executed, and shall Commission all the Officers of the United States.

REMOVAL FROM OFFICE

Provisions for removing the President from office are contained in Article II, section 4 of the Constitution:

The President, Vice President and all civil Officers of the United States, shall be removed from Office on Impeachment for, and Conviction of, Treason, Bribery, or other high Crimes and Misdemeanors.

THE PRESIDENTIAL VETO

Article I, section 7 of the Constitution contains the following provisions:

Every Bill which shall have passed the House of Representatives and the Senate, shall, before it becomes a Law, be presented to the President of the United States; if he approve he shall sign it, but if not he shall return it, with his Objections to that House in which it shall have originated, who shall enter the Objections at large on their Journal, and proceed to reconsider it. If after such Reconsideration two thirds of that House shall agree to pass the bill, it shall be sent, together with the Objections, to the other House, by which it shall likewise be reconsidered, and if approved by two thirds of that House, it shall become a Law. . . . If any Bill shall not be returned by the President within ten Days (Sundays excepted) after it shall have been presented to him, the

Same shall be a Law, in like Manner as if he had signed it, unless the Congress by their Adjournment prevent its Return, in which case it shall not be a Law.

The Constitution thus provides not only for a regular veto, which Congress may override by a two-thirds majority of both Houses, but also for a "pocket veto"—if the President opposes a bill sent to him ten days before the adjournment of Congress, he can, instead of vetoing it, merely ignore it, or "pocket" it, and prevent it from becoming a law.

The following list shows the number of bills vetoed by each President. Noted in parentheses after each total are the figures comprising the total: first, the number of regular vetoes; second, the number of pocket vetoes; third, the number of vetoes sustained by Congress; and fourth, the number of bills passed over his veto.

Washington—2 (2, 0; 2, 0)

J. Adams—0

Jefferson—0

Madison—7 (5, 2; 7, 0)

Monroe—2 (1, 1; 1, 1)

J. Q. Adams—0

Jackson—12 (5, 7; 12, 0)

Van Buren—0

W. H. Harrison—0

J. Tyler—10 (6, 4; 9, 1)

Polk—3 (2, 1; 3, 0)

Taylor—0

Fillmore—0

Pierce—9 (9, 0; 4, 5)

Buchanan—7 (4, 3; 7, 0)

Lincoln—6 (2, 4; 6, 0)

Johnson—28 (21, 7; 13, 15)

Grant—92 (44, 48; 88, 4)

Hayes—13 (12, 1; 12, 1)

Garfield—0

Arthur—12 (4, 8; 11, 1)

Cleveland (first term)—414 (304, 110; 412, 2)

B. Harrison—44 (19, 25; 43, 1)

Cleveland (second term)—170 (42, 128; 165, 5)

McKinley—42 (6, 36; 42, 0)

T. Roosevelt—82 (42, 40; 81, 1)

Taft—39 (30, 9; 38, 1)

Wilson—44 (33, 11; 38, 6)

Harding—6 (5, 1; 6, 0)

Coolidge—50 (20, 30; 46, 4)

Hoover—37 (21, 16; 34, 3)

F. D. Roosevelt—631 (371, 260; 622, 9)

Truman—250 (180, 70; 238, 12)

Eisenhower (first term)—97 (36, 61; 97, 0)

Total—2,109 (1,226, 883; 2,037, 72)

Franklin Delano Roosevelt holds the record for having vetoed the greatest number of bills —631—but this embraced a twelve-year period. During a two-term period, Grover Cleveland vetoed 584 bills.

The President who had the largest number of vetoes overridden—15—was Andrew Johnson.

PRESIDENTIAL AND VICE PRESIDENTIAL SALARIES

The First Congress fixed the salary of the President of the United States at $25,000 a year, to be paid quarterly, in full consideration for his respective service with the use of the furniture and other effects now in his possession. This act of September 24, 1789 (1 Stat.L.72) also fixed the salary of the Vice President at $5,000 a year.

The act of March 3, 1873 (17 Stat.L.486) raised the salary of the President to $50,000 and that of the Vice President to $10,000. The law became effective with the new term which followed the next day. Consequently, President Grant served his first four-year term at a salary of $25,000, and his second four-year term at $50,000.

The act of June 23, 1906 (34 Stat.L.454) authorized an additional sum not exceeding $25,-000 for the traveling expenses of the President, "such sum when appropriated to be expended in the discretion of the President and accounted for on his certificate solely."

The act of March 4, 1909 (35 Stat.L.859) raised the salary of the President to $75,000, and that of the Vice President to $12,000. The first President to receive the increased salary was Taft.

The act of June 25, 1948 (62 Stat.L.678) increased the President's traveling expenses to $40,000 a year.

The act of January 19, 1949 (63 Stat.L.4) increased the rates of compensation of the President, the Vice President, and the Speaker of the House of Representatives. The act authorized a salary of $100,000 a year for the President to be paid monthly and an additional expense allowance of $50,000 a year "to assist in defraying expenses relating to or resulting from the discharge of his official duties, for which expense allowance no tax liability shall accrue and for which no accounting shall be made by him." The Vice President's salary was increased to $30,000 a year, with an additional expense allowance of $10,000 in equal monthly installments "to assist in defraying expenses, relating to or resulting from the discharge of his official duties for which no tax liability shall occur or accounting be made by him."

An act of October 20, 1951, subjected the expense allowance to income taxes.

President Truman was the first President to receive the $100,000 yearly salary.

The act of March 2, 1955 (69 Stat.L.11) increased the salary of the Vice President to $35,000.

PRESIDENTS' PENSIONS

The first pensions to former Presidents were authorized by act of Congress signed August 25, 1958, by President Dwight David Eisenhower. The act granted former Presidents a pension of $25,000 a year and their widows $10,000 a year. They were also granted unlimited free mailing, free office space, and up to $50,000 a year for office help. The first checks were mailed October 4, 1958, to Herbert Hoover and Harry S Truman.

OTHER PERQUISITES OF THE PRESIDENCY

In addition to his salary, a President is the beneficiary of many perquisites, which may vary from time to time. He and his family live rent-free at the White House; a fleet of automobiles is at his disposal; and a squad of about twenty-five secret service men, paid by the Treas-

ury Department, guard him. A yacht, belonging to the Navy and maintained by regular Navy appropriations, is assigned to his use, as well as a presidential airplane owned by the Air Force. Horses for riding are supplied by the Army and a private Pullman car that is armor-plated with bullet-proof windows is at his disposal. He is attended by a personal physician supplied by the armed forces and has access to any of the Army and Navy hospitals. A library, supplied by booksellers, is at his disposal in the White House. A separate police force of over one hundred is assigned to guard the White House and its grounds. The President is served by domestic servants (but must supply them with food).

THE PRESIDENTS, THE COURTS, AND ARRESTS

A misconception prevails that the President may not be summoned to court and is immune from arrest. Actually, the President may be summoned to court and is liable to arrest. There is nothing in the Constitution which grants him immunity.

Thomas Jefferson was summoned on June 10, 1807, to appear as a witness in the trial of Aaron Burr for treason, but refused to attend. (See page 47.)

This action established a precedent but did not bind future Presidents.

In 1853, Franklin Pierce, driving home by carriage from the home of William Morgan in southeast Washington, D.C., ran down an aged woman, Mrs. Nathan Lewis. Pierce was arrested by Constable Stanley Edelin, but the case was dropped as Pierce was not proved guilty.

Ulysses Simpson Grant, driving his carriage west on M street, between 11th and 12th streets, Washington, D.C., was stopped for speeding by a Negro police officer. When the officer learned the identity of the driver, he hesitated before issuing a ticket. Grant told him to do his duty and accepted the ticket. He put up twenty dollars collateral, which he forfeited when he failed to appear for trial. Grant later wrote a letter to the officer's superior, commending his obedience to duty.

Since the advent of the automobile, police officers have frequently stopped automobiles carrying Presidents, but no arrests have been made.

PROTECTION AGAINST THREATS

On June 25, 1948, Congress enacted a law (62 Stat.L.740) which made threats by mail against the President punishable by a thousand-dollar fine or imprisonment for not more than five years or both. On June 1, 1955 (69 Stat.L.80), this protection was extended to the President-elect and to the Vice President.

THE PRESIDENT'S FLAG

Before 1916 several Presidents had flags, but these were not official and were really nothing but emblems.

The official President's flag—the President's seal in bronze upon a blue background with a large white star in each corner—was adopted on May 29, 1916, by President Wilson's executive order No. 2,390.

President Truman, by executive order No. 9,646, dated October 25, 1945, made several further changes and increased the number of stars to forty-eight, one for each state.

Legislation altering the number of stars to provide for Alaska and Hawaii has been undertaken.

SALUTE TO THE PRESIDENT

The President is customarily honored with a twenty-one-gun salute. The twenty-one-gun salute is given also to former Presidents, sovereigns, members of a royal family, and Presidents of other republics. It is claimed that the twenty-one-gun salute commemorates the year 1776, and for that reason salutes are often fired thus: one-seven-seven-six.

TERMS OF OFFICE

Eighteen Presidents served one term or part of one term.

Ten of these eighteen Presidents served a full four-year term: John Adams, John Quincy Adams, Van Buren, Polk, Pierce, Buchanan, Hayes, Benjamin Harrison, Taft, and Hoover.

Four died without completing their first term: William Henry Harrison, Taylor, Garfield, and Harding.

Four succeeded to the presidency and filled unexpired terms: Tyler, Fillmore, Johnson, and Arthur.

Fifteen Presidents served more than one term.

Eight of these fifteen Presidents served two full terms: Washington, Jefferson, Madison, Monroe, Jackson, Grant, Cleveland, and Wilson.

One—Franklin Delano Roosevelt—served three full terms and part of a fourth term.

Two were reelected for a second term but died before completing it: Lincoln and McKinley.

Three who succeeded to the presidency and filled unexpired terms were also elected on their own and served a second term: Theodore Roosevelt, Coolidge, and Truman.

President Eisenhower completed his first term and was elected for a second term (1957-1961).

The following list shows the range in length of service of past Presidents:

W. H. Harrison—32 days

Garfield—199 days

Taylor—1 year, 128 days

Harding—2 years, 151 days

Fillmore—2 years, 237 days

Arthur—3 years, 166 days

Johnson—3 years, 322 days

Tyler—3 years, 332 days

J. Adams—4 years

J. Q. Adams—4 years

Van Buren—4 years

Polk—4 years

Pierce—4 years

Buchanan—4 years

Hayes—4 years

B. Harrison—4 years

Taft—4 years

Hoover—4 years

Lincoln—4 years, 43 days

McKinley—4 years, 194 days

Coolidge—5 years, 213 days

T. Roosevelt—7 years, 171 days

Truman—7 years, 283 days

Washington—7 years, 308 days (first term began Apr. 30 instead of Mar. 4)

Jefferson—8 years

Madison—8 years

Monroe—8 years

Jackson—8 years

Grant—8 years

Cleveland—8 years (two non-consecutive terms)

Wilson—8 years

F. D. Roosevelt—12 years, 39 days (first term ended Jan. 20 instead of Mar. 3)

CABINET CHANGES DURING PRESIDENTIAL ADMINISTRATIONS

Three of the Presidents who did not live to complete their terms in the White House retained their original cabinets during their incumbency. They were William Henry Harrison, Taylor, and Garfield. Except for ad interim appointments and appointees carried over from the preceding administrations for a few days, these Presidents had only one cabinet officer for each post.

The only President to retain a cabinet for a full four-year period was Franklin Pierce.

John Quincy Adams, with two different secretaries of war, had the next closest retaining record.

The President who had the greatest number of changes in his administration was John Tyler, who succeeded to the presidency upon the death of William Henry Harrison. When Tyler became President in 1841, the consensus of the six-man cabinet was that he be designated "Acting President." This suggestion angered Tyler, and a few months after taking office he caused all of the members of his cabinet to resign, with the exception of Daniel Webster, who finally resigned in 1843. In less than four years in office, Tyler made 26 changes in his cabinet. In all fairness to him, however, it should be noted that 6 of the changes were made to replace appointees of Harrison, 11 were interim appointments, several others were occasioned by death, and still others were necessitated by the transfer of cabinet members to different departments. Tyler himself appointed 2 secretaries of state, 3 secretaries of the treasury, 3 secretaries of war, 2 attorneys general, 1 postmaster general, and 4 secretaries of the navy. His ad interim appointments included 4 secretaries of state, 3 secretaries of the treasury, 1 secretary of war, 2 secretaries of the navy, and 1 postmaster general.

PRESIDENTIAL SUCCESSION

Article II, section 1 of the Constitution of the United States provides for presidential succession as follows:

> In Case of the Removal of the President from Office, or of his Death, Resignation, or Inability to discharge the Powers and Duties of the said Office, the Same shall devolve on the Vice President, and the Congress may by Law provide for the Case of Removal, Death, Resignation or Inability, both of the President and Vice President, declaring what Officer shall then act as President, and such Officer shall act accordingly, until the Disability be removed, or a President shall be elected.

A law was enacted by Congress on March 1, 1792 (1 Stat.L.239) which provided that

> in case of the removal, death, resignation, or disability of both the President and the Vice President of the United States, the President of the Senate pro tempore, and in case there shall be no President of the Senate, then the

Speaker of the House of Representatives for the time being shall act as President of the United States until such disability be removed or until a President be elected.

Although the Twelfth Amendment, ratified in 1804, did not change the order of presidential succession, it provided that both the President and the Vice President be elected separately, voiding the system whereby the presidential candidate with the second largest vote became Vice President and thus eligible to succeed to the presidency.

No change was made in the order of succession from 1792 until the Presidential Succession Act of January 19, 1886 (24 Stat.L.1) was passed during Grover Cleveland's administration. This act, entitled "An Act to provide for the performance of the duties of the office of President in case of the removal, resignation or inability both of the President and the Vice President," provided that the succession should devolve upon the departmental secretaries according to the order of the creation of their respective departments. The order was State, Treasury, War, Attorney General, Postmaster General, Navy, Interior, Agriculture, Commerce and Labor (easily remembered by the mnemonic *St Wapniacl*). Actually, the order of succession was incorrect as the Department of War was established prior to the Treasury Department.

The Presidential Succession Act of July 18, 1947 (61 Stat.L.380) established the succession as follows: the Vice President, the Speaker of the House of Representatives, the President *pro tempore* of the Senate.

In 1955, the succession was elaborated as follows: the Vice President, the Speaker of the House of Representatives, the president *pro tempore* of the Senate, the secretary of state, the secretary of the treasury, the secretary of defense, the attorney general, the postmaster general, the secretary of the interior, the secretary of agriculture, the secretary of commerce, the secretary of labor, and the secretary of health, education and welfare.

No President and Vice President died during the same administration, and no cabinet officer succeeded to the presidency as a result of death.

Statisticians have calculated that the death of both President and Vice President in the same administration is not likely to occur more than once in 840 years.

The Presidents and Their Vice Presidents

PRESIDENTS AND VICE PRESIDENTS

There have been 34 Presidents (33 individuals, with Grover Cleveland counted twice since his two terms were not consecutive). Only 30 of the 34 had Vice Presidents; 4 who succeeded to the presidency were not subsequently elected in their own right and never had Vice Presidents. Since 6 of the 30 had 2 Vice Presidents, and since 1 had 3 Vice Presidents, there have been 38 presidential-vice presidential "teams." (Actually, only 36 individuals have held the office of Vice President; 2 are counted twice since each served under 2 Presidents.)

NEW YORK STATE THE BIRTHPLACE OF EIGHT VICE PRESIDENTS

The number of Vice Presidents born in New York State has been greater than the number born in any two other states combined. The eight Vice Presidents born in New York were George Clinton (who served under Presidents Jefferson and Madison), Daniel D. Tompkins (under President Monroe), Martin Van Buren (under President Jackson), Millard Fillmore (under President Taylor), Schuyler Colfax (under President Grant), William A. Wheeler (under President Hayes), Theodore Roosevelt (under President McKinley), and James Schoolcraft Sherman (under President Taft). Three of the eight succeeded to the presidency: Van Buren, Fillmore, and Theodore Roosevelt.

YOUNGEST AND OLDEST VICE PRESIDENTS FROM KENTUCKY

The two Vice Presidents who were the youngest and the oldest

at their respective inaugurations were both natives of Kentucky. The youngest was John Cabell Breckinridge, born at Lexington, Ky., who was 36 years and 42 days old when he was inaugurated Vice President under President James Buchanan in 1857. The oldest was Alben William Barkley, born near Lowes, in Graves County, Ky., who was 71 years and 57 days old when he was inaugurated Vice President under President Harry S Truman in 1949.

VICE PRESIDENTS ELECTED FROM STATES OTHER THAN THEIR BIRTHPLACES

The ten Vice Presidents listed below were elected from states other than their native states. The name of each is followed by (1) the state from which he was elected and (2) the state in which he was born.

Burr—New York, New Jersey

King—Alabama, North Carolina

A. Johnson—Tennessee, North Carolina

Colfax—Indiana, New York

Wilson—Massachusetts, New Hampshire

Hendricks—Indiana, Ohio

Morton—New York, Vermont

Stevenson—Illinois, Kentucky

Fairbanks—Indiana, Ohio

Coolidge—Massachusetts, Vermont

Dawes—Illinois, Ohio

INDIAN ELECTED VICE PRESIDENT

Senator Charles Curtis of Kansas, whose mother was a full-blooded member of the Kaw tribe of Indians, was elected Vice President of the United States to serve from March 4, 1929, to March 3, 1933 under President Hoover.

UNSUCCESSFUL VICE PRESIDENTIAL ASPIRANT ELECTED PRESIDENT OF CONFEDERATE STATES

Jefferson Davis of Mississippi became president of the Confederate States of America on February 18, 1861. Nine years earlier, he had been a contender for the vice presidential nomination at the Democratic national convention held at the Maryland Institute, Baltimore, Md., June 1-5, 1852. On the first ballot New York cast two votes for Davis; on the second ballot, Illinois cast eleven votes for him.

OCTOGENARIAN NOMINATED FOR VICE PRESIDENCY

The oldest nominee for the presidency or the vice presidency was Henry Gassaway Davis of West Virginia, a former senator, who was 80 years and 235 days old when he was nominated at the Democratic convention at St. Louis, Mo., in July 1904.

NEGRO CONTENDER FOR THE VICE PRESIDENTIAL NOMINATION

At the Republican convention held at Chicago, Ill., in June 1880, Blanche Kelso Bruce, United States senator from Mississippi, received eleven votes in the balloting for the vice presidency. He was the first Negro candidate for the vice presidential nomination of a major political party.

VICE PRESIDENTIAL TERMS

Sixteen of the thirty-six Vice Presidents served full four-year terms. They were Thomas Jefferson, Aaron Burr, Martin Van Buren, Richard Mentor Johnson, George Mifflin Dallas, John Cabell Breckinridge, Hannibal Hamlin, Schuyler Colfax, William Almon Wheeler, Levi Parsons Morton, Adlai Ewing Stevenson, Charles Warren Fairbanks, Charles Gates Dawes, Charles Curtis, Henry Agard Wallace, and Alben William Barkley.

Seven Vice Presidents did not complete their full four-year terms as they succeeded to the presidency upon the death of their predecessors. They were John Tyler, Andrew Johnson, Chester Alan Arthur, Millard Fillmore, Theodore Roosevelt, Calvin Coolidge, and Harry S Truman. (Three of the seven —Roosevelt, Coolidge, and Truman—were also elected to the presidency in their own right.)

Six Vice Presidents died before completing their four-year terms. They were William Rufus De Vane King, who served 45 days; Thomas Andrews Hendricks, 266 days; Elbridge Gerry, 1 year and 264 days; Henry Wilson, 2 years and 263 days; Garret Augustus Hobart, 2 years and 262 days; and James Schoolcraft Sherman, 3 years and 240 days.

Seven Vice Presidents were reelected for second terms. They were John Adams, George Clinton, Daniel D. Tompkins, John Caldwell Calhoun, Thomas Riley Marshall, John Nance Garner, and Richard Milhous Nixon.

Of the seven who were reelected, two served their second terms under different Presidents: Clinton under Jefferson and Madison, and Calhoun under John Quincy Adams and Andrew Jackson. Neither Clinton nor Calhoun completed his second term. Clinton was reelected to serve under James Madison from 1809 to 1813, but he died April 20, 1812, leaving the nation without a Vice President for 318 days. Calhoun was reelected to serve under Jackson from 1829 to 1833, but he resigned December 28, 1832, after his election to the Senate to fill the vacancy caused by the resignation of Robert Young Hayne of South Carolina. Calhoun served 82 days less than eight full years.

Technically, only two of the thirty-six Vice Presidents served eight full years in office. They were Tompkins, who served under James Monroe, and Marshall, who served under Woodrow Wilson. (Nixon will be the third Vice President with eight full years in office at the expiration of his second term under Dwight David Eisenhower in 1961.) However, two other Vice Presidents served two full terms. Adams served 47 days less than eight full years because he did not assume office until April 21, 1789 (nine days before George Washington was inaugurated). Garner served 43 days less than eight full years because his second term under Franklin Delano Roosevelt expired on January 20, instead of the previous March 3 date.

PRESIDENTIAL AND VICE PRESIDENTIAL TEAMS SELDOM REELECTED

Only five of the forty-three elections from 1789 through 1956 resulted in the reelection of a President and his Vice President. However, there were in all only eleven elections in which Presidents were reelected for a second consecutive term.

The five Presidents who carried their Vice Presidents into office for a second term were Washington (1789-1797), Monroe (1817-1825), Wilson (1913-1921), Franklin Delano Roosevelt (1933-1941), and Eisenhower (1953-1961). The Vice Presidents elected with them were respectively Adams, Tompkins, Marshall, Garner, and Nixon. (Roosevelt's Vice Presidents for his third and fourth terms were Wallace and Truman.)

In 1804, when Jefferson was elected for a second term, Burr was replaced by Clinton. At this election, the President and the Vice President were on separate ballots and it would have been possible to elect one and not the other.

Three Presidents had different Vice Presidents during their second terms because of the death or resignation of their Vice Presidents. Clinton, who had served as Vice President during the second term of Jefferson, died in office during the first term of Madison, and Gerry was elected to serve during Madison's second term. Hobart died during the first term of McKinley, and Theodore Roosevelt was selected for the second term. Calhoun resigned during the first term of Jackson, and Van Buren served as Vice President during Jackson's second term.

Lincoln had two Vice Presidents, Hamlin and Andrew Johnson. Grant's Vice Presidents were Colfax and Wilson.

Cleveland was elected for two nonconsecutive terms (1885-1889 and 1893-1897), and he had a different Vice President each term. Hendricks died while in office during the first term, and Stevenson served during the second term.

PRESIDENTIAL AND VICE PRESIDENTIAL CANDIDATES

Only one Republican presidential and vice presidential team has been elected twice: Eisenhower and Nixon.

Two Democratic teams were elected for second terms: Wilson and Marshall and Franklin Delano Roosevelt and Garner.

The only Republican Vice Presidents elected to the presidency were Theodore Roosevelt and Coolidge. The only Democratic Vice Presidents elected to the presidency were Van Buren and Truman.

The only presidential and vice presidential teams defeated for a second term were Van Buren and Johnson (1836) and Hoover and Curtis (1932). Several other Presidents were defeated for reelection, but each had a different vice presidential running mate.

VICE PRESIDENTS— STATUS AFTER HOLDING OFFICE

Three Vice Presidents were elected to the presidency after completing their vice presidential terms: John Adams, Thomas Jefferson (who served as President for two terms), and Martin Van Buren.

Seven Vice Presidents succeeded to the presidency upon the death of the Presidents under whom they had served: John Tyler, Millard Fillmore, An-

drew Johnson, Chester Alan Arthur, Theodore Roosevelt, Calvin Coolidge, and Harry S Truman.

Three of the seven who succeeded to the presidency were elected for additional four-year terms: Theodore Roosevelt, Calvin Coolidge, and Harry S Truman.

Five Vice Presidents served in the Senate after their vice presidential terms: John Caldwell Calhoun (who resigned as Vice President to serve in the Senate), John Cabell Breckinridge, Hannibal Hamlin, Andrew Johnson (who was elected to the Senate after serving as President), and Alben William Barkley.

Seven Vice Presidents died in office: George Clinton (who died during his second term), Elbridge Gerry, William Rufus De Vane King, Henry Wilson, Thomas Andrews Hendricks, Garret Augustus Hobart, and James Schoolcraft Sherman.

VICE PRESIDENTS IN THE PRESIDENCY

Ten men who were elected to the vice presidency also served as chief executive.

The seven who succeeded to the presidency when their predecessors died served the unexpired terms as follows: John

Tyler, 3 years and 332 days; Millard Fillmore, 2 years and 236 days; Andrew Johnson, 3 years and 323 days; Chester Alan Arthur, 3 years and 166 days; Theodore Roosevelt, 3 years and 171 days; Calvin Coolidge, 1 year and 214 days; Harry S Truman, 3 years and 283 days—a total of 22 years and 265 days during which the country was run by men who had not been elected to presidential office.

Three of the seven were elected for additional four-year terms: Roosevelt, Coolidge, and Truman.

Three others were elected to the presidency after the expiration of their vice presidential terms: John Adams, Jefferson (who served as President for two terms), and Van Buren.

EIGHTH AND TENTH VICE PRESIDENTS BECAME EIGHTH AND TENTH PRESIDENTS

Martin Van Buren, who was the eighth Vice President (March 4, 1833-March 3, 1837) was elected to the presidency and served as eighth President (March 4, 1837-March 3, 1841).

John Tyler, who was the tenth Vice President (March 4, 1841-April 4, 1841) succeeded to the presidency when William Henry Harrison died, and thus became the tenth President.

VICE PRESIDENTS—AGE AT INAUGURATION AND AGE AT DEATH

The average age at inauguration was 55 years and 7 days. (In this computation Clinton—who served as Vice President under Jefferson and Madison—and Calhoun—who served as Vice President under John Quincy Adams and Jackson—are each counted twice.)

The oldest Vice President to succeed to the presidency upon the death of the President was Truman, who was 60 years and 339 days old when he became President after the death of Franklin Delano Roosevelt.

The youngest Vice President to succeed to the presidency upon the death of the President was Theodore Roosevelt, who was 42 years and 322 days old when he became President after the death of McKinley.

The average age at death of the 32 Vice Presidents who are no longer living was 74 years and 296 days.

INDEX

Listed in this Index are the names of the Presidents and Vice Presidents; the names of political parties represented in national elections; general topics relating to all Presidents (e.g., *Inaugurations*); and special subjects associated with a single President (e.g., *Emancipation Proclamation*).

To find detailed information about a specific President, see the entry noting the individual biographical chapter in Part I. (Each chapter is arranged as follows: general summary, family history, nomination and election, appointments to the Supreme Court, important dates, Vice President, additional data.)

To find information about the Presidents collectively, see the subject entries noting the Comparative Data in Part II.

469